Healing the Fragmented Selves of Trauma Survivors

Healing the Fragmented Selves of Trauma Survivors integrates a neurobiologically informed understanding of trauma, dissociation, and attachment with a practical approach to treatment, all communicated in straightforward language accessible to both client and therapist. Readers will be exposed to a model that emphasizes "resolution"—a transformation in the relationship to one's self, replacing shame, self-loathing, and assumptions of guilt with compassionate acceptance. Its unique interventions have been adapted from a number of cutting-edge therapeutic approaches, including Sensorimotor Psychotherapy, Internal Family Systems, mindfulness-based therapies, and clinical hypnosis. Readers will close the pages of *Healing the Fragmented Selves of Trauma Survivors* with a solid grasp of therapeutic approaches to traumatic attachment, working with undiagnosed dissociative symptoms and disorders, integrating "right brain-to-right brain" treatment methods, and much more. Most of all, they will come away with tools for helping clients create an internal sense of safety and compassionate connection to even their most disowned selves.

Janina Fisher, PhD, is assistant education director of the Sensorimotor Psychotherapy Institute, an EMDR International Association (EMDRIA) consultant, and a former instructor at the Trauma Center, a clinic and research center founded by Bessel van der Kolk. Known for her expertise as a clinician, author, and presenter, she is also past president of the New England Society for the Treatment of Trauma and Dissociation, a former instructor at Harvard Medical School, and coauthor (with Pat Ogden) of *Sensorimotor Psychotherapy: Interventions for Trauma and Attachment*.

Healing the Fragmented Selves of Trauma Survivors

Overcoming Internal Self-Alienation

Janina Fisher

Routledge
Taylor & Francis Group

NEW YORK AND LONDON

First published 2017
by Routledge
711 Third Avenue, New York, NY 10017

and by Routledge
2 Park Square, Milton Park, Abingdon, Oxon, OX14 4RN

Routledge is an imprint of the Taylor & Francis Group, an informa business

© 2017 Janina Fisher

Library of Congress Cataloging-in-Publication Data
A catalogue record for this title has been requested.

ISBN: 978-0-415-70822-7 (hbk)
ISBN: 978-0-415-70823-4 (pbk)
ISBN: 978-1-315-88616-9 (ebk)

Typeset in MinionPro
by codeMantra

To my most gifted teachers:

All the trauma survivors who gave me a window into their inner worlds, who were my experts, who taught me what always to say and what never to say, and who, to this day, inspire me to find new ways to help them heal at the broken places.

A special debt of gratitude to Barbara Watson, who taught me the importance of inspiring instead of treating, laughing instead of crying, and holding on to belief when all others have lost hope.

And my eternal thankfulness to Camille for being "the wind beneath my wings."

Contents

List of Figures

Acknowledgments

As a child, my ambition in life was to become a writer, a life goal I quickly gave up when I got to college and began to see what it might actually entail in terms of blood, sweat, and tears. The invitation to write this book for Routledge gave that young part of me satisfaction in finally becoming an author, but I must confess that the process was just as difficult as other parts told me it would be decades ago!

The inspiration behind the ideas presented in this book comes directly from my patients who, over the years, taught me everything I understand today about the impact of trauma from "inside the volcano." They helped me to understand the experience of living with the enduring threat of annihilation, of hating themselves when they could not risk hating those who harmed them. They helped me to see that the deepest pain of all is connected to the failure of those they loved to cherish them and, for that reason, provide them safety and care. No arms reached out to break their fall, dry their tears, or comfort the ache of loneliness. There was no balm for the shame. When I finally understood that, to find peace, they needed a way to love the wounded children inside them, an insight came to me: it is the quality of our *internal* attachments that determines how safe we feel "inside," how easy or difficult it is to be "me." When we ignore, despise, or disown out littlest selves, we can't help but feel their pain: once again, they are not welcome. And when we learn how to offer them and ourselves an unconditionally "loving presence," wounds can heal and hope is renewed.

To get from an idea to a finished manuscript, though, takes a cast of thousands, to all of whom I am indebted. I would not have written a book at all if it were not for my longtime friends and chosen family, Stephanie Ross, and

Deborah Spragg, who first had the thought, "You should write a book!" And then never, ever let me forget it—for years. They became a Greek chorus that would not stop reminding me of what I "had" to do. Thank goodness for the wind at my back!

Every new writer also needs guides who have traveled the same journey and know the way. My dear friend, Lisa Ferentz, would not let me off the hook either, encouraging and supporting me over years now. Having already published her first two books, Lisa was not only my cheerleader but could give me wise advice, emotional "chicken soup," and a map to guide me along the way.

Thanks to Bessel van der Kolk, my friend and mentor, I have been able to fulfill a professional mission first inspired when I heard Judith Herman speak about trauma 27 years ago. In that moment, my course was set. I am eternally grateful for my years as a supervisor and instructor at Bessel's Trauma Center, for the opportunity to learn from him as he led the neurobiological revolution in psychotherapy, and for his mentoring of my teaching and writing career. The understanding of trauma described in this book comes directly from his contributions to the field and is inspired by his belief that "the body keeps the score."

My thanks, too, to Pat Ogden for her friendship, professional and personal support, and for the gift of Sensorimotor Psychotherapy. From Pat, I have learned how to use the resources of the body as a vehicle for communication that goes "beyond words." The therapist's own self is always the instrument in psychotherapy, and it behooves us to learn how to use our own internal states, body language, and tone of voice (the way mothers do with babies) to induce states of comfort, curiosity, and excitement that transform the client's state of distress. I also want to thank my Sensorimotor Institute "family" for their support—even when this book meant that I didn't have time for them!

I have appreciated Dick Schwartz's generosity and supportive presence since we first met as faculty at Bessel van der Kolk's annual trauma conference, and my gratitude for his IFS model goes back even further. When I discovered IFS 20 years ago, I was overwhelmed by the responsibility for a caseload of clients with dissociative disorders—all of whom were in crisis. The discovery of Dick's concept of "self"-leadership allowed me to step back and allow the inherent strengths in each of *them* to come to the rescue. In this field, experts and founders can be territorial and self-protective. But Dick is welcoming of all parts of each person he encounters, and I thank him for trusting me to honor his work—as I hope I have done with the affection and respect he has earned.

I am blessed also to have a family of colleagues around the world who have sent me their support, implored me to finish the book (at least for their sakes), or given me feedback when I've needed it. I want to thank Licia Sky, Carol Japha, Gil Levin, Benjamin Fry, and Sally LoGrasso for their willingness to read chapters in progress. Their insightful suggestions and encouragement helped enormously. In Norway, I am grateful to my dear friends, Kirsten Benum and Trine Anstorp, who always inspire me to dream bigger and then ply me with food and wine to entice me into our next project! In the United Kingdom, Benjamin Fry has given me the opportunity to translate my vision of "trauma treatment" into the ongoing work of Khiron House's clinical programs, while the uniquely talented staff inspire me in a different way: by speaking on behalf of the complex needs of their traumatized clients. In Italy, Giovanni Tagliavini and Paola Boldrini have generously offered me a stage from which to share my work. Their equally passionate devotion to serving the needs of traumatized clients (and their parts) makes them "family." A special thanks to Giovanni for his offer to translate this book into Italian, and thanks to Julian Baillet for offering to do the French translation. In Spain, I have "true believers" in this way of working, Dolores Mosquera and Esther Perez, whose encouragement was important to remember each time I questioned what I was doing. Thanks, too, to my wonderful UK colleagues and friends: Catherine Cox, Helen-Jane Ridgeway, Sally-Anne Bubbers, Linda Beton, and Liz Hall, among others. In Boston, my dear friend, Lana Epstein, contributed the gift of laughter—endless laughter—the perfect antidote to the stress of an author's journey. In New York, I want to give special thanks to Ken Frank, Sandy Shapiro, and Ken's study group for their enthusiastic reading of early chapters. I've found that a writer needs every crumb of that enthusiasm to keep going through such a long, often agonizing process.

My gratitude, too, to Dan Brockett, Steve Pierce, and the dedicated State of Connecticut Young Adult Services staff who participated in "test-driving" this model with their very traumatized, high-risk clients. The response we got from our clients affirmed that even severely suicidal and self-harming clients could benefit from understanding their fragmentation and learning to work with it.

There are so many more friends and colleagues and fellow travelers that I could thank, and I hope you will consider yourself thanked even if I have neglected to mention you by name.

Last, but surely not least, I want to thank my children and grandchildren for their love, support, and patience. No one can appreciate what they have sacrificed for "the book": weekends, evenings, vacations, outings, family dinners—for months at a time. On top of that, they have had to be supportive! And they have been. To Jadu, Jason and Kelli, Ruby, and Nika, I am so grateful! I don't know what I would do without your smiling faces and the best hugs ever. You have my heartfelt love and gratitude.

Introduction

How This Book Came To Be

Having no way to understand the entrenched self-alienation or intense self-hatred of their traumatized clients, therapists often feel frustrated, baffled, and inadequate to the task of trying to help. Why do they seem to be at war with themselves? Or with us? Although the client has come seeking relief from a burden of trauma-related symptoms and issues, the task of exchanging self-alienation for self-compassion can feel overwhelming or distasteful. Neither client nor therapist has a language with which to explain the internal struggles being played out inside the client's mind and body. In a mental health world that rejects the notion that personality and identity can be fragmented and compartmentalized, therapists are rarely trained to see the splits, much less the life-or-death battle for control being waged by "selves" with opposite aims and instincts.

My intention in writing this book was to share a way of conceptualizing the most complex and challenging clients who come to us, often carrying "terminal" diagnoses, such as personality disorder, bipolar II, even schizophrenia. Over three decades in the trauma treatment field, my compatriots and I have learned about trauma "the hard way," by letting the clients teach us about their inner worlds, their intrusive, overwhelming symptoms, what it is like to live in a body organized to expect annihilation or abandonment. Lacking approaches specifically tailored to the needs of traumatized clients, all of us "winged it," creating new techniques and interventions, seeing what "worked," and retaining what did—either because the interventions were effective or because the clients liked how they felt.

In the 1990s, as an instructor and supervisor at Bessel van der Kolk's Trauma Center, I was profoundly influenced by the neuroscience research that began to revolutionize our way of understanding trauma and by Bessel's belief that "the body keeps the score" (Van der Kolk, 2014). We began then to see trauma-related disorders not as disorders of events but as disorders of the body, brain, and nervous system. The neurobiological lens also resulted in another paradigm shift: if the brain and body are inherently adaptive, then the legacy of trauma responses must also reflect an attempt at adaptation, rather than evidence of pathology.

1

Through that neurobiological lens, what appears clinically as stuckness and resistance, untreatable diagnoses, or character-disordered behavior simply represent how an individual's mind and body adapted to a dangerous world in which the only "protection" was the very same caretaker who endangered him or her. Each symptom was an ingenious solution by the body to create some semblance of safety for the developing child or endangered adult. The trauma-related issues with which the client presents for help, I now believe, are in truth a "red badge of courage" that tell the story of what happened even more eloquently than the events each individual consciously remembers.

As I came to be known as an expert in treating trauma, increasing numbers of clients sought me out for consultation, asking, "Why am I not getting better? My therapist and I have a wonderful relationship, but none of my symptoms are diminishing. Am I doing the wrong kind of therapy? Or is there something wrong with me?" Time after time, as I heard from clients and therapists what had been tried and failed, I could not find a "mistake" or misguided choice of treatment. More often, what could be seen from the consultant's perspective was something both therapist and client could not see: the client was fragmented. What it had taken to adapt was a splitting of self and identity sufficiently severe that the individual's inner world had become a war zone. What I also noticed was the relief these clients experienced as I educated them about dissociative splitting as a normal adaptation to trauma. First describing to them the theory of Structural Dissociation (Van der Hart, Nijenhuis & Steele, 2006), I would then translate their struggles using the language of parts and the language of animal defense survival responses, the cornerstone of the Structural Dissociation theory. Often, as I spoke, I observed a look of recognition on their faces, as if I were telling them nothing new but simply giving them a language to describe at long last what they already recognized but had no words to explain. Rather than feeling stigmatized or "crazier," the Structural Dissociation model seemed to be reassuring to them. Its central principle, that splitting had simply allowed them to adapt and survive more successfully in an unsafe world, helped even very proud, narcissistic individuals to experience the fragmentation as a validation of their survival, not further proof of their defectiveness.

As I worked in this way with a range of clients, it became increasingly clear that when they "adopted" or came to love their hurt, lost, and lonely parts, something remarkable happened. Their self-disparagement, self-hatred, and disconnection began spontaneously to yield to self-compassion. Whereas the idea of being "nice," "taking care of" or being "compassionate" to *themselves* was met with disgust and avoidance, every client could be helped to "see" his or her child parts and to extend kindness and care. And as they developed internal attachment relationships to these young selves, I could see them healing.

What it means to "heal" is subjective, of course: for some clients, it implies the ability to function again, to simply reclaim their lives. But, as I observed the clients who began forming loving attachment bonds to their young selves,

I could see healing at a much deeper level. Seeing them "bond" with the child they had once been and feeling their shame and self-hatred melt away convinced me that the left brain "adult" side of each one was capable of relating to the right brain "child" side, experiencing him or her as innocent and little, spontaneously evoking warmth and protectiveness. By bonding to the lost children inside, their internal states transformed, creating a warm, loving environment that felt safe at last. Best of all, it was evident that this work was not only transformative but also easy for the clients once they learned the basic skills needed to form internal attachment relationships to their parts.

The book is intended for use by a wide range of therapists and for an even wider range of clients. In writing it, I hoped particularly to address the challenges faced by chronically traumatized individuals much like those who have sought me out for consultations. These are clients young and old who battle to recover from their legacies of trauma, confused that these have not resolved despite good therapy, effective treatments, supportive relationships, or even rich full lives in the present. I also wanted to describe an effective and respectful way of working with traumatized clients who have lost their hope and ability to function or who depend upon hospitals, families, and loved ones to care for them as they struggle with self-destructive impulses driving suicidal, self-harming, addicted, or eating disordered behavior. Despite decades of research attesting to the relationship between early abuse and a later diagnosis of borderline personality disorder, it is rare for clients with borderline diagnoses to be treated as trauma patients or to be recognized as individuals whose "borderline" symptoms stem logically and tragically from the unsafe environments of their early lives. Thanks to enlightened Departments of Mental Health in the states of Massachusetts and Connecticut, I have had the invaluable opportunity to try out the treatment model described in this book with some of their most high-risk patients and to find that, with a treatment model organized around trauma-related splitting and compartmentalization, these patients could begin to stabilize, to live outside of institutional walls, and to understand their attacks on the body as a valiant attempt by one part to gain quick short-term relief from the painful implicit memories of other parts. This book is also meant for traumatized clients who have "overcome," who have prestigious jobs and loving families of choice, whose lives are rich and full, but who still struggle to *enjoy* the quality of life they have fought to create. And the book is also intended to offer hope to individuals who may be stable but whose internal quality of life is still as dark and painful as the traumatic past despite the safety, support, and meaningful work in their external lives.

The treatment paradigm described in this book is not intended for the treatment of any one particular diagnosis. It is meant to be used with and on behalf of all survivors of trauma, whether the client carries a diagnosis of post-traumatic stress disorder (PTSD), has been given a common trauma-related diagnosis such as ADHD, bipolar disorder, borderline personality, or a dissociative disorder, or has never met a mental health professional. If you, the reader, have been failed, attacked, threatened, abandoned, terrorized, or abused by other human beings, and if you still carry with you the emotional and physical legacy of those experiences, or if you work to help those who do, I believe this book will speak to you.

Fragmentation and Internal Struggles

Ten years ago, in the context of consulting with traumatized clients who came to me as an "expert," seeking to understand why they were not making progress in treatment, I began to observe a very characteristic pattern: these clients had something unique in common. Each was superficially an integrated whole person but also manifested clear-cut signs of being internally fragmented. They experienced intense conflicts between trauma-related perceptions and impulses (for example, "the worst is going to happen," "I will be abandoned if I don't get out first") versus here-and-now assessments of danger: "I know I'm safe here. I wouldn't let my children live in this house if it were not safe." They suffered from paradoxical symptoms: the desire to be kind and compassionate toward others or to live a spiritual life, on the one hand, and intense rage or even impulses to violence, on the other. Once their conflicts were described, the patterns became more easily observable and meaningful. Each side of the conflict spoke to a different way of surviving the unsurvivable, of reconciling the opposites that are so often part and parcel of traumatic experience. With an explanatory model that described each reaction as logical and necessary in the face of threat or abandonment and that reframed them as the survival responses of different parts of the self, to which the individual could relate, each client started to make faster, more sustainable progress. The theoretical model that best explained the phenomena they described was the Structural Dissociation model of Onno van der Hart, Ellert Nijenhuis, and Kathy Steele (2004). Rooted in a neuroscience perspective and well-accepted throughout Europe as a trauma model, it was a good fit for me as a firm believer and spokesperson for a neurobiologically informed approach to trauma and trauma treatment. The theory describes (Van der Hart, Nijenhuis & Steele, 2006) how the brain's innate physical structure and two separate, specialized hemispheres facilitate left brain-right brain disconnection under conditions of threat. Capitalizing on the tendency of the left brain to remain positive, task-oriented, and logical under stress, these writers hypothesized that the disconnected left brain side of the personality stays focused on the tasks of daily living, while the other hemisphere fosters an implicit right brain self that remains in survival mode, braced for danger, ready to run, frozen in fear, praying for rescue, or too ashamed to do anything but submit. In each individual client, I could see that some parts were easier to identify with or "own" and some parts were easier to ignore or dismiss as "not me." Internally, the parts were also in conflict: was it safer to freeze or fight? To cry for help? Or to be seen and not heard? What I also noticed was that the internal relationships between these fragmented aspects of self reflected the traumatic environments for which they had once been solutions. The left-brain-dominant present-oriented self avoids the right-brain-dominant survival-oriented parts or judges them as bad qualities to be modified, while the right brain implicit selves of the parts are equally alienated from what they perceive as a "weak" or absent other half. The functioning self carries on, trying desperately to be "normal"—at the cost of feeling alienated from or invaded by the intrusive communications of the parts.

The Price of Self-Alienation: A "False Self"

Survivors of abuse, neglect, and other traumatic experiences often report functioning better as a result of their compartmentalization but then suffer from feelings of fraudulence or "pretending." Not realizing that each side of the personality is equally "real" and necessary from an evolutionary standpoint, clients easily misinterpret the intense, palpable feeling memories of the "not me" child as more "real" than the experience of the "going on with normal life self," doggedly "putting one foot in front of the other," or "keeping on keeping on" even in the face of overwhelming pain. Without an explanatory paradigm that makes sense of these contradictions, there is no way for individuals to know that their intense feelings and distorted perceptions are evidence of fragmentation, not proof of internal defectiveness or fraudulence masked by the ability to function.

Over time, self-alienation can only be maintained by most individuals at the cost of increasingly greater self-loathing, disconnection from emotion, addictive or self-destructive behavior, and internal struggles between vulnerability and control, love and hate, closeness and distance, shame and pride. While longing to be loved, safe, and welcome, many traumatized clients find themselves alternating between anxious clinging and pushing others away, hating themselves or having little patience with the flaws of others, yearning to be seen and yearning to be invisible. Years later, they present in therapy with symptoms of anxiety, chronic depression, low self-esteem, stuckness in life, or diagnoses such as PTSD, bipolar disorder, borderline personality disorder, even dissociative disorders. Unaware that their symptoms are being driven not just by the traumatic events but by an internal attachment disorder mirroring the traumatic attachment of early childhood, therapist and client have no framework for understanding the chaos and/or stuckness that may soon elude their best efforts at treatment.

Traumatic Attachment as a Complication in Trauma Therapy

In the trauma treatment world in which I have practiced professionally over the past 25 years, generations of "best treatment" models have been repeatedly challenged by client vulnerability to being triggered by apparently innocuous stimuli, swept into the "trauma vortex," and overwhelmed with painful emotions and physiological responses. For some clients, the present feels little better than the past. Since my postdoctoral fellowship in Judith Herman's clinic in 1991 and arrival at Bessel van der Kolk's Trauma Center in 1995 as a supervisor and instructor, my colleagues and I, led by Bessel van der Kolk, have been on a quest to find new methods or interventions that might help free our clients from the insidious impact of the traumatic past—but, even as each is an improvement on the last, we always come up somewhat short. Each new understanding or sophisticated treatment method helps some clients we haven't before been able to reach, but it doesn't bring resolution for all—or each brings relief in some symptoms while not alleviating others. And for some traumatized clients, the course of treatment even over the long term seems to consist of two effortful steps forward followed by a slide backward— pushing the proverbial boulder up a steep hill this week only to find by the next session that it is right back at the bottom again. Even more challenging, some clients find that their trauma-related wishes and fears of relationship are so equally intense that therapy and the therapist evoke painful yearning, mistrust, hypervigilance, and anger, or fear and shame, rather than feelings of safety and comfort. It was my hope in writing this book that the treatment approach described here would create a way for these clients and their therapists to navigate these challenges and resolve them.

Stuckness: Trauma-Related Internal Conflicts

Often, at this point, the client reports feeling worse instead of better, and the therapist begins to question his or her ability. Each wonders, "Am *I* doing something wrong?" What neither client nor therapist realizes is that stuckness in treatment reflects trauma-related internal conflicts between fragmented selves being played out on the stage of the psychotherapy. In questioning our ability as therapists or generalizing client behavior as "transference" or "resistance," we miss the opportunity to become witnesses to the reenactment occurring inside the client's fragmented inner world. Not understanding that fragmentation of the personality can result in simultaneous, strongly held opposing goals, such as "I want to die" and "I am determined to live," or "I want to be connected, but I don't want anyone to know I care." Or "I loathe and despise myself, I look up to others above me, and then I loathe and despise them when I see that they're not better than any other authority figure."

Although written for the therapist committed to finding ways to better help clients for whom other methods haven't been quite right or complete, this book is also written on behalf of the trauma survivor who comes to therapy as a client. Since the early 1990s, I have been looking for gentler, less retraumatizing ways of treating the effects of traumatic experience. It never made sense to me that a therapy for those who have been badly hurt should have to cause the same intensity of pain. I have always believed that it was bad enough for my clients to have lost their childhoods or adolescence, but it was absolutely unacceptable to allow the legacy of trauma to deprive them of their adult lives, too. And it has equally felt unacceptable that processing trauma should be as frightening and overwhelming as the early experiences themselves, that all subsequent relationships, even the therapeutic ones, should feel as threatening as those in childhood. When we are young, our caregivers have almost total control over our inner worlds and the power to evoke in us both painful and pleasurable emotions as well as lay down expectancies for how relationships work. When we have survived to adulthood with its promise of autonomy, we finally have the ability to move away from painful experiences, to choose how much or how little to trust, to negotiate boundaries and intimacy—but that's not how survivors of trauma feel. Their bodies still remember the experience of "no control" over pleasure or pain. My purpose in developing this approach was to describe a way of coming to terms with trauma that felt healing; that spoke to survival, not victimization; that created warm and pleasurable feelings in the body rather than terrifying ones.

This book is intended to appeal to clients and therapists working with trauma, attachment disorders, and dissociation as these manifest in complex and paradoxical symptoms, alienation from self, internal conflicts, and troubled therapeutic relationships or impasses. Therapists routinely are stymied by the effects of self-alienation on the therapy: shame, punitive self-hatred, separation anxiety and fear of abandonment, self-destructive behavior, inability to self-soothe or self-care, fears of hope, happiness, and compassion for self. Psychotherapist training programs provide little information on traumatic attachment, or on how undiagnosed trauma-related fragmentation or splitting can complicate straightforward resolution of trauma, or on the treatment of dissociative disorders as one of a constellation of trauma-related disorders. Healing traumatic wounds and trauma-related fragmentation is ultimately dependent upon the individual's relationship to self—or to his or her "selves." Self-alienation will always impede resolution of the past by creating an internal Berlin Wall standing in the way of acceptance that "it" happened and an ability to welcome home the child who endured and survived it.

How This Book Is Organized

Like all books, this one reflects its author's experience and theoretical paradigms. For me, as a practicing clinician whose professional homes have been Bessel van der Kolk's Trauma Center (since 1996) and Pat Ogden's Sensorimotor Psychotherapy Institute (since 2003), the theoretical models for understanding trauma to which I am committed have their origins in neuroscience and attachment research. It is important to me that we as therapists understand why we are choosing one treatment or intervention over another. Even when the interventions I choose are not immediately "successful," I can still look to the theory to help me understand why—so that my next intervention can be informed by what was missing in the last. In the chapters that follow, I will be integrating a theoretical understanding of trauma, dissociation, neurobiology, and attachment with a practical, "hand's on" approach to the treatment of these issues that is intended to be accessible to both client and therapist. To help clients reach below the level of "talking about," interventions drawn from a number of therapeutic approaches were integrated into this way of working, including Sensorimotor Psychotherapy (Ogden et al., 2006), Internal Family Systems (Schwartz, 2001), mindfulness-based approaches (Pollack, Pedulla & Siegel, 2014), and clinical hypnosis.

As I set out to create a way of working clinically with the Structural Dissociation model, being a practitioner and teacher of Sensorimotor Psychotherapy (Ogden & Fisher, 2015; Ogden et al., 2006), it was only natural to start by integrating my understanding of the body and nervous system with what I knew about parts from working with clients with dissociative identity disorder (DID). Because each part in Structural Dissociation theory is driven by an animal defense response (i.e., fight, flight, etc.), the connection to the body was easy to make. How the body organizes to flee is distinctly different than how it organizes to fight or feign death. But Sensorimotor Psychotherapy speaks the language of the body, so I still needed a language of parts. Richard Schwartz' (1995) Internal Family Systems (IFS) approach, upon which I had drawn heavily in my work with DID clients years earlier, teaches therapists to become fluent in speaking the language of parts. Not only are they asked to speak the language with their clients, but they are also expected to become mindful of their own parts. Because both IFS and Sensorimotor Psychotherapy are mindfulness-based treatment models, they also fit perfectly with my "mindfulness of parts" approach in which I help clients learn at first just to mindfully scan their bodies and feeling states for the communications from their fragmented selves.

What had drawn me originally to IFS for help in working with DID was the concept of "self" and "self"-leadership. (Schwartz, 2001) "Self" refers to innate qualities possessed by all human beings in undamaged form, no matter how much abuse and trauma they have experienced. These qualities include curiosity, clarity (the ability for meta-awareness or perspective), creativity, calm, courage, confidence, and commitment. Healing in IFS is the outcome of providing these qualities as an antidote to the painful experiences suffered by exiled child parts. With my DID clients, I had found it immensely stabilizing to help their adult selves grow these "C" qualities and to help the child parts learn to turn to a "self-led" wise adult self who could reassure their fears and loneliness. As I began to see that fragmentation was not limited just to clients with dissociative disorders, the Structural Dissociation model and IFS provided some welcome support. Structural Dissociation theory is a trauma theory, applying equally to clients with PTSD, complex PTSD, and borderline personality disorder. IFS is a parts theory, applying equally to all human beings, not just traumatized individuals with dissociative disorders. Feeling supported by these ideas, I began to use my "blend" of sensorimotor and IFS interventions and techniques with complex PTSD clients, with clients who came for consultations and were willing to try out different approaches. I also increasingly used it whenever I encountered a client who was stuck, in crisis, in turmoil or "terminal ambivalence." Just as with borderline clients, the mindfulness approach and the attribution of each and every symptom to parts (drawn from IFS) created "breathing space" that allowed clients to be curious about these parts, less afraid, even to feel empathy for them.

Chapter 1, Alienation from Self: How We Survive Overwhelming Experience, sets the stage by describing dissociative splitting and fragmentation as an adaptive response to abnormal experience. To create distance from overwhelming events and preserve a sense of "a good me," individuals must disown the self-states of which they are ashamed, intimidated, or experience as "not-me," allowing them to also disown the trauma (Bromberg, 2011). The ability to encode two parallel sets of experiences in one brain and body is supported by the "split-brain research" in the 1970s and 1980s (Gazzaniga, 1985) and by the neuroscience brain scan research in the late 1990s and 2000s demonstrating how traumatic events come to be encoded as implicit emotional and physical states, rather than being encoded in the form of chronological narrative. The introduction of the Structural Dissociation model in 2000 provided the first neuroscientific understanding of dissociative splitting and compartmentalization (Van der Hart et al., 2000). Unlike earlier models of dissociative fragmentation, this theory does not emphasize the compartmentalization of memory. Instead, its central tenet is that structural dissociation is a survival-oriented adaptive response to the specific demands of traumatic environments, facilitating a left brain-right brain split that supports the disowning of "not me" or trauma-related parts and the ability to function without awareness of having been traumatized. The splitting also supports development of parts driven by animal defenses that serve the cause of survival in the face of danger. Chapter 1 provides a theoretical foundation for understanding both neurobiologically informed trauma work and the need for a parts approach to treatment. Working with a parts approach allows therapists to work more effectively with complex and personality disorder clients. In this model, these clients are not "acting out," "manipulative," "resistant," or "unmotivated." Their trauma-related parts, activated by normal life stimuli, driven by implicit trauma responses, experience the sense of threat and automatically engage instinctive responses: fight, flight, cry for help, freeze, or "feign death" (Porges, 2011).

In Chapter 2, Understanding Parts, Understanding Traumatic Responses, we explore the implications of the neuroscience research on traumatic memory as a basis for understanding and recognizing the signs of fragmented parts as they will appear in client presentations. A simplified understanding of the emergency stress response to threat is presented and how the legacy of trauma becomes encoded in the body. It is important to know how body-based trauma responses drive animal defense impulses to unsafe behavior, why the left-brain-related "normal life" self may observe helplessly but cannot hold back the impulses to action. Underlying automatic hypervigilance, reactivity, suspiciousness, and impulsive action-taking is the body's autonomic nervous system, which governs action and inaction, strong emotions and numbing. In the wake of trauma, the nervous system adapts to a threatening world, conditioned to be "at the ready" for impending danger and therefore biased to mobilize sympathetic hyperarousal or parasympathetic hypoarousal or both, depending on the environment in which these responses were conditioned (Ogden et al., 2006). This chapter asks therapists to make a paradigm shift from a focus on traumatic events to prioritizing attention to the role of implicit memory in trauma treatment. In order to recognize, understand, and help clients work with their trauma-related parts, the therapist must help clients understand their responses to triggering so that they can accurately identify triggered, implicitly remembered feelings, beliefs, and survival responses. Lastly, this chapter addresses the question: What does it mean to "process memory"? When the memories are implicit feelings, body sensations, changes in activation, and disregulated impulsive behavior held by young parts, "what" gets processed? Modern views on memory emphasize its unstable nature: that is, the brain seems to be organized to update and rewrite past experiences, integrating them with prior and subsequent events. Rather than focusing on desensitizing the event memories, experts now advise prioritizing transformation or repair of trauma-related states through the cultivation of new experiences. Instead of focusing on developing a trauma narrative, clients are instead advised to rewrite their "self-defeating" stories and create a healing story that allows them to make meaning of what happened (Michenbaum, 2012).

Chapter 3, Working with Changing Roles for Client and Therapist, begins with a discussion of fundamental shifts in perspective and approach necessitated by a neuroscientifically informed view of traumatized clients. The treatment begins with education for the therapist on the nature of trauma and dissociation, geared to explain the symptoms with which a client struggles and to provide information to reassure him or her that these are normal, logical responses to trauma. Additionally, psychoeducation helps to equalize the inherent power differential by "making public" the knowledge base that will be used in the therapy, empowering clients to become educated consumers in their own treatments (Herman, 1992).

Most therapists have been trained in "uni-consciousness" models of personality and are less familiar with working in a "multi-consciousness" paradigm. Psychodynamically trained therapists have been trained to play a less directive, educational role than required in trauma treatment; cognitive-behavioral therapists may not have been trained in the skills of attunement and resonance. Both are critically important in the context of trauma and in a parts approach. The client's instinctive avoidance of the trauma and trauma-related parts will continue to re-enact the behavior of non-protective bystanders if not guided to a different way of working.

Mindfulness skills must be explicitly taught, along with the language of parts necessary for identifying them. The beginning stages of the therapy involve the therapist's attuned building of a collaboration based on what the client needs, not just on what he or she wants. To create a new story about whom he or she is in the aftermath of the painful and traumatic events requires learning new habits of observation and discovery: the "op-ed" stories clients have been writing about themselves have been biased, not in their favor. They need help in acquiring the skills of mindful observation of both positive and negative feelings and sensations without interpretation or judgment. Next, they learn to use the language of parts or "selves" to describe their often confusing or paradoxical actions and reactions as they happen moment-to-moment clients but without "identifying with them," or interpreting them as data about the immediate present. Identification invariably intensifies any emotion or evokes shame. Learning to describe an experience without "identifying with it" allows clients to notice its "building blocks" (Ogden & Fisher, 2015): "As I talk about my father, I'm noticing a tightness in my chest and my heart beating fast" or "I'm noticing that a part of me is anxious." Learning to dispassionately notice allows for the next steps in this approach to unfold: increased ability to hold a curious or even compassionate attitude toward whatever feelings or reactions are observed and, following that, an ability to "befriend" the emotion. In Buddhism, acceptance, welcoming, avoiding "attachment or aversion" (identifying with the feeling or fighting/judging it) are an essential part of finding equanimity, a state of calm, peacefulness, and composure. Translated into psychotherapy, this practice helps clients learn to tolerate and accept even the most painful, humiliating, or frightening emotions and sensations.

Rather than beginning with an exploration of the "old world" of painful, humiliating experiences and overwhelming feelings, the therapist is encouraged to focus on increasing the client's curiosity and interest in feeling states, parts, thoughts, and body responses. The goal of this approach is not remembering: it is *repair* of the injuries suffered as a result of the traumatic events, whether remembered explicitly as narrative or implicitly as feelings and reactions.

In Chapter 4, Learning to See Our "Selves": An Introduction to Working with Parts, therapist and client are taught the fundamental skills necessary for working in a parts paradigm. This early stage of the treatment is intended to help clients learn the basic skills necessary for working in a parts paradigm. First and foremost, clients are introduced to the Structural Dissociation model and asked to describe what resonates with their experiences and difficulties. How do they recognize themselves in the model? The Structural Dissociation model also offers a client-friendly entrée into identifying the signs of parts. Each animal defense survival response is associated with certain behaviors frequently associated with trauma. These are introduced to clients in diagram form to help them focus attention and take in this new information with greater interest and curiosity. Another approach to increasing awareness of parts activity is to ask clients to "assume" that all distressing thoughts, feelings, and body responses are communications from trauma-related parts. (This assumption is consistent with split-brain neuroscience findings on the activity and abilities associated with each of the two hemispheres.) Teaching schemas that facilitate ready identification of parts activity allows clients easier access to their internal experience, enabling them to differentiate "their feelings," rather than identify with all emotions as "mine." Clients are also taught to be mindful of internal conflicts, ambivalence, or confusion as manifestations of struggles between parts triggered by each other as well as by trauma-related stimuli.

Chapter 5, Befriending Our Parts: Sowing the Seeds of Compassion, focuses on interventions that begin a process of fostering the increased self-understanding and self-compassion so necessary for healing. Asked to have compassion for themselves or to better care for themselves, most traumatized clients have a strong negative reaction. But when an emotion such as fear or shame is connected to the felt sense of a young child, the same client can often feel empathy or even indignation for that child. In mindfulness-based treatment, it is not necessary that we differentiate between compassion "for ourselves" versus compassion "for the child." The felt emotional and somatic sensations of compassion are the same, no matter who is the intended receiver, and it is those sensations of compassion that help to soothe and heal traumatic and attachment wounding. It is also not necessary to have detailed narrative memory of the client's traumatic experience: it is only necessary for the client to have a felt sense of what the child part has been through. Having a "sense" or a synopsis of the client's trauma history allows the therapist and client to acknowledge what younger selves have been through without overwhelming the client's nervous system or capacity for affect tolerance. Acknowledging the parts' traumatic experiences feels validating without triggering traumatic reactions. At this stage of the work, the emphasis is on cultivating compassion for the parts, one by one. Compassion is challenged by overwhelming emotions or disturbing body responses. The goal is to help the client feel "just enough" of the part's suffering that empathy is evoked. It is important for the therapist to remember that, in trauma treatment, feeling too much interferes with empathy and compassion as much as feeling too little. At this stage, clients are also taught to recognize "blending" (Schwartz, 2001) or identifying with their parts, making them vulnerable to being flooded or acting out the impulse of some part, and to practice "unblending" and dis-identifying.

In Chapter 6, Complications of Treatment: Traumatic Attachment, we address the internal conflicts and struggles created by a history of traumatic attachment. If the hallmark of traumatic attachment is a reversal of roles in which the object of safety (the parent figure) becomes the object of fear and life threat, any intimate relationship thereafter, even the therapy, evokes danger signals. Growing closeness in relationship can convey threat or a promise of comfort and connection, evoking emotional memories of the longing for an attachment figure that never came alongside implicit memories of the abandonment and betrayal that did happen. Because attachment and fear have become intertwined in the client's experience, a therapy focused on the narrative memories or on the transference is likely to ignite an internal struggle between the hunger for closeness in young attachment-seeking parts and their fear of abandonment versus the defensive responses of fight, flight, and total submission. In dissociative disorder clients with parts that are more disconnected and autonomous, this internal struggle becomes even more easily activated in personal relationships or in the therapy, harder to decode or deconstruct, and more difficult to manage behaviorally.

How therapists anticipate this phenomenon and how they help their clients accept and work with it can lead either to deeper healing or to a reopening of attachment wounds in the therapy itself. If either clinging or devaluing is interpreted as an interpersonal issue between client and therapist, they are often exacerbated. If we understand them as "intra-personal," indicators of an internal attachment disorder still operating within the client, then the therapist can become an ally for both sides of the struggle and a facilitator of "earned secure attachment" (Siegel, 1999). In "earned" secure attachment, the insecure or disorganized attachment of childhood and/or adulthood is resolved to the point that individuals can reflect back on their early attachment relationships without becoming disregulated, without idealizing or demonizing their attachment figures, and feel a sense of acceptance. In this model, earned secure attachment is the outcome of the clients' growing ability to bond with their own young wounded selves as innocent children who deserved the loving care of a compassionate adult but never received it. Rather than the therapeutic focus being centered on attachment to the therapist, the emphasis is consistently on building empathy and attunement to the parts.

In Chapter 7, Working with Suicidal, Self-Destructive, Eating Disordered, and Addicted Parts, unsafe and high-risk behaviors are recontextualized as manifestations of parts-related animal defense survival responses. Addictive, eating disordered, suicidal, and self-injurious behaviors are all reinterpreted through a neurobiological lens. The neurobiological premise assumes that human bodies have the same self-righting, self-healing tendencies as do the bodies of other mammalian species. If that is so, then self-destructive behavior must also have a self-righting intention. Viewed in this way, unsafe behavior historically labeled "self-destructive" can be better understood as a desperate attempt to survive, a way to tolerate shame, rage, and fear, to inhibit flashbacks and nightmares, or to use endogenous or exogenous substances to regulate a traumatized nervous system. As part of an informal, clinically oriented pilot project offering new forms of treatment to trauma patients in a Connecticut Department of Mental Health system, participating clinicians have been gathering informal data on what precedes and follows episodes of unsafe behavior. They have observed that episodes of self-harm or suicide attempts most commonly follow relational disappointments, separations or ending of relationships, preoccupation with shame and self-loathing, and intrusive memories or flashbacks. This finding implies that such events evoke the experience of threat and generate trauma-related emotional responses that feel unbearable until some impulsive behavior diminishes their intensity or creates emotional and bodily numbing. After these episodes, there is a corresponding tendency for patients to report exhaustion, loss of energy, and intense feelings of needing rest—the same indicators characteristic of parasympathetic responses following a fight or flight response. Historically, this classic post-traumatic unsafe behavior has been interpreted clinically as attention-seeking, manipulation, or avoidance. With the implementation of this neurobiologically informed approach, in which patients are helped to reframe impulsive or unsafe behavior as communications from a part driven by the animal defense of fight, the frequency of unsafe behavior has diminished. By externalizing the impulses and assigning them to a defensive part, the patients are able to keep an observing prefrontal cortex available to help them manage the impulses as "not mine—it's the fight part." Better yet, when these patients are taught the Structural Dissociation model, there appears to be a decrease in negative self-judgment and an increase in their curiosity, both of which are antidotes to impulsive behavior. Teaching these clients the basic skills outlined in Chapters 4 and 5 and asking them to practice their use seems to have a stabilizing effect in and of itself. In addition, clients are given psychoeducation about the biological effects of their unsafe behavior and how it "works" to regulate the nervous system, helping them to gain a perspective on the body's role in these issues. As their ability to "unblend" from impulsive parts increases, and there is more access to an uninhibited prefrontal cortex, these clients are better able to notice the parts' distressing emotions and unsafe impulses and regulate them, rather than react to them.

In Chapter 8, Treatment Challenges: Dissociative Systems and Disorders, we address the unique issues posed by clients who have diagnosable dissociative disorders (DID, DDNOS, depersonalization disorder). A dissociative disorder diagnosis reflects a more extreme degree of compartmentalization, affecting the ability for continuous consciousness, the ability to know moment-to-moment "who I am," to make coherent choices and decisions and carry them through to completion, to manage impulses, to have accurate perceptions of cause-effect or time and space, and to integrate the traumatic past and normal, safe present. Clients with dissociative disorders are often underdiagnosed or misdiagnosed despite their statistically significant dissociative symptomatology (Korzekwa et al., 2009a). Most often, they present with diagnoses of borderline personality disorder, bipolar disorder II, and ADD or ADHD. This chapter reviews the diagnostic signs indicating a possible DID diagnosis, discusses assessment approaches, and suggests criteria for making a formal diagnosis. The same treatment approach outlined in Chapters 3–5 is very effective for DID and DDNOS clients, with adjustments to how the therapist works to account for the failures of memory and continuity.

Because the approach described in this book is mindfulness-based, it tends to be stabilizing for clients and to facilitate deconstructing problems encountered in normal life, as well as trauma-related issues. The language of parts allows both client and therapist to keep in mind the central challenge of working with dissociative disorders: holding in mind that the client is still one physical individual with one body and one brain, while equally appreciating that this one brain and body are fragmented and hold many parts of different ages, stages, attachment styles, and defensive responses. To feel empathy for each part's plight, while not losing sight of the fact that the client is an adult with functional capabilities is a mental ability that often has to be practiced before it becomes second nature. With dissociative disorders, the therapist is working with clients who are not an integrated "she" or "he." Viewing them as such is often confusing, rather than helpful, just as viewing clients as inner children without adult resources equally causes confusion.

The duality of whole and part, or a whole with parts, is always front and center in DID treatment. When the therapist asks the client to distinguish the parts responsible for a problem behavior and then becomes curious about their emotions, beliefs, motives, and defensive responses, he or she engages the left brain-driven part of the personality to "help" solve the issues and challenges raised by right brain-driven trauma-related parts. This skill is even more crucial in the treatment of clients with dissociative disorders than it is in work with fragmented individuals without DID. When right brain dominant parts can act independently outside the conscious awareness of the client, the need to have the balancing, stabilizing presence of a left brain self is especially crucial.

In Chapter 9, Repairing the Past: Embracing Our Selves, the premise is that resolution of traumatic experience is dependent upon overcoming survival-related self-alienation. By cultivating the growing attunement between child selves and grownup normal life self, each aspect of self feels an increasing comfort in the other's presence, greater safety, and a warmth in connection. But in order to foster attachment bonds between traumatized individuals and their young selves, the therapist first must help clients acknowledge, connect, and identify with the normal life adult inside themselves—the self that has the ability to care for and express caring, that has always been instinctively driven to seek safety, normality, and stability, that can "be here now" for a small child in need of safe attachment.

Distorted cognitions associated with shame and self-loathing often interfere with clients' ability to feel connected even to strengths they are aware they possess. Perhaps it was unsafe as a child to have strengths or a desire for mastery without traumatic consequences. The parts may be triggered by normal life activities (such as a job, a partner relationship, responsibilities, or simply having to be visible), undermining the client's ability to handle them. Internal conflicts between parts may debilitate or destabilize the normal life self or block attempts at developing a life after trauma.

Using clinical examples to illustrate in detail how the therapist can foster the innate compassion of the normal life self on behalf of wounded child parts, the reader is given a template for how internal acceptance is built by drawing on the client's strengths and life experiences as resources for the young child selves. While the left brain self has been learning and storing competencies, these abilities have not been available to the right brain selves. This chapter illustrates interventions that bring the two sides into contact and evoke pleasurable moments of attunement and togetherness that become the building blocks of internal secure attachment. The human brain's complexity allows us to heal ourselves: it endows upon us the unique ability to access acquired capacities and engage them on behalf of other parts sharing the same brain and body.

In Chapter 10, Restoring What Was Lost: Deepening the Connection to Our Young Selves, the healing work takes another step forward. First, clients must earn the parts' trust, made challenging by their implicit memories of inadequate bonding and failed trust that both increase the yearning to trust but also increase hypervigilant resistance to trusting. The therapist consistently asks the client, on behalf of the parts, to communicate, collaborate, and extend compassion to them, slowly building up a felt sense of an internal attachment figure, one who shares the same brain and body, one who might have once been the age of the parts but now is a strong, caring adult committed to creating a life different from the past: safe, nourishing, and relational.

In Chapter 11, Safety and Welcome: The Experience of Earned Secure Attachment, we address "integration" not as a goal of treatment but as a process that occurs organically when we use mindfulness-based techniques to bring awareness and compassion to the system of traumatized parts. As defined by Daniel Siegel (2010), "Integration results from differentiation coupled with linkage." Asked to bring focused attention to a young part in distress, the client is asked to imagine a young child of the same age with the same emotions in the room, "standing right there before you." By bringing the child part inside "alive," the therapist facilitates the client's access to right brain-based inherently compassionate intuitive responses. Using guided visualization, the therapist evokes images of the child's face, body language, and plight to increase the sense of connection or empathy between child and normal life adult and the latter is asked to notice, "And how do you feel toward that part now?" Repeatedly, client and part are asked to mentalize the other's mentalization, to notice how one impacts the other, stimulating a felt sense of connection, then enhancing the bond by sharing their responses again and again: "Ask the little girl how it feels to hear you say, 'I'm glad I'm here—I want her to feel safe'." While internal bonds of secure attachment are built through the dyadic interchanges between adult and part, the normal life self of the client is also asked to repair the distressed state of the child or create a new ending to the story of distress, just as secure attachment figures do. Imaginal experiences of healthy, safe attachment can generate the same feelings and sensations and evoke the same "attunement bliss" that babies and mothers enjoy, and, by simply focusing mindfully on these moments, they can be encoded as readily as a concrete, physical experience of safety and attunement (Hanson, 2014).

Chapter 11 stresses again that emotional healing of traumatic wounds has to be attachment-based. Like long-lost young relatives, the alienated disowned parts must be invited to the table and welcomed into the heart and mind and arms of the client. This process can be very moving for both client and therapist but is not without its challenges. The trauma-related fear of self-compassion is strong and unbending, leaving the therapist with the job of holding a calm, clear, courageous stance that alienation from or rejection of any part leaves us less than whole. Without welcoming each and every part "home" and offering safe, unconditional acceptance, survivors can't fully heal the wounds left by the failed empathy of the caretakers who harmed them or allowed them to be harmed when they were too little, too alone, and too vulnerable to defend themselves. For those clients traumatized as adults, the therapist has to be absolutely clear that resolution still depends upon all parts finding safety after trauma: young parts whose needs were not reliably met in childhood or who interpreted the traumatic events in the light of insecure attachment, adolescent parts whose fight and flight responses have been reactivated, despairing submissive parts who "took the fall" in an inescapable situation, even suicidal parts who would rather turn their swords on themselves rather than be humiliated or abandoned.

Dan Siegel's conceptualization of "earned secure attachment" reflects the belief of many in the attachment field (Main, Schore, Lyons-Ruth) that childhood attachment wounds can be modified through life experiences that "grow" states of secure attachment, even in adulthood. These experiences might include raising one's own children, healthy friendships and intimate relationships, or creating secure attachment relationships with one's parts. Each of these avenues for earned security capitalizes on the brain's ability to grow new neural networks and encode new, pleasurable feeling states. By imaginally evoking new implicit memories of safety and attunement, parts feel the inner sensate experience of healthy attachment, moments that can be encoded alongside the painful memories of failed or frightening attachments, changing the ending of the story. "Earned security" is measured by the degree of "coherence" exhibited by individuals reflecting on their early attachment relationships on the Adult Attachment Inventory, that is, the degree to which they have integrated the bitter and the sweet of their lives, the pain then and the pleasure in relationships now.

Only the human brain can create a new story of safety, closeness, and compassion by evoking states of well-being connected either to imagined or remembered experiences. For neuroplastic brain change to occur, only three ingredients are needed: first, clients have to be helped to inhibit their habitual emotional, physical, and cognitive patterns. Next, they have to practice a new pattern with which they'd like to replace the old—and then practice the new pattern over and over again without losing the felt connection to the child and to their own bodies. It could be as simple as bringing the right hand over the heart to communicate calm or repeating the words, "It's okay now" or "I'm here now."

A client's new "healing story" might sound a bit like this: "Once upon a time, my parts felt as unsafe and unlovable as I did as a child. Now I don't feel anxious that I'll be rejected and abandoned, and neither do they. I know I'm OK, and I know they're OK—I feel connected to my parts and to myself, and I'll always be here to keep them safe. They are special to me and always will be."

In the appendices that follow Chapter 11, therapists and clients will find some additional tools to help them with the tasks presented throughout the book. Appendix A consists of a simple protocol for learning how to unblend from parts, especially parts with intense feelings that hijack the prefrontal cortex and destabilize the client. Appendix B consists of a meditation circle practice for parts. Appendix C presents the Internal Dialogue protocol that, practiced over and over again, builds the ability to communicate internally, calm and comfort distressed parts, and grow the bonds of compassion. Appendix D presents a treatment paradigm for internal attachment repair. Appendix E consists of a worksheet, the Dissociative Experiences Log, for helping clients increase the ability to track and differentiate the signs of parts' activity and communication. And Appendix F provides a script for the Four Befriending Questions, a technique that builds inner communication and bonds of love and trust.

Psychotherapists have wondered and worried and philosophized for hundreds of years about the nature of healing. This book describes one theory about healing the effects of trauma and traumatic attachment that emerged from my clinical observations: healing is the outcome of reversing long-standing patterns of self-alienation and building the capacity to love and accept our "selves." When we reclaim our lost souls and wounded children, befriend them, and allow ourselves to trust deeply felt compassionate impulses to reach out to them and build bonds of secure attachment, they feel safe and welcome at long last. And we feel whole.

References

Bromberg, P. (2011). *The shadow of the tsunami and the growth of the relational mind.* New York: Taylor & Francis.

Gazzaniga, M. S. (1985). *The social brain: discovering the networks of the mind.* New York: Basic Books.

Hanson, R. (2014). *Hardwiring happiness: the new brain science of contentment, calm, and confidence.* New York: Harmony Publications.

Herman, J. L. (1992) *Trauma and recovery.* New York: Basic Books.

Ogden, P. & Fisher, J. (2015). *Sensorimotor psychotherapy: interventions for trauma and attachment.* New York: W.W. Norton.

Ogden, P., Minton, K. & Pain, C. (2006). *Trauma and the body: a sensorimotor approach to psychotherapy.* New York: W.W. Norton.

Pollack, S.M., Padulla, T., & Seigel, R.D. (2014). *Sitting together: essential skills for mindfulness-based psychotherapy.* New York: Guilford Press.

Porges, S.W. (2011). *The Polyvagal theory: neurophysiological foundations of emotions, attachment, communication, and self-regulation.* New York: W.W. Norton.

Schwartz, R. (1995). *Internal family systems therapy.* New York: Guilford Press.

Schwartz, R. (2001). *Introduction to the internal family systems model.* Oak Park, IL: Trailhead Publications.

Siegel, D.J. (1999). *The developing mind: toward a neurobiology of interpersonal experience.* New York: Guilford Press.

Siegel, D. J. (2010). *The neurobiology of 'we.'* Keynote address, Psychotherapy Networker Symposium, Washington, D.C., March 2010.

Van der Hart, O., Nijenhuis, E.R.S., & Steele, K. (2006). *The haunted self: structural dissociation and the treatment of chronic traumatization.* New York: W.W. Norton.

Van der Hart, O., Nijenhuis, E.R.S., Steele, K., & Brown, D. (2004). Trauma-related dissociation: conceptual clarity lost and found. *Australian and New Zealand Journal of Psychiatry*, 38, 906–914.

Van der Hart, O., van Dijke, A., van Son, M., and Steele, K. (2000). Somatoform dissociation in traumatized World War I combat soldiers: a neglected clinical heritage. *Journal of Trauma and Dissociation*, 1(4), 33–66.

Van der Kolk, B.A. (2014). *The body keeps the score: brain, mind and body in the healing of trauma.* New York: Viking Press.

CHAPTER 1

The Neurobiological Legacy of Trauma: How We Become Fragmented

"If the elements of the trauma are replayed again and again, the accompanying stress hormones engrave those memories even more deeply into the mind. Ordinary, day-to-day events become less and less compelling. Not being able to deeply take in what is going on around [us] makes it impossible to feel fully alive. It becomes harder to feel the joys and aggravations of ordinary life, harder to concentrate on the tasks at hand. Not being fully alive in the present keeps [us] more firmly imprisoned in the past."

(Van der Kolk, 2014, p. 67)

In the face of abuse and neglect, especially at the hands of those they love, children need enough psychological distance from what is happening to avoid being overwhelmed and survive psychologically intact. Preserving some modicum of self-esteem, attachment to family, and hope for the future requires victims to disconnect from what has happened, doubt or disremember their experience, and disown the "bad [victim] child" to whom it happened as "not me." By holding out some sense of themselves as "good" disconnected from how they have been exploited, abused children capitalize on the human brain's innate capacity to split or compartmentalize. That "good child" might be precociously mature, sweet and helpful, perfectionistic, self-critical, or quiet and shy, but, most importantly, he or she has a way to be acceptable and safer in an unsafe world. Splitting or fragmenting in this way is an ingenious and adaptive survival strategy—but one with a steep price. To ensure that the rejected "not me" child is kept out of the way (i.e., out of consciousness) requires that, long after the traumatic events are over, individuals must continue to rely on dissociation, denial, and/or self-hatred for enforcing the disconnection. In the end, they have survived the failure of safety, the abuse, and betrayal at the cost of disowning their most vulnerable and most wounded selves. Aware that their self-presentation and ability to function is only one piece of who they really are, they now feel fraudulent. Struggling to stay away from the "bad" side and identify with the good side, they have a felt sense of "faking it," "pretending," or of being what others want them to be. For some, this conviction of fraudulence engenders resentment; for some, shame and self-doubt. For both groups, the legacy of the trauma remains alive rather than resolved.

As children of abuse continue to grow through latency into adolescence and subsequently adulthood, this splitting of the self supports another important aspect of surviving trauma: mastering normal developmental tasks, such as learning in school, developing peer relationships, finding interests on which to focus and even enjoy. The "good" part of the child is free to develop normally while that other part of the child bears the emotional and physical imprint of the past, scans for signs of danger, and braces for the next set of threats and abandonments. To make the individual's situation more complicated, neither the "me" nor the "not me" self is likely to have well-developed chronological memories of the traumatic events that could provide a context for self-understanding. Due to the nature of traumatic memory, what can be "recalled" tends to appear in the form of intrusive images, emotions, and physical reactions (Van der Kolk, 2006; 2014) that occur spontaneously without warning, not a sequence of narrative memories that make a clear-cut case for what happened "beyond a reasonable doubt."

The "Living Legacy" of the Past

Without a clear chronological record of what happened but vulnerable to the uninvited activation of trauma-related feeling and body memories, individuals are left with a legacy of symptoms and reactions with no context that identifies them as memory. Survivors of trauma later present in therapy with descriptions of their anxiety, depression, shame, low self-esteem, loneliness and alienation, problems with anger, and impulsivity or acting out. They might be troubled by chronic expectations of danger: intrusive fear and dread, hypervigilance ("eyes in the back of my head"), chronic shame and self-hatred, a conviction that the worst is about to happen, hopelessness and helplessness, fear of abandonment, numbing and disconnection from emotions. Or they may come to therapy as a last resort because they are fighting a losing battle against addiction, self-harming impulses, eating disorders, or a longing or even determination to die. Often, they can tell us very little about what evokes these self-destructive impulses that bring quick short-term relief at great risk to their safety: "I do it to punish myself," "I hate myself," "I don't deserve to live," "I'm disgusting—I wish I were dead." They sometimes struggle with how to connect these patterns to the past—but, more often, they prefer not to think about what happened then or minimize it: "It wasn't that bad."

In the early history of trauma treatment, therapists relied on the "talking cure," the most commonly accepted practice in psychotherapy from the time of Freud to the present day (Rothschild, in press), to address the strong emotional reactivity of traumatized clients coupled with their lack of clarity for the traumatic events. Clients were generally encouraged to keep retrieving the memories of "what happened" until they had established a detailed narrative of the chronological events. But, when therapists adopted this approach, rather than resolving the traumatic past, clients became flooded with overwhelming implicit memories and traumatic reactions, increasingly symptomatic rather than at peace (Herman, 1992; Van der Kolk, 2014). Talking about the events of the past, therapists discovered, led to more implicit "reliving" of it. Unwittingly, the therapist and the "good child," now a grown-up client, were at long last validating the events experienced by the disowned "not me" child—while at the same time, activating the trauma-related parts and triggering their implicit memories. Feeling endangered yet again, the "not me" children were crying for help, still without being heard.

I have long believed that trauma treatment must address the *effects* of the traumatic past, not its events. Being able to tolerate remembering a horrific experience is not as important a goal as feeling safe right here, right now—or being able to reassure oneself that the racing of the heart is just a triggered response, not a sign of danger—or being able to relate to shame, grief, and anger as the feeling memories of child selves too young to comfort themselves. In my view, resolution of painful past events cannot truly be achieved without reclaiming the lost children and disowned parts of ourselves, extending to them a helping hand, welcoming them "home" at long last, creating safety for them, and making them feel wanted, needed, and valued. It took many decades of scientific research for the clinical world to accept that child abuse constituted an epidemic, not a rare occurrence, and that untreated post-traumatic stress resulted in tremendous social costs, not just individual suffering. Only in the last ten years have the concepts of implicit memory and bodily-driven responses to trauma become increasingly widespread (Ogden et al., 2006; Van der Kolk, 2014), but, even now, theoretical ideas about splitting, parts of the self, and dissociation are still controversial and often avoided. We as a field have not yet accepted that compartmentalization is normal under stress and much more common than we generally recognize. In a parallel process, the mental health world has had a history of disowning the prevalence of child abuse, dissociation, and fragmentation of the personality, either by ignoring its manifestations or by invalidating it as "factitious" or "malingering." To be the "good child" in the psychiatric treatment world, therapists have been under pressure to "un-see" signs of dissociation, to diagnose voices as a psychotic symptom, and to treat fragmented clients "as if" they were whole integrated human beings. To be an integrated human, as Dan Siegel (2010) insists, requires "differentiation—with linkage," that is, it necessitates the ability to make distinctions between different parts of the self, to name them as parts, but also to link them to other parts and to the whole of which they are a part. Disowning parts of one's self and over-identifying with other parts does not facilitate integration and a sense of being whole, nor does it engender an internal sense of safety that could counteract the after-effects of an unsafe, unwelcoming hostile world.

Parallel Lives: The Disowning of Dissociation

In the history of the trauma field, the concepts of dissociation and splitting have been repeatedly observed as complications of trauma but consistently rejected as "not me," that is, as not valid or believable within the prevailing diagnostic systems and therefore to be avoided. One of the difficulties with gaining acceptance for the existence of dissociative splitting and especially dissociative disorders has been an absence of studies demonstrating a scientific basis for such dramatic, difficult-to-treat symptoms. Theories of parts tend to be metaphorical rather than biologically or brain-based. In the dissociative disorders world, the explanatory hypothesis has historically been stress-related: when events are traumatic, the theory asserts, they exceed the brain's capacity to tolerate or process them as wholes. Therefore, they must be split or compartmentalized so that overwhelming event memories are shared by dissociated parts of the same age, each carrying some portion of the memory. In this model, each part is viewed as a repository of memory, representing the history of the client at a specific time. In treatment, the parts are encouraged to "download" or disclose their memories so that the "host" can share their pain and accept their shared past. Only then could the parts begin fusing into one homogenized whole (Putnam, 1989). Although this hypothesis makes intuitive sense to many clinicians and clients, it lacks the scientific validity necessary to overcome the skepticism and disowning of dissociation by the mental health world.

Another theory is that multiplicity is normal, that all human beings have multi-consciousness rather than uni-consciousness. A mindfulness-based approach to understanding parts based on this hypothesis is Internal Family Systems or IFS (Schwartz, 1995; 2001). Known for its compassionate tone and cultivation of mindful awareness, IFS also depends upon a metaphorical theory, this one based on intrapsychic defenses: the "not-me" child is termed an "exile," hidden from conscious awareness by the activity of "managers." When the manager parts do not offer enough protection to keep exiles out of awareness, acting out by another set of parts, the "firefighters," creates distraction and crisis. Healing occurs in the IFS model when the exiled parts are reclaimed, can feel safe enough with "self," the higher self of the client, to share the disowned memories and be "unburdened" of the painful emotions and beliefs connected to the trauma.

But to bring credibility to such a controversial "not us" topic as dissociation, good clinical models without a theoretical basis are not sufficient. It took the neuroscience revolution to provide a scientific explanation for the concept of "splitting" and even to the terminology of "parts of the self." It has taken years of research to challenge the fixed negative beliefs about dissociation and dissociative disorders so prevalent in the field (Brand et al., 2016).

Compartmentalization under Stress: Exploiting the Fault Lines

A biological basis for understanding compartmentalization under stress lies in the brain's innate "fault lines," the fact that its functions are tied to and governed by different regions and differentiated structures within each region (Van der Hart et al., 2004). One "fault line" for splitting available even at birth is the right hemisphere-left hemisphere split. Though children are born with both left and right hemispheres, they are right brain dominant for most of childhood (Cozolino, 2002; Schore, 2001). The slower developing left brain has spurts of growth around the age of language development and again at adolescence, but the development of left brain dominance is only achieved very gradually over the course of the first eighteen years of life. In addition, the corpus callosum, the part of the brain that makes possible right brain-left brain communication, also develops slowly and only becomes fully elaborated around the age of twelve (Cozolino, 2002; Teicher, 2004). Thus, in the early years of childhood, right brain experience is relatively independent of left brain experience, lending itself to splitting should the need arise. Studying brain development in children and adolescents, Martin Teicher has observed a correlation between a history of abuse and/or neglect and under-development of the corpus callosum compared to normal controls (2004), which would also support the hypothesis that trauma is associated with independent development of right and left hemispheres and that deficits in communication between the two brains may hinder right-left integration, leaving clients with "two brains" (Gazzaniga, 2015) instead of one integrated brain.

The "split-brain research" of the 1970s (Gazzaniga, 2015) was the first research to show the degree to which left and right hemispheres of the brain operate independently and quite differently. "Split-brain" research refers to studying patients whose right and left hemispheres have been separated by injury or surgery or who have suffered damage to the corpus callosum. Although these patients demonstrate that there seems to be some shared knowledge available to both hemispheres, only the left hemisphere uses language to describe experience and information, while the right hemisphere is more visual, better able to recognize differences and similarities between stimuli but lacking words to describe it. The right hemisphere tends to remember episodically and implicitly, whereas the left is specialized for autobiographical memory and acquired knowledge. But the left hemisphere's ability to encode information verbally does not imply that its recollection of events is more "accurate." "The left hemisphere has a tendency to grasp the gist of a situation, make an inference that fits in well with the general schema of the event, and toss out anything that does not. This elaboration has a deleterious effect on accuracy but usually makes it easier to process new information. The right hemisphere does not do this. It is totally truthful and only identifies the original [information]" (Gazzaniga, 2015, p. 152); that is, the right hemisphere does not "forget" the nonverbal aspects of experience and does not interpret it. Emotions, these researchers discovered, are experienced on both sides of the brain but can only be verbalized by the left hemisphere; the right hemisphere might act on the emotion but could not describe it in words. And without an exchange of information via the corpus callosum, researchers observed that the left hemisphere might have no memory of the right hemisphere's emotion-driven actions and reactions.

Attachment research has also contributed to the literature supporting the concept of an innate tendency to compartmentalize under stress. In longitudinal studies of attachment behavior (Lyons-Ruth et al., 2006; Solomon & George, 1999; Solomon & Siegel, 2003), researchers have demonstrated that children with disorganized attachment status at age one are significantly more likely to exhibit dissociative symptoms by age 19 and/or to be diagnosed with borderline personality disorder or dissociative identity disorder in adulthood. When attachment figures are abusive, the child's only source of safety and protection becomes simultaneously the source of immediate danger, leaving the child caught between two conflicting sets of instincts. On the one hand, they are driven by the attachment instinct to seek proximity, comfort, and protection from attachment figures. On the other, they are driven by equally strong animal defense instincts to freeze, fight, flee, or submit or dissociate before they get too close to the frightening parent. Liotti (1999) hypothesizes that dissociative splitting is necessitated to manage this irresolvable struggle between two such strong emotional and physical drives and two very different internal working models: biologically, the attachment figure automatically elicits the cry for help response or proximity-seeking drive, yet approaching abusive or threatening adults also elicits fear and fight and flight responses.

Van der Hart, Nijenhuis, and Steele (2004; 2006) cite yet another set of fault lines along which dissociative compartmentalization can occur: the "action systems" or drives that propel the stages of child development and adaptation to the environment. One set of drives can be seen in children's innate propensity to attach, explore, play, and develop social engagement and collaboration skills and then, as older children and adults, learn to regulate their bodily needs, mate and reproduce, and care for the next generation (Panksepp, 1998; Van der Hart et al., 2006). Equally, though, children have to depend upon their instinctive animal defenses (hypervigilance, cry for help, fight and flight, freeze, collapse and submission) to quickly inhibit exploration, social engagement, and regulating functions to ensure automatic self-protective behavior. For children raised in unsafe environments, both types of action system are necessary in response to changing internal and external demands: for example, going to school requires a part of the personality that can explore, pay attention in class, learn, and socially engage with peers and teachers. At home, with parents who may be withdrawn or neglectful at some times and violent at others, the ability to rapidly shift from state to state as needed to deal with different threats could be essential: for example, in response to the sound of the abuser's voice or footsteps, panic or fear could alert the individual to danger. Playfulness might lift the parent's irritable mood and facilitate a positive connection by making him or her laugh (social engagement). At times, it might be helpful to capitalize on the submission response to become the precociously responsible child who tries to protect younger siblings in the face of the violent behavior, but at other times, it could be safer to rely on hypervigilance, staying "on guard," carefully observing the parents' mood, and reacting in whatever ways best defend against their "frightened or frightening" behavior. These patterns of compartmentalization can be conceptualized as trauma-related procedural learning: it is safer to adapt using a system of selves rather than becoming a fully integrated "self."

Extrapolating from the observations by Charles Myers of "shell-shocked" World War I veterans, Van der Hart and colleagues (2004) labeled these different drives or systems "part(s) of the personality." Although "part of the personality" remains a very controversial term in the mental health world, it has certain advantages: first, use of the word "part" clearly suggests that there is a whole person and personality—of which we are studying just one piece. Secondly, it is a word so commonly used to describe normal ambivalence or inner conflicts (e.g., "Part of me wants to eat that piece of cake so badly, but another part won't let me") that it is easily adopted by clients. And lastly, research has demonstrated the propensity of the brain to develop neural networks holding related neural pathways that consistently "fire" together, and these neural systems often encode complex systems of traits or systems (Schore, 2001) that represent aspects of our personalities or ways of being. For example, if neural pathways activating the proximity drive fire consistently in the presence of the attachment figure, along with neural pathway holding feelings of loneliness and yearning for comfort and a neural network holding the tendency to believe that "she loves me—she would never hurt me," the result might be a neural system representing a young child part of the personality with a toddler's yearning for comfort and closeness along with the magical thinking that the attachment figure will be safe and loving, yet also the uneasy feeling that something is not right. Such neural systems can be complex with a subjective sense of identity or can be a simpler collection of traits associated with different roles played by the individual.

Van der Hart et al. (2006) borrowed the language of Myers in describing the aspect of self driven by daily life priorities as the "apparently normal part of the personality" and parts driven by animal defense responses as the "emotional parts of the personality," or, individually, the fight, flight, freeze, submit, or attach for survival parts. In this book, I will use terms that I have found more useful in clinical practice: the "going on with normal life part" and the "trauma-related parts" of the personality. In avoiding the words, "apparently normal," my goal is to emphasize the positive evolutionary function of parts of us driven to survive or persevere and to challenge clients' tendencies to see their ability to function as a "false self" and their trauma-related responses as the "true self." In addition, emphasizing the positive aims and goals of the "normal life" part encourages clients to strengthen their ability to regulate the tumultuous emotions and autonomic dysregulation of the animal defense-related parts, rather than either trying to ignore them or interpreting them as "the true self." Connecting different parts to the survival responses that drive their actions and reactions challenges the client's automatic shame and self-doubt: experiences of feeling rage make more sense when tied to a "fight part" triggered by an act of unfairness; automatic passivity and the inability to say "no" feels less shameful when connected to a young child submit part whose sense of safety is tied to pleasing others or feeling "less than." The concept that each part represents a way of surviving dangerous conditions, that each represents a different approach to self-protection, gives meaning and dignity to the fragmentation. The parts in this view are not repositories of memory; they were a means of surviving the 'worst of the worst,' not a means of remembering it. As I often say to my clients, "We wouldn't be sitting here together today if each part had not done its job well, if each hadn't helped you to survive." But as carriers of our instinctive survival responses, the parts remain poised for the next threat or the next trauma-related trigger for decades after "it" is over.

Recognizing the Signs of Structurally Dissociated Parts

Just as each individual responds to trauma differently, we would expect each client's structurally dissociated personality system to be unique. Clients whose histories of chronic trauma and/or multiple types of abuse and/or neglect necessitated more complex structural dissociation are likely to have a well-developed going on with normal life self and several different parts driven by the survival responses of fight, flight, freeze, submission, or cry for help. But even in these clients, fragmentation can be more subtle and permeable or more dramatic and rigid: some clients (e.g., those carrying PTSD or bipolar II diagnoses) might shift between clear-cut states (sometimes irritable, sometimes depressed, at other times anxious). Clients with borderline personality disorder might present at times as regressed and clinging; at other times, cold and angry; then, at still other times, hopeless and passively suicidal, while all the while functioning fairly well at work. With mild to moderate dissociative disorder not otherwise specified (DDNOS), the therapist might encounter clearly observable compartmentalization and some difficulty with memory (e.g., not clearly recalling the intense anger and aggressive behavior of their fight parts or the neediness of a young child part with separation anxiety). In clients with dissociative identity disorder (DID), not only will the number of trauma-related parts tend to be greater overall, but these clients are more likely to have other subparts serving the priorities associated with the going on with normal life self, for example, a professional self, a parenting part, or a part with special talents or social skills. In addition, as the neural systems governing each part become more elaborated and autonomous, DID clients start to exhibit switching and time loss as they are "hijacked" by parts who, when triggered, act outside the conscious awareness of the going on with normal life self.

> While updating her curriculum vita, Celia, a successful organizational consultant, was surprised to discover that she had won an award in 1990 for which she had no memory. Not only could she not recall winning it, she couldn't recall what she had done to deserve it! Annie also discovered disturbing evidence of missing time and dissociative hijacking when she received a letter from her oldest friend asking

her never to contact him again under any circumstances. "I will never forgive you for what you said to me last week—it was cruel, and I don't want to be hurt anymore." Lacking a memory of having spoken to him recently, she could not imagine why 'she' had been angry at him and what 'she' could have said that upset him so much.

Characteristically, while the going on with normal life part tries to carry on (functioning at a job, raising the children, organizing home life, even taking up meaningful personal and professional goals), other parts serving the animal defense functions of fight, flight, freeze, submit, and "cling" or attach for survival continue to be activated by trauma-related stimuli, resulting in hypervigilance and mistrust, overwhelming emotions, incapacitating depression or anxiety, self-destructive behavior, and fear or hopelessness about the future, that is, the difficulties that often lead clients to seek psychotherapy.

Symptoms as Communications from Parts

Many clients come for treatment after being flooded or "hijacked" by the trauma responses and implicit memories of the animal defense-related parts; others come when their attempts to disconnect or deny these trauma responses lead to chronic depression or depersonalization. Although some clients may present with diagnosable dissociative disorders, many more will come to therapy with trauma-related symptoms that appear initially straightforward, such as PTSD, anxiety and mood disorders, or personality disorders. However, certain symptoms can alert us to the presence of underlying structural dissociation: for example, see the following.

Signs of Internal Splitting

The client functions highly at work when stimulated by "positive triggers" (work assignments, collaboration with peers, responsibilities) while regressing at home or in personal relationships because of the trauma triggers associated with those environments. Or the client might report alternating fears of abandonment followed by pushing away those who try to get close or a tendency to initially idealize others followed by disillusionment and anger when they fail the client in some way. The fears of abandonment represent communications of the attach or cry for help part as closeness to others exacerbates that part's separation anxiety; the pushing away is the response of a fight part activated by the risk of vulnerability or hurt. Splitting often manifests in paradoxical behavior: fears of triggers might be intense, while the client lacks appropriate fears for real threats; the client plans a family vacation for the following summer while simultaneously ruminating on her determination to suicide; or he describes himself as "enlightened," kind, and reasonable, while family and friends portray the client as typically angry, arrogant, and demanding.

Treatment History

The client reports a number of previous treatments that have resulted in little progress or clarity, or describes those treatments as rocky and tumultuous or having ended in some unusually dramatic way. The therapist or previous therapists report feeling "in over my head," "inadequate for what he or she needs," "don't have the skills," while the client reports fearing therapist abandonment more than therapeutic inadequacy.

Somatic Symptoms

Unusual pain sensitivity or uncharacteristically high pain tolerance, stress-related headaches, eye blinking or drooping, narcoleptic symptoms, even physical symptoms with no diagnosable medical cause can be trauma-related or a symptom of dissociative activity. One of the most common indicators of structural dissociation is atypical or non-responsiveness to psychopharmacological medications (Anderson, 2014). In these instances, parts are communicating somatically: blinking or drooping of the eyelids often signals dissociative switching; a collapsed left shoulder and a tense, raised right shoulder might be evidence of a submissive part on the non-dominant side of the body and a part ready to fight connected to the physically stronger dominant side of the body.

"Regressive" Behavior or Thinking

Sometimes, the client's body language seems more typical of a young child than an adult of his or her chronological age: he or she might appear shy, collapsed, fearful, unable to tolerate being seen, or unable to make eye contact. The message might be: "I'm scared—don't hurt me" or "Please notice me—please like me" or "Please don't leave me." Verbal and cognitive style can also reveal the presence of younger parts of the self: concrete or black/white thinking, words or style of expression more typical of a child than an adult. Children use shorter sentences, express themes related to separation, caring, and fairness, and are more likely to feel empathically failed when not well understood.

Patterns of Indecision or Self-Sabotage

Often misinterpreted as "ambivalence," a client's inability to make small everyday decisions or problems with carrying out his or her expressed intentions can reflect conflicts between parts with opposite aims. Often this phenomenon manifests in frequent changes of job, career, or relationship, or a history of success in life alternating with self-sabotage or inexplicable failure, high functioning alternating with decompensation, hard work being suddenly undone by self-destructive actions. Very crucial life decisions can be involved, but often this pattern appears in difficulties in daily living such as an inability to choose what to wear in the morning, what to eat for breakfast, or whether to keep a date with a friend for lunch.

Memory Symptoms

While memory gaps and "time loss" are cardinal symptoms of dissociative disorders, more subtle memory problems can be indicative of structural dissociation. For example, all of the following memory issues are common manifestations of parts activity: difficulty remembering how time was spent in a day, difficulty remembering conversations or the focus of therapy sessions, "black outs," getting lost while driving somewhere familiar (such as going home from work), forgetting well-learned skills (such as how to drive), or engaging in behavior one does not recall.

Patterns of Self-Destructive and Addictive Behavior

Many studies have demonstrated correlations between suicidality and self-harm and addictive behavior with a history of trauma, so it should not be surprising that therapists encounter traumatized clients who struggle against their own self-destructive behavior. My assumption is that unsafe behavior consistently reflects the activation of fight and flight-driven parts by trauma-related triggers. While the going on with normal life self of the client seeks therapy because he or she is committed to life, to wanting "all the things everyone wants," fight parts engage in high-risk behavior or attempt to harm the body or end life in the effort to get relief from the implicit memories at any cost. Parts driven by the flight response tend to engage in eating disorders that result in numbing or addictive behavior that alters consciousness, allowing distance from unbearable feelings and flashbacks. Fight-related parts are prone to more violent actions, whether aggression toward others or self-harm and suicidal behavior. In a pilot study using the structural dissociation model with a group of severely symptomatic inpatients hospitalized for 2–10 years to prevent intentional or unintentional suicide, six of the eight subjects demonstrated marked improvement after a year of psychoeducationally based treatment focused on identifying the parts connected to the unsafe behavior and strengthening the ability of the going on with normal life self to identify and separate from the impulses of self-destructive parts (Fisher, in press).

By the time the trauma survivor appears at our doorstep, the neurobiological and psychological effects of a dysregulated autonomic nervous system, disorganized attachment patterns, and structurally dissociated parts will have become a set of well-entrenched, familiar, habitual responses. He or she will be unconsciously driven by post-traumatic implicit procedural learning activated by trauma-related triggers. The symptoms and triggered reactions now will be so familiar and automatic that, subjectively, they feel like "just who I am." Although apparently unrelated to the past, these "just who I am" responses are the conveyors of a narrative that cannot be fully remembered or put into words, a history held by different parts of the personality with different perspectives, triggers, and survival responses.

> For Gillian, the anger, shame, and hopelessness she felt at age 26 had that quality: she didn't have to account for why she felt those feelings because they were so familiar, so much a part of her. She didn't think to be curious about how fearless she could become when angry or how quickly shame and hopelessness could take over her body and stop her words in mid-sentence. Nor was she curious about how confident she was in her ability as an artist, unafraid to market her work yet so afraid of displeasing people in personal relationships. Gillian didn't even feel alarmed by what her therapist called the "suicidal part"; she simply accepted as normal her strong wish not to live. Normal life was a distant memory—something that had once been important to her—but now long gone. She didn't see the subtle but meaningful signs that her going on with normal life part was still alive and well and had always been, even during the worst times. She was still a wise, mature mother figure for her little sister and the emotional support of her mother—a role that gave her a sense of control over the chaos in the family. Secondly, she had used her aesthetic and creative abilities as a safe haven as a child—that was the side of her with which she identified as "the good side," leading her to become a professional ceramicist in her early twenties. She minimized it: "Hey, if I didn't have an alcoholic mother, I'd probably go in for drugs, so I'm addicted to making things—so what?"

As Gillian attests, trauma survivors all too often develop other symptoms that represent neurobiologically regulating attempts to cope with the trauma: self-injury and suicidality, risk-taking, re-enactment behavior, caretaking and self-sacrifice, revictimization, and addictive behavior. All of these behaviors represent different ways of modulating a dysregulated nervous system and preparing for the next threat: self-injury and planning suicide induce adrenaline-related responses of power, icy calm, control, and physical strength but also a relaxation effect from increased production of endorphins; restricting, binging and purging, and overeating all induce emotional and bodily numbing; and addictive behaviors can be tailored to evoke either numbing or increased arousal or a combination of both. Historically, in the mental health field, we have addressed these issues first by stabilizing unsafe behavior and then treating the traumatic events. But narrative memories are connected to intense states of autonomic arousal. Because the activation "readies" us for danger, remembering is likely to reactivate self-destructive impulses. Even "thinking about thinking about" the memories (Ogden et al., 2016) is often enough to cause a reactivation of the nervous system as if the events were recurring in the here-and-now. The neurobiological research and a better understanding of the somatic legacy of trauma advise us to take a new and different course in treatment (Van der Kolk, 2014; Ogden et al., 2006). (See Chapter 2 on Understanding Parts, Understanding Traumatic Responses and Chapter 7 on Working with Suicidal, Self-Destructive, Eating Disordered, and Addicted Parts.)

Helping Clients and Their Parts "Be Here" Now

When their symptoms represent implicit memories held by trauma-related parts expressing emergency and survival responses, individuals continue to feel unsafe, and their parts continue to defend, as if threatened now. When trauma responses are misinterpreted in these ways, it threatens the parts: it feels like proof that they are endangered, defective, or trapped in a hopeless situation. Once again, the felt sense is that they are in danger, alone, without protection. Our first priority in treatment must be to challenge this subjective perception that their symptoms are indicative of current danger or proof of their defectiveness or "just who they are." Therapists need to counteract the habitually triggered danger signals and trauma responses by calling attention to these reactions as communications from parts. When clients are provided with psychoeducation about structural dissociation, encouraged to become mindful and curious instead of reactive, helped to develop new responses to triggers, they begin to build the capacity to self-regulate and to "be here now." Then, by pacing the exploration of the past in such a way that the autonomic nervous system gets a chance to experience regulation instead of dysregulation, clients can experience moments of what I call "being present in the present," moments of feeling calm in the body, being able to think clearly, knowing they are safe.

In the next chapter, we will explore how to understand the issues and symptoms described by our clients as manifestations of the "living legacy" of trauma. Without an understanding of post-traumatic implicit memory or structural dissociation, not knowing they have been triggered by some cue reminiscent of the past, they interpret fear, shame, and anger as signs of imminent danger or deep-seated inadequacy. It can be a relief to discover that their stuckness, resistance, chronic depression, fear of change, entrenched fear and self-hatred, crisis and conflict, even suicidality all can be communications from parts who fear for their lives, unaware that the dangers they are bracing against are now in the past. Disappointment, criticism, closeness, or distance, even authority figures, may no longer be life-threatening, but each nonetheless evokes trauma-related implicit memories and the parts that hold them. Helping clients learn to become curious and interested in their symptoms and able to identify the voices that speak through their reactions can change their relationship to themselves and to the past from one of shame and dread to one of compassion. Knowing that each part is charged with the mission to survive, each in its own way, helps clients to see that how they survived was more crucial than how they were victimized. Understanding how each part participated in survival increases the sense of "we, together" and challenges the sense of being abandoned and alone. Feeling warmth and empathy for young wounded selves feels healing and comforting.

References

Brand, B.L., Sar, V., Stavropoulos, P., Kruger, C., Korzekwa, M., Martinez-Taboas, A., & Middleton, W. (2016). Separating fact from fiction: an empirical examination of six myths about dissociative identity disorder. *Harvard Review of Psychiatry*, 24(4), 257–270.

Cozolino, L. (2002). *The neuroscience of psychotherapy: building and rebuilding the human brain*. New York: W.W. Norton.

Gazzaniga, M. S. (1985). *The social brain: discovering the networks of the mind*. New York: Harper-Collins.

Gazzaniga, M. S. (2015). *Tales from both sides of the brain: a life of neuroscience*. New York: Harper-Collins.

Herman, J. L. (1992) *Trauma and recovery*. New York: Basic Books.

Liotti, G. (1999). Disorganization of attachment as a model for understanding dissociative psychopathology. In J. Solomon and C. George (Eds.). *Attachment disorganization*. New York: Guilford Press.

Lyons-Ruth, K. et al. (2006). From infant attachment disorganization to adult dissociation: relational adaptations or traumatic experiences? *Psychiatric Clinics of North America*, 29(1).

Ogden, P., Minton, K., & Pain, C. (2006). *Trauma and the body: a sensorimotor approach to psychotherapy*. New York: W.W. Norton.

Panksepp J. (1998). *Affective neuroscience: the foundations of human and animal emotions*. New York: Oxford University Press.

Putnam, F.W. (1989). *Diagnosis and treatment of multiple personality disorder*. New York: Guilford Press.

Schore, A.N. (2001). The effects of early relational trauma on right brain development, affect regulation, and infant mental health. *Infant Mental Health Journal*, 22, 201–269.

Schore, A.N. (2010). Relational trauma and the developing right brain: the neurobiology of broken attachment bonds. In T. Bardon, *Relational trauma in infancy: psychoanalytic, attachment and neuropsychological contributions to parent-infant attachment*. London: Routledge.

Schwartz, R. (1995). *Internal family systems therapy*. New York: Guilford Press.

Schwartz, R. (2001). *Introduction to the internal family systems model*. Oak Park, IL: Trailhead Publications.

Siegel, D. J. (2010). *The neurobiology of 'we.'* Keynote address, Psychotherapy Networker Symposium, Washington, D.C.

Solomon, J. & George, C. (1999). *Attachment disorganization*. New York: Guilford Press.

Solomon, M.F. & Siegel, D.J., Eds. (2003). *Healing trauma: attachment, mind, body and brain*. New York: W.W. Norton.

Teicher, M.H. et al. (2004). Childhood neglect is associated with reduced corpus callosum area. *Biological Psychiatry*, 56(2), 80–85.

Van der Hart, O., Nijenhuis, E.R.S., Steele, K., & Brown, D. (2004). Trauma-related dissociation: conceptual clarity lost and found. *Australian and New Zealand Journal of Psychiatry*, 38, 906–914.

Van der Hart, O., Nijenhuis, E.R.S., & Steele, K. (2006). *The haunted self: structural dissociation and the treatment of chronic traumatization*. New York: W. W. Norton.

Van der Kolk, B. A. (2006). Clinical implications of neuroscience research in PTSD. *Annals NY Academy of Sciences*, 1–17.

Van der Kolk, B.A. (2014). *The body keeps the score: brain, mind and body in the healing of trauma*. New York: Viking Press.

CHAPTER **2**

Understanding Parts, Understanding Traumatic Responses

"When the images and sensations of experience remain in 'implicit-only' form …, they remain in unassembled neural disarray, not tagged as representations derived from the past … Such implicit-only memories continue to shape the subjective feeling we have of our here-and-now realities, the sense of who we are moment to moment, but this influence is not accessible to our awareness."

(Siegel, 2010, p. 154)

Trauma often leaves its legacy in ways that don't fit traditional diagnostic or treatment molds. Rather than finding relief in disclosing their secrets, clients feel ashamed, mistrustful, or exposed. Instead of feeling better, they experience difficulty remembering or generalizing their new learning outside of therapy and return like Winnie the Pooh to the very same place over and over. Or there is no one "she" or "he" with whom the therapist can work. The agitated, angry client of last week is often replaced by someone who is depressed, shut down, unable to say more than a few dark words. Then, the next week, plans for the future are the subject of discussion rather than despair and suicide. When we mention last week's disclosure of sexual abuse, the client is surprised; the disclosure has been forgotten as if it hadn't occurred. Whereas, last week, therapy was the client's only safe place, today it feels unsafe and threatening. Worse yet, the determination to change has given way to the fear of change. Not only is the therapist confused by these shifting states of mind, so too is the client.

In the context of life threat, survival is a necessity. Being able to consciously witness the experience, preserve a sense of time, place, and identity, and clearly encode a memory of what happened frame-by-frame is an unnecessary luxury when human beings are in immediate danger. Faced with potential threat, the brain and body instinctively mobilize the emergency stress response, preparing the individual to take action: fleeing, fighting, ducking, and hiding. As danger cues are perceived by the sensory system, a chain reaction of neurochemical events is set in motion. The *amygdala* (a structure that serves as the brain's smoke detector and fire alarm) begins to "fire" more rapidly, activating another limbic system structure, the *hypothalamus*, to initiate an adrenaline release to "turn on" the sympathetic nervous system. As the adrenaline release speeds up heart rate and respiration to increase oxygen flow to muscle tissue, the body prepares to engage fight-flight impulses. The individual feels braced and strong; the events unfold in slow motion; an icy calm replaces fear; the eyes narrow; and the body prepares for action, clenching fists, engaging the leg muscles, biceps, and shoulders. As fight and flight responses unfold, release of another neurochemical, cortisol, begins to activate reciprocal activity in the parasympathetic nervous system. The parasympathetic system is best known for its role in recuperation, rest, and states of calm and is often referred to as an "energy conservation system" in contrast to the "energy expending" sympathetic system (Ogden et al., 2006). As the body mobilizes for fight and flight, the parasympathetic system prepares the body to freeze (like a deer in the headlights) to avoid exposure or to submit or "feign death" (Porges, 2011) if the individual is trapped with no way out, no way to defend. The parasympathetic system also helps the body recover from the massive expenditure of energy involved in fighting and fleeing, facilitating feelings of depletion, exhaustion, "just need to sleep," or numbing.

In traumatogenic environments where the threat of danger is ever-present, it is more adaptive for both children and adults when their bodies are conditioned to maintain a readiness for potential danger. These automatic patterns of response may be sympathetically activated (biased toward hypervigilance, high arousal, readiness to take action, impulsivity) or parasympathetically dominant (without energy, exhausted, slowed, numb, disconnected, hopeless and helpless). For children or victims of domestic violence who endure day-in-day-out conditions of threat or for whom being seen and not heard is the safest adaptation, it is common to see parasympathetic patterns of passivity, slowed thinking, and depression or shame dominating the individual's experience. In sympathetically dominant clients, it is more typical to see hyperactivity, reactivity, feelings of anger or fear, a readiness to act first and think later, and mistrust or hypervigilance.

Because survival depends upon sympathetic highs and parasympathetic lows to drive animal defense responses, these clients' nervous systems have been conditioned to dysregulate under stress. The parts connected to sympathetic arousal (fight and flight parts, the attach part, and the freeze part) and those connected to parasympathetic arousal (submit, the going on with normal life self) are primed for activation as the nervous system responds to triggers. Under traumatic conditions, individuals fail to develop or lose the capacity for a "window of tolerance" (Ogden et al., 2006; Siegel, 1999). The "window of tolerance" refers to the individual's bandwidth or capacity to tolerate intense emotions at the sympathetic end and bored, numb, or "low" feelings at the parasympathetic end. Because most threatening conditions for traumatized children are recurrent or "enduring" (Saakvitne, 2000), there is generally very little opportunity to develop a window of tolerance. To adapt, their bodies have had to be on high alert, ready for action, or to be disconnected, numb, passive, and able to endure whatever comes. When they are triggered later in childhood or as adults, their nervous systems are already conditioned to activate the same autonomic responses and animal defenses that served them best as children (Ogden et al., 2006). As Grigsby and Stevens (2000) stress, "An activity that previously has been adaptive is likely to recur because the brain functions automatically, but probabilistically, to produce that [same] behavior in similar circumstances" (p. 51). The body's instinct to prepare for the next threat, while ensuring survival, is inconsistent with the opportunity to recover from what has just happened, to feel a sense of "it's over now," or to reset the nervous system to a calm, resting state. Years later, clients often report a feeling of anxiety when they begin to access feelings of calm: "It feels so weird," they complain, "I'm not comfortable with it."

In addition, when the autonomic nervous system is repeatedly activated, the *hippocampus* (the part of the brain responsible for putting experience into chronological order and perspective preparatory to being transferred to verbal memory areas) is suppressed (Van der Kolk, 2014). Without a functioning hippocampus or prefrontal cortex, the individual is deprived of an opportunity to witness what happened or to process it and is left instead with only the "sensory elements [of the experience] … unintegrated and unattached" (Van der Kolk, Hopper, & Osterman, 2001). For the very worst of human experiences, the body's survival responses have impeded the mind and body from making meaning of what has happened. Survivors are left with a confusing array of unfinished neurobiological responses and "raw data," i.e., the overwhelming feelings, physical reactions, intrusive images, sounds, and smells associated with the event encoded as implicit memories and therefore unrecognizable as "memory."

With the advent of brain scan technology in the mid-1990s, it became possible to study traumatic memory by observing the brain's response to "script-driven provocation," a type of research in which subjects recall the details of a specific trauma while their brain activity is scanned and recorded. Bessel van der Kolk (2014; 1994) had been arguing for years that "the body keeps the score:" that traumatic memories did not resolve as did ordinary memories because they were physiologically driven rather than subject to deliberate recall. He believed that this underlying physiology accounted for the occurrence of "re-enactment behavior" in trauma patients and a host of other symptoms we associate with post-traumatic stress disorder (PTSD). In addition, most trauma survivors tended to have either too many unbidden intrusive memories or "not enough" memory to feel certain of what happened, very different from their memories of ordinary events that could be willingly recalled.

The brain scan research slowly but surely revealed the causes of these unique characteristics of traumatic memory: when research subjects recalled a traumatic event in their own words, the language and narrative areas of the prefrontal cortex became inactive, while emotional memory centers in the right hemisphere limbic system, especially the *amygdala*, became highly activated. With the left hemisphere language centers inhibited, these subjects were speechless, leaving the amygdala to "fire" (i.e., stimulate an emergency stress response) unchecked—as if the event were happening all over again. This research thus confirmed another characteristic of traumatic memory: even if it could not be deliberately retrieved and verbalized, it could be activated by triggers (i.e., stimuli in some direct or indirect way connected to traumatic events), even decades after the events were over. Gillian provides us with a good example of these characteristics of traumatic memory.

> Gillian's traumatic experiences of 10 years before were reflected in triggered implicit memory states: swings from anger to numbing, shame and self-doubt, difficulty attaching to others but also difficulty tolerating aloneness or separation, feeling overwhelmed and wanting to die "to get it over with." She didn't remember clearly her mother's neglect or older brother's incestuous behavior, and she would never have thought to connect her extreme feelings to the events she could recall, but as a 26-year-old still living in her parents' home, she was constantly triggered by apparently benign stimuli. Though her mother was now less depressed and her brother was an adult and out of the home, the house was full of "landmines." The most innocuous stimuli (e.g., being alone in the house, not being "heard" when she tried to express her feelings, disappointment that no one understood her) evoked strong feelings that she still wasn't "safe."

Uninvited Remembering

As difficult as it can be to deliberately recall traumatic experiences as a past event, the brain's "negativity bias" (Hanson, 2014), its tendency to perceive and prioritize negative stimuli more quickly than positive stimuli, results in long-term sensitivity to all cues related to previous danger. Even very subtle cues (e.g., Gillian's being alone at home or feeling disappointed) can stimulate the implicit memories and inadvertent uninvited "remembering." Without stimulus discrimination, unavailable when the prefrontal cortex is inhibited, the body responds as if the individual was facing life-or-death threat now. It instinctively mobilizes the same survival defense responses as if the client were in immediate danger. For survivors of trauma now in their 40s, 50s, and 60s, this reactivation of memory via triggers has been especially costly. Many have been victims of triggering for many more years than they were exposed to the actual traumatic events. Without awareness that their triggered responses are evidence of body and emotional memory, they "believe" the pounding heartbeat, burning shame, braced muscles, inability to breathe, numbing, and/or explosive rage are signs that they are in danger. When it becomes clear that they are not at risk, other fears arise: maybe they are going crazy, or have proof they are defective, or maybe they are just going through the motions of life "pretending." On the basis of this "evidence," many traumatized individuals isolate and withdraw, end healthy relationships prematurely or explosively, or can't end unhealthy ones.

Many function but avoid living life fully to reduce their exposure to triggers, and others engage in self-destructive behavior to manage the overwhelming feelings and activation, only to feel more damaged and defective.

"Remembering" Actions and Reactions

With a more scientific understanding of the neurobiology of trauma, traumatic memory can now be understood as a highly complex phenomenon. How each individual encodes memories of the traumatic past is unique and different, but what each has in common is the way in which memory is fragmented and unintegrated. Some trauma survivors have more explicit memories for events; some have little to none. All have a host of implicit memories, including trauma-related emotions, autonomic arousal responses, muscle and body memories, cognitive distortions, and visceral memories, as well as tactile-olfactory-visual and auditory memories.

And to a greater or lesser degree, all "remember" via trauma-related procedural or conditioned learning (Grigsby & Stevens, 2000), too. The procedural memory system is a subset of implicit or nonverbal memory that encodes function, action, and habit: that is, riding a bike, driving a car, social behavior like shaking hands or smiling on greeting others, and well-learned abilities from playing the piano to playing golf or tennis. Survival "habits" are also encoded as procedurally learned behavior—for example, tendencies to automatically disconnect from strong emotion or to feel overwhelmed by it, difficulty making eye contact, need for a certain physical proximity or distance from others, withdrawal or isolation, difficulty asking for help or disclosing feelings and personal information, a tendency to say "too much" or "too little," phobias of emotions or emotional expression, avoidance of having one's back to others or to doors and windows, habits of freezing, fighting or fleeing in response to stress or triggers.

To the extent that the individual has difficulty identifying implicit emotional, physical, or procedural memories as "memory," reality-testing can become compromised, creating a kind of self-triggering. When particular people or situations are experienced as unsafe, there is a tendency for them to become "demonized," that is, to become associated with danger or menace. Once the trigger is also a trigger, the body responds to it as a danger signal in its own right; the prefrontal cortex shuts down; and there is no witnessing brain to discriminate memory from present reality. Gillian's fear of helping professionals illustrates how innocuous or even positive stimuli can become associated with a sense of threat and thereafter experienced as dangerous. It also demonstrates that if the implicit memories and trauma responses are associated with a child part, reality-testing will be even more challenging because a child part's cognitive style, limited by the age or developmental stage of that part, is likely to be more concrete.

> Gillian developed a fear of therapy and therapists in her early teens: as the family's identified patient, she was sent to one therapist after another to be "fixed." None of them "got" what her behavior was communicating about her mother's alcoholism or her brother's abuse and

focused on strengthening her relationship with her family by getting her to be more compliant. "Not being understood," "not being heard," or "no one getting it" are all very powerful triggers for traumatized individuals. Without realizing it, the therapists' automatic assumption that this was a healthy but overly permissive family with a challenging child made them triggering stimuli and therefore dangerous. Isolated from her peers, the "best friend" of her fragile mother, dependent on her father's financial assistance, and triggered by the helping professionals, Gillian regarded therapy as a dangerous place she had to navigate rather than as a source of help and safety. Had she known that her fear was a communication from a young child part that longed for help but was triggered by the failure of former therapists to "believe her," Gillian would have been able to make a connection between the past and present. She might even have felt protective of this little girl and tried to stand up for "her." She might have been able to reassure the child that, even if no one else did, Gillian believed her unquestionably. Gillian knew what had happened. She might even have been able to tell the little girl that not being understood or believed was hurtful but it wasn't dangerous—as long as she was in Gillian's care.

For trauma treatment to be effective, no matter what methods we employ, survivors have to be able to integrate past and present. Concretely, this step requires education: about what traumatic memory is and is not, about triggers and triggering stimuli, about learning to accurately label triggered states ("this is a feeling memory"—"a body memory"), and cultivating the ability to trust that triggered states "tell the story" of the past without the necessity to either recall or avoid recalling specific incidents. When the therapist can also help clients connect implicit memory states to young parts of the self, it is easier to address them as a record of old dangers instead of signs of current threat. Also, when the triggered sensations, emotions, and images are reframed as "the child part's feelings," clients are better able to tolerate their intensity. Feeling compassion or protectiveness for younger selves also helps the clients to feel their "big-ness," to appreciate the physical size differences, the adult capabilities and resources, and the greater respect which individuals are accorded as adults and the greater safety it enables them to count on.

Finding "Now," Not "Then"

It is not difficult for traumatized individuals to re-experience the past, explicitly or implicitly. What is more challenging is how to "be here now" when one's body is communicating "danger, danger—red alert!" We now know that, as important as it is to acknowledge the past, it is even more crucial for traumatized individuals to stay connected to present time: "Right now, I can feel my feet—I can see where I am—this is just a moment—it will pass." The past does not have to be denied or avoided. It simply is (Rothschild, in press). Acknowledging the past without exploring it or observing the past intruding into present experience is very validating for traumatized clients: "Of course you are sensitive to disappointment! After a childhood of neglect and false promises, who wouldn't be sensitive to disappointment?" Acknowledgment of the past while lingering in the awareness of the present is much more helpful to clients in the early stages of therapy than exploring the past in detail and inadvertently evoking its implicit components.

When the implicit aspects of memory reactivate the sense of danger "now" instead of conveying that we are remembering dangers that are over, we can't look back on the past. There is no vantage point in the here-and-now from which to look back and view what happened "then." Rather than remembering what happened, once thought to be the goal of trauma treatment, we know now that resolution of the past requires *transforming* the memories. As Bessel van der Kolk wrote over 20 years ago, "[The] goal of treatment is to find a way in which people can acknowledge the reality of what has happened without having to re-experience the trauma all over again. For this to occur, merely uncovering memories is not enough: they need to be modified and transformed, i.e., placed in their proper context and reconstructed into neutral or meaningful narratives. Thus, in therapy, memory paradoxically becomes an act of creation, rather than the static recording of events ..." (Van der Kolk, Van der Hart, & Burbridge, 1995, p. 2).

"Transformation" or "reconstruction" of traumatic memory occurs as the individual's relationship to both the implicit and explicit memories undergoes change, as tolerance for triggered or dysregulated states expands so that he or she can "be here now," live more fully in the present, and slowly reorganize the unprocessed implicit elements into a new narrative that, as Donald Meichenbaum (2012) says, tells a "healing story."

References

Gazzaniga, M. S. (2015). *Tales from both sides of the brain: a life of neuroscience.* New York: Harper-Collins.

Grigsby, J. & Stevens, D. (2000). *Neurodynamics of personality.* 1st Edition. New York: Guilford Press.

Hanson, R. (2014). *Hardwiring happiness: the new brain science of contentment, calm, and confidence.* New York: Harmony Publications.

Meichenbaum, D. (2012). *Roadmap to resilience: a guide for military, trauma victims and their families.* Clearwater, FL: Institute Press.

Ogden, P., Minton, K. & Pain, C. (2006). *Trauma and the body: a sensorimotor approach to psychotherapy.* New York: W.W. Norton.

Porges S. W. (2011). *The Polyvagal theory: neurophysiological foundations of emotions, attachment, communication, and self-regulation.* New York: W.W. Norton.

Rothschild, B. (in press). *The body remembers, volume 2: revolutionizing trauma treatment.* New York: W.W. Norton.

Saakvitne, K.W., Gamble, S.J., Pearlman, L.A., & Lev, B.T. (2000) *Risking connection: a training curriculum for work with survivors of childhood abuse.* Baltimore, MD: Sidran Institute Press.

Siegel, D.J. (1999). *The developing mind: toward a neurobiology of interpersonal experience*. New York: Guilford Press.

Siegel, D. J. (2010). *The neurobiology of 'we.'* Keynote address, Psychotherapy Networker Symposium, Washington, D.C.

Van der Kolk, B. A. (1994). The body keeps the score: memory & the evolving psychobiology of post-traumatic stress. *Harvard Review of Psychiatry*, 1(5), 253–265.

Van der Kolk, B.A. (2014). *The body keeps the score: brain, mind and body in the healing of trauma*. New York: Viking Press.

Van der Kolk, B.A., Hopper, J., & Osterman, J. (2001). Exploring the nature of traumatic memory: combining clinical knowledge with laboratory methods. *Journal of Aggression, Maltreatment & Trauma*, 4(2), 9–31.

Van der Kolk, B. A., van der Hart, O., & Burbridge, J. (1995). Approaches to the treatment of PTSD. In S. Hobfoll & M. de Vries (Eds.), *Extreme stress and communities: impact and intervention*. NATO Asi Series. Series D, Behavioural and Social Sciences, Vol 80. Norwell, MA: Kluwer Academic.

CHAPTER 3

Changing Roles for Client and Therapist

"We think that by protecting ourselves from suffering we are being kind to ourselves. The truth is, we only become more fearful, more hardened, and more alienated. We experience ourselves as being separate from the whole. This separateness becomes like a prison for us, a prison that restricts us to our personal hopes and fears and to caring only for the people nearest to us. Curiously enough, if we primarily try to shield ourselves from discomfort, we suffer. Yet when we don't close off and we let our hearts break, we discover our kinship with all beings."

(Pema Chodren, 2008, p. xxxx)

In the aftermath of trauma, individuals' symptoms and difficulties reflect how their minds and bodies once tried to adapt to circumstances beyond their control. "Not feeling alive in the present" might have once served as an antidote to the threat of annihilation: if we don't feel alive, the threat loses its power to terrify us. Depression might once have provided a cushion against disappointment and being overwhelmed. Hypervigilance enables even children to stand guard over themselves. Numbing and loss of interest allow the individual protection against grief and disappointment: if you don't care, it doesn't matter anymore. Anger pushes others away before they cause harm or, worse yet, before the survivor develops an attachment to them. It would be rare in the mental health treatment world to think of these symptoms as adaptive strategies made possible by the body's instinctive survival defenses. But from a neurobiologically informed perspective, they are "survival resources" (Ogden et al., 2006), ways that the body and mind adapted for optimal survival in a dangerous world. In the worst of circumstances, our survival resources save us—at a cost. By disowning the trauma, or the anger, or the need for contact with others, we lose or deny important aspects of ourselves. By over-identifying with the trauma-related shame, hopelessness, and fear of being seen, we constrict our lives and make ourselves smaller than we need to be. Both strategies, adaptive in a time of danger, become liabilities when the individual is ready to live a "life after trauma," free of the constrictions and restrictions needed for living in a trau-matogenic environment.

In the absence of a context of meaning (i.e., a narrative) to explain their bewildering reactions, afraid to be curious or even more afraid to face the events that created a need for these responses, clients assume the worst: they are crazy or damaged or inadequate. Without specialized training in trauma, most therapists would not know to be curious about differentiating normal emotional responses from traumatic reactions, desperate communications from parts, ingenious survival strategies, or implicit memories. Because the client presents in crisis or chaos with emotional pain or signs of a "mental disorder," we feel a responsibility to diminish or alleviate the symptoms—curious about their origin in the childhood past perhaps but not necessarily curious about their role or their original purpose.

When the therapist subsequently encounters "resistance" or trauma treatments become "stuck," our theoretical models make meaning of it, but rarely do these theories assume a creative, adaptive explanation. When clients continue to live from crisis to crisis or complain that they are not improving in therapy nor have energy for change, one hypothesis might be that they are "help-rejecting complainers" or "passive-aggressive." Or the therapist might theorize that these clients are "borderline," "attention-seeking," or manipulative, "acting out" for some secondary gain. The ashamed, chronically depressed client might be described as having "low self-esteem." Whether objectively accurate or not, these types of interpretations have gained clinicians little in terms of practical or successful client interventions for trauma.

Working with the Neurobiological Legacy of Trauma

In a neurobiologically informed treatment, a different set of theoretical principles guides our thinking. The root causes of the client's difficulty, we now know, is not just the original event but the reactivation of implicit memories by trauma-related stimuli that mobilize the emergency stress response as if the individual were in danger again (Van der Kolk, 2014). A trauma-informed treatment therefore focuses on recognizing and working in present time with the spontaneous evoking of implicit memory and animal defense survival responses rather than on creating a verbal narrative of past experiences. But since implicit memories encoded in nonverbal areas of the brain are subjectively experienced as emotional and physical reactions not distinguishable as "memory," the first task of therapy is often to help clients recognize and "befriend" their triggered reactions, rather than react to them with alarm, avoidance, or negative interpretations.

Many traumatized clients come to therapy with unusually difficult, painful histories: severe childhood physical, emotional and/or sexual abuse, neglect, abandonment at an early age, abuse/neglect coupled with other types of trauma, multiple perpetrators, or sadistic and malevolent abuse accompanied by mind control practices, child pornography, or forced witnessing of violence. These complex histories often are accompanied by "borderline" presentations, more severe compartmentalization, and dissociative disorders or by more severe self-destructive, suicidal, and addictive behavior—or both. For over twenty years, the "gold standard" of trauma therapy has been the Phase-Oriented Treatment Model (Ogden & Fisher, 2015; Van der Hart, Nijenhuis, & Steele, 2006; Herman, 1992), a sequential approach in which the consequences of autonomic dysregulation are treated first and then, only after a period of symptom stabilization, the traumatic memories and their implicit components are addressed. Only when the past is no longer "alive" in the client's body can integration of past and present, child and adult, part and whole be completed. But for clients with chronic, multi-layered trauma histories and severe dissociative symptoms, dysregulated unsafe behavior, or chronic stuckness, the goal of stabilization can be elusive. Years of treatment focused on self-regulation and avoidance of traumatic content sometimes leads only to small steps forward—or bigger steps forward followed by setback after setback. For fear of exacerbating the dysregulation, the therapist might inadvertently collude with the client's tendencies to ignore the trauma; or fearing empathic failure, the therapist might make the opposite mistake: allowing clients to say too much and, then having triggered themselves, become overwhelmed or unsafe. Often, the therapist comes to feel equally overwhelmed by the conflicting challenges of helping the client stabilize while also feeling heard and validated and to resolve the past.

A Multi-Consciousness Approach to Treatment

A parts approach offers some new possibilities for addressing these challenges. First and foremost, working with symptoms as manifestations of parts allows the therapist to incorporate mindfulness-based practices: helping clients "notice" their experience rather than "get in touch with it." In traumatized clients, the heightened intensity (or numbing) caused by autonomic dysregulation makes "getting in touch with feelings" either overwhelming or deadening, either of which can evoke anxiety, depression, or impulsive behavior. "Noticing" as in mindful awareness allows the client to achieve "dual awareness," the ability to stay connected to the emotional or somatic experience while also observing it from a very slight mindful distance. Secondly, a parts approach allows us to titrate emotions or memories: if one part is overwhelmed by emotional pain, other parts of the mind and body can be calm, curious, or even empathic. If one part is remembering something alarming or devastating, other parts can offer support, validation, or comfort. As meditation practices, clinical hypnosis, and other uses of mindfulness attest, the human brain is capable of holding multiple states of consciousness "in mind" simultaneously, and this ability has important therapeutic uses. The left hemisphere is associated with more positive moods and the right hemisphere with more negative states (Hanson, 2014); the medial prefrontal cortex supports an observing consciousness that enables us to "hover above" whatever we are feeling so it can be experienced as a feeling in the body rather than lead to retraumatization (Van der Kolk, 2014). Using "dual awareness," we have the capacity to fully inhabit the present moment: to feel our feet on the ground through awareness of body sensation while our visual perception takes in details of the room in which we are sitting—while, in the same moment, we can evoke an image from an earlier time in our lives that takes us "back there" to a state-specific memory.

Describing these phenomena using the language of the brain, however, would not have the same result as does using the language of parts. To say, "I can sense my medial prefrontal cortex is curious about the negative mood state connected to the right subcortical areas of my brain" does not evoke interest, emotional connection, or self-compassion. When the therapist teaches clients to observe, "I can sense in myself some curiosity about the depressed part's sadness," they are more connected and attuned to their emotions and sensations—the first step toward achieving the ability to have compassion for themselves. Research shows that when the medial prefrontal cortex is activated, there is a decrease in activity in the right hemisphere amygdala (Van der Kolk, 2014). It is most likely activation of the amygdala by trauma-related triggers that results in flashbacks, intrusive implicit memories, automatic animal defense responses, or parasympathetic responses of disconnection, numbing, or spacing out.

Pathogenic Kernels of Memory

If the purpose of modern trauma therapy is no longer to treat traumatic events, what should be the focus?

Van der Hart, Nijenhuis, and Steele (2006) have suggested that trauma treatment prioritize the effects or "pathogenic kernels" of the trauma, that is, those aspects of the post-traumatic legacy that still exert a traumatic effect on the client or constrict full participation in normal life even to this day. For example,

> Even after years of therapy, Annie was still afraid to leave the house, resulting in a pattern of isolation—even though she hated feeling alone and lonely and stuck in the house. Although Annie was aware that it was safe in her small rural town, the shaking and trembling she experienced each time she tried to go out seemed more "real" than her factually based appraisal of her environment.
>
> When I asked her, "What would have happened if you walked out the door in the home you grew up in?" she replied, "Anyone could get me—anyone." There was a long pause. "No wonder I can't even open the front door now—it wasn't safe even to peek out my mother's door back then!"
>
> Though differentiating the implicit memory from factual reality gave her insight, it did not change her ability to leave the house—because

the implicit memory was held not by Annie but by a structurally dissociated young part of her. Once we identified the part "who is afraid to leave the house," I asked Annie to inquire of the part, "Ask her if she'd be willing to show you a picture that would help you understand what she's afraid will happen if you walk out this door ..." An image immediately came up connected to the experience of having been kidnapped at the age of seven. "Is that what you're afraid of?" she asked the child part. She could feel her head wanting to nod. "Did you think it could happen again?" Another nod. Spontaneously, Annie said to the part, "Did you know that can't happen at my house?" She felt her head nodding again. "Do you know why? Because I'm too big now, and no one can see you because you're inside me." She could feel a sense of relief and tension relaxing in her body each time she said again, "No one can see you—they only see me because you're safe inside."

Although there were many different traumatic events connected to the kidnapping, the "pathogenic kernel" that continued to affect her life and distort her reality was the experience of being away from home and alone—that is, what led up to the kidnapping. As we worked on ways of demonstrating to the part that Annie was too big to be kidnapped, such as measuring Annie's height on the door jam and asking the little girl to show us how tall she was, the words that consistently regulated the little part were the words, "They can't see you because you're inside me! All they can see is my big, tall body."

Another pathogenic kernel was the absence of a protective adult who would have supervised a seven-year-old that night and made sure no one would take her. That also needed to be addressed.

Unless her parts felt that someone cared about her/them, Annie disclosed, she had trouble feeling any safety even in her home—or in her body—because their fears were so intense. As the parts explained to her, "If someone cares about you, they watch over you to make sure nothing happens." In her previous therapy, Annie had complied with the therapist's insistence that she repeatedly recall and re-experience the traumatic events, stimulating recurrent flashbacks in and out of therapy. She remembered wanting to tell the therapist that the excavation of memory was making her worse. But, under the influence of young "attach for survival" parts wanting the therapist to care about them, she just did as the therapist said.

Influenced by widespread belief in the "talking cure," the pioneers in the trauma field initially assumed that creation of a narrative and being able to "tell the story" to a witness were sufficient to process "what happened" and resolve the symptoms (Rothschild, in press). A corollary assumption was that the worst effects on the individual would be dictated by the worst aspects or details of the trauma. Therefore, one might think it important to process those "worst" memories.

These assumptions leave therapists trained to use the phase-oriented treatment model in a quandary: while it does not feel empathically attuned to ask clients to avoid telling their stories, the prioritizing of stabilization requires focusing away from traumatic events. On the other hand, meeting the client's "need to 'get it out'" is also risky. The former risks empathic failure; the latter risks destabilization. What does the therapist do when caught between "a rock and a hard place?"

Acknowledging the Past Without Exploring It

When we start to understand traumatic memory from a neurobiological perspective, client memories do not have to be avoided or discharged. We simply have to help clients develop a different *relationship* to both their explicit and implicit memories. It is the details of memory and chronological scene-by-scene retelling that activates associated implicit memories, dysregulates the nervous system, and can have a retraumatizing effect on the client. Acknowledging the trauma or implicit triggered memories is never unsafe, especially when we allude to the "bad things that happened" in a more general way without vivifying the details of them or using triggering language, such as "rape," "incest," or "penetration." When the therapist alludes to the "unsafe world you grew up in," or "the years when nowhere was safe," most clients feel validated and supported. This kind of matter-of-fact acknowledgment of the past often calms the traumatized nervous system rather than activating it: it conveys, "Someone knows how it was."

In addition, when they talk about a traumatic event, therapist and client have a choice of focus: they can concentrate on the experience of horror (most likely to trigger implicit memories), or on the victimization and objectification (most likely to trigger shame), or they can bring attention to how the individual survived. How did he adapt to a traumatogenic environment? How did she "fight" or "flee" without incurring more punishment? How did he get up and go to school the next morning?

> Annie's fear of leaving the house and the need to have proximity to a protective figure were reflections of how she survived: via hypervigilant anticipation of danger, constriction of her activities to what was safe, and a focus on pleasing people and gaining their loyalty. Though other parts longed to be a part of "normal life" and yearned for closer connections to others, the fearful agoraphobic 7-year-old had been dictating defensive avoidance for many years. As Annie learned to correctly interpret "her" fear of leaving the house as a communication from a frightened little girl, she could more easily work with her "agoraphobia." She began by bringing up images of the door the little part was afraid to open (i.e., the door of her childhood home) and praising the seven-year-old for figuring out that she should never, ever, ever open that door. Then Annie would call up images of the

door in her own home that she wanted to open to a safe neighborhood and community. She visualized taking hold of the seven-year-old's hand, somatically communicating that she was there and would not let anyone harm her. Over many weeks of Annie's patient reassurance and help in orienting her to the present by focusing on the images, this young child part was increasingly able to trust that the door she and Annie opened was not the same door that had once led to a dangerous world.

A Different Approach to Traumatic Memory

In today's trauma treatment world, therapist and client have many more choices when it comes to treating traumatic memory. We can choose what kind of memory to treat: implicit or explicit memory? Memories of dehumanizing events or memories of ingenious survival? Memories as held by parts? Cognitive schemas? Incomplete actions? Or procedural memories of habitual actions and reactions? We can touch on memory by acknowledging it, naming it as a part's memory or as an implicit feeling or body memory. The therapist can help the client observe how it continues to exert its effects through pathogenic kernels that may or may not have any obvious connection to narrative. What is different is that the therapist no longer has to be focused preferentially on becoming a witness to the client's narrative regardless of its effects on his or her symptoms and stability. Instead, the trauma therapist's job is to create in the therapy hour a neurobiologically regulating environment that enables the client's nervous system to experience greater safety and therefore an expanded capacity for tolerating both past and present experience (Ogden et al., 2006).

A Different Kind of Witness

Although many clients are relieved to know that "telling the story" is a choice but not a requirement of the therapy, some profess a longing or intense feeling of need to tell someone "what happened." A neurobiologically informed therapist can also bear witness to the individual's story but in a different way than in traditional models. As witness in a psychodynamic approach, the therapist is a receptive listener who can tolerate hearing the story, even its horrifying details, and still "be there" for the storyteller. A good witness in this approach never interrupts even when the client becomes autonomically activated or makes meaning of the events by constructing a "self-defeating narrative" (Meichenbaum, 2012), such as "it was my fault." In a neurobiologically oriented world, this approach raises concerns: a story told chronologically and in detail to a silent witness is more likely to trigger trauma-related autonomic responses and implicit memories, reactivating the neural networks as if the client were again in danger. As a silent listener without a way to keep track of the client's autonomic dysregulation or cortical activity, we have no way to know: is the client overwhelmed? Is the client able to mentalize and thereby witness being witnessed? Or is the prefrontal cortex shut down? If clients are dysregulated and cortically inhibited, they cannot take away a corrective memory or coherent narrative of having been heard.

Differentiating Past from Present

The ability to differentiate being triggered and being threatened is key to trauma treatment. We have to know we are safe *now* in order to effectively process how unsafe it was *then*. The therapist has to be curious: can this client differentiate objectively between a trauma and a trigger? Or does he interpret the triggering as "danger now"? Without education about the phenomenon of implicit memory and a prefrontal cortex capable of taking in this new information, post-traumatic dysregulation, hypervigilance, impulsivity, and/or shutdown will be repeatedly reinforced by the simple phenomenon of triggering. In the example below, Sheila insisted that telling her story was the only way she could resolve the intense pressure she felt inside that kept communicating to her: "I have to tell someone."

> After setting a particular appointment time for this important moment of "telling," Sheila arrived a few minutes late, a little breathless. First, I invited her to take a moment to let her breath settle: "We have all the time we need—all the time in the world," I said slowly and gently (a technique drawn from Sensorimotor Psychotherapy [Ogden & Fisher, 2015]). "Take your time … and while you're getting your breath back, let's talk for a few minutes about this important process you want to have today. I know it's something you've felt an intense need for … to be heard and believed. But it is also going to bring up a lot. I just want to be sure that it's OK if I interrupt you from time to time—to ask how you're doing, check on how your nervous system is coping, or slow things down so you can settle. It's my philosophy: on my watch, I don't want the telling of your story to be retraumatizing, so I might be annoying from time to time because I am going to interrupt to make sure that doesn't happen. Is that OK?" (Getting the client's explicit permission for an intervention is another important principle of treatment in Sensorimotor Psychotherapy.)
>
> Sheila begins to describe the environment in which the abuse took place: "My mother was not the right match for my super-intellectual father—she wanted nice clothes and pretty things—he was frugal and worried about money. He didn't like conflict or emotionality; she was always highly emotional. It was hard to be around her because she'd suddenly go into a rage." Seeing her activation rising as she recalled her mother's rages, and noticing how little she was breathing, I interrupted.
>
> ME: "How are you doing right now, Sheila? That's a lot to remember."
> SHEILA: "I'm a little overwhelmed but managing OK—when I was talking about my mother and her anger, I suddenly remembered

something: she used to beat me when I was 'too emotional,' especially if I cried or I got angry ... She could cry and scream at me, but I couldn't scream back."

ME: "*She* could yell, but you couldn't ... [I mirrored her words so she could hear them and take them in.] And you were just a little girl ..."

SHEILA: [begins to cry]

ME [speaking as she is crying]: "Yes, lots of feelings coming up—painful feelings?" [She nods] "Of course ... You were just a little girl, and you couldn't get mad and you couldn't cry ... lots of feelings there. ... Just notice, though: right here, right now, that little girl inside is crying, and no one is getting mad at her ... You and I are hearing her cry and hearing her feelings, and we're not mad ... we feel for her ... Ask her to notice that it's different here—it's different with you and me. Right this minute, she's being heard and we are feeling for her."

In a more traditional psychodynamic approach, the therapist would most likely have spoken less and certainly interrupted less. But all of the "interruptions" had a purpose: to help Sheila stay "here" instead of going "there," to help her slow down and pay attention to her breathing and activation, to keep her prefrontal cortex online to make sure she could witness being witnessed, and to provide a different experience, an antidote, for her young child self.

Witnessing Being Witnessed

To achieve the purpose of witnessing, it is of crucial importance to remember that the longing to be heard may be a natural human response to having to keep terrible secrets, but it is also an implicit memory. Few children "tell their stories" to someone at the time of the abuse, leaving a feeling memory of the longing or impulse to tell that was never satisfied. Often, the clients who are desperate "to tell" are being driven by that implicit memory. In addition, the wish to tell or be heard does not guarantee that client can remain fully present in the moment when activated by the details of the narrative. The syndrome of "post-traumatic stress disorder" reflects the degree to which traumatic reactions can intrude upon and "upstage" the experience of "being here now." The research (Van der Kolk, 2014) is clear that trauma-related stimuli, including one's own narrative, stimulates the body to alarm responses, animal defense reactions, and inhibition of prefrontal activity—all of which prevent witnessing the therapist's attentive presence. In Sensorimotor Psychotherapy (Ogden & Fisher, 2015), the therapist periodically directs the client's attention back to the present moment by asking clients to: "Pause for a moment and just notice what's happening right now: you are telling your story ... and I'm hearing you ... I'm hearing you and I believe you ... Notice what that's like to feel me here with you, listening to you ... and believing you." In a parts approach,

I might ask: "What's it like for the parts to hear those words, 'I believe you'?" In Sensorimotor Psychotherapy, the therapist would next ask, "What happens in your body when you notice that?" Or "What happens inside when I say the words, 'I hear you, and I believe you'?"

I can also bring the client's attention to the difference between now and then: "I am hearing you, and … I believe you," "I'm hearing you, and I'm not angry," "I'm hearing you and I'm not going away," "I hear you, and I am not shocked, not horrified … Just notice that. What's it like to have someone hear you without shock or horror?" At these moments of recognition (when the client can experience how different "now" is, how attentively someone listens now, how it feels to be believed), the old experience is changed: there is a different ending to the story now—and that changes the feelings inside.

The Therapist as "Auxiliary Cortex" and Educator

In a neurobiologically informed treatment approach, the issues presented by traumatized clients are seen as stemming from dysregulated autonomic arousal, implicit memories, disorganized attachment, and structural dissociation, requiring that the therapist play a somewhat different role in the treatment. In traditional models, it has always been assumed that individuals had access to words that could describe the traumatic experiences but without the opportunity to express them.

In the light of the neuroscience research, however, that assumption has to be re-examined. Brain scan evidence on traumatic recall of events is clear that traumatic memory evokes "speechless terror" and experiences "beyond words" (Ogden & Fisher, 2015; Van der Kolk, 2014), not a clear-cut narrative that can be verbalized. In brain scan studies, narrative recall resulted in inhibited cortical activity, including inhibition of expressive language centers in the left brain, leaving the subjects "speechless," while the limbic system, especially the right hemisphere amygdala, became highly active (Van der Kolk & Fisler, 1995). These findings describe what therapists often observe in traumatized clients: when the prefrontal cortex, inhibited by autonomic responses to traumatic memory, cuts them off from language areas of the brain, their ability to observe even their own experience verbally and sequentially is lost. The overwhelming emotions and physical impact are too big to be captured by language. After the events are over, many victims attempt to put words to what has happened but can only approximate a "feeling of what happened" biased by whatever meaning-making they have attached to the event (Damasio, 1999). Often these stories are distorted by the experience of degradation, humiliation, terror, and abandonment: they do not capture the event itself but rather how the victims experienced themselves as a result of it. Shame, feeling dirty or disgusting, or painfully exposed is not a description of an event. They are the implicit memories of the effects of that event on them.

A neurobiologically informed therapist is aware that clients do not know these facts about traumatic remembering. They have not read the brain scan research, and do not know why they can't remember at all or why they remember only in fragments that feel "unreal," or why they feel so much shame or are afraid of remembering at all. They experience themselves as crazy or inadequate or damaged without understanding the role of the trauma in biasing their interpretations. Without the words and without a template to make meaning of what has happened, let alone understand the resulting symptoms, our clients will not be able to make headway in therapy or in their normal lives. It therefore becomes imperative for the therapist to act as an educator and temporary "auxiliary cortex" (Diamond, Balvin, & Diamond, 1963, p. 46). When the therapist is willing to reinterpret the client's "self-defeating story" and give it psychoeducationally informed meaning, it has a different effect than providing empathy or challenging distorted cognitions. When the therapist provides a template for understanding the trauma-related symptoms or the phenomenon of triggering, and makes sense of their prefrontal shutdown and animal defenses, clients are reassured that there is logic to their actions and reactions: what I call "trauma logic." Lillian provides us with an illustration of these issues and how I dealt with them on the occasion of our first meeting.

> Seventy years old and a recently retired pediatrician, Lillian appeared barely able to walk, even with the help of her son who had set up a consultation to "find out what's wrong with my mother." Shaking, trembling, her head hanging, she made her way into the office and sat on the couch, rocking back and forth like a small child. "All I can say is I feel like a frightened child, and I don't know why," she said. "I'm afraid of my own shadow—I can't look at you—I can't go out of the house by myself."
>
> I asked, "When did this frightened child appear? When did the fear begin?"
>
> After a terrifying childhood, Lillian described herself as having become a headstrong, independent young adult, determined to become a doctor and help children around the world. That fearlessness persisted for many decades: in her pediatric career, raising her children as a single mother, and then volunteering for Doctors Without Borders after retirement. Then she came home from Africa at the age of 70 without a job, structure, or a cause. "I was just alone in the house all day—I felt lonely and useless and of no value—and then the fear started."
>
> I said excitedly, "I just realized what must have happened, Lillian—can I tell you the story about what is going on right now?"
>
> She nodded.
>
> "A very brave young woman left home fifty years ago, walked away from the trauma and the intimidation, and she never looked back. There was a lot of trauma in her body—a lot of traumatized young parts—but she had a strong drive to build a normal life, and she did! With that strong, determined normal life self, she created a family, chose a

career, and even fulfilled her goal of helping children just as afraid as she was once. She never looked back—even once. But after the return from Africa, there were no more goals for the normal life part to pursue, no more people to help or kids to raise—nothing to keep her going. The empty house and the loneliness triggered the young traumatized parts she'd been able to ignore for so many years. Triggered by being alone in the house, they began to have intense feeling and body memories of feeling hopeless, unlovable, alone, and, most of all, scared out of their minds. This fear you are having is a memory, their feeling memory of what it was like to be in their home—in your family's home."

"What do I do?" she asked.

ME: "Think as a mother and a pediatrician for a moment: what do we do when a child is feeling scared and doesn't know she's safe? When the scary feeling is a memory?"

LILLIAN: "We'd reassure her that she's safe …"

ME: "OK, and what would you do if she didn't believe you right away?"

LILLIAN: "We'd have to tell her over and over again—tell her that we're there, that nothing can hurt her now."

ME: "You know children well, don't you? Yes, you'd have to tell her over and over, wouldn't you? Can you start now? Just tell her with your feelings and your body that you're here."

Lillian was quiet for a moment, then she chuckled: "Smart kid—she says if there's nothing scary happening, why am I so scared?"

ME: "Explain to her that you did get scared—you got frightened when she got scared—always tell the truth to her because no one ever did that before."

Lillian was quiet again, her attention inside: "She likes me admitting that I got scared, too, but then I told her that I looked around, and nothing bad was happening. And that is why I came here today even though I was scared."

ME: "Right—it isn't that grownups never get scared, but they do something different with their fear than kids do."

LILLIAN: "Yeah, and now I have to remember not to get scared when she gets scared."

ME: "That's right—you don't want to blend with her fear—because then she has no one. You want her to have access to your confidence and courage so it will be there for her, too."

In this single session, it was immediately clear to me that Lillian's return from Africa had stimulated a flooding of implicit memories of terror, loneliness, shame, and fears of abandonment. She had neither the knowledge base nor the words to explain her sudden transformation from confident globe-trotter to quivering child other than "I feel like a frightened child." Notice that the therapist/educator does not hesitate to make psychoeducational meaning of the client's symptoms and story, to introduce words like "trigger," "part," "feeling memory," "dysregulation." A therapist/educator does not deflect or interpret a question such as, "What do I do?" Knowing that the question is a request from the normal life self for a roadmap, the therapist provides both concrete information and the opportunity to experiment with using it.

Clearly, Lillian's frightened part had "hijacked the body" (Ogden & Fisher, 2015), inhibiting her prefrontal cortex from being able to conceptualize an answer to the question, "What is wrong with me?" If the therapist's role is to educate, rather than elicit the client's interpretation of what is wrong, then this question provides an opportunity to teach the client about autonomic dysregulation, implicit memory, and structural dissociation. Lillian's description, "I've turned into a frightened child," immediately opened the door to the discussion of child parts, and although it was only the second or third sentence she uttered, I did not hesitate to say, "Yes, you have. You've been hijacked by a very young, very scared little girl." Another client might have described it as, "My body is running amuck—I can't sleep, I can't stop shaking, I am paralyzed," calling for psychoeducation about the body's participation in trauma-related symptoms. Some narratives might have emphasized deficiencies: "I've fallen apart—I'm so ashamed—I don't want anyone to see me like this—I'll never be the person I used to be." For clients with shame-related cognitive schemas, psychoeducation becomes imperative to help them disidentify from the self-defeating story of failure and inadequacy. They will need education about their symptoms: "Yes, it feels as if you've fallen apart, and you don't want anyone to see you. The good news is that you haven't fallen apart—your body is just remembering feeling broken, shattered. The shame is a feeling memory, too, that often helps keep children safer." When clients lament that they'll never "be the person I used to be," they can often be reassured that the "person I used to be" is alive and well in their left hemispheres. They are experiencing "limbic hijacking," which inhibits cortical functioning and thereby disconnects them from the "person I used to be."

As illustrated in the session with Lillian, another important part of the therapist/educator's role is to help clients connect not only to their vulnerability but also to their strengths. Historically, trauma treatment has emphasized helping clients get in touch with vulnerable emotions of fear, grief, and shame and with their rage—with the expectation that grief and anger will empower, dissipate shame, and free them to let go of the past. However, clients often get stymied when the anger and grief are overwhelming rather than empowering or when shame is exacerbated rather than relieved by access to grief. In addition, focus primarily on trauma-related emotions creates a bias in the treatment by leaving out a very important aspect of any traumatic experience:

how the child's survival resources and animal defenses enabled him or her to remain intact, to "keep on keeping on."

A Creative Adaptation to Abnormal Experience

Even when the only option is to "feign death" (go numb, pretend to be asleep, float up to the ceiling, or go unconscious), the body instinctively chooses the defensive response most likely to succeed in limiting the injury, shock, or pain. When we freeze, inhibit active defenses, and can't speak, it is also adaptive: what could we say that wouldn't provoke the aggressor? When children fight back, even if it's a losing battle, their animal defense systems may instinctively assess that, in *this* situation, it is safer to fight than to submit—even though it might result in punishment. It seemed important to emphasize the strengths connected to Lillian's going on with her normal life self, to reassure her that we can temporarily lose access to a part of the brain, but, unless we sustain a brain injury, those strengths are still encoded and potentially accessible. The intrepid, determined woman she had been most of her adult life was still intact and available for reconnection.

At the moment a trigger precipitates flooding of implicit memories held by structurally dissociated parts, the client frequently loses access to verbal information or conceptual thinking. For the time being, Lillian was going to need her therapist to be an auxiliary cortex, providing psychoeducation about trauma and parts, helping her "test-drive" different interventions and practice those that worked, and mapping out step by step how to stop the flooding and access her normal life self once again. Her biggest risks were going to be regression and avoidance. Without a therapy that emphasized the importance of using mindful observation, curiosity, and psychoeducation to gain access to her normal life self, Lillian would be at risk to "blend" with the parts (Schwartz, 2001) and become a frightened child rather than building relationships with them. Or, having reconnected to her going on with her normal life self, she might feel so much relief that it might be tempting to ignore and suppress the trauma-related parts again. In the initial consultation session, it was important to establish a way of working that emphasized that she could heal and go on with her life—if she were willing to build a protective, caring relationship with her young parts by calling upon the same determination to help suffering children that had been her strength and motivation since her twenties.

A New Role for the Therapist: Neurobiological Regulator

In early attachment relationships, parent figures provide not only an auxiliary cortex for their infants but also externally mediated neurobiological regulation or soothing. Successfully regulating a child's immature nervous system is necessary not only for his or her sense of attunement and well-being but also critical for growing affect tolerance via an expanding "window of tolerance"

(Ogden et al., 2006; Siegel, 1999) that allows children to increasingly regulate and tolerate a range of emotions. Childhood neglect, trauma, early loss, witnessing of violence, or "frightened and frightening" caregiving (Liotti, 2004; Lyons-Ruth, 2006) all interfere with attachment formation and therefore with developing a spacious and flexible window of tolerance that fosters resilience. With or without childhood trauma, adult traumatic experiences, such as combat, assaults, rape, and domestic violence, disrupt previously established autonomic patterns and prime the nervous system to respond to environmental stressors with over- or under-activity.

The result is a client who enters therapy with a dysregulated nervous system and a truncated window of tolerance, with a brain conditioned to activate the emergency stress response in the presence of trauma-related stimuli. Unless the therapist is prepared to offer interactive neurobiological regulation, a dysregulated client will encounter difficulty with some of the basic aspects of traditional psychotherapy: the request to "free-associate" or say what comes to mind, the ability to connect to affect, to trust the therapist's good intentions, to focus, conceptualize (why he or she is there, what hopes or goals bring the client to therapy), connect past/present, and "sit with" whatever emotions and physical reactions are activated in the course of the therapeutic hour without hyper- or hypoarousal, dissociation, or impulsive responses. This is a challenging expectation, one for which a window of tolerance and a prefrontal cortex are necessary prerequisites.

> At her first visit, Carla, a 45-year-old attorney, was visibly shaking as she described why she was there. Her speech pressured, she leaned forward as if ready to leap out of her chair at a moment's notice. "I haven't been able to eat or sleep in months. My last therapist said she couldn't help me, and this new one lets me out early each week because I get too overwhelmed to do 'the work,' as she calls it." Holding out her shaking hands for me to see, she asked, "Why isn't 'the work' helping me with all this? Why does the work have to be about the abuse? I don't know how I'm managing at my job, but it's the only place I almost feel like my old self."
>
> Talking very slowly and calmly to slow the pace of conversation, but with a smile to signal that things were not so bad as she felt, I said, "I have good news and bad news for you—which do you want first?" [More smiling.]
>
> "The bad news," Carla said, "Better to get it over with."
>
> "The bad news is you are flooded with trauma-related feelings and body memories, and your nervous system has gone through the roof into extreme hyperarousal. Want to hear the good news? The good news is that you are not going crazy! [The therapist laughs and smiles, and Carla does, too.] In fact, there is a very simple remedy for this! Would you like to hear it?
>
> "Yes!"

"To help your nervous system and stop the flooding of feeling memories, we need to get your frontal lobes back online. That's why you feel better at work: your job requires you to think—it 'pulls' your prefrontal cortex to do what it does so well."

In this vignette, I use a number of "tools" available to all therapists: my tone of voice, pacing of speech, smiling and laughing versus a serious facial expression, choice of focus (beliefs, affect, body, vulnerability, strength, parts), projecting a confident energy versus a questioning, more tentative energy. Focusing attention on the client's strengths often elicits a moment of recognition and reconnection to resources long forgotten; reframing negative interpretations or providing corrective information helps to change the story, elicit curiosity, and even regulate the nervous system.

To help facilitate getting her prefrontal cortex back online, I next provide some psychoeducation by reinterpreting Carla's difficulties as dysregulation: "No one can think clearly or manage intense feelings when the nervous system is in a state of traumatic activation—it's too overwhelming. So, let's go very slowly and stay curious. I'm going to ask you to pause and just notice what your body is doing right now."

"The shaking has gone down," she observed in a less pressured tone. "I feel less speedy and on edge—actually, as soon as you said, 'we just need to get your frontal lobes back online,' I felt better."

"Great! Your body really responds to those words: 'all we have to do is get your frontal lobes back online.' Now, let's be curious about what else gets your frontal lobes back online other than going to work. Over the years, has your prefrontal cortex been a resource for you?"

"Oh yes! I'm a civil rights attorney. I have to inspire people, challenge them, out-argue them, make them see what needs to be done."

"Wonderful—your prefrontal cortex is a resource, and so is your sense of purpose, being more determined than the other side. Now we need to focus your determination on getting your frontal lobes back online. Here's what I want you to do: I want you to notice when you're speeding up and starting to feel more shaky and overwhelmed, then pause and just keep saying to yourself, 'I'm just triggered—these are feeling memories'—or body memories—which do you prefer? Feeling memory? Or body memory?"

"Body memory—it feels like my whole body, not just my feelings."

"Wonderful—then remind yourself that it's just your body being triggered, just body memory, and then become interested and curious in what's happening rather than panicking." As the session continued, the therapist kept watching for the signs that Carla was getting hyperaroused again, asked her to pause periodically and then use her frontal lobes to be curious and interested in these body memories without trying to figure out to what event they were best matched.

Each time, the observing and curiosity slowed her down, increased activity in the prefrontal cortex, settled her nervous system a bit, and allowed her to think more clearly.

The neurobiologically astute therapist has one primary goal: to ensure that each intervention, including even the physical presence of the therapist, has a regulating effect on the client's nervous system. We can be confident that trauma-related material will be dysregulating and that trusting the therapist, being the center of attention, revealing avoided emotions or secrets, feeling too close or not close enough will all be triggering. Even the proximity to another human being in a small, enclosed space may be activating for some clients. Once committed to therapy, the potential triggers keep multiplying: changes in schedule, not feeling "gotten," inadequate time or words to express all one wants to say, disappointed hopes for some particular response, separation between sessions, distorted beliefs, and projections.

Unlike traditional models of treatment, the assumption in neurobiologically informed trauma treatment is that clients are just as likely to be dysregulated by therapy than to feel "safe," more likely to come to therapy with limitations imposed by trauma-related hypo- or hyperarousal, sensitivity to triggering, and some degree of structural dissociation. The most complex regulating challenges are posed by clients with dissociative disorders and more severe structural dissociation (see Chapter 8 on Treatment Challenges: Dissociative Systems and Disorders).

Tessa came to her first therapy session with a very sophisticated question, "How does one deal with the effects of attachment trauma in personal relationships?" But as she talked about her new dating relationship, it became increasingly clear that she was describing structural dissociation: "I really like him, but when we're together, I start feeling very ambivalent. I begin questioning: should I have come on this date? Should I let him hold my hand? What if he becomes sexual?" The picture she described suggested conflicts between several parts: a part that liked him and longed to be his girlfriend, a part that pulled away and began questioning as soon as things got closer, a part that wanted sex, and a part disgusted and frightened by the thought. "So I keep my distance when we're out taking a walk, but then I get home to an empty apartment, and I feel a longing for him, and I wish I'd let him take my hand. I hate this—I can't think about anything else at home, but then I get ambivalent in his presence."

ME: "Of course it's a battle ..." I knew that validating the normality of her internal conflicts would help her feel understood. "How could it not be? This is what relational trauma leaves as a legacy: the terrible longing when you're not together and a 'yuck, don't get too close' feeling in his presence."

The "of course" is said with conviction but also a softness and sadness. "How could it not be?" is said with a smile that normalizes and lightens it. "Terrible longing" conveys the yearning in its tone; "yuck" is equally spoken with conviction but also toughness. Both are expressed as if each is entirely normal and to be expected.

"What generally happens next?" I ask.

TESSA: "I don't know ... I try to be honest about my ambivalence but at the same time, he's all I ever think about ... Usually, these guys stop returning my texts and emails, and I don't know why, so I get very upset and keep texting to explain myself. And then I get brushed off. He isn't ready for commitment either, he'll say. But what's the 'either'? What makes him think I'm not ready for commitment?" [Note that she is out of touch in this moment with the part of her that speaks openly to her dates about feeling ambivalent.]

ME: [Again, I mirror her words so she can hear herself better:] "So the ambivalent part discourages him, and then the part that yearns for connection encourages him—the guy must get very, very confused!" [Laughs softly.]

TESSA: "Why do you keep talking to me like I'm some multiple personality?" she suddenly says in a new gruff, irritated tone.

I use an authoritative but empathic tone: "Because I can hear both sides in your story, Tessa. Both sides of you are there. This is what happens when we have relational trauma when we're young: a battle starts up inside whenever we might possibly, maybe get close to someone." [The last few words are said with a tone of regret or sadness.]

If clients like Tessa are willing to embrace the structural dissociation model, learn to consciously and voluntarily "split off" the intense affects and assign them to younger, more vulnerable parts, they can achieve the necessary mindful distance to feel some relief without having to resort to denial or disconnection. Only when they are able to "see" the parts in these paradoxical responses will they be able to begin healing their wounds. But they cannot successfully learn the abilities needed without help and direction from the therapist.

The Therapist as Director, Coach, and Pace-Setter

Many therapists have been carefully trained to avoid directing the treatment for fear that clients will become automatically compliant and lose an opportunity to get "in touch" with an inner sense of direction. But because dissociative fragmentation results in multiple senses of direction and an inhibited prefrontal cortex, because of the risks of retraumatization or stuckness and avoidance, the therapist has to be unafraid to gently direct the focus and pacing of treatment.

One way of conceptualizing this aspect of the therapist's role is to think of it as providing a roadmap for clients whose traumatic reactions inhibit consistent access to the prefrontal cortex, leaving them confused and overwhelmed with no sense of direction. Or, because we are working with fragmented systems of parts, the more active role of family therapist is also a good model for trauma therapists, especially in the face of the need to prevent chaos and crisis. As family members engage in old, unhealthy patterns of behavior in the session, the family therapist has no choice but to guide and direct the session to prevent increased conflict and help family members begin to develop increasing acceptance of and compassion for each other. The therapist working with a fragmented client is in the same role—made more challenging by the fact that he or she can't actually see the other family members!

As clients are taught by the therapist to mindfully notice the child parts' distress and understand it as "her" or "his" pain, they are next encouraged to empathize with "the child part's feelings." This is not always an easy step for clients whose way of distancing the "not me" parts has been to loathe and despise their feelings. But the therapist whose compassion for the parts is genuine and spontaneous can create a contagion effect, evoking compassion even in the client who resists. To evoke empathy for the child, the therapist has to ask the client to pause and be curious about this child part that is afraid, ashamed, or hurt and lonely. How old is he or she? Can the client see the part? What does he or she look like? What expression does the client see on that little face? Acknowledging the enormity of what this child part has experienced can also evoke compassion, as long as the therapist is clearly asking, "What kinds of things has *this child* experienced?" rather than "What happened to you at this age?" The latter is more likely to trigger implicit reliving, while the former helps the client "see" the child as a helpless, innocent victim. Lastly, the client is next taught to use the resources characteristic of the normal life self to "help" the child parts that are so frightened and in so much distress.

In session after session, as clients present the issues or feelings most troubling on that day, the therapist continues to ask them to notice "which part" is upset today and what has triggered that part. The assumption that upset is always a communication from a part is not a scientific fact, of course—it represents a way of relating to triggered states or implicit memories in a mindful, compassionate, non-pathologizing way.

Underlying this assumption is a mindfulness-related bias that noticing our thoughts, feelings, and body experience with interest, curiosity, and compassion is likely to lead to positive change (Davis & Hayes, 2011; Ogden & Fisher, 2015). If we as therapists consistently encourage the normal life self to take a mental step back, increase curiosity about the younger parts that are "having a hard time," notice the bodily and emotional signs that communicate "their" feelings, and then experiment with what might help the parts feel safer, better protected, less ashamed, we will be "processing" post-traumatic memory. Simply by noticing spontaneously evoked implicit memories and assigning the feelings to younger selves, clients can learn to feel less afraid of their triggered responses and more connected to and protective of their parts, rather than ashamed and alienated.

The Body as a Shared Whole

When I help clients foster empathy for their vulnerable or protector parts, they cannot help but feel that empathy in their bodies. If I were to ask, "Do you feel compassion for yourself, too?" the answer would be "Absolutely not!" But when they say, "I feel badly for that little part—I feel sad for him [her]," I can observe their faces softening and their bodies relaxing a little bit. They can feel the empathy extended to a young child part or brave protective fight part, can feel the part responding positively, and it feels good inside the shared whole of the body. Although human beings tend to put words to experiences of empathy ("I feel understood—it feels like someone 'gets it'—I feel like you believe me"), attunement and empathy are actually nonverbal somatic experiences of warmth, relaxation, being able to breathe more deeply, and feeling emotionally closer and more connected.

Because, despite the presence of many parts, there is only one shared whole of a body, it also means that any intervention having a positive effect on body experience will have a positive effect in some way on each part. For example,

Ted had been "hijacked" or taken over by a depressed, ashamed submit part many years previously when early professional success unexpectedly triggered a flooding of post-traumatic implicit memory, sending him into a tailspin from which he had never recovered. Now, twenty years later, he was still depressed, still struggling to function, still ashamed of his "fall from grace" as he termed it. A tall, thin man, his shoulders and spine were collapsed; he walked with a duck-footed awkwardness; and he tended to look down at the floor rather than at me. His refrain was: "You don't understand." He was correct about that: it was hard for me to understand how this bright, talented man had just given up and given in to the depression—until one day, as I listened to his self-punitive confession of the week's failures, I felt myself collapse. My spine and shoulders sunk; I began to feel energy-less and helpless; I found myself questioning my ability as a therapist.

Without consciously choosing to disclose, I heard myself saying, "You know, Ted, as you talk, I can feel myself collapsing in my chair, going numb, feeling absolutely helpless, questioning my adequacy ... I may not be as good at this as I thought I was ..."

Suddenly, he sat up: "That's how I feel!" he said. "You finally got it! Now you know what I'm going through."

ME: "I do." [Still slumped in my chair with no energy to meet his energy.]

TED: "I feel so much better now that I know you 'get' it!" Now he was sitting up with his back straight and aliveness in his face and tone of voice.

ME: "It seems like you felt better as soon as you sat up, though. Is it OK if I do that, too?" [I imitate his posture of excitement and pleasure] "Oh, that is so much better—thank you."

TED: [Sitting up even straighter with his shoulders back] "Yes, that does help, doesn't it?"

ME: "Would it be OK if we stood rather than sit? Maybe that would help me with this hopeless feeling ..." [We both stood up.]

TED: "This is much better!" [He suddenly looked like a new person: more assured, more masculine, more related to me instead of alone in his depressive world.]

ME: "It sure is—what a difference! In you, too—it's like your grownup self is standing tall and sending a whole new message to the depressed part!"

TED: "I feel like a man," he said. "It's been a long time since I felt like a real man. If that makes the depressed part feel better, I'm glad."

ME: "Maybe before, your physical collapse communicated to him that he was right—he should be depressed and hopeless and question himself. Now your body is sending him a really different message, isn't it?"

Utilizing movement interventions drawn from Sensorimotor Psychotherapy (Ogden et al., 2006; Ogden & Fisher, 2015), Ted transformed his internal experience, especially that of the depressed submit part. His new body language communicated to the depressed part that he wasn't a little boy alone in an intimidating world, that he wasn't "less than," and that the boy could hold his head high along with Ted. By combining a parts perspective with the somatic interventions of Sensorimotor Psychotherapy, Ted and I could work simultaneously with the parts and the whole, rather than feeling pressure to choose one approach or the other.

The Changing Role of the Therapist

Not only does a parts approach require role changes for the therapist (from listener to educator, from individualistically oriented to systems-oriented, from facilitator to role model), but so do the demands of neurobiologically informed trauma treatment. The emphasis on greater differentiation between parts as a vehicle for mindful self-observation conflicts with the prevailing view in the field that the therapist must de-emphasize parts language and emphasize that the patient is one whole person in one body. However, when that one mind and body is in chaos or bent on self-destructive behavior or so fragmented that reality-testing is compromised, the goal of treatment must be to restore order and provide a period of stability during which clients can learn to identify the different perspectives inside them, develop more conscious and effective defenses, and differentiate their normal life selves from the impulsive, ashamed, or critical voices they hear inside. When the client reports many years of traditional talking therapy without the kind of progress in treatment one might expect, or describes having been stuck in an ongoing internal conflict over months or years without much success in resolving it, or describes the signs of structurally dissociated parts, it should be clear that treating the client as one person in one integrated body has not worked. Traditional talking therapy approaches might work well with individuals who are less fragmented or traumatized, but it does not work with clients whose habits of self-alienation and self-rejection recreate the rejections and humiliations of childhood.

Processing Experience Instead of Events

Therapists often feel pressure to address traumatic memory as early in treatment as possible because they have been taught that "trauma processing" is the gold standard of trauma therapy. Often unaware of changes in the standard of care in the field or familiar with new mindfulness-based treatments, they assume the need to access event memories.

But in the model of treatment described here, the focus is not on traumatic events but on the "legacy of trauma" as it is carried by the parts and continues to intrude even decades later into the minds, bodies, and ongoing lives of survivors. "Processing the trauma" is equated in this model with "transforming" how the parts have encoded the *effects* of the traumatic events and transforming the client's *relationship* to the parts from one of alienation to one of unconditional acceptance and "earned secure attachment." For therapists with years of event-focused trauma treatment experience, it is often hard to shift from a narrative approach to a "repair" perspective. What they need to remember is that the event focus of the early trauma treatment field simply reflected an extension of the "talking cure" to trauma therapy (Rothschild, in press), not the creation of an approach specifically tailored to the in-depth understanding of traumatization available to therapists today (Van der Kolk, 2014).

Throughout treatment, the therapist will encounter event-related issues. There will inevitably be parts that want to "tell all" or parts that tell and retell stories of the same events over and over again. Equally likely are parts that resist the therapist and the therapy in order to keep the secrets of the past intact or avoid "going there." Because therapists will encounter all these different points of view in their clients, it helps to keep in mind that the goal in trauma treatment is not remembering what happened but the ability to be "here" instead of "there" (Van der Kolk, 2014).

When individuals can be conscious and present in the here-and-now and tolerate the ups and downs and the highs and lows of normal life, they are ready to heal the injuries caused by the trauma—the injuries to innocence, to trust, to faith—the injuries to the body and the injuries to the heart and soul. Remembering the past is helpful only to the extent that it helps to heal rather than reopen the wounds. However much remembering plays a role in trauma treatment, it should never be used in the service of reliving the painful past or asking the parts to relive it.

Remembering in fact should serve a larger purpose: to help the client "be here now" by transforming the past and changing the ending to each part's story. Remembrance should be used as a catalyst to evoke a deeper appreciation of how the client has survived "with heart and soul intact" and a gratitude for all the parts that helped the client survive and now deserve to be part of a safe and healthy present.

References

Chodron, P. (2008). *The pocket Pema Chodron.* Boston: Shambhala Publications.

Damasio, A. (1999). *The feeling of what happens: body and emotion in the making of consciousness.* New York: Harcourt, Brace.

Davis, D. M. & Hayes, J. A. (2011). What are the benefits of mindfulness? A practice review of psychotherapy-related research. *Psychotherapy,* 48(2), 198–208.

Diamond, S., Balvin, R., & Diamond, F. (1963). *Inhibition and choice.* New York: Harper and Row.

Hanson, R. (2014). *Hardwiring happiness: the new brain science of contentment, calm, and confidence.* New York: Harmony Publications.

Herman, J. L. (1992) *Trauma and recovery.* New York: Basic Books.

Liotti, G. (2004). Attachment, trauma and disorganized attachment: three strands of a single braid. *Psychotherapy: Theory, Research, Practice, Training,* 41, 472–486.

Lyons-Ruth, K. et al. (2006). From infant attachment disorganization to adult dissociation: relational adaptations or traumatic experiences? *Psychiatric Clinics of North America,* 29(1).

Meichenbaum, D. (2012). *Roadmap to resilience: a guide for military, trauma victims and their families.* Clearwater, FL: Institute Press.

Ogden, P. & Fisher, J. (2015). *Sensorimotor Psychotherapy: interventions for trauma and attachment.* New York: W.W. Norton.

Ogden, P., Minton, K., & Pain, C. (2006). *Trauma and the body: a sensorimotor approach to psychotherapy.* New York: W.W. Norton.

Rothschild, B. (in press). *The body remembers. Volume II: revolutionizing trauma treatment.* New York: W.W. Norton.

Schwartz, R. (2001). *Introduction to the internal family systems model.* Oak Park, IL: Trailheads Publications.

Siegel, D.J. (1999). *The developing mind: toward a neurobiology of interpersonal experience.* New York: Guilford Press.

Siegel, D. J. (2010). *The neurobiology of 'we.'* Keynote address, Psychotherapy Networker Symposium, Washington, D.C.

Van der Hart, O., Nijenhuis, E.R.S., & Steele, K. (2006). *The haunted self: structural dissociation and the treatment of chronic traumatization.* New York: W.W. Norton.

Van der Kolk, B.A. (2014). *The body keeps the score: brain, mind and body in the healing of trauma.* New York: Viking Press.

Van der Kolk, B.A. & Fisler, R. (1995). Dissociation and the fragmentary nature of traumatic memories: overview & exploratory study. *Journal of Traumatic Stress,* 8(4), 505–525.

CHAPTER 4

Learning to See Our "Selves": An Introduction to Working with Parts

"The essence of trauma is that it is overwhelming, unbelievable, and unbearable. Each patient demands that we suspend our sense of what is normal and accept that we are dealing with a dual reality: the reality of a relatively secure and predictable present that lives side by side with a ruinous, ever-present past."

(Van der Kolk, 2014, p. 195)

"['T]he self' who was in the camp wasn't me, isn't the person who is here, opposite you. No, it's too unbelievable. And everything that happened to this other 'self,' the one from Auschwitz, doesn't touch me now, doesn't concern me, so distinct are deep memory and common memory. ... Without this split, I wouldn't have been able to come back to life."

(Langer, 1991, p. 5)

The brain and body are inherently adaptive, instinctively prioritizing survival demands over other drives, such as socialization, exploration, sleep and rest, hunger and thirst, and play (Van der Hart et al., 2006; Schore, 2001). In infancy and early childhood, the attachment drive is an even more powerful mobilizer than fight/flight instincts, reflecting the child's need to physically depend on parent figures. In adolescence, the balance shifts the other way: fight/flight responses are mobilized as or more readily than proximity-seeking behavior. When other defenses fail us or increase the danger, freezing and submission responses are automatic at all developmental stages. In the face of inescapable threat to life, the brain and body instinctively "feign death" (Porges, 2005), shutting down, going unconscious and/or limp, or "pretending to be asleep," as human beings often describe it. The innate ability to neurocept or sense the severity of the threat is accompanied by an instinctive tendency to engage the safest, most effective defensive response in a given context.

In the same way, human beings instinctively seek psychological distance from traumatic events or from "deep memory" to avoid being overwhelmed by the remembrance. To keep on "keeping on," we must psychically split off from what is happening right now, what did happen a moment ago, and what might happen next. Whether in wartime, in a concentration camp, or in the context of childhood abuse and neglect, some sense of self must be kept separate from the horrifying events around us even if that self just goes through the motions of life. To get up each morning and face death, abandonment, assaults, or imprisonment requires somehow disowning the horror and fear left from the day before and the dread of what is to come. Disowning "the other one" inside is a survival response: the overwhelming feelings are no longer ours; that shame does not belong to us but to "him" or "her;" the white-hot rage and violent impulses certainly aren't "me." By disowning our traumatized parts and/or "not me" self-states (Bromberg, 2011), by disconnecting from them emotionally or losing consciousness of them via dissociation, we preserve our hearts and souls from growing as bitter as our circumstances. We hold out hope for the future and we keep going.

Distancing from the trauma serves another important function in childhood, another way of surviving: it allows us not just to keep going but to keep growing and developing despite whatever befalls us. With distance or disconnection from the trauma, children can focus on mastering age-appropriate developmental tasks and developing a repertoire of functional abilities. When part of the child can concentrate on "normal" activities, such as going to school, can experience new learning and mastery, can play sports and make friends, there is an opportunity for normal development of exploratory and social drives. The going on with normal life self, unaware of what is happening or only dimly aware of it, might become a "parentified child" by day, a good student at school, a lover of nature or horses or books or making things with his hands. The worse the trauma or neglect and the less safety, the more distance will be needed from the knowledge of his or her emotional and physical vulnerability. For example, in times of war, in abusive families, or in a concentration camp, it might also be adaptive to disown normal physical needs, attachment-seeking, or the wish to be comforted. When we disown needs that can't be met or feelings that are unacceptable, we protect ourselves from unbearable disappointment or punishment (e.g., "I'll give you something to cry about!"). One way to accomplish this challenging task is to split the sense of desperate needing and the refusal to need anything between two parts: one part that actively seeks proximity, comfort, or needs-meeting and one that just as actively pushes others away or keeps a hypervigilant, suspicious distance. Disowning one's sad or lonely or needy parts, as well as angry, hypervigilant, or counterdependent parts, prevents self-acceptance and self-care, but it is safer. When the individual must adapt to an environment that punishes or ignores a child's basic needs and feelings, self-compassion too becomes "dangerous." It cannot be "me." Depending upon what best promotes safety and optimal development in each unique environment, children might have to identify with their angry, aggressive, hypervigilant parts and disown their innocent, trusting, attachment-seeking parts, or they might have to reject the parts that bore the brunt of the abuse so that the trauma can be blamed on "their" vulnerability. Alienation from self is often necessary, too, to maintain

some semblance of attachment to grossly neglectful and abusive caretakers—
an under-rated but important survival instinct when we are young enough to
be dependent on our caretakers. If the "good child" is distasteful to attachment figures, it can be more adaptive to disown the "good me" or even the
going on with normal life self and identify with the bad, ashamed, disgusting
child who doesn't threaten dangerous or neglectful caretakers. Whichever
parts endanger the child's adaptation must be walled off; whatever parts are
necessitated by the environment must be identified with as "me."

The Cost of Adaptation

Disowning requires selective attention, a focusing away from whatever is "not
me." The senses fail to register what is taking place around us; we don't feel our
emotional responses, good or bad; we are in a zone. We can't "own" our anger or
dependence or fear when we don't feel them. We can't "own" traumatic events
that we haven't witnessed. We can't know ourselves as whole human beings because only those qualities valued in a traumatic environment are accessible to
consciousness. Segregating intense feelings, though, results in affect intolerance:
if we can escape our emotions by automatically and involuntarily shifting into a
different part of the self or different feeling state, we never get the opportunity
to exercise our "emotional muscles," and all feelings gradually become more
and more intolerable. Inner conflicts are never resolved, just distanced.

When that happens, acting out (self-destructively or addictively) and "acting in" (through self-hatred, self-judgment, punitive introspection) become
the only avenues for regulating emotions and autonomic arousal. Splitting or
fragmentation must become more complex and creative. For example, some
parts may become more autonomous, "emancipated" from cortical control,
or so split off from other parts there is no intrapersonal awareness between
them. Whereas continuous consciousness across states might be typical of
complex PTSD, development of increasingly severe trauma-related disorders
(borderline personality disorder, dissociative disorder not otherwise specified
[DDNOS], and dissociative identity disorder [DID]) increasingly becomes a
risk the more prolonged and severe the traumatic events. (See Chapter 8 for
more on Treatment Challenges: Dissociative Systems and Disorders.)

The therapist's job of normalizing compartmentalization is made easier by
the nature of the Structural Dissociation model: it is simple, straightforward,
and positive in approach, yet its grounding in neurobiology gives it credibility even when clients are skeptical and intellectually hypervigilant. Using the
diagram in Figure 4.1, I explain to clients that human brains are designed to
be able to split if things get "too much" or "too overwhelming." Because right
and left brains are separate brain structures, it makes intuitive sense to clients
that, when they are exposed to trauma, the split between the two hemispheres
enables the left brain aspect of self (what Cozolino [2002] calls "the verbal lin-
guistic self") to "keep on keeping on," earning it the title of the "going on with
normal life part," while the right brain mobilizes the "corporeal and emotional
self" (Cozolino, 2002), with its more physical survival resources, to prepare for

the next threat, thus its name, "the trauma-related part." It is also easy for most clients over the age of 12 to understand that no one could survive in just one way—for example, just by fighting. It is easy for them to comprehend that they have additional subparts as well, each of which contributes a different survival strategy. And then, to ensure that the clients can connect personally to the theoretical model, I ask them what they already know about each part. Do they recognize their going on with normal life selves? Do they recognize a part that knows how to ask for help? A part that knows how to fight or get angry? Do they recognize a frightened part? An ashamed or compliant part? Which parts are most difficult for the client to deal with? Which does the client like best?

With the help of the diagram, I try to demonstrate how each part sees the world through a different lens, is driven by a different animal defense imperative, and how it relates to others based not only on its history but on its biological role. Each holds different implicit memories and interpretations of what happened; each has a different job to do.

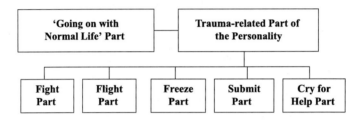

Figure 4.1 Structural Dissociation Model.

Years after the traumatic experiences, clients come to treatment describing their symptoms or issues, not knowing that they are describing traumatized parts and their implicit memories. The animal defense survival strategies that once reduced the level of harm or enhanced their survival have now become split off automatic responses activated by trauma-related stimuli. Divorced from the original events that necessitated them, they are long outdated and often extreme or maladaptive in the client's normal life today (Figure 4.2).

The paradoxical quality of these symptoms is rarely captured by traditional diagnostic models. Clients report symptoms of major depression (the submit part), anxiety disorders (freeze), substance abuse and eating disorders (flight), anger management or self-harm issues (fight), and they alternately cling to others or push them away (the characteristic symptoms of disorganized or traumatic attachment). Sometimes they come with co-occurring issues: suicidality, chronic pain, obsessive-compulsive disorder, inability to function, or loss of previous functioning. Often, they are diagnosed with borderline personality disorder or, because of their autonomic hypo- and hyperarousal responses, with bipolar II. Only occasionally, when memory gaps and losses of consciousness have been observed, do such clients receive dissociative disorder diagnoses. But whether traumatized individuals have been given one diagnosis (e.g., depression, borderline personality, anxiety disorders) or have been given many, standard treatments rarely have had a lasting impact, and many structurally dissociated clients have spent years in therapy with little to no change in their symptoms. Studies (Foote et al., 2006; Karadag et al., 2005) have consistently shown that the dissociative disorders (dissociative amnesia, dissociative fugue, dissociative disorder not otherwise specified [DDNOS], and DID) are consistently under-diagnosed in both inpatient and outpatient settings relative to the more widely known diagnoses of borderline personality, bipolar disorder, attention deficit disorder, and substance abuse disorders. These studies also indicate that there is a correlation between severity of symptoms and having an undiagnosed dissociative disorder. That is, when symptoms of dissociation are present but not diagnosed or included as an issue in the treatment, we can expect increased rates of high-risk behavior, more frequent relapses, and more instances of suicidal behavior, not just ideation (Karadag et al., 2005; Korzekwa & Dell, 2009). Perhaps because DID remains a controversial diagnosis even to this day, evidence of more common dissociative disorders (especially DDNOS) is often overlooked or the symptoms are interpreted as signs of other diagnoses. It is crucial that therapists know of the well-documented correlation between borderline personality and dissociative symptoms: a series of studies by Korzekwa et al. (2009a; 2009b) and by Zanarini (1998) have consistently found evidence that approximately two-thirds of borderline patients have statistically significant levels of dissociative symptoms, and one-third tend to have sufficient symptoms to justify a diagnosis of DID.

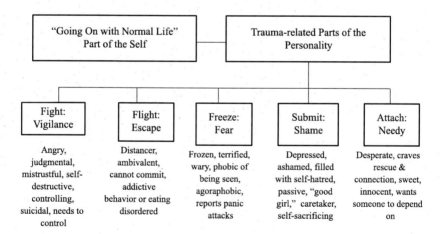

Figure 4.2 Recognizing Parts by the Role they Play.

"Getting to Know You"

Aaron described the reasons for which he had come: "I start out by getting attached to women very quickly—I immediately think they're the 'one.' I'm all over them, can't see them enough … until they start to get serious or there's a commitment. Then I suddenly start to see everything I didn't see before, everything that's wrong with them. I start feeling trapped with someone who's not right for me—I want to leave, but I feel guilty—or afraid they'll leave me. I'm stuck. I can't relax and be happy, but I can't get out of it either."

Aaron was describing an internal struggle between parts: between an attachment-seeking part that quickly connected to any attractive woman who treated him warmly and a hypervigilant, hypercritical fight part that reacted to every less-than-optimal quality she possessed as a sign of trouble. His flight part, triggered by the alarms of the fight part, then would start to feel trapped with what felt like the "wrong person," generating impulses to get out—an action that his submit and cry for help parts couldn't allow. Guilt and shame for the commitment he'd promised (the submit part's contribution) and fear of loss (the input from his traumatically attached part) kept him in relationships that his fight and flight parts resisted with equal intensity. Without a language to differentiate each part and bring it to his awareness, he ruminated constantly: should he leave? Or should he stay? Was she enough? Or should he get out now? Often, suicide seemed to him the most logical solution to this painful dilemma, yet at the same time "he" dreamed of having a family with children and a loving and lovely wife. "He" didn't approve of his wandering eye, yet "he" couldn't stop trolling for prospective partners. Who was "he"? The suicidal part's threat to end it all was in direct conflict with his wish for a wife and family; the "trolling for women" part was at odds with the person he wanted to be and believed he should and could be.

Nelly presented herself as "depressed" but when asked to describe her symptoms, instead she recounted a series of beliefs about herself: "I'm disorganized, lazy—I can't seem to get off the ground—I'm ashamed to think of myself as a competent person, though people tell me I am." Her first thought each morning was "another day for me to make a waste of," and then she would feel overwhelmed and pull the covers over her head and sleep until early afternoon. Appointments were forgotten; dishes didn't get washed; there was nothing to eat in the house—confirming her belief that she was a failure and generating a series of harsh judgments that drained her energy and generated the impulse to go back to bed. Now in her fifties, she could recall what it was like to be the underachieving child in an achievement-oriented family, "hiding in plain sight" to avoid angering her abusive narcissistic father who was threatened by his children's accomplishments and wounded by their failures. Her funny, charming personality had won him over, and seeing her as a bright, ditzy, disorganized kid was acceptable to him—at least marginally acceptable. She had promise, even if she didn't have achievements.

Now, all these years later, Nelly found herself confused about who "she" was. For so long, she had been "hijacked" (Ogden & Fisher, 2015) by the under-achieving, self-denigrating, quirky child part that had once helped protect her from her father's wrath and win his heart. The dominance of this submissive part's role in Nelly's life was supported by that of an equally familiar critical part whose words and worldview were eerily like her father's. Without a parts model on which to draw, it was easy for her therapist of many years to mis-take Nelly's self-loathing for low self-esteem and to interpret her wry sense of humor as "a defense against core emotion."

> But Nelly felt best when her going on with normal life self broke free, and she could be focused professionally, witty, charming, and self-disparaging in a humorous yet self-compassionate way. Sadly, the critical part succeeded in convincing her that these abilities were just those of a false self whose role it was to hide what a waste of human life she had ended up becoming. Even when she felt good, the critical part found a way to communicate judgment! She needed a "no fault" paradigm for understanding herself and for seeing each part's contribution as a communication from the past. Inside, the submit part was afraid to let Nelly actualize as the talented professional she was for fear she would "get a swelled head;" the critical part hypervigi-lantly worried about failure; and the freeze part was afraid to leave the house for fear that all human beings would be scary like her father.

And because all this was happening in one body, Nelly made the logical as-sumption that these were all "her" feelings—never questioning the paradoxi-cal reactions that revealed evidence of an internal war among parts.

Developing Curiosity: Who Is "I"?

In most psychotherapy models, no differentiation is made between the "I" that feels shame or the "I" that explodes in anger or the "I" that is always afraid. Each emotion is treated as an expression of the individual's whole self. In a parts model, however, each distressing or uncomfortable thought, feeling, or body sensation is treated as a part (Schwartz, 1995). By deliberately and con-sistently using the language of parts rather than the language of "I," the ther-apist helps the client to observe each trauma-related feeling or reaction as a message from a part or parts: "Which 'I' feels ashamed and apologetic? And which 'I' is disgusted by all the apologizing?" When we ask these questions, we evoke curiosity and facilitate mindful observing. There is now a very slight distance between the observer and what is being observed. The client can still feel the feeling or reaction but with a decrease in intensity, presumably due to increased activity in the medial prefrontal cortex and reduced amygdala activation. The word "part" introduces new information, generating interest and often curiosity.

Aaron and Nelly had long lost any curiosity they might once have had about their symptoms: they accepted the input of angry, suicidal, demoralized, lonely, self-critical, and self-loathing parts as "my feelings," ignoring the fact that these were contradictory emotional states. Wanting to attach to someone is in direct conflict with wanting to flee; wanting to feel mastery, competence, and energy is in direct conflict with "flying below the radar" or appearing "less than" to avoid threatening others. But both were so identified with the parts' struggles and conflicts that these paradoxical responses escaped their notice. The first task in therapy was to challenge their assumptions and ignite their curiosity in two ways: first, by using the "language of parts" (Schwartz, 2001), rather than the language of "I," and, secondly, by asking them to use mindful observation, instead of their automatic negative interpretations, to "track" (Ogden et al., 2006) the moment-to-moment signs of their parts' thoughts, feelings, visceral reactions, and movement impulses as they responded to triggers around them with competing survival responses.

Mindful Noticing of the Inner Landscape

To the extent that clients continue to ruminate on their trauma-related emotions and cognitive schemas, the more often they are triggered by environmental stimuli, the more dysregulated their nervous systems will become and the more activated the parts. The more the prefrontal cortex is inhibited or shut down by trauma-related dysregulation, the harder it becomes for the normal life self to stay curious and present. Without an observing prefrontal cortex to differentiate past and present, repeated activation of neural networks holding traumatic memory further sensitize these pathways to future triggering, exacerbating trauma-related symptoms (Van der Kolk, 2014). Learning to observe rather than react and to attach neutral labels to what is noticed (e.g., scared child part, angry part, etc.) is the foundation of a parts approach.

With the help of a therapist who persistently reframes problematic emotions and issues as communications from parts, clients learn to identify the key features that indicate signs of a part's presence. They are taught to observe distressing or uncomfortable physical sensations, overwhelming or painful emotions, negative or self-punitive beliefs, internal struggles, procrastination, and ambivalence. Automatic reactions, the same thoughts repeatedly coming to mind, repetitive responses to triggers, negative reactions to positive events or stimuli, or "over-reactions" should also be flagged as likely signs of parts activity. The practice of being asked repeatedly to be curious and notice all of these phenomena as possible signs of parts activity has a number of benefits. Mindful observation evokes activity in the prefrontal cortex, counteracting trauma-related cortical inhibition and inducing a very slight sense of separation from the feeling, thought, or part. For the first time, clients might notice that they can have a relationship to the feeling rather than be consumed by it or over-identified with it. Another benefit of mindful awareness is its effect on autonomic dysregulation: activation of the medial prefrontal cortex (the part of the brain that engages when we meditate) is associated with decreased activation in the amygdala (the brain structure associated with initiation of the emergency stress response). In addition, when individuals become curious and interested and focused on what they are observing, they intuitively slow their pace and increase concentration to increase observational capacity.

When clients have greater access to their going on with normal life selves (or what is called "self" (Schwartz, 2001) in the Internal Family Systems model), they benefit significantly from the advantages made possible by increased activity in the prefrontal cortex: they can use mindful noticing to separate from the intense reactions of a part; they can have a relationship of curiosity or compassion toward the part's feelings or perspective; they can create ways of soothing or managing the emotions; and they can choose to react differently to foreseeable events or triggers than they have in the past. In contrast, parts under the influence of implicit memory will have the same reactions over and over again: separation anxiety, irritability or anger, shame and hopelessness, fear, self-destructive impulses, etc. Even if available to the client, coping skills and problem solving are less likely to work when parts are triggered because the "problem" to be solved is most often an implicit memory, not a current stress or challenge. And when "the problem" is the result of competing states engaging in a struggle for control, adult coping ability has little to no effect on it.

Survival-Related Internal Struggles

Certain internal struggles between parts are inevitable and predictable. The cry for help or attach for survival response will automatically evoke flight-related distancing impulses—or fight-related protective reactions such as mistrust, hypervigilance, anger, or judgment. Critical thoughts expressed by the fight part, often experienced by clients as "self-loathing," are likely to trigger the submit part's feelings of shame, hopelessness, and inadequacy. Interpersonal closeness can trigger either the attach part's yearning for more proximity, the freeze part's fear of being harmed, and/or the warning alarms of the fight and flight parts—or all of these reactions simultaneously. Professional or family responsibilities can feel like a repetition of bearing old burdens to the submit part, even when the work is self-initiated by a competent normal life self who enjoys completing chores that once felt overwhelming to a small boy or girl. Sometimes, it is the steps forward in life taken by the normal life part that most alarm the trauma-related parts and even trigger their conflicts and crises. "Being seen" positively (e.g., being given a compliment, praised for something, or evoking attention for one's accomplishments), successful performance, and achievement awards can all evoke the fear of visibility in the freeze part and the expectation of being used or abused in the fight part. We often forget that some kind of special attention or "grooming" often precedes sexual or even physical abuse, making traumatized clients hypervigilently sensitive to being treated kindly as well as to being ill-treated.

As Donald Meichenbaum (2012) reminds us, trauma is an experience beyond words, and the beliefs or stories that individuals attach to a traumatic event bias their meaning-making, leading to what he calls the creation of "self-defeating stories." Which parts might write a self-defeating story? The submit part would be likely to write a shame-based, hopeless story of victimization; the cry for help part a story of how no one came or cared; the fight part would communicate that it's better to die than to continue to be used and abused. The going on with normal life self has access to the wider perspective of the prefrontal cortex and can learn to understand that the belief one is "faking it" might be adaptive in a traumatic environment, while continuing to believe it later in life would be maladaptive. When beliefs are consistently differentiated from emotions, visceral reactions, tension versus relaxation, and actions, when all of these inputs are connected to the parts contributing them, clients begin to get a clearer sense of who they are as a whole and why they have struggled so hard.

> Danny was an overachiever professionally, driven by a judgmental critic and an anxious part that feared failure. Whatever he achieved, it wasn't enough for the critic and didn't reassure the fearful part. A new boss who was never satisfied with his work but who took credit for Danny's accomplishments provided the trigger that opened the floodgates of implicit memory. Suddenly, his fight part was confronting and challenging the boss, the submit part was feeling so ashamed and victimized that it was hard to go to work, and Danny was experiencing a painful sense of not being wanted or valued anywhere, the emotional memories of an attach part. Each held a piece of his survival: the fight part's indignation at the misuse of power by both parents, the submit part's self-defeating, self-blaming story, and the heartbreaking emotions of a young boy who felt an unmet yearning to be special to someone. As Danny "unblended" from these parts and used his meditation skills to observe them as younger selves, he felt an immediate compassion for the young boy who felt so hurt. "That's why I've been pushing myself to achieve—to win praise so that this boy feels special to someone!" Instinctively, he felt protective of the young boy: he could feel a determination in his body: this boy should not be hurt again, he thought. He would have to make this little boy feel special—he would have to communicate the acceptance his parents had withheld.

Selves-Acceptance

"Befriending" one's parts is not simply a therapeutic endeavor: it also contributes to developing the practice of self-acceptance, one part at a time. When clients pause their reactions to "befriend" themselves, to be curious and interested rather than dismissing and reactive, they slow time. Autonomic arousal settles; there is a relaxing of the sense of urgency to do or be anything different. They feel more at peace because their parts can be more at peace. Self-alienation, that is, disowning of some parts and identifying with others exclusively, does not contribute to a sense of well-being, even when it is absolutely necessary in order to survive. Self-alienation creates tension, pits part against part, communicates a hostile environment (often much like the traumatic environment), and diminishes the self-esteem of every part. Befriending means that we "radically accept" (Linehan, 1993) that we share our bodies and lives with these "room-mates" and that living well with ourselves requires living amicably and collaboratively with our parts. The more we welcome rather than reject them, the safer our internal worlds.

References

Bromberg, P. (2011). *The shadow of the tsunami and the growth of the relational mind.* New York: Taylor & Francis.

Cozolino, L. (2002). *The neuroscience of psychotherapy: building and rebuilding the human brain.* New York: W.W. Norton.

Jimenez, J. R. "I am not I." *Lorca and Jimenez.* R. Bly, Ed. Boston: Beacon Press, 1967.

Karadag, F., Sar, V., Tamar-Gurol, D., Evren, C., Karagoz, M., & Erkiran, M. J. (2005). Dissociative disorders among inpatients with drug or alcohol dependency. *Clinical Psychiatry,* 66(10), 1247–1253.

Korzekwa, M., Dell, P.F., & Pain, C. (2009a). Dissociation and borderline personality: an update for clinicians. *Current Psychiatry Reports,* 11, 82–88.

Korzekwa, M., Dell, P.F., Links, P.S., Thabane, L., & Fougere, P. (2009b). Dissociation in borderline personality disorder: a detailed look. *Journal of Trauma and Dissociation,* 10(3), 346–367.

Langer, L. L. (1991). *Holocaust testimonies: the ruins of memory.* New Haven, CT: Yale University Press.

Linehan, M. M. (1993). *Cognitive-behavioral treatment of borderline personality disorder.* New York: Guilford Press.

Meichenbaum, D. (2012). *Roadmap to resilience: a guide for military, trauma victims and their families.* Clearwater, FL: Institute Press.

Ogden, P. & Fisher, J. (2015). *Sensorimotor Psychotherapy: interventions for trauma and attachment.* New York: W.W. Norton.

Porges, S. W. (2005). The role of social engagement in attachment and bonding: a phylogenetic perspective. In Carter, C.S. et al. *Attachment and bonding: a new synthesis.* Cambridge, MA: MIT Press.

Schore, A.N. (2001). The effects of early relational trauma on right brain development, affect regulation, & infant mental health. *Infant Mental Health Journal,* 22, 201–269.

Schwartz, R. (2001). *Introduction to the internal family systems model.* Oak Park, IL: Trailheads Publications.

Steele, K., van der Hart, O., & Nijenhuis, E.R.S. (2005). Phase-oriented treatment of structural dissociation in complex traumatization: overcoming trauma-related phobias. *Journal of Trauma and Dissociation,* 6(3), 11–53.

Van der Hart, O., Nijenhuis, E.R.S., & Steele, K. (2006). *The haunted self: structural dissociation and the treatment of chronic traumatization.* New York: W.W. Norton.

Van der Kolk, B.A. (2014). *The body keeps the score: brain, mind and body in the healing of trauma.* New York: Viking Press.

Zanarini, M.C., Frankenberg, F.R., Dubo, E.D., Sickel, A.E., Trikha, A., Levin, A., & Reynolds, V. (1998). Axis I co-morbidity of Borderline Personality Disorder. *American Journal of Psychiatry, 155*, 1733–1739.

CHAPTER 5

Befriending Our Parts: Sowing the Seeds of Compassion

"Mindfulness is an act of hospitality. A way of learning to treat ourselves with kindness and care that slowly begins to percolate into the deepest recesses of our being while gradually offering us the possibility of relating to others in the same manner. ... [The] process simply asks us to entertain the possibility of offering hospitality to ourselves no matter what we are feeling or thinking. This has nothing to do with denial or self-justification for unkind or undesirable actions, but it has everything to do with self-compassion when facing the rough, shadowy, difficult, or uncooked aspects of our lives."

(Santorelli, 2014, p. 1)

Reclaiming Our Lost Selves

While yearning to "like" ourselves, the disowning of traumatic experiences or the vulnerable, ashamed, angry, or depressed parts holding implicit memories of those experiences results in a profound alienation from self: "I don't know myself, but one thing is clear: I don't like myself." The ability to be compassionate or comforting or curious with others, which comes so easily to many trauma survivors, is not matched by the ability to offer themselves the same kindness. What it took to survive has created a bind. It was adaptive "then" to avoid comfort or self-compassion, to shame and self-judge before attachment figures could find them lacking, but now it has come to feel believable that others deserve or belong or are worth more—while, at the same time, it also feels that these "others" are not to be trusted; they are dangerous or uncaring.

It is a well-accepted premise that, to feel safe in any relationship, human beings need compassion both for themselves and for the other. Internal attachment bonds or "earned secure attachment" (Siegel, 1999) give us emotional resilience. The internalization of secure attachment allows individuals to tolerate hurt, loneliness, anxiety, disappointment, frustration, and rejection—all the risks inherent in any close relationship. But in order to unconditionally accept ourselves and "earn" that resilience, we need to develop a relationship to *all* of us: to our wounded and needy parts, to the parts hostile to vulnerability, to the parts that survived by distancing and denial—to the parts we love, the parts we hate, and even the parts that intimidate us.

Embedded in most methods of psychotherapy is the belief that "healing" is the outcome of a relational process: that if we are wounded in an unsafe relationship, the wounds must heal in a context of relational safety. But what if the quality of our *internal* attachment bonds, rather than our interpersonal attachments, is a more powerful determinant of our ability to feel safe? What if attachment to ourselves is a bigger contributor to the sense of well-being than the attachment we feel to and from others? What if being witnessed as we recall painful events does not heal the injuries caused by those experiences? And what if compassion for the child who lived through these events is more important than knowing the details of what happened? If that is so, and I believe it is, then trauma treatment must focus less on painful and traumatic events and more on cultivating compassion for our disowned selves and their painful experiences. When all parts of us feel internally connected and held lovingly inside, each can experience feeling safe, welcome, and worthy, often for the first time. The first step is to become curious about this "other" inside whom we do not really know.

The Role of Mindfulness: How We Can "Befriend" Ourselves

To observe and identify the signs indicating parts activity requires a witnessing mind capable of focused concentration or "directed mindfulness" (Ogden & Fisher, 2015). Mindfulness has an important role to play in the treatment of trauma because of its effects on the brain and body. Mindfulness practices counteract trauma-related cortical inhibition, regulate autonomic activation, and allow us to have a relationship of interest and curiosity toward our feelings, thoughts, and body responses—or parts. In brain scan studies, mindful concentration has been associated with increased activity in the medial prefrontal cortex and decreased activity in the amygdala (Creswell et al., 2007).

Mindfulness is key to trauma work not only because of its regulating effect on the nervous system but because it also facilitates the capacity for "dual awareness" or "parallel processing," allowing us to explore the past without risk of retraumatization by keeping one "foot" in the present and one "foot" in the past (Ogden et al., 2006). "Dual awareness" is a habit of mind or mental ability that allows us to simultaneously hold in mind more than one state of consciousness. When the client can stay present in a mindfully aware relationship to both present moment experience and an implicit or explicit memory connected to the past, he or she is in dual awareness. When individuals can connect to a felt sense of the child self's painful emotion while simultaneously feeling the length and stability of the spine, the in and out of the breath, the beating of the heart, and the ground under their feet, intense emotions can be held and tolerated. Sensorimotor Psychotherapy, Internal Family Systems, and hypnotic ego state therapy (Phillips & Frederick, 1995) are all mindfulness-based methods, as are the other popular treatments for trauma most frequently sought out by clients—Eye Movement Desensitization and Reprocessing (EMDR) (Shapiro, 2001) and Somatic Experiencing (Levine, 2015).

From Whose Perspective Should We Observe?

Observations of the environment through the telescopic lenses specific to each part often create a distorted perspective for the client. Each part has partic-ular biases that narrow what it picks up as data and what it never sees. The fight part is not scanning for safety cues: it is hypervigilantly oriented toward threat stimuli. Attach sees only the warm smile, the reassuring words, the polite manners—and never sees the danger signals that indicate grooming or seduction. The submit part doesn't see the respect of his colleagues, the approval of his boss or family members, but he is likely to be hypersensitive to data that confirm beliefs in unworthiness or not belonging. When clients learn to identify the lens through which they are looking ("the little part is hoping to see someone who likes her," "the depressed part is looking at Susan's expression and thinking the worst"), they can begin to see the actions and reactions of their parts from a meta-awareness perspective. Rather than being flooded with overwhelming emotions, they learn to separate from the intense reactions of a part, acknowledge the feelings as "his" or "her distress," and bear witness to the child part's painful experience. Perhaps for the first time, clients can have a relationship to a distressing feeling rather than being con-sumed by it or identifying with it as "mine." The feeling or reaction is still palpable but with a decrease in intensity that is consistent with the ability to sustain curiosity and interest in it, rather than react. Mindful "interest," rather than "attachment or aversion," helps individuals tolerate emotions and sensations that may have previously felt frightening, and it supports a neutral stance toward whatever is observed or discovered. In addition, when individ-uals become curious and interested and focused on what they are observing, they intuitively slow their pace to increase concentration and observational capacity. Being "interested" is the first step toward getting to know another being, even when that other is a part of one's self. From this new perspective, it is easier for most individuals to find ways of soothing the parts' emotions and anticipating events or triggers that might overwhelm a child without support from someone older and wiser.

In an Internal Family Systems approach (Schwartz, 1995; 2001), the ob-server role is ascribed to "self," an internal state that draws upon eight "C" qualities: curiosity, compassion, calm, clarity, creativity, courage, confidence, and connectedness. "Self" is not just a meditative state or dependent upon having positive experiences in life: each quality is an innate resource available to all human beings no matter what their past or present circumstances. Most importantly for the purposes of psychotherapy, access to these states creates an internal healing environment.

In the model I am describing here, integrating approaches drawn from Sensorimotor Psychotherapy and Internal Family Systems, there is also a fundamental assumption that these "C" qualities are accessible to any human being. They are never lost, no matter how sadistic and prolonged the traumatic experiences. However, I find that, for many lower-functioning clients with habitually inhibited precortical activity, it may be necessary to practice in order to access these states consistently. Some individuals may have to learn how to regulate autonomic activation sufficiently to keep the prefrontal cortex online before they can connect even to their curiosity. Some clients may be triggered by feelings of compassion, calm, courage, even curiosity. In these instances, I ask the client to pick one of the "C" qualities from Internal Family Systems and just focus on the practice of accessing that quality.

> Sarah at first picked compassion but quickly found that she felt so overwhelmed when she opened her heart to the young parts that, in the end, she couldn't feel *for* them because she was too blended: she felt only the tidal wave of their emotions. Then she chose calm as the quality she wanted to cultivate but found that triggering, too. "I think it's too close to having to be quiet and not move," she realized. Finally, as her third choice, she picked curiosity. That didn't trigger the parts, but because she blended so quickly with their intense reactivity, she often missed the chance to be curious. For her, it was easiest simply to observe her body responses: to mindfully notice when she was triggered and observe the activated thoughts, feelings, and body sensations as "things of interest," rather than interpret or describe them in a narrative.

Adopting an attitude of mindful noticing or dual awareness also allows clients to slow down their thoughts, feelings, and physical reactions enough to listen more attentively to the parts. The therapist at first must support them by prompting them to "notice what's happening," "notice 'who' is here with us," and by observing each thought or feeling as a separate communication: "I hear a part of you speaking today that feels overwhelmed and scared—do you notice that part, too? Can you be curious about what's scaring her?"

"See how that ashamed part immediately interpreted the chaos in your apartment as her fault! Maybe because the critical part was having such a fit about it ..."

"There's quite a battle going on today inside you, huh? A lot of thoughts focused on whether or not to commit to your boyfriend—a lot of emotions and tears coming up. Notice the perspectives of both sides: what part wants you to stay connected no matter what? What part is afraid of him leaving? What part thinks *you* should get out while the going is good?"

"The hopeless part is really struggling today, isn't he? He doesn't want to feel this way—he doesn't want to be stuck in the past—but hopelessness and shame are his 'safe place,' and he's afraid it's not safe to have hope."

Differentiating Observation versus Meaning-Making

As Donald Meichenbaum (2012) reminds us, trauma is an experience beyond words, and the beliefs or stories that individuals attach to a traumatic event bias their meaning-making, leading to what he calls the creation of "self-defeating stories." Which parts might write a self-defeating story?

The submit part would be likely to write a shame-based, hopeless story of victimization; the cry for help part a story of how no one came or cared; the fight part would communicate that it's better to die than to continue to be used and abused. Only the going on with normal life with its access to the wider perspective of the prefrontal cortex has the ability to conceptualize at a higher level, to make meaning out of the apparently paradoxical feelings, beliefs, and instinctual reactions of the whole system. It requires higher order cognitive processing to comprehend that the belief one is "faking it" might be adaptive in a traumatic environment, while continuing to believe it later in life would be maladaptive. When beliefs are consistently differentiated from feelings, visceral reactions from perceptions, tension from relaxation (Ogden & Fisher, 2015), and when all of these inputs are connected to the parts contributing them, clients begin to get a clearer sense of who they are as a whole and the trauma logic underlying their actions and reactions.

Blending, Shifting, and Switching of Parts

Parts do not wear name tags, nor do personality systems come with road maps or instruction manuals. Every part of the client shares the same body, the same brain, the same environment. When we have a feeling or thought, it could be the expression of any part. To know "whose" feeling or thought requires familiarity: a personal relationship with the part that allows immediate recognition when we hear its voice. Or to know requires that we pause, listen carefully, and piece together the data or clues: which part would have reacted to that trigger? What kind of part would feel ashamed right now? But any of these acts of curiosity and interest are impossible when we identify with the part, when we "blend" with its feelings and reactions, interpreting them as our own. The term "blending," created by Richard Schwartz (2001) and used in Internal Family Systems, refers to two confusing phenomena described by trauma clients: the tendency to identify with parts ("I am depressed," "I want to die.") and the tendency to become so flooded with their intense feelings and body responses that who "they" are and who "I" am become indistinguishable.

Catherine was on vacation with her husband in the Caribbean, a place they'd visited many times before and to which both felt a deep connection. The second morning of their trip, she woke up to inexplicable feelings of loneliness. She felt sad and empty, far away from her husband, even though he was only inches from her. "Believing" the feelings were hers, she found herself interpreting them: "He really doesn't understand me—he means well, but he's not really there for me." By the time her husband woke up, she was in tears, accusing him of not truly caring. Only later in the day, when she was better connected to her normal life part, did she realize that the lonely feeling came from a young part who, disconnected and split off from Catherine's present day life, didn't experience the safety, support, and companionship she'd found in her marriage. The little part just needed reassurance that she wasn't all alone.

Catherine had not only become blended with the young part but had shifted into an altered state during her dream sleep so that, on awakening, she was in another time and place. Now in the implicit memory state of a little girl in a very lonely, frightening family environment, she lost any connection to her present day perspective altogether. Gone was her happy marriage, gone the successful creation of a new life, a new safety, and a new family in which she was welcome and valued. She was back in Michigan, and it didn't feel safe.

Rachel alternated between feeling depressed and feeling irritated— sometimes irritated more with herself, sometimes annoyed by others. The depression took hold most powerfully when her partner, Susan, was busy with work and friends, leaving little time or energy for Rachel. At such times, the depression often convinced her that it would be better to die than to live, but, knowing how much it would hurt her partner to lose her, she would fight the impulse to act on her suicidal feelings. When she felt the irritability, on the other hand, she lost the empathic perspective toward her partner: feeling annoyed and "morally correct" in her judgment, she had no qualms about hurting Susan's feelings. The depression and abandonment feelings were triggered by the loss of Susan's attention, whereas the critical feelings were usually triggered by Susan's tendency to "rescue" friends and family who "needed help," even if it meant being disconnected from Rachel and absorbed in the crises of others.

When Rachel was asked to notice the depression as a depressed part and to be curious about how old that part was, the number "12" immediately came to mind. "That was a tough age," she recalled. Asked to focus on the depressed 12-year-old and to notice what other feelings went with the depression, Rachel could feel a sense of not belonging, of not being wanted or worthy of notice, as well as fear that being noticed might bring something bad instead of good. During her childhood, Rachel's mother could barely manage the stress of having six children she hadn't truly wanted; being noticed was a mixed blessing because more often than not, it led to anger or demands to perform rather than reassurance and closeness. It made sense that this part would be triggered by a partner who had too many people depending on her. Despite how loving and validating Susan tended to be, Rachel's 12-year-old part held a different reality. When Susan was busy, she re-experienced the implicit memories of a cold, unaffectionate mother whose attention was divided. When asked to notice the irritability as another part, Rachel immediately thought of her mother: "Oh, my God! The irritable part sounds just like my mother—frugality and avoidance of "excess" emotion were moral issues for her." When she was asked to "unblend" or mindfully separate from the irritable part and notice it as a part, she became aware that "she" (i.e., her normal life self) prized the unconditionally accepting relationship she and Susan had developed much more than the judgmental part did. The judgmental part was still trying to enforce her mother's rules decades later, Rachel realized with a laugh—as if her mother's approval were still necessary for survival!

Rachel exemplifies the phenomenon of "blending," while Catherine exemplifies "shifting" of mental states. Rachel could easily reality-test her perceptions; she could step back from them; and she could even be curious about why she was having such strong reactions. Catherine, on the other hand, experienced palpable changes in both emotional state and perspective during which she had no memory or connection to other feelings and states. On the first day of their vacation, she had felt a sense of appreciation for being in such a beautiful place with a loving, supportive husband. But after "time-traveling" in her sleep, she woke up to profound feelings of loneliness. There was no curious "Why am I feeling this way?" in her mind, only a frantic sense of urgency to end the painful feeling.

Nelly, on the other hand, had dissociative identity disorder (DID) and often "switched" from state to state, a cardinal symptom of DID in which changes in state are sudden, frequent, and often accompanied by losses of consciousness. (For example, had Catherine "switched," she might not have recognized her husband at all; she might not have known where she was or even how old or what her name was.)

When Nelly was "in" her depressed "default setting" part, there was no other reality, no other perspective. During the day, she found she could switch states by making lunch dates with friends. Their affection and interest acted as a positive trigger, facilitating a switch into her going on with normal life self. One moment, she would feel shame and self-loathing, questioning why she had made a lunch date at all, then, as soon as her friend arrived, the normal life part that had made the appointment would be present. At night, feeling better after seeing her friends, "she" would make a commitment to herself to get up in the morning and start the day, no matter how badly she felt. But when she woke up "hijacked" by the depressed part, she would have no memory of the commitment "she" had made the night before. Then "she" would go back to sleep, not wanting to face the day, and when "she" woke up again in the early afternoon, the ashamed part would feel "pathetic" and inadequate. It was not important that Nelly's dissociative disorder be diagnosed, but identifying the switching was important. Without realizing that she switched, she could only interpret her behavior through the lens of failure.

All of these clients, regardless of diagnosis, were learning to separate from the feelings, beliefs, activation, and body responses of their parts, rather than automatically assuming that all of their mental and emotional life belonged to one self. They were practicing mindful noticing and the ability to identify parts as they appeared moment by moment rather than identify with those parts as "who I am." Over and over again, they became aware that each time they noticed a part as "she" or "he," rather than automatically identifying with its feelings, they felt some relief—a little or even a lot. When, in addition, they became more deeply curious about a part, they began naturally to feel compassion toward him or her—in spite of themselves or in spite of the parts that were hostile toward the other parts. There was a gain in perspective, a feeling of greater calm, and that calming would often "turn on" the prefrontal cortex, facilitating more creative solutions to problems that represented internal conflict between parts.

Facilitating Empathy

Not only does the therapist model bearing witness to each part's qualities, emotions, and trauma-related perspective, she or he must also provide the missing link of empathy for each part. Knowing that simply observing and naming what they observe as a "part" is challenging enough for clients, I try to model mindful use of the language of parts. I notice their "voices," feelings, and points of view, often before the client does, name their appearance, and then I deliberately add a tone of warmth or communicate pleasure and appreciation for each part. I describe their plight ("What was a little boy supposed to do?") when clients are struggling with compassion. I try to verbalize appreciation for their contributions to the client's survival: "Had he not given up and given in, what would have happened to all of you? How would your stepfather have reacted?" Most importantly, I share my own personal experience of the client's parts to bring them alive and make them "real." Using language that evokes positive feelings and associations, I try to communicate that they are much more than disembodied implicit memories without a context. I might admire the ingenuity of a very young part: "That little girl was one smart cookie, wasn't she? Oh my!" Or the courage of an adolescent part: "That 15-year-old was one determined young lady, huh? But, you know, she was always very creative, too—who would have thought to 'hide out' in a hospital where her parents couldn't get to her? It was pretty amazing how she pulled that off. It's not so easy to keep being admitted to hospitals to get away from your parents!" If we are speaking about an adolescent male part, I might say, "Wow, he took some big risks. Always getting in trouble so he could get help for all of you when he could have been killed." I can also cultivate empathy by "defending" or "sticking up" for the parts, as in the following example:

> Nelly responded to my helping her notice the depressed part by judging its behavior: "Well, she's a loser—she doesn't let me even get out of bed!"
> I immediately challenged her: "Are you suggesting a depressed 11-year-old part chose to be this way? She volunteered at birth to be a 'loser'? [I raised my hand as if to volunteer, and we both laughed.] No baby in the crib volunteers to be depressed or to hate herself ... let's be curious about how she lost her hope ...'"

"Seeing" the Parts: Externalized Mindfulness

When individuals are too identified or too blended with the their parts' feelings and beliefs to access mindful observation, as is common with very dysregulated clients, therapists need other ways of facilitating dual awareness—enough dual awareness that the normal life self develops a perspective on and a relationship with the trauma-related part rather than blend with it.

There are a number of ways to achieve dual awareness, even in very decompensated individuals, but all depend upon multi-modal interventions. Because visual focusing seems to increase curiosity and activate the medial prefrontal cortex, trauma therapists can benefit from including an easel or large clipboard as part of their office equipment (as I do). For example, I might ask a client to draw a picture of some part with which he or she has been struggling and then invite the client to look at the picture with curiosity: what does the drawing tell him about this part? What is he learning from the drawing that challenges what he's previously believed about the part? How does he feel toward this part now?

Or we can help clients decode struggles between parts by creating a "flow chart" that tracks the internal relationships between the parts in conflict, starting with an initial trigger and then noting step by step which part or parts were activated. Drawing a rectangle at the top of the page to depict the going on with normal life self, clients are asked to observe retrospectively, frame by frame, the sequence of triggers and parts that set the internal conflict in motion. The trigger is usually represented by a large arrow shape that I color in red. Next, the client is asked to recall which part reacted first to the triggering stimulus, and that part is depicted by a circle within which the therapist can write the approximate age or some description of the part (i.e., "depressed part," "anxious part") by which to recognize it in the future. The therapist next asks: "How did this part react to [the trigger]? How did he feel?" Then the therapist writes down the words connected to that part below its circle, making sure to identify its feelings and beliefs: "Believes she is disgusting and worthless—'just wants to crawl into a hole'."

Following that, the client is asked to observe, "What part got triggered by the ashamed part?" For example, Nelly would have said, "Then the hopeless part gets triggered: she just keeps saying, 'It's all bad and it will never get better.'" That part in turn gets represented by a circle within which is written its age and "name" or descriptor and below which are the words that describe its perspective and emotions. Typically, internal struggles occur between 3 to 6 different parts, and the flow-charting continues until a full picture of the conflict or problem emerges and can be appreciated. In the following example, the client came in feeling distressed and suicidal, so dysregulated that she could not unblend from the parts, so I asked her if we could diagram what was happening so "we can both really 'get' it—we know there are some pretty distressed parts, but we don't understand what's triggering them."

Clients rarely refuse to diagram because it tends to feel less threatening than talking about their emotions, but I can add, "And if we start diagramming, and you find it too overwhelming or not helpful, just tell me." "Let's start with what happened first—there was some trigger, and then the first feelings you felt were ... what?"

> CLIENT: "I felt so lonely and unwanted—like no one was there—I've just been abandoned."
>
> ME: "A little part was triggered, huh? [While she talks, I draw a circle for the young part and describe her distress in the same words used by the client.] Back to that place of painful loneliness where no one wanted her. How sad! And then what happened next? What part came up next?"
>
> CLIENT: "Then I felt such intense shame—it was overwhelming—I felt so disgusting and dirty that no wonder no one wanted me."
>
> ME: "So the little part triggered the shame part and the shame part blamed herself! And not just for the little part's being alone but for everything—she just took it all on her shoulders. It was all her. That's what she does, doesn't she? She always assumes it's her."

Much like the diagram in Figure 5.1, what feels like an internal struggle to the client usually appears in the diagram as a series of parts, each of which triggers each other in succession, leading to some impulse to give up, hurt the body, die, or run away—some desperate measure for what feels like desperate times.

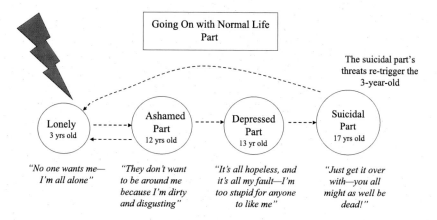

Figure 5.1 Drawing the "Problem."

The visual images symbolizing each different part and his or her feelings tend to spontaneously invite unblending. As they study the diagram, I can often see a shift in clients' body language or tone of voice indicating to me that the normal life self is noticing the parts instead of blending with them. And if unblending does not occur spontaneously, I can ask the client to focus specifically on each element of the drawing separately and increase curiosity about each part, observing each set of feelings and thoughts and noticing how each has made meaning of the implicit feelings triggered by other parts.

"Notice how it all began when your boyfriend was late, and he triggered the little part—she was so hurt! She felt so disappointed and unimportant, and then the hopeless part triggered her more and triggered your fight part—and she was beside herself! Can you see how it worked?" Observing on the diagram how suicidal, addictive, acting out, or self-destructive parts get triggered by the emotions of the vulnerable parts and then emerge to offer the young parts a "way out" of their distress further clarifies that the underlying purpose of trauma-related self-destructive behavior is to bring relief and regulation to the body: the very opposite of trying to die. Once curiosity and even compassion are elicited, the next step is to diagram a solution—in this case, a solution for the lonely part and a solution for the suicidal part. A solution or intervention is always best if it emerges organically out of the concern or protectiveness of the going on with normal life self (Figure 5.2).

The first diagram(s) depicts for the client how the system of parts became activated and polarized as a result of the triggering. The second diagram is used to depict how the normal life self can now provide healing and care for the child parts, making the suicidal part's "attempt to help" unnecessary. Had I treated the suicidal part's "offer to help" as life-threatening suicidal ideation and tried to hospitalize the client, both the fight part and the attach part would have been further triggered. The attach part would have felt more

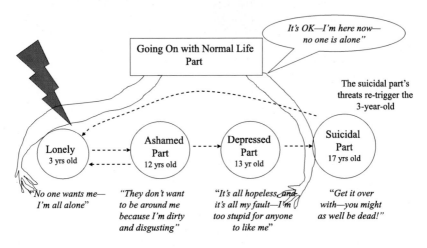

Figure 5.2 Diagramming a Solution for the System.

alone, banished to the hospital, and the fight part would have felt hostility and entrapment by a controlling authority figure.

In this example and many others, the solution to what could have been a life-or-death crisis results from a comforting reparative experience being offered to the vulnerable little part. A compassionate normal life self is asked to take the lonely, ashamed, hopeless child parts "under her wing," communicating a sense of care and protection. Even if the client is struggling with compassion, the visual image of the arms encircling the young parts evokes positive sensations in the client's body: warmth, protectiveness, a smile, the impulse to move toward the drawing and thus the parts. The advantage of the diagrams is the ability to introduce something foreign and potentially challenging through non-verbal communication. Had I asked this client to say, "I will take care of you," to the younger parts, I might have received the answer: "No, I don't want to take care of them!" But when I draw the arms and describe the intervention as a gesture, "See what happens when you take these young parts under your wing so they aren't so overwhelmed and scared," no client protests. As I speak, I make a gesture with my right arm as if taking someone under my wing, and I repeat the gesture again each time I say the words "under your wing." The somatic communication speaks directly to the parts themselves. The left brain, specializing in words, may react negatively to the verbal communication but cannot block the somatic message intended for the right brain (Gazzaniga, 1985). The younger parts can feel the "wing" in the drawing and in my gesture.

Another means of externalizing the parts' struggles and conflicts so they can be witnessed is to use objects to represent them: sand tray figurines, animal figures, stones and crystals, even rubber ducks. Notice that all of these figures are appealing to a child's mind, not just an adult mind and body. The therapist must never forget that the client is not a "he" or "she" but is a system composed of parts of all ages from infants to wise elders.

> Cath came for a consultation to assess whether a DID diagnosis would be more appropriate for her than psychotic disorder, the label given to her each time she reported hearing voices. She was challenging to interview, though, because she was constantly distracted by what seemed to be a very heated internal conversation among her voices. Her mouth moved as if she were talking, though she emitted no sound; she would gesture as though angry, a scowl on her face. Occasionally, I could read her lips as she shook her head vigorously and mouthed "No, no!" Each time I used the word "part" or asked her about the voices that were talking to her, the dialogue might pause for a moment, but there was no clear sign I had been heard—until the third appointment to which Cath came carrying a little plastic bag. "Here, these are the parts," she said, and she dumped the contents of her little bag on the table and promptly returned to her internal conversation. A small pile of miniature rubber ducks sat on my coffee table, a gift from Cath representing the parts she couldn't yet tell me about because she was too overwhelmed by their sheer number and the intensity of their feelings and conflicts.

Following that session, Cath gradually learned to describe her week-to-week internal problems and conflicts using the ducks, choosing different sizes and colors of little rubber ducks to represent different parts. Weeks later, she even brought in a rubber stress ball in the shape of a human brain to represent, "that big brain you keep talking about," proof that she had been listening to me after all when I talked about the "wise mind" part she had in her grownup brain. Each week, we would address whatever issue she brought in by using the ducks to create a psychodrama-like sculpture that depicted how inner conflicts between parts had resulted in a crisis or problem. Then I would describe duck by duck what she had shown me:

> "When the little orange duck [I pointed to it to focus her attention] got triggered by the angry man at the post office, the green duck started to run out of the building, which freaked out Jeremy [the medium-sized red teenage duck]. He thought the man was after him, so he jumped in the car and started driving away too fast, and that scared all the young parts! He drove so fast, and he was so mad and scared that it frightened the other ducks even more. What they need is to have the big brain help them at the post office so the angry man doesn't yell at them. What does the part with the big brain think should be done about this? The child parts like to go to the post office, but they always get yelled at because people get confused when child parts are talking in a grownup's body. They think the grownup is

being weird. Maybe they shouldn't be going into stores alone without a grownup—what do you think?"

Invariably, with some coaching from me, the rubber brain would come up with a creative solution that reflected wider perspective-taking made possible by Cath's being able to observe the duck tableau's depiction of the whole system and the whole of an experience. The internal intensity and the "noise" of the voices made it difficult for her to be mindful, but she could focus on the ducks and access more curiosity. Cath began to see the patterns of chaos and crisis that resulted when she switched into younger parts and then they were triggered by an external stimulus. Their hyperaroused emotional reactions would then trigger the defensive responses of fight and flight parts like Jeremy, retriggering the young parts all over again. Whether achieved through mindful observation, drawing, diagramming, or "duck therapy," externalization or visual depiction of the parts in interaction facilitates a wider field of awareness, greater curiosity and interest, a sense of perspective ("I'm safe now even though my parts don't believe it"), and increasing capacity to access the better judgment of the wise mind.

Blending and Reality-Testing

Because her survival strategy had historically been to automatically blend with whatever part was activated in a given moment, Annie had never questioned the information she regularly received through her body (tension, held breath, elevated heart rate, shaking and trembling), her thoughts (disparaging, hopeless, scathing), or her emotions (shame, panic, dread). Small, unremarkable daily events, including positive experiences like being asked by a potential friend to go to lunch, repeatedly triggered the parts and their implicit memories, which triggered other parts. "That's why it's easier to have a beer at 10 in the morning and go back to bed." For example, being invited on a lunch date triggered an insecure child part afraid she wouldn't know how to act, which then triggered hypervigilant parts guarding childhood secrets by discouraging close friendships, which then triggered judgmental, humiliating parts: "How stupid! What a ridiculous idea! Why would anyone want to be friends with you? She'll see how dumb you are in a minute." Between the sense of danger evoked by normal life triggers and the shame triggered by the judgmental parts, it was natural that, in her blended state, Annie assumed her world must be humiliating and dangerous and she was defective and unwanted.

Blending Keeps the Trauma "Alive"

How could any individual resolve traumatic experience in what subjectively feels like an unsafe, hostile environment? Clients and therapists alike often collude in believing that trauma can be resolved by processing the events even when critical voices are still attacking the individual at will, using the same words or scathing tone as the perpetrator. Similarly, both may equate "safety" with freedom from self-harm or a non-abusive home environment, as I did when I first met Annie. It might not occur to us that a "felt sense" of safety is likely to be unattainable if the client is habitually blended with child parts who still feel unwelcome, frightened, or ashamed or suicidal. Although the external environment may now be safe from an objective perspective, clients who are blended with their implicit memories and parts may have no bodily or emotional sense of safety that could reassure the parts that "it" is over. Before trauma can be resolved, the client must learn how to unblend from parts so that the realities of both brains can be appreciated. From an unblended, dual awareness perspective, the normal life self can learn to orient to the immediate environment by focusing visual attention, can correctly evaluate the level of safety, but also feel the parts' fear and bracing for danger as "their" evaluation. From the perspective of "present reality," as I call it, the normal life part can bear witness to the parts' past reality and often feel empathy for their still being "there."

Learning to Unblend

Because it takes practice to detect when one is blended, often the therapist becomes the observer who notices blending: "Hmmm, I can see you're really blended with the ashamed part today," "It's hard not to blend with that anxious part—you're so used to 'insta-blending' with her." "Insta-blending" is the term I use to describe procedurally learned habits of automatically blending with whichever parts have the strongest feelings, often so quickly that mindful noticing doesn't catch it. To be able to identify these patterns as they happen, it is important for clients to have a language for what is happening to them that is non-interpretive and non-pathologizing and helps them to notice potentially problematic conditioned learning. Clients also benefit from "unblending protocols," skills and steps for what to do after they've noticed that they are blended. (See Appendix A for a model of unblending protocol.)

> Suzanne came into her session with the guarded facial expression I had learned to expect as the expression connected to her hyper-vigilant part. This "bodyguard" part was always primed for disappointment or betrayal, both of which had been daily experiences in Suzanne's childhood. "I can't do it," she said. "I can't do it. I can't do what you and Dr. G. want from me." (Both her primary therapist and I had been trying to help her learn to unblend, but she was more often blended than not.) "Why do you keep trying to make me do something I can't do?!" As she spoke, her voice got more emotional and higher-pitched, a sign to me that this was a part speaking.
>
> ME: "Notice the part that keeps saying, 'I can't—I can't!' Can you separate from that part a little bit? See if you can feel her without 'becoming' her ... so she knows you're hearing her."

SUZANNE: "No, I told you, I can't do that stuff you guys want me to do!"

ME: "Suzanne, I know it's hard to learn to unblend when you're so used to thinking of all these parts as 'just you.' But would you be willing to try something? [She nods.] See what happens if you say, '*She* is afraid I can't do it—*she's* afraid.' What happens?"

SUZANNE: "It's not quite as intense."

ME: "Yes, it's not as intense when she hears you say, 'She's afraid.' Can you keep saying 'she'?"

SUZANNE: "OK."

ME: "Ask her: what is she worried about if she can't 'do it'?"

SUZANNE: [pauses, appearing to be listening inside.] "She's afraid you'll give up on her and then you won't help her."

ME: "Of course, she's worried about that! Because she had a mother whose motto was 'my way or the highway,' that's always a worry for her, isn't it?"

SUZANNE: "But it feels like my worry, too. Can I tell you the problem I have with this unblending thing? When I try to do it, when I step back from the parts' feelings, then I can't feel them at all. I just feel numb. Either I feel all of it, or I can't feel it at all."

ME: "Well, that is a problem, isn't it?" [Note that I validate her issues with unblending as normal and natural, trying to imply that my standards are different from her mother's.] "If the little part hadn't been so worried that we would reject and abandon her, maybe you'd have been able to tell us about this problem. And it's such a common one." [I now shift to some psychoeducation for her normal life self as a context for understanding her difficulties in unblending.] "Many trauma survivors find it hard to have what we call 'dual awareness': awareness of your being and awareness of the parts' feelings at the same time. But let's see if I can teach you some ways of unblending that might help with that. Would you be willing to try five steps to unblending?" [I deliberately chose a very structured approach, broken down into concrete small steps, to make the learning easier than she was primed to expect.]

SUZANNE: "OK."

ME: "First, notice the feeling of 'I can't'—can you still feel it?"

SUZANNE: "Yes, I can—it's not as intense, but it's still there."

ME: "Start by noticing the feeling and repeating again, 'She's afraid I can't do it.' That's Step One."

SUZANNE: "Say it out loud or to myself?"

ME: "Whichever feels more comfortable for you. If you are feeling distress, just assume that it belongs to a part and say to yourself or out loud, 'She's afraid … or 'She's upset.'" [I give her a minute or two to try out this new language with herself.] "Is that better or worse?"

SUZANNE: "Better."

ME: "Ready for Step Two?"

SUZANNE: "OK."

ME: "Here's Step Two: engage your core—slightly tense the muscles in your core so she can feel your presence. ... Can you still feel her?" [Remembering that Suzanne had been an athlete as a child, I chose to try out using the body as a resource here.]

SUZANNE: "I can!"

ME: "Great! Now ask her if she can feel you."

SUZANNE: "She can."

ME: "Wonderful! You can both feel each other! Great work! Hooray!! Does she like that?"

SUZANNE: "She does. She's telling me that's why the parts are so freaked out all the time—because they don't think anyone hear them."

ME: "A good reason for us to work on this, huh? Now you are both ready for Step Three! OK, now lengthen your spine a little bit from your lower back up—like you're putting space between the vertebrae ... Ask her if she can feel how tall you are now ..."

SUZANNE: "She's surprised—she didn't know I was that tall."

ME: "Good work! Now you can feel *her*, and she can feel *you*, and you're talking! Does she like that?"

SUZANNE: "Yes, she likes it a lot. And I like it because I hate it when I try to unblend and then I can't feel the part at all."

ME: "Ask her if it feels good to hear you say that you want to be able to feel her with you."

SUZANNE: "She likes that, but she says she's still worried that I won't get it, and you and Dr. G. won't like her ..."

ME: "Good, I'm glad she can tell you her worries. That's a good thing. Just be careful not to blend with her worries. Let's practice Step 4: connect to your department supervisor role for a moment. Imagine that this part is coming to you as her supervisor, and she's worried that she's not getting things fast enough and that she'll be fired. What would you tell her?"

SUZANNE: [Thinks for a moment.] "I'd tell her not to worry—to just keep trying to learn the job and trust that if she keeps trying, she will get it."

ME: "Wonderful advice, Suzanne—your staff are lucky to have such a wise, compassionate supervisor—now to Step 5: ask her if it helps her to hear that or if she still needs something else."

SUZANNE: "She says it does help, she wants me to keep saying it because she needs to hear it over and over ..."

ME: "Good point! She hasn't heard it often enough in her life to believe it and take it in. Do you think you could remember to keep telling her that she'll get it if she keeps trying? Would it help if you put it on your calendar and asked your phone to remind you? I know you keep track of your kids' schedules that way, and this part is a kid, too."

SUZANNE: [now clearly in her going on with normal life part] "I'll put her in my schedule, but it would also help if you wrote down those five steps for me so I can remember and practice." [This request told me that her normal life part was more present than I had seen before: she could think about how to achieve a goal that involved the parts.]

ME: [Talking as I write down the five steps we just practiced.]"That would definitely reassure her, Suzanne! And now, before we end today, let's thank her for telling you she was so worried! That was important. How else would you know? Maybe we can also schedule a time for her or other parts to tell you about their worries ... Let's be thinking about that."

Less afraid to connect to her young self because she was provided with a set of structured steps and not expected to connect to "too much" vulnerability too soon, Suzanne was able to not only unblend but also begin a dialogue with the little part who had been so upset. Like Suzanne, clients often spontaneously experience compassion for their parts once they are no longer blended with them: "I feel really sad for her—I want to just pick her up and hold her." Here, the therapist might feel tempted to stay with the emotion of sadness rather than continue with the parts focus. But the therapist's role at this point is keep the client in a mindful state and centered on the child: "What is it like for her to feel your sadness for her? To feel that someone actually cares how she feels?" "See what happens if you reach out to her and just offer your hand." As clients imagine reaching out to their younger selves or even make a reaching out gesture, a technique drawn from Sensorimotor Psychotherapy (Ogden & Fisher, 2015), their internal state usually transforms: they feel a sense of warmth; their bodies relax; they feel calmer. To ensure that these positive internal states are more than momentary, the therapist must continue focusing on "what happens inside" to deepen the felt connection to the child part and increase closeness and compassion.

Sometimes clients become expert at saying all the right words to their parts but without an embodied connection to the words or the part. It is very important that the therapist ask clients to linger on the changes in emotion or sensation that occur when the normal life self says or does something nourishing or comforting for the parts. He or she can ask, "What changes in her feelings when she senses you are really 'there'?" Or ask her, "How can she feel that you are sincere? What tells her that?" Sometimes, the therapist has to interweave psychoeducation with the parts work, as I did with Suzanne above, to make the point that change will come only through repetition of new patterns: "The more you hold her, the safer she will feel, and then the calmer you will feel. She can't let you feel calm and centered if she's terrified."

Sometimes, the child's predicament has to be "translated" by the therapist to help the normal life self "get it":

> "She's saying that she likes you here with her, but she doesn't trust it yet. ... That makes sense, doesn't it? Can you feel her holding back a little? It just means that she's been through a lot—as she certainly has, right? And that makes it hard for her to trust. For her to believe that someone will really be there for her, you'll need to keep on showing up, day after day after day, communicating that you care how she feels. That's what she would need to truly believe you are there for good, and she can finally relax and feel safe."

Providing Hospitality

In the late 1980s and early 1990s, when early experts in dissociation were trying to put words to what they observed in patients with "multiple personality disorder," the term chosen for what we now know as the going on with normal life self was "host." Although that label was meant to convey the sense of an empty vessel holding the traumatized parts, another meaning we could assign to the term "host" is that of homeowner and provider of hospitality. In fact, if the going on with normal life self is in charge of the body's health and well-being, must provide food, shelter, and other necessities, and is focused on present moment priorities, it is quite literally the "host" or home base for all parts of the self. In addition, given its access to the medial prefrontal cortex, the going on with normal life self has the unique ability to see a wider perspective, to conceptualize, to reconcile opposites or at least keep them simultaneously in mind. The normal life self has the capacity to hold in dual awareness both past and present, part and whole, animal brain and thinking brain. However, when clients finally come for treatment, the going on with normal life self is often demoralized or depleted, identified with certain parts and intimidated by or ashamed of others. Although the normal life part has the innate ability to learn to observe them all, to decrease autonomic dysregulation, and to become interested in rather than afraid of the parts, he or she may need education to recognize them as young child selves trying to communicate their trauma-related fears and phobias.

Welcoming the Lost Souls and Traumatized Children

But why should the normal life self become a warm and welcoming host to trauma-related parts when they are turning his or her daily life upside down? Just as therapists have to make a convincing case that connection to emotion or remembering the past or practicing skills is of benefit to clients, it is our job to make the link between the hopes and dreams that brought the client to therapy and the ability to recognize and befriend the parts. Think about what the client is seeking from therapy: what is the wish that drove her to your door? What is he hoping for as a result of treatment? Why is he or she here? Is this client seeking relief or self-actualization? Trying to stay alive or trying to make meaning of his or her experience?

Notice that each explanation I give to a client is generally positive, normalizing, and speaks to the "best self" of the client:

> "I know you wish the parts would just go away, but would that be fair? To neglect them the way you were neglected? I don't believe you're that kind of person. The person I know you to be would never reject wounded children because they were upset or inconvenient."
>
> "Think of the parts as your roommates—you all share the same body, the same home. You have a choice: you can learn to accept each other and get along, or you can struggle to win every battle!"
>
> "We wouldn't be sitting here today if it weren't for your parts. By taking on the survive-at-all-costs role, they allowed you to leave home, go to college, and start a life far away from the world of your childhood. It's only fair to take them with you to this better, safer world—it could be a way to thank them. It's not much of a thanks to leave them 'there' while you go forward."
>
> "Rightly or wrongly, you and the parts are inseparable: as long as their distress becomes your distress. For you to live a life freer of fear, anger, and shame, the parts need to welcomed—they have to feel safe."

Notice that the meaning-making of the therapist challenges the going on with normal life self while at the same time expressing support for the parts. Each statement or question communicates that the therapist will be an advocate for the young, vulnerable, and traumatized. There is no emphasis on discovering what happened in the past: the focus is on the relationship between parts and normal life self *now*, what is happening between them in the present moment. There is an implicit assumption that they are driven by the experiences of the past, by painful body and emotional memories. That can be acknowledged, but no effort is made to connect the parts' reactions now to specific events then. When clients spontaneously associate a part with particular image or event, the therapist reframes the intrusion of memory as the part's way of communicating why it is afraid or ashamed or angry.

> "When we talk about the part that fears abandonment, that same image always come up, doesn't it? That image of your mother driving away angrily, and this little part of you running down the street after her … I wonder if that little girl is trying to ask you, 'Will you get overwhelmed and run away from me, too?'"
>
> "If that image were a message from some young part of you, what would he be trying to tell you? Would he be saying, 'Yes, *that's* why I'm so scared all the time'? Or 'Help me!' or "Don't let anyone hurt me.'

It's important to know, isn't it? Otherwise he's going to have to keep
giving you disturbing pictures to make his point."

Initially, therapy sessions must be used as the opportunity to practice these
new habits of noticing the parts, naming what is noticed, and unblending.
But practice requires a therapist who will consistently ask: "'Who' is speaking right now? What parts are reacting to the conversation we're having?
What part is having this strong emotional reaction?" As noted in Chapter 4,
most human beings are in the habit of assuming that all thoughts, feelings, and physical reactions are "mine," that what "I" am feeling represents
"my" emotions. It takes week-after-week practice to help clients relinquish
that automatic assumption and learn instead to assume that anything they
might be feeling or thinking could be an expression of any one of many
parts.

To help individuals reclaim their fragmented, disowned, alienated parts,
the therapist must be relentless and persistent in using the language of parts
in therapy and asking the client to use it, too: "What happens when you say,
'She is feeling ashamed'? Do the feelings get more intense or less?" Each time
I invite clients to name what they feel as "his" or "her" feelings, they notice a
slight relaxing or relief—as if by naming the emotion as "his" emotion conveys to the part a sense of being heard or being understood.

Most clients have evolved a procedurally learned habitual strategy for dealing with the intrusive or underlying communications from parts. Some try to
control the intrusive feelings and impulses, ignore the tears or self-denigrating
thoughts or voices. Others interpret each feeling, impulse, or belief as "my feeling" or "how I feel," forgetting that they may have felt differently even seconds
before. The former strategy yields a more emotionally cut-off, controlled way
of being that interferes with the enjoyment of life. The latter leads to chaos or a
feeling of being overwhelmed, out of control, crazy, on the verge of implosion
or explosion. Not only do these patterns need to be noticed and translated into
parts language, but it is also important that the therapy emphasize strengthening the normal life self and enhancing the qualities associated with "self" or
"self energy" in the Internal Family Systems approach (Schwartz, 2001). The
normal life self must develop the capacities of "wise mind": staying connected
to present time, capable of meta-awareness or the capacity to hover above,
seeing all of the parts, and the ability to make decisions for the sake of the
whole. The concept of 'self' in Internal Family Systems helps clients connect
to states of compassion, creativity, curiosity, and perspective, while the going
on with normal life self of the Structural Dissociation model emphasizes the
importance of developing the functional ability to take action to implement
decisions for the sake of the system. If we put the two models together and
encourage the development of wise mind or "self energy" in the going on with
normal life self, then we have leadership informed by clarity of view, compassionate acceptance, and the capacity for behavior change. The challenge
is how to access a going on with normal life part and convince that aspect of

self to not only assume a leadership role but also cultivate the qualities of self: curiosity, compassion, clarity, calm, creativity, courage, commitment, and connection.

Forming a Connection to a Wise Compassionate Adult

Because the actions and reactions of the parts are driven by autonomic activation and animal defense survival responses, it is common for survivors of trauma to "own" and become identified with some parts just as they disown other parts. Some identify with their normal life selves, as did Carla; some identify with their suicidal parts or angry parts; some identify with the attach part's desperate proximity-seeking and end up "looking for love in all the wrong places." Some identify with the submit part and become the caretakers even for family members who have abused them. But when clients identify with trauma-related parts or blend with them, they can quickly lose access to the prefrontal cortex and the normal life self. The intensity of the parts' trauma responses tends to "drown out" a felt connection to the left brain self who can remember to grocery shop even though the freeze part is having panic attacks today. It is not surprising that the normal life self's dogged persistence in making a normal life possible comes to be interpreted as "pretending" or "fraudulent." It is counterintuitive to conceive of a part that thinks and acts rationally and functionally despite the overwhelming sensations and emotions as reflecting an authentic self, much less a self that embodies how the client survived the years of abuse, neglect, or captivity without losing the capacity or drive to "go on."

Many clients immediately reject the concept of having a normal life self: "There's no adult here—I don't even like adults," said the law student who came to see me for a consultation, promoting the agenda of the little part that needed care because she was "home alone" with no one. "I used to function," said an artist. "I used to have a life but no more. I couldn't handle things—I couldn't function in so much pain." After a romantic breakup, her depressed part became intensely hopeless and encouraged by friends and therapist to see it as grief, the artist blended with the depressed part, making it harder and harder to function.

> I asked the artist, "Do you remember what it was like when you could function, when you had a life?"
>
> CLIENT: "I do—I had so many interests and things I loved to do." [Her face lit up.]
> ME: "When you remember those days, what happens in your body?"
> CLIENT: "I feel more energy—more hope—then I think, 'Who am I kidding? There's no hope for me.'"
> ME: "That's what the depressed part keeps telling you! And you believe her which doesn't help either of you. Would you have done

      that with your students in art class? If one of them told you the
      same thing, would you have agreed with her?"

CLIENT: "No, of course not!" [Getting a bit irritated with me. But from a
      body perspective, irritation is an antidote to depression, so I am
      encouraged, not discouraged, by the irritation.]

ME: "What would you tell your student?"

CLIENT: "I'd tell her, 'Do what you love—that's all you have to do. Hope
      will follow from that, not the other way around.'"

ME: "Right, she doesn't need hope to follow her heart! Good point.
      And if she does, she will feel more hopeful. See what happens if
      you tell that to the depressed part ..."

Here, I could challenge the over-identification with the depressed part by accessing her normal life part's career experience and inherent compassion. The left-brain wisdom available to her right brain depressed part was still there in her normal life self. Sometimes, when clients are as adamant as the law student that they would never have a normal life or adult part, I challenge them with a simple biological fact: "Unless you have had a brain injury you forgot to mention, or brain surgery, the normal life self is still alive and well in your prefrontal cortex [I tap my forehead to demonstrate where to find that part of the personality]—it's still there even if you haven't been able to function for years." Or as I said to the artist, "I'm happy to tell you that the brain is like the Library of Congress—it doesn't lose information. If you have ever had even a day or hour of curiosity or clarity of mind or confidence, those abilities are still within you. You've just lost access to them because the depressed part hijacked you just trying to get you to see how upset she was." By stressing that parts blend, hijack the body, intrude flashbacks and images in order to get the attention and help of the normal life self, I can often spontaneously evoke empathy for the part: "Really?! You mean she only brought me so low because she wanted me to see how much pain she was in? Because she wanted help?!"

Connecting to the Resources of a Competent Adult

The easiest, most direct route to the normal life self is through those activities and life tasks or experiences with which this part is or was once identified. Is the client a parent? An administrator? Teacher? Attorney? Health care professional? Is there a hobby or cause that has meaning? If functioning has been problematic for an individual, we can ask: What "normal life" roles did he or she play earlier? Is there a wish or dream for a normal life that is important to the client? Does he or she play any role that requires prefrontal cortical activity? In using this model with young adults from inpatient and residential settings in a regional mental health system, we repeatedly described the normal life part to patients who, because of their abuse and neglect, had never functioned in normal life, even as children. Nonetheless, when our team from the Connecticut Department of Mental Health Young Adult Services described the Structural Dissociation model to these clients, almost all identified with having anormal life self: "That's the part of me that wants out of this hospital!" "Yes, that's the part that wants to be normal, not a mental patient." "That's the 'me' who wants to go to college and get a job." "I recognize my normal life part: she's the one who wants to get married, live in a real home, and have kids." Others could begin to feel a more palpable connection to their normal life selves once they began to associate their symptoms with the different parts and could disidentify from them, that is, differentiate what "I" want from what the parts seemed to be seeking. Whatever past "normal life" experience or vision of a future a client may have, it can become the vehicle for developing a stronger felt sense of having an adult body and mind (Ogden et al., 2006). I have helped clients find a normal life part on inpatient units (the part that organized a ping-pong tournament for her peers), in activities such as jewelry-making, playing tennis, horseback riding, volunteer work with animals or children, even in serving as the voice of wisdom and support for others in their lives.

Each time I point out, "That's your going on with normal life self—sticking with what's important—putting one foot in front of the other no matter what," I bring the client's attention to the influence of the normal life self in their lives. When the client protests, "But that's just a false self—I just fake it," I challenge their curiosity: "So the belief is that your normal life self is just a fake—how interesting ... But how could that be? Even if you are 'faking it,' it's still you. If I faked it, I would do it differently."

I underscore the courage and instinctive drive to seek normal even in an abnormal environment: "Think of it this way: the normal life self is the part of you that keeps trying to be OK even when all the other parts are freaking out, and that takes a lot of courage and determination—to 'keep on keeping on' when your parts are freaking out. A 'false self' wouldn't have to work that hard!"

Selves-Acceptance

"Befriending" one's parts is not simply a therapeutic intervention: it also contributes to developing the practice of self-acceptance, one part at a time. When clients pause their emotional reactivity to "befriend" themselves, to be curious and interested rather than dismissing or judgmental, they slow time. Autonomic arousal settles; there is a relaxing of the sense of urgency to do or be anything different. With their bodies in a calmer state, they can be more at peace, and, as a result, their parts feel more at peace. Self-alienation (i.e., disowning of some parts and identifying with others exclusively) does not contribute to a sense of peace or well-being, even when it is absolutely necessary in order to survive. Self-alienation creates tension, pits part against part, communicates a hostile environment (often much like the traumatic environment), and diminishes the self-esteem of every part.

As I made my case for accepting and welcoming her parts to a young graduate student, Gaby, she grew thoughtful. "These are good ideas. What about having a daily meditation circle?" she asked. "I could sit and invite them to join me in the circle. They wouldn't have to talk, but if they wanted to tell me about things they were worried or upset about, they could. It would be a safe place for all of us." The next week, she reported back. "It was amazing to see them all there—to know they came to meet me and to see if I would really listen. A lot of them were upset about how stressful my job is and the memories it brings back. I told them I'd talk to you about how to make it easier for them." [See Appendix B, Meditation Circle for Parts.]

"Befriending our parts" means that we "radically accept" (Linehan, 1993) that we share our bodies and lives with "roommates" and that living well with ourselves requires living amicably and collaboratively with our all of our selves, not just the ones with whom we feel comfortable. As Gaby's Meditation Circle taught her, the more we welcome rather than reject our owned and disowned selves, the safer our internal worlds will feel.

"I am not I.
I am this one
walking beside me whom I do not see,
whom at times I manage to visit,
and whom at other times I forget;
who remains calm and silent while I talk,
and forgives, gently, when I hate,
who walks where I am not,
who will remain standing when I die."

(Juan Ramon Jimenez, 1967)

References

Creswell, J.D., Way, B.M., Eisenberger, N.I., & Lieberman, M.D. (2007). Neural correlates of dispositional mindfulness during affect labeling. *Psychosomatic Medicine, 69*, 560–565.

Gazzaniga, M. S. (1985). *The social brain: discovering the networks of the mind*. New York: Basic Books.

Hanson, R. (2014). *Hardwiring happiness: the new brain science of contentment, calm, and confidence*. New York: Harmony Publications.

Jimenez, J.R. (1967). I am not I. *Lorca and Jimenez*. R. Bly, Ed. Boston: Beacon Press.

Levine, P. (2015). *Trauma and memory: brain and body in search of the living past*. Berkeley, CA: North Atlantic Books.

Linehan, M. M. (1993). *Cognitive-behavioral treatment of borderline personality disorder*. New York: Guilford Press.

Meichenbaum, D. (2012). *Roadmap to resilience: a guide for military, trauma victims and their families*. Clearwater, FL: Institute Press.

Ogden, P. & Fisher, J. (2015). *Sensorimotor Psychotherapy: interventions for trauma and attachment.* New York: W.W. Norton.

Ogden, P., Minton, K., & Pain, C. (2006). *Trauma and the body: a sensorimotor approach to psychotherapy.* New York: W.W. Norton.

Phillips, M. & Frederick, C. (1995). *Healing the divided self: clinical and Ericksonian hypnotherapy for post-traumatic and dissociative conditions:* New York: W.W. Norton.

Santorelli, S. (2014). Practice: befriending self. *Mindful,* Feb. 2014.

Schwartz, R. (1995). *Internal family systems therapy.* New York: Guilford Press.

Schwartz, R. (2001). *Introduction to the internal family systems model.* Oak Park, IL: Trailheads Publications.

Shapiro, F. (2001). *Eye movement desensitization and reprocessing: basic principles, protocols, and procedures,* 2nd edition. New York: Guilford Press.

Siegel, D.J. (1999). *The developing mind: toward a neurobiology of interpersonal experience.* New York: Guilford Press.

Van der Hart, O., Nijenhuis, E.R.S., & Steele, K. (2006). *The haunted self: structural dissociation and the treatment of chronic traumatization.* New York: W.W. Norton.

CHAPTER 6

Complications of Treatment: Traumatic Attachment

"Attachment is [a reflection of] the infant's need to be safe from danger. We are not born securely attached. To the infant, the world is not a safe place."

(Solomon, 2011)

"In human infancy, experienced threat is closely related to the caregiver's affective signals and availability rather than to the actual degree of physical or survival threat inherent in the event itself. Equipped with limited behavioral or cognitive coping capacities, the infant cannot gauge the actual degree of threat."

(Lyons-Ruth et al., 2006, p. 6)

The "Missing Experience" of Secure Attachment

In the first few minutes after birth, newborn and mother generally meet heart against heart as the baby is laid across the mother's chest. These and other early experiences of attachment are body-to-body experiences: holding, rocking, feeding, stroking, gaze-to-gaze contact. Rather than using words, we communicate to infants with coos, mmmmm's, and terms of endearment that evoke a lilt in the voice and bring a smile to our lips. Preverbal children take in the warm gaze, the smile, the softness or playfulness and respond with smiles, vocalizations and chuckles of delight, relaxing or brightening in a dyadic dance with their caregivers (Schore, 2001a). But infants and young children are equally equipped to perceive the body tension of the caregiver, the still, expressionless face (Tronick, 2007), the irritable tone of voice, or the rough movements. A baby's immature nervous system is easily alarmed by intense emotional reactions, loud voices, sudden movements, or manifest anxiety in the mother (Lyons-Ruth et al., 2006). Whether the quality of parental care promotes secure attachment or is "frightened or frightening" (Lyons-Ruth et al., 2006) as in traumatic or "disorganized attachment," these early bonding experiences are later remembered not as visual or verbal narratives but in the form of "implicit" or "emotional memories" and procedurally learned autonomic, motoric, visceral, and behavioral responses.

Relational Habits: One Way of "Remembering" Early Attachment

The better the quality of our early attachment experiences, the greater our capacity to tolerate distress as we develop into adulthood. Our capacity for affect tolerance, self-soothing, and achievement of an integrated sense of self later in life is dependent upon the self-regulatory or self-soothing abilities acquired during the first 2 years of life (Shore, 2003), including both the ability for interactive regulation (to be soothed by others) and auto-regulation (the ability to soothe ourselves). Affect tolerance in adulthood appears to be directly tied to the smooth acceleration, braking, and deceleration of the autonomic nervous system (Ogden et al., 2006) developed in very early secure attachment relationships. The experience-dependent development of the *right orbital prefrontal cortex* (Shore, 2001b), the brain's "self-soothing center," is also facilitated by secure attachment in early life. In order for children's nervous systems to develop a "window of tolerance" (Ogden et al., 2006; Siegel, 1999) for the highs and lows of emotional arousal, they require repeated emotional-somatic experiences of "interactive regulation," that is, a caregiver who soothes, comforts, reassures, or otherwise down-regulates their states of distress or who distracts, cuddles, or playfully up-regulates their moods in the context of fatigue, boredom, depression, or shutting down. If an "attachment style" represents a child's adaptation to a particular caregiving environment and a given caretaker, then we might think of attachment strategies as "procedurally learned," that is, habits of action and reaction stored in the brain's nonverbal memory system for function and habit. Many different memory systems interface in attachment relationships: "what we do with one another," how we relate, reflects the procedural memory system. Autobiographical memory for family relationships and events captures "what we know about one another," and emotional memory determines how our emotional states are altered in relationship to one another (Grigsby and Stevens, 2002). The attachment "habits" of each individual also reflect implicit memories describing what ratio of closeness to distance created the most safety and what was the best adaptation to the attachment demands in a particular family environment. Some clients may automatically tense up in response to proximity or human touch. Some may have developed habits of avoiding those closest to them, and others habits of preferential orienting just to family members or significant others, away from strangers and acquaintances. For some, eye contact may have been a lifeline, leaving the client with little ability to disengage from "staring" at others; but, for some individuals, eye contact might have been an aversive experience of looking into frightening eyes, resulting in habits of disengaging or looking away later noted by therapists as "poor eye contact" without awareness that habits of eye contact tell us valuable information about early attachment experiences. Where clients sit (closer or farther from the therapist), whether their bodies are oriented toward or away, lean toward or pull back from the therapist, already provide us with important information about the client's attachment style and history.

Trauma and Attachment: The Source of Safety Becomes the Source of Danger

> "[W]ith a [frightened/frightening] caregiver, infants are caught in a relational trap: their defense systems motivate them to flee from the caregiver, while at the same time their attachment system motivates them, under the commanding influence of separation fear, to strive for achieving comforting proximity to her or him."
>
> (Liotti, 2011, p. 235)

Because children's innate attachment behavior is organized around proximity-seeking and social engagement, caregivers who are neglectful and abusive pose a double threat: not only does their frightening behavior evoke fear/flight/fight responses but it also intensifies the child's yearning for proximity. The result is what Main and Hesse (1990) first termed "disorganized" or Type D attachment, the result of what Main termed "fright without solution." When parents are "frightened or frightening," Main and Hesse concluded, the child's instinctive source of comfort and safety becomes the source of danger. Rather than attachment figures providing protection and interactive regulation for the child, their behavior is alarming. Frightening, frightened, and/or abusive parents stimulate proximity-seeking drives and activate the child's survival defenses of fight and flight, or they evoke rapid activation of the parasympathetic dorsal vagal system to initiate freezing, shutting down or "playing dead." Beatrice Beebe's infant research (2009) has demonstrated that, as early as 3 to 6 months, babies develop what she calls "expectancies," patterns of behavior that anticipate interactions with their caregivers. In her observations of infants with disorganized attachment, these expectancies range from shutting down and going limp to matching the mother's dysregulated states (e.g., imitating maternal laughter in response to their distress). In both instances, the infants succeed in regulating their responses to their mother's alarming behavior but in ways that, if procedurally learned, set the stage for longer term autonomic dysregulation: either automatic parasympathetic shutdown or mimicking of maternal sympathetic responses.

Because infants and young children, dependent on their caretakers for survival, cannot effectively flee or fight, their repertoire of survival responses is limited to the resources of their young bodies (Ogden et al., 2006). Driven to seek proximity to attachment figures when alarmed or hurt, they defend against threat by backing away, closing their eyes, hiding, shutting down, or dissociating. When the source of danger *is* the attachment figure, the mind and body must find a way to maintain an attachment bond while simultaneously mobilizing animal defense survival responses to protect the child. These two powerful innate drives (to attach and to defend) each remain highly activated, one drive dominating at times and then the other. The result is a child (and later adult) caught between two equally strong "pulls": the yearning for proximity and closeness and the animal defenses of fight, flight, freeze, and submission. "Too much" closeness feels dangerous, but so does "too much" distance. Without any narrative memory, without a conscious thought, Karin's story illustrates how powerful early nonverbal attachment learning can be.

> Karin had no narrative or event memories of the first year and a half of her life spent in a Romanian orphanage, but she had many unrecognized implicit and procedural memories: her body remembered that closeness is dangerous, propelling her to push away boyfriends as the relationship grew closer, especially if they were kind and loving. As these romantic relationships endured despite her negative reactions to the closeness, she found herself becoming increasingly hypervigilant, suspicious, and reactive to any failure of attunement or attention. Each time she felt abandoned, unseen, or unheard, she would erupt in anger and threaten to leave. When, after many months of conflict and rejection, the young man finally succumbed to being pushed away, Karin would feel overcome with feelings of loss, abandonment, and separation anxiety: "How could he leave me?" she would ask. "Maybe he didn't love me ..." Once he was gone, the urge to push him away suddenly yielded to the intense yearning to pull him closer.

As Liotti (2011) describes it, "[In the context of frightened/frightening caregiving], 'the caregiver becomes at the same time the source and the solution of the infant's alarm' (Main & Hesse, 1990, p. 163). Fear comes to paradoxically coexist, in the infant's experience, with the soothing provided by proximity to the caregiver" (p. 234). The tragedy for children like Karin is the strong association that develops between soothing or proximity and fear. The warm, positive feelings evoked by her boyfriends' loving behavior very quickly activated fear and vigilance, leading to crisis after crisis in the relationship until finally they abandoned their efforts to win her.

Not only do children like Karin fail to develop a window of tolerance, but worse yet, their nervous systems become biased toward sympathetic hyperactivity, impulsive proximity-seeking, and fight-flight behavior, often diagnosed as oppositional-defiant disorder in childhood and borderline personality disorder in adulthood. Or they become parasympathetically dominant: shut down, inhibited, hopeless and helpless, without initiative or energy, a state frequently mistaken for depression. There are no stronger evolutionary instincts than the attachment drive and its polar opposite, the animal defense survival responses. The tendencies of babies and young children to seek and maintain proximity, to explore the environment while using caregivers as a "safe base," and to seek a parent figure when alarmed or distressed have contributed to

child safety and protection for centuries. Even when a parent appears frightened and is therefore frightening, the proximity-seeking drive can still be
activated by anxiety about a parent's safety or moods. Primitive signs of this
conflict between proximity and safety can be observed in orphanage-raised
adoptees: at first, they often arch away from the adoptive mother's body or
stiffen on contact, look away rather than toward the caregiver. In contrast,
babies in secure attachment relationships actively search the faces of adults to
establish gaze-to-gaze contact and then socially engage by smiling, laughing,
and cooing.

"Controlling Attachment Strategies" and Trauma

By the preschool years, now possessing language and motor skills they
did not have in infancy, children with disorganized attachment status are
observed by researchers to develop "controlling tendencies": a pattern of
behavior that manages or controls the caregiver's actions and reactions
in one of two characteristic ways (Liotti, 2011). One subgroup exhibits
"controlling-caretaking" behavior, a parentified style of relating by soothing, reassuring, and helping their mothers. The other subgroup exhibits
"controlling-punitive" behavior: attacking the mother verbally and/
or physically, humiliating and devaluing her. Researchers note that the
controlling-caretaking pattern is more common in girl children and more
common when mothers exhibit role-reversal (i.e., are needy and childlike)
and guilt-inducing behavior; controlling-punitive behavior is more common in boys, especially in response to maternal hostility. In each case, the
child has found a way to defend and attach simultaneously: to remain close
to the parent while inhibiting the dependency needs usually associated with
attachment.

"Phobia of Therapy and the Therapist"

This legacy of disorganized attachment and controlling strategies affects
all later adult relationships, including the therapeutic one. Van der Hart,
Nijenhuis, and Steele (2006) call this latter phenomenon "phobia of therapy
and the therapist." To the extent that traumatized clients come to therapy
craving the relief, understanding, and care offered by the therapist (proximity-
seeking), they are equally likely to experience fear and distrust of both the
relationship and the process either early in treatment or as the relationship
with the therapist grows. The prospect of trusting someone, of being seen, of
disclosing one's secrets does not bring relief: it brings trepidation.

As Jessica Benjamin (1994) describes it, "To be known or recognized is
immediately to experience the other's power. The other becomes the one
who can give or withhold recognition: who can see what is hidden; who can
reach, conceivably even violate, the core of the self" (p. 539). The lived experience of traumatized individuals has created an unavoidable and painful

paradox: closeness cannot be trusted, but distance or aloneness is also not safe. Their experience was that being alone and without protection created greater vulnerability, while being in proximity was also not safe. Because they could not depend upon the protection of the non-offending caretaker, these clients are either loathe to depend upon the therapist, or they assume the opposite: that their only safety lies in dependency. The yearning to self-disclose tends to conflict with the fear that self-disclosure will be used against the client, that secrets will not be believed, that he or she will be humiliated, not validated. Simon illustrates the dilemma in which therapist and client can find themselves: in coming to therapy, he expressed his wish for help, but his parts could not allow him to accept help, much less trust it!

> Each time I brought more warmth to my tone, more determination to help him, the more I could see Simon's body tensing up. When I leaned forward to make contact with him, I felt him pulling back. Although he verbalized a wish for help, I could feel him withdrawing from whatever I offered. If I leaned forward to emphasize a point, I could see his body stiffen and pull back.

> ME: "Seems like you want to take in what I'm saying, but it's hard, isn't it?"
> SIMON: "It feels like you're trying to sell me something and I should be careful because it might not be safe."
> ME: "Yes, I can tell it doesn't feel safe. Your body is just trying to protect you, huh? It's saying, 'Be careful—don't just accept whatever you're told' …"

Simon was paralyzed by an internal conflict: he wanted help with his debilitating thoughts and feelings, but somehow he couldn't allow himself to accept the help offered.

> To further complicate Simon's dilemma, different parts of him were in head-to-head conflict about the therapeutic relationship. His judgmental, cynical fight part questioned the therapist's credentials, methods, and orientation. His more intellectual going on with normal life self, who had researched my work in advance, thought the approach seemed "appropriate." His lonely, lost child part just yearned for the therapist to "say something nice," something that would put a balm on his emotional wounds. The submit part whose depressive beliefs about himself kept Simon perpetually dysphoric both liked and felt threatened by the therapist's challenging of those beliefs as just a survival strategy. Not knowing which internal pull or voice was "his," Simon alternately identified with all of them. At some appointments, he would be open to working on changing his relationship to the depression by understanding it as that of a young boy who had learned

to keep himself quiet and shut down, so he could "fly below the radar." At other times, he would express ambivalence about continuing in therapy or even anger that, "I've wasted all these years seeing therapist after therapist—this is just one more failed attempt."

Each structurally dissociated part, driven by a particular animal defense response or combination of responses, tends to be biased in its perspective on attachment versus safety. As each is evoked on different days by different aspects of the treatment, the therapist can become confused and disoriented if he or she does not recognize the fragmentation and identify the parts. The attach parts often idealize the therapist and actively seek a relationship that at first may seem like healthy therapeutic collaboration: "I need help, and you have expert help to give me." But, over time, the client, blended with the attach part, becomes progressively more childlike or needy, develops separation anxiety, or is increasingly in crisis. Driven by their innate proximity-seeking instincts, the bias of the attach parts is that the only safety lies in closeness, in being cared about, not being separated. One day, Annie and I decided to gather more information about what "caring" meant to the parts who repeatedly questioned whether I really cared about her or them, who incessantly worried that they would displease me and provoke abandonment—to the point that their anxiety made it difficult to focus on issues other than their preoccupation with me.

> When I asked why her little parts were so focused on evoking evidence that I cared, Annie became quiet and turned her attention inside to better hear the internal conversation. "They're saying that if someone cares about you, they'll protect you. They won't leave you alone to get taken—they'll watch out for you." The night she had been kidnapped at age 7, no adult was watching out for her—she was all alone. The parts' implicit memories of that experience made "caring" all important, but no matter how many times Annie or I reassured them that I had proven I cared many times over, they could be momentarily reassured if they felt "cared for" but then that moment of relief would immediately quickly trigger more anxiety.

Awakening the Yearning for Care

Rather than feeling comforted by the therapeutic relationship or by the growing closeness that usually occurs as a natural, healthy outgrowth of psychotherapy, the attach parts can often have the opposite reaction. As they feel "closeness" at long last, it is both a relief and a trigger. Their fears of abandonment and sensitivity to empathic failure typically intensify, often leading to increasing demands on the therapist's time and energy. Concerned by the increasing levels of distress, volume of calls, mounting instability, or accusations of empathic failure, therapists may not realize that their valiant attempts to create safety and attunement in the therapy are instead evoking implicit memories. The feeling memories of painful yearning for someone to care, to comfort, to be close often evoke a hunger for contact that can become obsessive and is often pathologized as psychotic or erotic transference. In addition, if therapists are not familiar with the Structural Dissociation model or have been trained to diagnose the symptoms of disorganized attachment as evidence of borderline personality disorder, they can be dysregulated by the shifting states and conflicting presentations of the client. The going on with normal life self might trust the therapist's offer of safety, might be willing to "work" in therapy with little need for reassurance. The attach parts will trust the therapist immediately and unconditionally but their yearning for closeness will also be triggered by kindness, warmth, and care, resulting in an increasing hunger for more and more proximity. Desperate for contact, the attach part often has difficulty leaving the therapist's office at the end of sessions and/or seeks "proximity" between visits—through voicemail, email, or text. Because these young parts are highly anxious and alarmed, their messages often appear to be signs of crisis to which therapists feel a responsibility to respond. Over time, however, the therapist may begin to notice a pattern: the same level of urgency is evoked by both large and small stressors; therapeutic reassurance is less rather than more successful over time; sensitivity to empathic failure becomes heightened; and the number of crisis calls does not diminish over time or may even increase. That is because the job of these parts is to "cry for help" and because their implicit memories of yearning for contact and fear of abandonment are exacerbated, rather than soothed, by proximity to an attachment figure. Without the therapist's awareness that these parts are just one aspect of an otherwise competent adult or that their distress represents activation of memory, he or she may feel responsible for soothing them.

One way for therapists to recognize when they are being "inducted into the system" (i.e., have taken responsibility for regulating and soothing a part whose job it is to maintain proximity to potential attachment figures) is to look at whether the treatment is successfully stabilizing the client and expanding the window of tolerance. When, despite the out-of-session support, the client needs more rather than less contact to remain stable, therapists can be quite certain that they have inadvertently been responding to an attach part whose job it is to elicit care, not an adult client needing some temporary support in resolving a crisis while developing more ego strengths and resources.

Recontextualizing Disorganized Attachment as an Internal Struggle

If therapists interpret the disorganized attachment as the expression of a whole integrated client, the symptoms are likely to be understood as a "personality disorder." Only when the assumption is made that these behaviors represent disorganized attachment associated with structurally dissociated parts can the therapist avoid becoming inducted into the system, whether as rescuer, potential victimizer, or uncaring bystander. Without the conceptual framework of structural dissociation, therapists can easily become confused and frustrated by the alternating appearances of attach parts expressing needs for more proximity and flight or fight parts distancing, controlling, or devaluing the treatment.

Often early on or as the attach part becomes more vulnerable, the flight part manifests in the therapy as a client expressing ambivalence about the treatment. "I didn't want to come today," that part typically announces. "I have nothing to talk about." "I'm not sure I want to continue." Flight parts' instinctual avoidance is likely to be triggered by therapy sessions. When the focus turns to painful emotion, the client might suddenly flee the session, or, just as the therapist feels the treatment is "deepening," the client's flight part might suddenly cancel remaining appointments. The attach part or normal life self then is likely to return in a crisis weeks or months later with no memory of why "he" or "she" left the therapy previously. The client's normal life self might come regularly to each appointment but then, hijacked by the flight part, shut down, become mute, or dissociate. Attempts to process these patterns as if they were those of a whole integrated individual are usually frustrating at best. Therapists often find themselves dismissing such clients as "resistant," "unmotivated," or "guarded," without realizing that they have been stymied by a series of parts whose job it is to distance in relationships, avoid the trauma, and detach emotionally.

When attach and flight parts alternate in therapy, the therapist often becomes even more confused and frustrated: for example, the "client" asks to talk on the phone between sessions, sends daily emails and texts, and expresses fears of abandonment, yet at each face-to-face appointment, this same "client" shuts down, cancels at the last minute, or expresses the wish not to have come at all. In this example, there is no one "client"; we are dealing with two different subparts with conflicting wishes and fears. If we tell the client's flight part that she is not obligated to come if she doesn't want to, the attach part will feel rejected and pushed away. If we tell the attach part that she seems ambivalent about the therapy, she will feel even more deeply wounded. She would come every day if we just invited her! If we ask the flight part to reflect on the urgent need to talk on the phone Wednesday evening followed by a disinterest in coming to therapy on Thursday, we are most likely to get a shrug of the shoulders as if to say, "I wouldn't know."

Another manifestation of the flight part is observed in eating disordered or addictive behavior. Rather than distancing externally, eating disorders and substance abuse provide a way of distancing or "fleeing" dysregulated emotions and sensations internally. In the treatment of both addictive behavior and eating disorders, it is helpful for therapists to make a clear distinction between the normal life self, often highly motivated to stay sober or engage in harm reduction, and the flight part, undeterred in its determination to numb or disconnect or facilitate a false temporary window of tolerance. If that differentiation is not made, therapists are likely to find themselves engaging in a struggle in which they become the spokespersons for abstinence, sobriety, and healthy behavior, while the flight part must defend the use of the substance or eating disorder against what feels like an enemy. Rather than engaging in a head-to-head battle with a flight part, it is more useful for the therapist to capital-ize on the compartmentalization by working with the normal life self, using its capacity for reflection to increase curiosity about the flight or addict part: what is its intention? What outcome does it want? (See Chapter 7 for more on working with parts and self-destructive behavior.)

Not One but Many Transferences

Because the therapist is an attachment trigger for all the parts, it is crucial to be aware of the different transferential relationships each part will tend to de-velop. Attach needs to feel the therapist is warm, connected, and attuned to its needs for care. Flight needs space and acceptance of its need to keep a distance or to come and go. Fight requires proof that the therapist will not "use" secrets against the client, will not try to use dependency to control the parts, and has no hidden agenda. "Proof" sometimes means that the therapist is subjected to tests of her patience, testing of boundaries, and tests of her ability to hold the treatment frame. Submit just wants to please by complying with whatever the therapist seems to want, often increasing the need for more testing by fight, and freeze just doesn't want to be hurt. To ensure that the therapy does not become derailed by these traumatic attachment issues, the therapist must be prepared for the issues posed by disorganized attachment and assume that the work will include negotiating multiple transferential relationships.

Recognizing the Transference of Parts

If disorganized attachment reflects the relationship between a proximity-seeking attach part and a hypervigilant, protective fight part, then other parts with similar goals will be active in the treatment and supportive of one or the other side. Although the submit part can appear as the "identified pa-tient," referred for chronic depression, issues of shame, or an inability to set limits and boundaries, the submit part also frequently serves the needs and goals of the attach part by trying to please those whose connection the attach part seeks, avoid displeasing potential attachment figures, and ensure that the demands of the attach part do not overwhelm the therapist.

In some clients, the submit part may be more burdened and submissive and, in others, more compliant and pleasing. The submit part might even strive to be the best client the therapist has yet encountered so as to increase the posi-tive feelings the attach part craves. But, when the "good client" is actually a sub-mit part, somehow the progress we would expect from a client with this level of intelligence, functioning, and willingness to engage does not happen. Instead, the client takes one step forward and one back, appears to make prog-ress but then mysteriously is back to wherever he or she started. The willingness to do whatever the therapist asks does not lead to integration of new information or new skills. It is as if we have been conducting the treatment with a child who listens and acts as if she understands but lacks the cortical functioning that would enable the information to be useful. Or, because submission as survival response is dependent upon parasympathetic dominance, the submit part has no access to energy for change and no influence on the other fragmented selves of the client.

Key indicators that a theme is being expressed by a part is the degree of rigidity associated with it: parts are likely to see the world as black or white, have difficulty comprehending new information or widening their perspective to take in multiple points of view. If therapists find themselves engaged in a struggle with clients or "resisting their resistance," that is often a sign that they are in dialogue with one part of the client, not the larger consciousness of a normal life self. If the therapist responds to submit by saying, "That's interesting—so there's a belief inside that 'nice people don't say No'—no wonder that's such a hard word to say," the submit part is likely to reply: "Well, that's true." This response is very different from what we might hear from a going on with normal life self who, despite being avoidant of overwhelming emotions or unsure if his or her childhood experience really qualifies as "traumatic," is likely to be more curious about the therapist's point of view: "Really, you mean other people have that experience, too?"

Creating an Alliance with the Fight Part

If disorganized attachment reflects an internal conflict between proximity-seeking drives and fight/flight responses, then the transferential relationship with the fight part will inevitably become an important focus of the therapy. First of all, fight parts are generally the most hypervigilant and wary of attachment, least likely to trust therapists or the process of therapy, especially to the extent that the treatment focuses on the client's vulnerabilities: on disclosing secrets, sharing deeply personal information, connecting to expressing strong emotions. Often, the presence of the fight part is felt subtly and indirectly: for example, in how much the client is comfortable sharing about his or her history or even daily life, in questions put to the therapist about office policies (especially around confidentiality, fees, and boundaries), or when the client starts to say something and then stops in mid-sentence, unable to recall what he or she wanted to say. We might also encounter indicators of an active fight part in the client's history: a previous therapy that ended "badly"; friendships that were dropped after recurrent conflicts; difficulties at work due to interpersonal struggles or confrontations; breakups in relationship. Or we might see the fight part play an active role in the treatment. When therapists "fail the client empathically," for example, they are informed of their failure by a fight part activated by the hurt feelings of young parts. "Empathic failure" generally describes a choice of words or actions that has disappointed or hurt the client's feelings—or, more accurately, the feelings of the attach part. Most of the time, these moments of "empathic failure" occur because the therapist is speaking to someone perceived to be an integrated adult, not realizing that the client is blended with a needy, lonely, sad, or ashamed child part. If spoken to an adult, the words or tone used may have been harmless or even compassionate, but spoken to a child part with urgent hopes for care or rescue, the words are deeply hurtful. For example, the therapist might raise a billing issue or a change in appointment time, announcement of a vacation or change in policy. Spoken matter-of-factly to a 40- or 50-year-old adult, the words, "I need to talk to you about billing issues" or "about my vacation," are simply information, but they feel cold or cruel to the child part. Rarely is the resulting empathic failure brought to our attention by that child part, though. Our clients do not generally look confused, hurt, or wounded, much less burst into tears, which would alert the therapist to the inadvertent rupture. Instead, therapists hear about these empathic failures from an indignant, angry, or even outraged fight part, making it more difficult for the therapist to understand much less empathize with what has happened. The vulnerability of the child part is vehemently defended by the fight part, but, unable to "see" the little part, the therapist feels put on the defensive, distanced or disrespected by an angry, indignant client—the very opposite of the attach part's needs and wishes. We are inducted into the disorganized attachment "system," feeling badly for having hurt the client but also defensive in the face of being criticized, devalued, and found wanting. Without the realization that an "empathic failure" represents the inadvertent wounding of a child part coupled with the defensive efforts of an angry part seeking restitution or protection of the little parts' vulnerability, the therapist's efforts at "repair" may also be misattuned.

Another manifestation of disorganized attachment can be a preoccupation with suicide, a tendency to self-harm, or a tendency toward promiscuous or unsafe sexual behavior. Suicidality and self-harm always reflect the role of the fight part because of its unique capacity for aggression. No other part has the physical strength and violent impulses that accompany the animal defense of fight. Submit may dream of going to sleep and never waking up; flight may wish to escape intense emotions, but neither has the physical ability to end life or harm the body. (See Chapter 7 for a more extensive discussion of treating suicidal and self-destructive behavior as manifestations of parts.)

What most often triggers suicidal and self-injuring parts are empathic failures, losses, painful loneliness—anything that reopens the emotional wounds of the attach part. Other common precipitants are intrusive memories or flashbacks, both of which can be linked to the attach parts' cry for help and both of which increase feelings of vulnerability and shame.

Vulnerability is the enemy of the fight part. At age one, three, six, even ten, there is little a fight part can do to defend against those on whom the child depends. In adulthood, any situation in which dependency and/or vulnerability are stimulated is likely to activate the fight part. That means that any therapy that appears to emphasize the creation of dependency or encourage vulnerability is likely to be highly threatening to those parts. Although most therapists would rightly insist that evoking vulnerability or dependency is not their conscious goal, we have to remember two things: first, that the fight part is hypervigilant and focused narrowly on threat. Even as normal a stimulus as the box of tissues sitting in the therapist's coffee table is a danger signal to the fight part. Secondly, most therapists do encourage self-disclosure, expression of feelings, and learning to ask for and receive support—all of which can be misconstrued as the encouragement of vulnerability—especially when the attach part is eagerly awaiting a sign that dependency will be welcomed by the therapist and the fight part is on guard against exactly that danger.

There is No "He" or "She"

Often, therapists are understandably confused by the relationship between the fight and attach parts. At the start of therapy they may encounter a "client" who is closed, counterdependent, guarded, and reluctant to disclose his or her secrets. Not realizing that they have encountered a *part* of the client, not an integrated whole, they encourage reaching out and asking for support—or they reach out to the client, believing that the gesture will reduce shame or fear. But beneath the militant counterdependence of the fight part, there is always an attach part whose longing and hurt are being defended, who is being "protected" by the avoidance of dependence. When the therapist attempts to help the counterdependent client or part "open up," the attach part is inevitably activated by the reaching out, resulting in a client who, in the therapist's mind, is now still counterdependent at times but can also be extremely dependent and easily wounded. The attach part's implicit memories and unmet yearning for connection have been stimulated, and both feel emotionally unbearable. The fight part's distrust of connection has been equally heightened.

When the therapist does not continue to reach out, believing that the client has successfully softened the counterdependence, the attach part's separation anxiety intensifies, and fight must go to its defense. If the therapist continues to reach out, concerned about triggering shame or fears of abandonment, the attach part's hunger for connection continues to be triggered, causing more distress and often the need for more and more contact. The more frequent the contact, the greater the fight part's sense of threat. To make matters worse, as the fight part pushes the therapist away or uses harm to the body to regulate unbearable emotions, the attach part is likely to feel more vulnerability instead of less, increasing demands for contact and further activating the fight part. Many therapists notice that as the need for contact intensifies and they try to meet the demand, they increasingly are accused of empathic failure: "I was suicidal, and you could only stay on the phone for 5 minutes?!" "You really think 'a few minutes' is enough when I'm in this living hell?" It is helpful to remember at those moments that the client's parts are re-enacting their early experience of disorganized attachment: caught up in a painful, wrenching struggle between the implicitly remembered need of little parts for more care and the implicit distrust connected to the dangers of neediness when attachment figures are abusive.

Diagnostically, the client with disorganized attachment is increasingly likely to fulfill criteria for borderline personality disorder, and if diagnosed as such, may be judged "attention-seeking" and "manipulative." The role of the trauma and traumatized parts is likely to go unrecognized and untreated; the manifestations of disorganized attachment will be confused with personality disorder symptoms. The worst fears of the going on with normal life self will also be realized: he or she is getting worse in therapy, not better. As with addicted and eating disordered flight parts, it is easy for therapists to become engaged in a struggle with self-destructive or suicidal fight parts centered on safety and risk management issues and to lose the opportunity to help clients use their normal life selves to work with parts bent on ending life rather than being rendered vulnerable. (See Chapter 7 for more information on how to manage issues of safety.)

A Therapist for All the Parts, Not Just for the "Client"

Most therapists take on a single client, not a motley collection of parts sharing a common body. But since structural dissociation and splitting is statistically likely in the context of trauma, therapists should assume that by taking on any traumatized client, they may be taking on his or her parts, too. That means that the therapist must listen, speak, and conduct the treatment somewhat differently than he or she otherwise would in treating more integrated clients whose early lives did not require splitting and self-alienation. As the therapist meets the client for the first time, hears the presenting issues and takes a history, he or she should already be attuned to the trauma-related themes likely to be echoed by different parts: painful loneliness and the need for connection, despair and self-defeating beliefs, fear and avoidance of being seen, addictions and eating disorders, the impact on relationships of problems with anger and hypervigilance.

Listening for the "Voices" of the Parts

Encouraging curiosity, providing psychoeducation about trauma and trauma treatment, mindful noticing of patterns and themes, and an introduction to the language of triggering are all important even in a first or intake visit. Even as we are gathering information from a new client, therapists should be listening intently for the "voices" of the different parts and also for signs of a normal life self: a home, career or job, relationships, interests, some areas of stability, and, most importantly, a functioning prefrontal cortex and the capacity to observe what happens moment to moment. The trauma-informed therapist is also alert for signs of dysregulation either visible in the session or reported by the client ("I just shut down," "I had to leave," "I just starting screaming"). Until the therapist is certain that the client has an adequate window of tolerance and equally sure there is an observing self that can relate to intense feelings (i.e., stay connected to the emotions without dissociating or becoming dysregulated), he or she does not pull for emotions (the landscape of the parts), only for an awareness of their different "voices." How clients regulate whatever emotions come up spontaneously tells the therapist more about the extent of their windows of tolerance. Aware that traumatic events are past events that intrude on the present when triggered by reminders of the past, the therapist introduces the language of triggering early in treatment—along with the language of parts.

Mark came to his first session with a paradoxical issue: his rich, satisfying life after trauma was missing one ingredient, a partner or spouse. "I've never fallen in love, never had a relationship that lasted more than 6 months—but on the other hand, I don't really see the need for one in my day to day life. I'm here just in case I might be missing something." The therapist replied, "So there's a part of you that has made sure you never fall in love, and another part that wonders if, someday, that will feel like a loss. Could we be curious about both of them?"

Jacqueline told her therapist: "I'm here because I have a long history of trauma. Do you want me to tell you all of the things that have happened?"

"Not unless there is something special that you want me to know—I'm really more curious about how the trauma has stayed with you, how it's still affecting your life day to day."

"It's ruined my life ..."

"Is it still ruining your life? What triggers it?"

She describes a pattern of many years: each time she has built a stable, satisfying relational and work life, she's found herself precipitously fleeing it to take care of one or another member of her family of origin, thereby losing everything she had built for herself.

I respond, "So, there is a very strong—very, very strong—going on with normal life part of you that keeps on rebuilding your life, no matter what, and then there's a very self-sacrificing part that feels compelled to give it all up to take care of your family, even those members who abused you as a child. Could we be curious about that pattern?"

ME: "What did you do?"

CLIENT: "I was a family medicine doctor—I loved it, but I couldn't handle the stress, especially after I stopped being able to drive."

ME: [Curious about any loss of normal life functioning] "You stopped being able to drive? What happened that made it no longer possible to drive?"

CLIENT: "I would start to go somewhere, and I'd suddenly forget where I was going or how to drive the car. I would panic! Then I'd have to call my secretary and tell her to come get me. I couldn't do it by myself."

ME: "It seems that driving and going to work and having a normal life must have been very threatening to your traumatized parts—they panicked, and you didn't know it was them—you thought it was you. How sad ..."

"I used to be able to function, but I haven't for a while now," Robert disclosed.

These three clients included a doctor, a therapist, and a teacher—all ideal candidates for therapy—all of whom reported symptoms that were paradoxical in some way. Putting aside what might be viewed as the "bigger" issue of the client's trauma history, I habitually listen for the subtle indicators of losses of functioning, internal conflicts, self-sabotage, and paradoxical behavior. In addition, I am not thinking of parts as tied to the clients' histories—I listen for how the parts' implicit memories are being triggered in the client's current life. Are they being triggered by the client's determination to live a normal life after trauma? By the client's exposure to certain kinds of trauma-related triggers (e.g., a boss who is controlling and critical, a child at an age at which the client was traumatized, family members connected to the perpetrator)? Or I am listening for some life event that is likely to stir up earlier trauma, such as a loss, betrayal or recent traumatic event, or even a happy life transition (engagement, marriage, birth of a child, promotion or graduation). Is there a pattern in the client's life that might be telling a story of unresolved trauma being re-enacted at an implicit level?

Becoming the therapist for all the parts begins with listening for their chorus of voices and themes, beginning to name the themes and the parts as they are heard, and evoking the client's curiosity about what has been happening. Most clients come to therapy with a feeling of confusion, desperation, unbearable pain, and unspoken fears that they are losing their minds. Although they may have created a story to explain their bewildering symptoms, the first few visits mark the point in time when they are often most open to hearing a new perspective that reassures them they are not crazy or defective. As I tell them a different story, one that makes sense of what they have been experiencing, often the relief is palpable.

> TO MARK, I SAID: "I get it, and you will, too! After what happened to you as a kid, some part of you inside you made a vow that he would never, ever, ever, ever let someone hurt him again. He's just trying to protect himself and you—even now."
>
> TO JACQUELINE: "Of course, that young girl who survived by taking care of her parents and her brothers and sisters, would feel no right to a life of her own—maybe having a life actually made her feel guilty and ashamed rather than safe and stable."
>
> TO ROBERT: "It makes so much sense: you created a very rich, challenging grownup life as a husband, father, and medical professional. You were being recognized in your community. That probably scared the parts so much that they couldn't let it keep happening—they felt exposed and in danger. They had to stop you, and they succeeded."

Speaking on Behalf of the Parts

It is common for clients to have difficulty sustaining access to the going on with normal life self, difficulty feeling empathy for their parts, difficulty maintaining access to the prefrontal cortex, even retaining their initial curiosity about this new way of thinking. Because the language of "I" is an automatic "default setting" for most of us, our procedurally learned tendency when we feel something is to say, "*I* feel this way." It takes repetition and practice to use the words, "a part of me feels this way," as comfortably or automatically. Often, the therapist feels discouraged by the slow pace or begins to question if the approach is helpful, but it is important to remember that we are changing a kind of learning that is meant to be indelible. Human beings never forget procedural learning: how to shake hands, how to drive a car, how to pick up a knife and fork, and we never lose the tendency to say "I." Learning to use the word "part" instead of "I," remembering to think in parts language, listening for their different voices: all of these skills take the same kind of practice involved in learning a foreign language.

Practice can come in many forms:

As a "practice" that reminds the client that all distressing emotions, thoughts, and life problems reflect communications from parts, I can include the language of parts in my opening greeting to the client: "How have the parts been this week? How did the week go for them?"

To interrupt and inhibit the automatic assumption of "I," I can repeatedly remind clients of the multiple points of view inside: "Which 'I' feels that way? And is there any 'I' who feels differently?"

I can reiterate the psychoeducation on structural dissociation: "Let me remind you about the structural dissociation model … Which part would have been most likely to be shamed by that experience? Yes, it would be submit—she always assumes it's her fault. And how did the fight part react to the same criticism? Very differently, huh?"

I can mirror what has just been said, reflecting the client's words while simultaneously translating them into parts language: "So, there's a part of you that feels very ashamed and unsure of himself today …"

To which the client might reply, "Yes, I almost cancelled because I didn't want to face you."

> **ME:** "Hmmm … So interesting … That part didn't want to face me. Who was he afraid I would be? How was he afraid I would act?"

Often, the client immediately free-associates to someone by whom he or she was once shamed or intimidated: "He's afraid you'll look down on him like all those teachers did because his clothes don't match and they're dirty and torn."

Here, the therapist must bring the normal life self's attention to the words and meaning just expressed by the child part to ensure that they are being heard. Using a mindful "contact statement" (Ogden & Fisher, 2015), the therapist repeats, "Yes, he's afraid I'll look down on him just like all those teachers did. He thinks I'll see that his clothes are torn and don't match, and I'll think he's no good."

> CLIENT: "Yeah, the teachers could see how neglected he was, and they thought he was trash."
> ME: "That's what their looks and eyes said: he was trash. And now that's what he's afraid I'll see, too."

As the client connects emotionally to the parts and reports the fears and phobias still affecting them, the therapist has an opportunity to speak "on their behalf" (Schwartz, 2001), to generate a deeper level of felt compassion in the client for the parts. Voicing a question used throughout Internal Family Systems work, the therapist asks: "When you hear those words, *how do you feel toward that part now?*" "Feeling toward" is a mindful phrase, different from "feeling for" (having sympathy) or "feeling about" (an attitude of mind). It asks the question, "What feelings do you notice having toward this part now?"

> CLIENT: "I feel sad for him."
> ME: "Yes, you feel sadness for him—it wasn't his fault he was so neglected, was it? Could you let him know that—not so much with words as with your feelings and your body? [Short period of silence] What's it like for him to sense someone caring how he feels?"
> CLIENT: "It's very new, but he likes it ..."
> ME: "Yes, you can tell he likes it, but it is very new ... Nobody ever felt for him ... Let him know you understand just how new it is and maybe hard to trust ..."

One of the keys to this work is the use of the therapist's own compassion and insight as an instrument. When the therapist communicates, "I get it" and when the normal life self and wounded part both feel "gotten" by each other, there is a shift in inner experience. When an increasingly warm inner dialogue between adult and child is facilitated by a therapist whose words and body communicate empathy and emotional connection to both, a spontaneous deepening and bonding takes place between them. The therapist is not just teaching the client to do "the work" or doing the work with a passive client. He or she is actively helping to build a relationship between a traumatized child and an innately caring adult, both held by the therapist as a compassionate third presence. That "is" the work.

Avoiding the Tendency to "Pick Sides"

Without realizing it, therapists and clients have a tendency to side with some parts over others. The therapist might find it hard to work with the level of risk caused by an eating disordered or addicted flight part or a self-injurious fight part. It might be easier to work with submit's willingness to go along with the therapist's agenda or with the attach part's neediness than with the resistance or devaluing of fight or the chronic ambivalence about therapy expressed by the flight part. Without doubt, the therapist will find it more rewarding to work with the normal life part's difficulties with daily functioning than to sit with a mute, shutdown freeze part or a fight part in "Level 4 lockdown" mode.

The biggest challenge for the therapist is being able to remember that these frustrating, alarming issues are driven by the internal conflicts between parts, rather than automatically assuming that the client is an integrated "he" or "she." When that happens, we are more rather than less likely to be drawn into what was an internal struggle.

Whether our agenda is to get the "client" to verbalize more, express more affect, or curb unsafe behavior, once we lose the parts framework, we can only contribute to the internal polarization. The more we emphasize with the client that this is a struggle between part and part, the outcome of which will be determined by the system rather than by us, the more quickly it will be resolved. The therapist's job then becomes twofold: first, to provide the bird's eye perspective of the internal conflicts and, second, to "dance" with each part and with the system as a whole.

Dyadic Dancing

Attunement to all parts and to the system as a whole is expressed through the therapist's body: the face softens or looks firm but calm or communicates warmth; the tone becomes one of curiosity, fascination, or determination. The therapist might lean forward or sit back in rhythm with the client. He or she uses the right brain perception to monitor the client's body and nervous system, and then mindfully adjusts breathing, tone of voice, energy level, and facial expression accordingly. Seeing that the client is getting agitated, the therapist slows respiration, slows the pace of speech, and softens the tone. Avoiding questions that require thinking, he or she asks the client to "notice" the agitation or notice the belief that goes with it. Rather than listening to the entirety of the client's statement or story before replying, as is the custom in most therapeutic methods, the therapist immediately engages in a "duet" or dialogue. The client makes an observation; the therapist responds by echoing the words or translating them into parts language; a reaction occurs, hopefully but not necessarily an increase in curiosity, and the therapist echoes that statement in parts language, makes a "bird's eye perspective" comment, or asks the client to simply stay mindful and interested. Long "filibuster" monologues are interrupted and, as often as possible, turned into dialogues centered on shifting the normal life self's attention to the interplay between parts or between parts and triggers.

The key to ensuring that clients feel no loss of empathy when they are interrupted or when their words are reinterpreted as a communication from a part is the sensitivity of the attunement. To the extent that the therapist is curious, excited, fascinated, awed, touched, tickled, or deeply sympathetic, clients and their parts will feel "met" by the interruptions, rather than cut off.

"Dyadic dancing" is the term Allan Schore (2001a) uses to describe the "co-regulation" of mother and infant in those interchanges in which they feed off each other's body language, sounds, smiles, and facial expressions in mutual attunement. The success of therapeutic dialogue rests on it feeling like a dyadic dance. In infant dialoguing, each maternal response either soothes or builds excitement, and the attuned caregiver makes sure to track the baby's signals to ensure that the infant is enjoying the exchange, neither over- or understimulated. Similarly, the attuned therapist observes the client's body language, tracks what elicits the going on with normal life self's curiosity and interest, what reassures submit or attach parts, what helps the fight part to feel less phobic of emotion or closeness, what regulates the autonomic nervous system so that the client's body is neither over- or understimulated.

What makes the exchange more challenging for the therapist is the need to attend not just to one but a number of parts at once. Our words of reassurance for a young part, for example, cannot be so touching that we trigger flight or fight parts' aversion to any emotion other than anger. While discussing fee increases, vacation plans, and other logistical issues, we have to take care not to provoke anxiety in the child parts, to reassure them even while discussing logistics with the adult client. Including the parts in our awareness instead of automatically reverting to an "I-thou" perspective can actually facilitate the success of these "housekeeping" conversations. I can announce my vacation dates to the normal life self, and then add reassurance for the attach part: "I know you [the normal life self] are fine with my taking vacations, but the little girl gets very nervous—she gets afraid no one will be here for her, and she'll have no one to protect her. She might like it if you were willing to meet with the person who is covering for me—the fight part would hate it, but the attach part might like it. It might reassure her that she's not going to be alone and unprotected. The other option is to offer to be her protector while I'm away. How do those two choices sound?" Another arena in which young parts can be triggered is the subject of billing, especially when the parts have feelings of shame connected to money. Here, too, the therapist can make sure to acknowledge the views of all parts: "I completely trust your normal life self's integrity, and I know you've had a lot of other things on your plate for the last few months, so don't feel badly that I had to remind you. And please, *please* reassure your child parts that *they* have done nothing wrong. It's OK for us to talk about things that come up."

The discussion of safety is another topic that can trigger parts' survival responses. Some parts might feel confused or frightened by the word "safety," having been told they were "safe" when they were not. If the flight and fight parts are engaging in unsafe behavior, it is very important for the therapist to voice respect for their different conceptions of safety. For them, "safety" is not to be found in asking for help or sharing their feelings. The therapist and normal life self might view the hospital as a safety net, forgetting that if fight and flight view it as "dangerous" or a "trap," hospitalization should not be the first line of safety planning. Contracting for safety can be reassuring to the normal life self but a red flag to the fight part, triggering feelings of being controlled or asked to depend. Decisions about safety planning and differentiating safe versus unsafe actions are best made by the normal life self, but if the goal is simply restraint of the fight or flight part, then the opportunity to reach higher-level goals will be missed. (See Chapter 7 on unsafe and self-destructive behavior) In this model, the higher-level goal of the treatment is the development of increasingly close emotional bonds between the going on with normal life survivor and the young parts that are still afraid, still grieving what they never got, still deeply ashamed and alone. The bonds of internal between parts and normal life self trust support trusting the therapist, but, more importantly, they support collaboration and consensus.

To the degree that the therapist speaks from a place of authentic respect, warmth, and admiration for all the parts and empathizes with each point of view, the going on with normal life self can begin to accept each part as a potential resource, not just a liability, and a "real" person worthy of compassion. To do so requires the therapist to speak to and about each part from the point of view of other parts.

> "The submit part must be so worried that fight's 'straight on don't mince words' style of speaking will displease or anger others."
>
> "What the fight part doesn't realize is that when we tell children to shut up and stop crying, they might do it, but they get more scared. The other way to get them to stop crying is to reassure them that you won't let them get hurt. Could you ask the fight part to give you a chance to see if that works faster?"
>
> "I know the little part wants to tell me about the bad people who hurt her, but I also know that the fight part believes that it's dangerous for her to tell. I am going to make a promise to the little part. In fact, the grownup Lucy and I could do that together—we need to promise her she won't be hurt anymore. She doesn't have to tell us what happened because we 'get it.' Then let's see if the fight part is willing to have her tell us—or whether, once she feels protected, it's not so important to tell us."
>
> "Could I be the defense attorney for the flight part for a moment? All these years, the flight part has tried to protect you by numbing your feelings and zoning you out on drugs. He knew you couldn't handle the emotions or knowing what happened, so he took you 'away.' I realize that it's gotten out of hand, that the addiction is now dangerous and has to be treated, but I don't want you to forget that the addict part was trying to help—he did help. You wouldn't be where you are today without him by your side."

Often therapists hesitate to use the language like "inner person" for fear that it will exacerbate the dissociative fragmentation, but to the extent that the parts are visualized and treated as if they were small children and teens, it will be easier for the going on with normal life part to gaze fondly at them. The more the normal life self experiences warm, open, relaxed interest in the parts, the less need for distancing or disconnection from them. Especially as clients stabilize, the survival contributions of fight and flight parts must be enthusiastically acknowledged. They must be treated like war veterans: the therapist or client might not believe that the war was necessary or useful, but these parts fought hard for a worthy cause: the survival of the client. So therapist and client together must honor their service.

The submit and freeze parts often benefit from being honored, too. Although their service consisted of avoidance strategies (freezing, becoming mute, serving others, pleasing and self-sacrifice, floating up to the ceiling), they too were essential to the client's survival and adaptation. Without them, most childhood survivors of neglect and abuse might have reacted in ways that threatened the abuser(s) and evoked far worse punishment. Often, the attach part won moments of support from grandparents, teachers, the mothers of friends, neighbors—moments that provided hope, role models, even the belief that they could be loved. Even though these parts still get triggered and continue to drive trauma-related symptoms, the therapist must emphasize, "How is this part still trying to help?" "What is this part worried about? How is this an attempt at a solution?"

> Annie reminded her therapist: "You know, they're all trying to fix it in their own ways."
> "Fix it?"
> "Yes, fix what was wrong then—when we were all young—they're still trying to do that now the way they learned to do it then."

References

Beebe, B. et al. (2009). The origins of 12-month attachment: a microanalysis of 4-month mother-infant interaction. *Attachment & Human Development,* 12(1–2), 1–135.

Benjamin, J. (1994). What angel would hear me? The erotics of transference. *Psychoanalytic Inquiry,* 14(4), 535–557.

Grigsby, J. & Stevens, D. (2002). Memory, human dynamics and relationships. *Psychiatry,* 65(1), 13–34.

Liotti, G. (2011). Attachment disorganization and the controlling strategies: an illustration of the contributions of attachment theory to developmental psychopathology and to psychotherapy integration. *Journal of Psychotherapy Integration,* 21(3), 232–252.

Lyons-Ruth, K. et al. (2006). From infant attachment disorganization to adult dissociation: relational adaptations or traumatic experiences? *Psychiatric Clinics of North America,* 29(1).

Main, M. & Hesse, E. (1990). Parent's unresolved traumatic experiences are related to infant disorganised attachment status. In Greenberg, M. et al., *Attachment in preschool years: theory, research and intervention.* Chicago: University of Chicago Press.

Ogden, P., Minton, K., & Pain, C. (2006). *Trauma and the body: a sensorimotor approach to psychotherapy.* New York: W.W. Norton.

Schore, A.N. (2003). *Affect dysregulation and disorders of the self.* New York: W.W. Norton.

Schore, A.N. (2001a). The effects of early relational trauma on right brain development, affect regulation, & infant mental health. *Infant Mental Health Journal,* 22, 201–269.

Schore, A.N. (2001b). The right brain as the neurobiological substratum of Freud's dynamic unconscious. In D. Scharff & J. Scharff (Eds.). *Freud at the millennium: the evolution and application of psychoanalysis.* New York: Other Press.

Siegel, D.J. (1999). *The developing mind: toward a neurobiology of interpersonal experience.* New York: Guilford Press.

Solomon, M. (2011). *The trauma that has no name: early attachment issues.* Presentation at the Psychotherapy Networker Symposium, Washington, D.C., March 2011.

Tronick E. (2007). *The neurobehavioral and social-emotional development of infants and children.* New York: W.W. Norton.

Van der Hart, O., Nijenhuis, E.R.S., & Steele, K. (2006). *The haunted self: structural dissociation and the treatment of chronic traumatization.* New York: W.W. Norton.

CHAPTER 7

Working with Suicidal, Self-Destructive, Eating Disordered, and Addicted Parts

"When neither resistance nor escape is possible, the human system of self-defense becomes overwhelmed and disorganized. Each component of the ordinary response to danger, having lost its utility, tends to persist in an altered and exaggerated state long after the actual danger is over."

(Herman, 1992, p. 92)

"[Abused children] will need to have the potential to mobilize an intense flight-fight response and to react aggressively to challenge without hesitation ... [These survival responses] markedly augment the individual's capacity to rapidly and dramatically shift into an intense aggressive state when threatened by danger or loss."

(Teicher et al., 2002, p. 18)

Surviving trauma, going on each day as if nothing has happened, coping with both the normal challenges of daily life and the abnormal challenges of traumatogenic environments—all tax an individual's belief in safety and erode the determination to live. Feeling helpless, overwhelmed, inadequate, vulnerable, terrified, and alone, the lived experience is that there is nowhere to turn, nowhere to hide, no one to help. The only resources upon which each individual can draw reside in the body: disconnection, numbing, dissociation, neurochemicals such as adrenaline and endorphins, and the animal defense survival responses of fight, flight, freeze, submit, and attach for survival. These are "desperate times requiring desperate measures."

It is not surprising that trauma and self-destructive behavior go hand-in-hand. "Road rage," sexual compulsivity, the inability to anticipate danger and take self-protective measures, indifference to normal safety concerns, inability to leave dangerous situations or relationships—all are congruent with past experiences of being treated as an object whose welfare doesn't matter, whose life has no purpose other than to be used. It is no wonder that the prospect of death can be comforting as an alternative to entrapment, not surprising that wishing to die rather than live with such pain could be procedurally learned as a way of surviving. There is scientific support for this hypothesis as well as clinical evidence. Suicidal ideation, threats of suicide, and suicide attempts have all been statistically correlated with a diagnosis of PTSD, as have substance abuse, eating disorders, and self-injury (Khoury et al., 2007; Krysinska & Lester, 2010; Min et al., 2007). Even after repeated treatments for these symptoms and disorders, rates of relapse are extremely high among those with trauma histories (Najavits, 2002), suggesting that these different forms of addictive behavior have a complex inter-relationship with the effects of traumatic experience. How can we understand the coexistence in one individual of a strong will to live and an equally intense longing to die at one and the same time?

A Way Out or a Way to Go On?

Surviving trauma requires immense determination to keep on "keeping on" while simultaneously taxing an individual's belief in safety and eroding the wish to live. Having to cope both with the normal challenges of daily life and the abnormal challenges of traumatogenic environments is a heavy load for any human being to bear, much less a child. Having a sense that there is relief in sight; an exit plan, a parachute, or a "Get Out of Jail Free" card, brings a glimmer of hope or lessening of helplessness: "There is something I can do." When we are very young, the only resources upon which we can draw reside in the body: disconnection, numbing, dissociation, our body's neurochemicals (adrenaline, endorphins, cortisol), and animal defenses of freeze, total submission, or cry for help. By the teenage years, there are more options afforded us by a more physically powerful body and rapidly developing brain. As we develop during puberty, the animal defense survival responses of fight and flight become effective actions rather than the wishes and fantasies of a small child.

Whether trapped under enduring conditions of threat or triggered by everyday stimuli, and whether we are three, thirteen, or thirty, the felt sense is that these are desperate moments requiring desperate measures to survive. The choice of "desperate measure" is only limited by our circumstances and our bodies. The sympathetic nervous system mobilizes the body to defend itself in the face of threat, but when fighting and fleeing are too dangerous, the body instinctively inhibits action by freezing or redirecting the impulse. We punch the wall; imagine ourselves crashing into a telephone pole; throw something; punch or bite ourselves. Immediately, there is a felt sense of control—just as we might feel when we duck for cover, get away, or push back the attacker.

Desperate Measures

Self-destructive behavior thus has its origin in the experience of feeling terrified of annihilation, isolated and abandoned, helpless against overwhelming emotions, and filled with despair and hopelessness. Whether these states are reactions to threat and violence or repeatedly triggered implicit memories, they feel equally true (and therefore equally frightening) now. To further amplify the desperation, manifestations of vulnerability feel unsafe, too. Emotions and emotional expression rarely result in greater safety for child victims and more often provoke intensified violence—to the point that many traumatized individuals become more afraid of their feelings than afraid for their lives.

The fact that the normal sensations and emotions resulting from any adverse event are experienced as threatening, not liberating, is something important for therapists to keep in mind. In the effort to help clients acknowledge their feelings, rather than shutting down or acting out, therapists often forget that these emotions were once a source of danger and are now connected to implicit memories of overwhelm, threat, or humiliation. When clients learn instead to associate emotions that feel overwhelming or unsafe to a young child part of the self, the relationship to the feeling is altered. The client can feel the emotion still, but perceiving it as a child part's feelings reduces its threat, reduces the client's sense of vulnerability. It is OK for a child to feel ashamed or lonely or sad. It is even understandable that the child's vulnerability triggers fight and flight parts. The client's job is to mindfully notice the emotions as communications from a child part, to name them as "the little one's sadness" or "the little boy's fear," and inhibit the automatic tendency to identify with the fight or flight part and act on their impulses.

Another contributor to self-destructive behavior in traumatized individuals is the absence of ways to soothe or regulate intense, autonomically driven feelings and sensations. The ability to self-soothe is directly related to consistent early experiences of soothing that condition the nervous system to settle and recalibrate until the child is in an "optimally aroused" state (Ogden & Fisher, 2015). Under conditions of inadequate early attachment followed by traumatic threat, our clients' nervous systems learn habits of sympathetic hyperarousal to drive hypervigilence and readiness for action or habits of parasympathetic hypoarousal to ensure inaction and numbing (Ogden et al., 2006). Lacking the ability to self-regulate, overwhelmed by apparently dangerous emotions and sensations, the child's felt sense is, "I can't survive these feelings—if I can't make them stop, I will explode into a million pieces—I will die." The result: both ordinary and autonomically exacerbated emotional reactions come to feel unbearable, intolerable, and life-threatening. On the other hand, the dangers associated with high-risk behavior seem "unreal." The client is used to surviving life threat by dissociating or minimizing the danger in order to "keep on keeping on." Dying is not what the client fears. The client fears his or her own feelings. What feels dangerous is the implicit memory: "I can't tolerate these emotions by myself—if no one can help me, I will die—I have to do *something*."

Mastering Unbearable Emotions

The most common error made by professionals and lay people alike in understanding high-risk behavior is the automatic assumption that self-harm, suicidality, eating disorders, and substance abuse are destruction-seeking, rather than relief-seeking. If we assume that self-harm induces pain, then we interpret it as masochism or self-punishment or a cry for help. If we assume that suicidal ideation reflects a conscious intention to die, we will interpret it as a life-threat or a scream for help. And if we do, we will miss the core issue in self-harm: the pursuit of mastery over unbearable feelings or relief-seeking.

At the heart of all self-destructive behavior is a simple fact: hurting the body, starving it, planning its annihilation, or compulsively engaging in addictive behavior result in welcome relief from physical and emotional pain. Ironically, based on its physiological effects, high-risk behavior seems to be an ingenious attempt to cope with pain, or to live through it, in the only ways the client knows how. If we can validate that clients currently have no better way of self-soothing, if we can acknowledge why self-harm or suicidal ideation and self-destructive behavior have been successful in bringing relief—albeit in a paradoxical way—we have the opportunity to develop a collaborative relationship with the client (and the fight or flight parts) in facing the challenges of relief-seeking. Rather than reacting immediately to suicidal ideation, active addiction, or self-harm as a safety concern, the therapist should begin by communicating curiosity: what problem might this be a solution for? What triggered this impulse? What is it the client is hoping for as a result of the action? Has he or she found relief in this way previously?

Providing psychoeducation about why these behaviors are so effective in regulating unbearable states mitigates client shame and secrecy. Describing the range of positive intentions that might underlie a self-destructive impulse makes it all the more likely that clients will volunteer their doubts and fears about achieving relief in these ways, rather than trying to convince the therapist that addictive or unsafe behavior is their only or best option.

Historically, treatments for unsafe behavior have often polarized client and therapist: the therapist's goal of reducing self-injury or preventing suicide is often in conflict with the client's need to hold on to the one kind of relief that can be counted upon to work. Or the therapist's agenda of "safety first" might evoke an interpersonal struggle by putting the therapist in a policing role. In this treatment model, my first priority is to help the client attend to the internal struggle: what feelings are activating fight and flight parts to such desperate measures? Which parts want to die? Which are trying to help? And which want to live? Are any of them frightened by the fight part's capacity for violence? Do the child parts see the fight part as a rescuer or are they afraid of being killed?

To effectively treat unsafe and addictive behavior, therapist and client must be able to share the intra-personal dilemma: if self-harming, eating disordered, or addictive behavior is the only means of managing what feels like life-threatening emotional arousal, how else does the client tolerate the pain? How do therapists encourage clients to acquire or make use of the skills, resources, or treatments that are healthier options when "ordinary measures" are slower and less effective than the desperate measures? When the client's internal experience is a sense of life-or-death urgency? Historically, the treatment approaches for trauma-related self-harm, addictive behavior, eating disorders, or suicidality have primarily addressed abstinence and safety as behavioral goals, only to discover that trauma-related triggers and an inadequate window of tolerance consistently undermine the client's attempts at stability. To understand the complex inter-relationship between trauma and unsafe, addictive behaviors requires comprehension of the effects of these behaviors on the body and how they facilitate relief and regulation.

Capitalizing on the Body to Gain Relief

Child abuse and neglect, torture, domestic violence, and many other categories of trauma share a common characteristic: the victim's body, mind, and emotions have been exploited by others, either to gratify their needs, exert control, or provide an outlet for release of tension (Miller, 1994). It is not surprising that children whose bodies have been used in this way might later become adults who instinctively use their own bodies to relieve tension or act out impulses. They have been deprived of the normal experiences of tension relief (i.e., the soothing of secure attachment), while the abuse has relegated the body to no more than a vehicle for releasing tension, with no other real value.

When distressed, most children seek connections to others, preferably adults, for soothing, reassurance, or comfort. Those who experience neglect or abuse, however, quickly learn to avoid connection, rather than seek it, and to rely almost exclusively on their own resources. Because they cannot trust or depend on others for support, they instinctively seek relief in a variety of behaviors that share one common characteristic: none requires reliance on other human beings. Some clients learned as teenagers to use drugs and alcohol to numb; others discovered in early puberty that self-starvation or binging and purging allowed them to achieve a similar state of calm or "non-feeling." Still others, often beginning when young children, develop a variety of relief-providing self-injurious behaviors: pinching, cutting, scratching, burning, hitting or punching, head-banging, and even blood-letting.

How Self-Destructive Behaviors "Work"

The biggest challenge in treating self-destructive behavior is how effective it is in producing relief—at least in the early stages before tolerance develops. Harm to the body (cutting, burning, hitting, ingestion of sharp objects) has the same effects as any injury or threat: first, the harm stimulates adrenaline production (resulting in increased energy, focus, feelings of power and control, and decreased emotional and body sensation), and then a heightened endorphin release, facilitating a relaxation/analgesic effect. Both responses occur quite quickly, providing almost instant relief for the client feeling terrified and overwhelmed by the level of intensity or the disconnection.

Although eating disorders have traditionally been conceptualized as resulting from a distorted body image or distorted sense of self, it is striking that their effects quite specifically address the hyperarousal-related symptoms of trauma. In eating disorders, relief can be achieved by under- or over-eating. For example, in anorexia, restricting food intake results in numbing of emotion and sensation while at the same time, due to the effects of ketosis, there is an increase in energy and feelings of well-being. Over-eating also results in numbing accompanied by relaxation, increased parasympathetic hypoarousal, disconnection from the body, spaciness, or drowsiness. Bulimia, too, in both the binging and purging phases, causes a reduction in hyperarousal and decreased pain sensitivity via activation of the dorsal vagal system (Faris et al., 2008), the same branch of the parasympathetic nervous system implicated in total collapse and feigned death survival responses. That bulimia is associated with a higher pain threshold compared to normal controls (Faris et al., 2008), presumably because of the numbing effects of both the binging and purging, may account for the increased number of young women being diagnosed with this disorder.

Both substance abuse and addictive behaviors also tend to result in quite specific effects on autonomic arousal—as reflected in the drug-related terms "uppers" and "downers." Cocaine, speed, MDMA (Ecstasy), Ritalin and Adderall, crystal meth, and other stimulants are the drugs of choice when clients begin to feel "dead" or "empty" but can also be used to increase feelings of power and control or maintain arousal at a heightened level in clients who fear relaxation or confuse it with insufficient hypervigilance. Similarly, alcohol, marijuana, benzodiazepines, and opiods, such as heroin, oxycodone, and morphine, all down-regulate hyperarousal symptoms and overwhelming emotions, but they can also be used to help individuals maintain a chronic state of hypoarousal in which they can be sure of not feeling or sensing "too much." Particularly in eating disorders and addictions, any sense of connection between the drug or behavior of choice and the trauma symptoms they treat has often long been lost. Habitually "using" or engaging in eating disordered behavior prevents the intrusion of feared emotions and sensations—until the client begins to develop tolerance and must restrict, binge and purge, or overeat more frequently or severely to induce the same effect. As clients develop tolerance, eating disorders often spiral out of control. Consistent with the split-brain research showing the tendency of the left brain to create rational arguments for right brain-driven irrational behavior, clients with eating and/or substance abuse disorders will have "stories" or rationales for their symptoms: for example, "I'd be as big as a house if I didn't _____." But those stories do not account for the relief experienced as a result of eating disordered behavior. They do not explain the panic triggered by the effects of increased tolerance, and the desperate need to numb the feelings again, causing increased eating disordered or addictive behavior.

It may be more than a coincidence that substance abuse, eating disorders, self-harm, and suicidal behavior typically begin in the years from 11 to 14—just at the height of a teenagers' mounting internal conflicts between the drive for independence/individuation and the fear of abandonment and separation.

Self-Destructive Behavior and the Attachment Drive

Most victims of trauma face some version of the same life-threatening dilemma: how to minimize the dangers facing them and maximize the relational resources that might afford protection while simultaneously avoiding vulnerability to those who might do them harm. To minimize danger, they must avoid antagonizing the predator; they must cultivate good will while simultaneously remaining guarded. For young children, this challenge is especially difficult due to their dependence on adults and the strength of their biological drive to attach or seek proximity. They need a solution that inhibits the attachment drive without increasing the risk of abuse or sacrificing any positive attention that might be available to them.

> While her mother and I conferred about her emotionally disturbed older brother's care, 2-year-old Anya ran in, tripped over a toy, and fell hard on her chin. She started to sob but made no eye contact or appeal to her mother for comfort, nor did her mother seem to notice her crying. Seemingly oblivious to either adult, Anya pulled herself up to a standing position and started to rock from foot to foot, quietly sobbing and rocking at the same time. In her own world now, her eyes unfocused, she kept rocking until she was calm and quiet.

Attachment researchers who study disorganized attachment have described behavior like Anya's beginning as early as age two, postulating that it reflects a solution to the challenge of experiencing simultaneous urges to seek proximity and impulses to distance or defend. Presumably wary of seeking proximity to their "frightened and frightening" caregivers when vulnerable or needy, these preschoolers begin to relate in ways that give them more control, termed the "controlling strategies" (Liotti, 2014). One group, described as "controlling-caregiving," engages in parentified or "tend and befriend" behavior: charming, directing, entertaining, soothing, precociously independent, and offering approval and comfort to the parent. The other group of children, termed "controlling-punitive," reacts to proximity in ways that are hostile, provocative, coercive, shaming, and sometimes aggressive or violent, putting them at risk for diagnoses of "oppositional-defiant disorder." It appears from this research that when caregivers are neglectful, dangerous, or unavailable, safety becomes equated with the choice between appeasement or parentification, on the one hand, and hostility or distancing, on the other. Or proximity-seeking and distancing alternate in the same individual, each impulse driven by a different survival defense response: the attach or submit part's using parentified behavior to gain greater control over closeness and the fight part's use of hostile engagement to push others away at the same time. Because closeness and safety are intertwined when we are dependent for survival on caregivers, the implicit message is: "It isn't safe to depend. It isn't safe to get too close or to love those closest to you." These patterns of attachment behavior persist into adulthood and when accompanied by structural dissociation, become increasingly sophisticated, polarized, and easily activated.

Animal Defenses and Unsafe Behavior

Structural dissociation facilitates negotiating unsafe attachment relationships: if the wish for closeness is held by an attach part, the ability to appease by a submit part, the need for distance by flight, the fear of attack by freeze, and the imperative to control the situation is instinctive for the fight part, then the individual has all the "ingredients" necessary to manage in a dangerous world. That each structurally dissociated part can operate somewhat independently of the others to pursue its goals creates an advantage. Quick, automatic transitions from hypervigilant to needy to distancing to robotic compliance facilitate defensive flexibility—important when you have easily provoked abusive caretakers. When perceiving trauma-related stimuli as dangerous increases the chances of avoiding trouble, and staying safe another day, this pattern is adaptive. But, once we are safe (i.e., no longer emotionally or physically dependent on abusive individuals), these defensive patterns are no longer useful. The parts still scan the environment for traumatic triggers salient to their aims and needs and react to each in their own characteristic ways. But their activation increases susceptibility to internal conflicts. The most threatening triggers every part will encounter are likely to be other human beings. Not only will angry, violent, aggressive individuals evoke strong defensive responses, so will authority figures, and even those to whom clients are closest: partners and spouses, therapists, family members, close friends, and love objects of all kinds. Tragically, those who might aid in the healing process are likely to be as triggering for the structurally dissociated parts as those who harmed them.

As these struggles inevitably lead to increasing polarization, the internal conflicts intensify. The attach part instinctively idealizes potential attachment figures (including the therapist), while the fight part is likely to become more guarded, hypervigilant, or hostile to those seeking closeness or whomever empathically fails the young parts by disappointing them, not "being there," not caring for them, or having other priorities. Because the others in the client's life believe they are in the company of an adult, not a child, even their most well-meaning and supportive efforts to "be there" can easily disappoint or hurt a young traumatized part's feelings. What is well-meaning and supportive to an adult is very different than "well-meaning and supportive" to a child, as Jessica attests.

Jessica counted on her friends and their friends to help her during difficult times, and they tried to come through. But their practical offers of rides, help with finding a new job, or being treated to lunch didn't register as "caring" to a 2-year-old attach part. She longed for a hug, for gaze-to-gaze contact, for someone who would hang on her every word, someone who wasn't in a hurry to go somewhere after lunch. As these were not experiences generally offered to a 45-year-old woman, Jessica's attach part was often left feeling hurt and disappointed. Complicating this situation was her fight part's constant alertness to behavior that would wound the attach part or offend the fight part's sense of fairness. Because Jessica's parents had both been hypersensitive and hypercritical, the fight part's alarms went off in the context of what her friends deemed very minor offenses. And once someone offended, the fight part remained hostile and vigilant for months or even years, refusing to allow Jessica to forgive and move on—or even to reassure the little part. Gradually, she became more and more isolated, unable to make new friends because the fight part inevitably found them "cold," "narcissistic," "mean," or "not healthy enough" for her. But isolation did not solve the underlying attachment wound: the child part's loneliness and rejection sensitivity only deepened, while the fight part's hypervigilence increased in tandem.

Particularly as children enter puberty, begin to individuate, and become physically stronger, the fight and flight parts become more active. By age 15, adolescent parts are often physically capable of standing up to authority figures and exercising power and control over the vulnerability of younger parts (yearning, neediness, hurt, disappointment) that could potentially be exploited. It is not a coincidence that eating and substance abuse disorders tend to appear around ages 11 to 12 at a time when separation-individuation instincts require inhibition of the attachment drive but also at a time when the child's physical strength and greater independence increase opportunities for disordered eating, self-harm, and access to substances. Sometimes this is also the stage at which a first suicide attempt takes place.

Annette could remember the time she first dreamed of dying as a solution to her situation. She was 6 years old, her mother was away at work all day, and her stepfather's abuse became increasingly cold, calculating, and sadistic. Every day, she would promise herself: "If you just get through today, you can die tomorrow." Then she could breathe, knowing there was an end in sight. "If you just get through today, you can die tomorrow." It was a promise that brought welcome relief and helped fortify her for what was to come. Even after her mother left her stepfather and the abuse stopped, the wish to die remained a "fail safe" solution each time she felt overwhelmed or abandoned. She made her first suicide attempt at age 14 after the end of a relationship with her first boyfriend: she downed a bottle of aspirin.

The paradox was that, initially, the wish to die had begun as a way to live through the abuse by exerting control: "I'll only put up with this one more day." That sense of control brought welcome relief each time she made that promise to herself. By age 14, however, just wishing wasn't enough to bring relief anymore. "That's why," she said, "I had to do something. I had to feel that I *could* end it." She was not relieved to be alive still nor was she disappointed. Once she'd taken the overdose, Annette felt a renewed sense of purpose: she did have a way out when she needed it. At the same time, she was cautious to avoid detection of her suicidality for fear of "being locked up." This continued to be the pattern until Annette was in her 30s: something or someone would hurt or trigger the younger parts' feelings, and the suicidal part would re-establish a sense of control by threatening suicide, self-harming, or taking non-lethal overdoses, often small enough just to render her unconscious for the night until she could wake up the next morning and go on about her life. Of more concern was her use of alcohol.

> After a hospitalization following the first suicide attempt at age 14, Annette felt trapped and fearful. If she couldn't control her impulses, she'd be locked up again, but if she gave up her suicidal longing, there would be no source of relief. She began to feel an internal battle. Her littlest part longed for someone to just love her and keep her safe, but that rendered her vulnerable to men looking for sex. Disappointment in not finding someone to care triggered the child's grief, and although the suicidal part bought a little relief by scratching her arms, Annette worried that the scratches would be viewed as signs she wanted to die. On her fifteenth birthday, some friends brought a bottle of wine, and as she drank her first glass, she began to feel "normal." The wine relaxed the tension and fearfulness, allowed her to laugh and smile at people's jokes—and then they smiled back, filling her little part with hope that maybe they liked her after all.

Even after individuals are safe, trauma-related triggers interfere with differentiating what is safe now from what was dangerous then. Once her stepfather was gone, Annette was finally safe from harm, but she and her parts didn't feel safe. Her little part still yearned for the safety of someone's love and protection; her suicidal part still brought relief by promising to end it all; and her addict part had to increase her consumption of alcohol to regulate trauma-related implicit memories and their accompanying autonomic arousal. When boyfriends left or girlfriends disappointed her, the little part panicked, and Annette was flooded with hurt and desperation—requiring yet more wine. As the years went on, though, her once trusty chemical support began to fail her: to make the feelings go away, the flight part now had to drink to blackout. But when she blacked out, what happened next re-exacerbated the disturbing feelings instead of easing them. All too often, her nights out at the bar with her trendy young professional "family" of drinkers ended in blackout, and she would find herself in a stranger's bed the next morning.

Treating the Causes of Self-Destructive Behavior

Self-destructive behavior stems from a "perfect storm" of variables: first, a trigger evokes trauma-related implicit memory. Second, the implicit memory's association with danger activates the emergency stress response, inducing a sympathetic nervous system reaction and shutting down the prefrontal cortex, impairing the individual's judgment and disempowering the normal life self. Now, parts with conflicting defensive responses have free rein to act on their survival instincts, leading to some action intended to bring relief—whether it is binging and purging, cutting, a suicide attempt, addictive behavior, or restricting food. For a short time, perhaps only minutes, clients report a temporary feeling of control or well-being that reinforces the connection between the aversive feelings, dysregulated arousal, and immediate need for an action that will bring "relief." Because often there is little felt connection between the apparently benign or mildly distressing trigger, the hurt and sadness or shame of child parts, and the impulsive behavior of fight or flight parts, even the client does not understand his or her behavior except as a statement about the actions taken: "I want to kill myself."

Stabilization of high-risk behavior requires addressing "the parts' part," a step not included even in newer, cutting edge treatments. Dialectical Behavior Therapy (DBT) addresses the skills needed by the normal life part to tolerate the dysregulated emotions of the traumatized parts but does not address fragmentation or how to differentiate the normal life self from the parts. Internal Family Systems (IFS) addresses the role of the parts but conceptualizes self-destructive behavior as an expression of "firefighter" parts trying to suppress vulnerable "exiles" (Schwartz, 2001). In IFS, the normal life self is thought to be a "manager" and its emphasis on functioning just another way to keep the exiles out of mind. In this model, the normal life self is a competent present-moment-oriented aspect of the individual able to provide social judgment and "top-down" behavior management but is also capable of curiosity, compassion, wisdom, courage, and calm. In IFS, those qualities (along with clarity, confidence, and commitment) are reserved for "self" or what I call "wise mind" or the "wise self." Sensorimotor Psychotherapy (Ogden & Fisher, 2015) is the only treatment model for trauma other than Somatic Experiencing, that focuses on the contributions of autonomic dysregulation and animal defenses to post-traumatic stress disorders but lacks, as does IFS, specific interventions to address unsafe behavior. Each (IFS and Sensorimotor) encourages a mindful interest and curiosity in the habitual patterns rather than a solution-oriented approach to safety issues.

In IFS, the therapist understands the firefighters as motivated to protect and defend the exiles. In Sensorimotor Psychotherapy, unsafe behavior is framed as a "survival response" to autonomic dysregulation.

Trauma-Informed Stabilization Treatment (TIST)

Trauma-informed stabilization treatment (TIST) (Fisher, 2015) is a treatment model developed to stabilize severe self-destructive behavior unresponsive to conventional treatments. TIST was initially developed in the context of a paradigm shift in the State of Connecticut's Young Adult Services, a division under the Department of Mental Health and Substance Abuse. In an attempt to help some of its most severe cases in the age range from 18 to 25, a daring decision was made to explore the impact of trauma-informed approaches, given that a high percentage of these chronically suicidal, self-destructive clients had histories of severe trauma. The patients for whom the program was first designed had been given many different diagnoses over years of mental health treatment in inpatient and residential settings. What they had in common was an early childhood history of trauma followed by symptoms of severe self-injury, suicidality, substance abuse, eating disorders, and aggression toward others, primarily staff. All of them had been hospitalized for more than six months and as long as 10 years. Their difficulties in benefiting from existing treatment models resulted from the lack of a method that could simultaneously address the separate components of their self-destructive behavior: its origins in their traumatic past, trauma-related triggering, loss of perspective and judgment due to cortical inhibition, and the degree of relief experienced as a result of the behavior. By using the structural dissociation model as the theoretical foundation for TIST, each separate variable contributing to unsafe actions in a client could be identified and each of the self-destructive impulses could be externalized and assigned to the appropriate part. That single intervention in and of itself immediately supported the clients' identification with the going on with normal life self, loosening the identification with the suicidal and self-harming impulses. To ensure that the model was not perceived as shaming by clients, all aspects of self (including the suicidal part) are consistently described in terms of their positive contribution to survival.

When treatment models conceptualize self-destructive behavior as pathological, "borderline," or manipulative, and judge inhibition of unsafe impulses as "healthy," attention is diverted away from the underlying issue: the internal struggle between conflicting drives. Should the client seek relief in impulsive action or find a way to bear the pain and go forward? Successful treatment of any conflict requires acknowledgment of all sides or parties involved, not just those toward whom we are biased. Although on the surface it seems that the answer should be easy, it is not. With no hope or belief in the future, with emotional vulnerability intensified by autonomic activation and adrenaline-driven fight-flight impulses wanting discharge, it is hard for traumatized clients to believe that "keeping on keeping on" has much chance of success. To resolve the struggle, clients have to learn to trust that all their parts are committed to survival in different ways; that even their most intensely suicidal parts "want to die in order to live."

Acknowledging Self-Destructive Parts

"I feel suicidal" is an utterance that strikes fear in the heart of any therapist because it implies that the whole being of the client wants to die, that danger is imminent. The TIST model makes a different assumption. It assumes that the wish to suicide reflects the point of view or impulse of one part but not necessarily all. The question we must ask before jumping to any conclusion is: which "I" feels suicidal? The depressed part? A suicidal part? What triggered this part or parts? What is driving the impulse or feeling?

Once broken down into its component parts, the suicide threat might just mean, "My little part is really sad and disappointed, and the fight part is trying to prevent her from future rejection by threatening suicide." Or it could mean that the suicidal part has been triggered by the child's tears and frightens her to stop the tears. Or perhaps it means that the depressed part just wants to go to sleep and never wake up again. Each of these answers would require a different solution—which we cannot provide without gaining an understanding of the parts. In addition, TIST would ask: where is the normal life self? Why is he or she missing in action? What could the normal life part do to find out more about what is happening or to soothe distressed parts? Is the normal life self temporarily disempowered by the intense emotions and impulses of the child parts or the fight and flight parts? Or is the going on with normal life self just watching helplessly from a distance?

Most human beings would agree that criticism is not motivating; that suppressing or blocking feelings results in either depression or anger. Yet these are often the treatment approaches used with suicidal, self-destructive, eating disorder and addicted clients. The message is: these impulses or behaviors are wrong—they are dangerous—and we are going to help you stop engaging in them. To fight and flight parts, this approach is tantamount to waving a red flag at the proverbial bull. It alienates and polarizes the parts whose trust we most want to win, whose motives we want to understand. It can undermine a normal life self who is sincerely trying to work with treatment providers but keeps being told she or he is not trying hard enough—when in fact no amount of "trying" by the normal life self can stop parts driven by adrenaline and convinced that their only safety lies in action. In the TIST model, the intentions of a part are differentiated from its actions: what is the suicidal fight hoping to accomplish? How is it trying to protect the client? The following example describes the first client treated with the TIST model as it was first being developed in a state hospital setting. Katya illustrates how switching from a uni-consciousness model to a parts model and from a treatment method for borderline personality to a treatment approach for trauma could quickly change the treatment picture:

Katya had been hospitalized now for well over 2 years because of her unrelenting suicidality and self-injury, drug use, and violence toward staff. Although Katya recognized the role of her fight part once the new treatment model was described to her and validated its contribution to her survival, its determination seemed to increase with each unsafe event. Sometimes, Katya could unblend and differentiate herself from the fight part's violent impulses by repeating as a mantra: "It's just the fight part—it's just the fight part—I don't have to do what it says." But sometimes the fight part hijacked her seemingly "behind her back," and suddenly an act of aggressive or self-harming behavior would occur. Worried that the suicidal fight part was treading too close to the edge, I decided it was time that Katya and I found out what was driving it. I inquired, "Could you ask the suicidal part what it's worried about if it pauses and takes some time to let you work on all this? What is the suicidal part afraid will happen if it stops trying to kill you?"

Even Katya was surprised by the answer. "The fight part says: 'It's the only way to push people away—they can't hurt you if they can't get close.'" In the hospital, she had developed close relationships to certain staff who would comfort her little parts, joke around with the adolescent parts, and connect to her normal life self. But the fight part had pushed away her family and successfully convinced her fiancé to end their engagement because he couldn't tolerate the fear that she might die. Hearing the suicidal part's agenda evoked panic in her attach part and worry in her normal life self: what about her wish to love and be loved? To marry and have children someday?

As I coached her, Katya asked the suicidal part: "What would you need from me to trust that I could handle these relationships that I want to have?" The suicidal part replied, "I would have to believe that you would be OK, that you couldn't be devastated." It would take many months for Katya to prove herself to the fight part and many more months to finally be approved for discharge from the state hospital.

Today, she lives on her own, with the love and companionship of her cat, the closest comfort to her attach part and the emotional center and regulator of any negative feelings. She is proud to have grown into the normal life she once dreamed about, a life that includes college classes as well as caring for herself, her apartment, and her cat. The fight part now trusts her to choose relationships well and to soothe parts that might feel hurt or rejected by others before their implicit memories are triggered and become overwhelming. She in turn trusts the fight part to discriminate when people are taking advantage of her or expecting too much. Now, with growing communication and collaboration, Katya can heed the fight part's warnings and set boundaries before it reacts aggressively to potential threat. Her ability to comfort the attach part reduces the sense of aloneness and vulnerability, allowing the fight part to sit back and leave her to do her job.

By learning to "ask inside," Katya learned how to dialogue with her fight part, rather than interpreting its behavior, until she finally discovered why it was so determined to lead her down a self-destructive path, even if that meant she was "incarcerated" on a locked ward in a state hospital. When the fight part acknowledged its primary purpose was to keep her safe from any attachment, even to her parents, the last few years suddenly made sense to her. Knowing how much she and her attach part yearned for closeness, she had immediately understood what she'd have to do to be free to live her life as she wished it to be, rather than the way her traumatic experiences had dictated that it be. Having almost died many times, it was clear that her fight part was unyielding and would ultimately have its way if she didn't do something different.

Today, Katya is not reliant on anyone other than her cat for regulating her emotions and actions. She takes no psychiatric medications, no longer goes to therapy, and has been discharged from the Department of Mental Health system. The parts seem to feel safe with her, safe enough to allow her to set up a Facebook page to make contact with others and share her story of survival and redemption. When she first was assigned to the new "trauma program" I developed in the hospital, the pilot version of what has become the TIST approach, she immediately felt a sense of pride: she wasn't sick; she had been harmed, and she was receiving special services as a result. With a basic understanding of trauma that helped her see her symptoms as logical and meaningful, she felt less unworthy. As a "trauma patient," she was being treated as someone who deserved something more than medication, restraints, and injury-proof hospital rooms, someone who was intelligent and capable of participating in her own recovery. She kept repeating to her staff, "I needed a trauma program, and I finally got one—this is what I've needed all this time."

The opportunity to change her relationship to her symptoms, to make meaning of them as a legacy of the trauma, and to externalize them as communications from her parts all helped Katya to "disidentify" or "unblend" from the parts, rather than continuing to interpret their actions and reactions as her own. She could begin to differentiate her willingness to work therapeutically as evidence of an intelligent, motivated normal life self and feel a greater alliance with the staff who wanted to help her, rather than "believing" the hypervigilant suspicions of her fight part or the desperate seeking of contact and validation coming from the attach part. As she identified with her normal life self, without a loss of compassion and loyalty to her young parts, they relaxed ever so slightly—enough that she was less often triggered and more often able to recognize when she was. This process of separating "whom she was meant to be" from the actions and reactions of the parts and learning to regulate their strong responses sufficiently so she could interrupt the fight part's acting out took several years. It required a few of the staff who embraced the TIST model to repeatedly and consistently help her translate her emotions into parts language, connect the feelings and impulses to those parts, feel empathy toward them, and, trusting that this process would allow her to avoid acting on the fight part's impulses, tolerate the risk that she might die before her team could help her learn how to help the parts.

Soothing the Vulnerable, Honoring the Protectors

As in Katya's case, suicidal and self-destructive parts are typically activated by the distress of younger parts associated with the experience of traumatic attachment. In the TIST model, the major focus is not on inhibiting the impulses of the fight and flight parts. It is on anticipating and soothing the emotional activation of young, vulnerable parts before the fight and flight parts take action. First, clients are helped to recognize the signs and symptoms of distressed child parts because even before the client has the ability to "help" them, their appearance can be used to anticipate unsafe situations. The therapist must model mindful observation of "domino effects," patterns in which triggered parts trigger other parts that trigger other parts that eventually trigger fight or flight.

> I decided it was important to make Terri aware of the relationship I was seeing between her suicidality and a disowned young part of her. Because I believe that timing and readiness are everything in psychotherapy, I had waited several months—until a moment when Terri expressed *her* own anxiety about the prospect of future crises: "My boss told me that if I'm hospitalized again, he can't keep me on in my job. No matter how good I am at it. I don't know what to do. I can't tell him I'll never make another suicide attempt!"
>
> ME: "Hmmm ... That is a problem, isn't it? Maybe there is a way around this. I'm observing a pattern: have you ever noticed that the suicidal part only gets activated when your depressed 13-year-old is having a hard time? I know you try to ignore her so you can keep working, but I think being ignored just reminds her of never being seen—never feeling she mattered to anyone. It seems to me that the suicidal part deserves to be thanked for getting us to listen to the 13-year-old at last! I don't think the suicidal part wants to die (or kill anyone), but it's clearly stating that it won't stand for her to be left alone to suffer." At first, Terri pooh-poohed this theory and insisted she didn't have parts, so it was irrelevant. I nonetheless

continued to watch for signs of the 13-year-old's deepening depressions so I could warn Terri that the suicidal part wouldn't be far behind.

In this instance, the depressed part was a very accurate barometer for anticipating the sudden impulsive actions of the suicidal part, which almost always resulted in months of hospitalization. By intervening to help the 13-year-old by acknowledging her distress before a crisis ensued, suicide attempts could be more predictably warded off in time to prevent threats to her job and threat to life.

Often, depressed parts are the triggers for unsafe behavior. Sometimes, parts who communicate via flashbacks and memories are instigators of fight or flight parts: the body and emotional memories of young parts intrude upon the consciousness of the normal life self to communicate that they are afraid they'll be hurt again, that no one will believe them, that they need protection. The somatic message that things are still unsafe might then trigger fight parts to protective action, for example, to end the risk of being hurt again forever. Ashamed parts are also triggering for the fight part, evoking a painful vulnerability that is intolerable to a part whose biological imperative is to gain control over the enemy. When the therapist can predict the risk ahead of time and help the client's normal life self provide soothing and a sense of no longer being alone to the vulnerable parts, the risk of impulsive behavior diminishes dramatically. Clients are taught the Internal Dialogue Technique (see Appendix C) and asked to practice it in therapy sessions until their ability to regulate parts' unbearable feelings grows sufficiently that they can use it independently of the therapist.

"No Part Left Behind"

"No part left behind" is the motto clients are taught and the standard to which they are held. This standard challenges the survival strategy of self-alienation. As functional as the normal life self might be, he or she will not be allowed to abandon the parts responsible for survival. The ashamed part, the frightened part, the addicted or eating disordered flight part, or the suicidal, the angry, self-injurious or justice-seeking fight part: all deserve respect and compassion.

When clients are held to the "no part left behind" standard in therapy, the threat of abandonment, which for children is as frightening as the threat of annihilation, is lifted. The parts, hearing the therapist speak on their behalf, have a reparative experience: someone has heard them. The normal life self, I know, will also feel grateful later on as the parts' attachment to him or her grows. Being loved by a small child feels pleasurable to both parties, as every parent knows. And when a mindful normal life self can interpret their implicit memories as "just a feeling" or "just a memory" and develop greater ability to soothe and regulate "their" responses, the parts begin to feel safer. Now a new, safer and more satisfying internal environment can be established.

In a world that feels safe or safer, traumatized clients can learn to use their capacity for inner communication to co-create a life they were "meant to have," rather than living a life dictated by the trauma. Each part can play a valuable role after trauma. Not only do the parts offer survival defense responses but other important resources as well related to their specialized roles. The fight response, for example, provides increased energy, "grit" or determination, a "backbone," refusal to give way, and the ability to guard our rights and privileges. As the client's normal life self learns to ask the fight part to "give me courage to say No," or "give me the strength to hold my ground," there is a surge of energy or increased strength in the core or spine. The normal life part now has other resources for change and growth; the freeze part feels a bodily sense of being protected; the submit part is not freely "used" by others, and there is energy to counteract its depressive hypoarousal; the flight part doesn't have to run for cover because the parts are safe "here now."

> Robert was a tall gaunt 70-year-old man, tormented since his early 20s by voices warning him that someone wanted to kill him. Having witnessed his mother beaten nearly to death by his abusive father, the fear of being killed was very familiar to him, and since he was a young boy, it could only be soothed by the longing for death. Only his devout Catholic faith prevented him from committing suicide, no matter how much he felt compelled to end his life.
>
> After 2 years of helping him stay alive, I was in his hospital room to say goodbye as he faced death from end-stage cancer. His "wish" was at hand, and he was terrified. "All my life, I've longed to die—but now that I'm really dying, I'm scared—wanting to die gave me control—dying is taking it away." In the 20 years since I said goodbye at his bedside, I've taken his wisdom with me: wanting to die is about taking control, not about wanting death.

References

Faris, P., Hofbauer, R., Daughters, R., Vandenlangenberg, E., Iversen, L., Goodale, R., Maxwell, R., Eckert, E., & Hartman, B. (2008). De-stabilization of the positive vago-vagal reflex in bulimia nervosa. *Physiology & Behavior, 94*(1), 136–153. DOI: 10.1016/j.physbeh.2007.11.036.

Fisher, J. (2015). *The trauma-informed stabilization treatment model.* Two-day workshop. Toronto, Canada: Leading Edge Seminars.

Herman, J. L. (1992). *Trauma and recovery.* New York: Basic Books.

Khoury, L., Tang, Y.L., Beck, B., Kubells, J. F., & Ressler, K.J. (2010). Substance use, childhood traumatic experience, and posttraumatic stress disorder in an urban civilian population. *Depress Anxiety, 27*(12), 1077–1086.

Krysinska, K. & Lester, D. (2010). Post-traumatic stress disorder and suicide risk: a systematic review. *Archives of Suicide Research, 14*(1), 1–23.

Linehan, M. M. (1993). *Cognitive-behavioral treatment of borderline personality disorder.* New York: Guilford Press.

Liotti, G. (2011). Attachment disorganization and the controlling strategies: an illustration of the contributions of attachment theory to developmental psychopathology and to psychotherapy integration. *Journal of Psychotherapy Integration*, 21(3), 232–252.

Miller, D. (1994). *Women who hurt themselves: a book of hope and understanding.* New York: Basic Books.

Min, M., Farkas, K., Minnes, S., & Singer, L.T. (2007). Impact of childhood abuse and neglect on substance abuse and psychological distress in adulthood. *Journal of Traumatic Stress*, 20(5), 833–844.

Najavits, L. M. (2002). *Seeking safety: a treatment manual for PTSD and substance abuse.* New York: Guilford Press.

Ogden, P. & Fisher, J. (2015). *Sensorimotor Psychotherapy: interventions for trauma and attachment.* New York: W.W. Norton.

Schwartz, R. (2001). *Introduction to the internal family systems model.* Oak Park, IL: Trailhead Publications.

Teicher, M.H. et al. (2002). Developmental neurobiology of childhood stress and trauma. *Psychiatric Clinics of North America*, 25(2), 397–426.

CHAPTER 8

Treatment Challenges: Dissociative Systems and Disorders

"Dissociation is the essence of trauma. The overwhelming experience is split off and fragmented so that the emotions, sounds, images, thoughts and physical sensations related to the trauma take on a life of their own. The sensory fragments of memory intrude into the present, where they are literally relived. As long as the trauma is not resolved, the stress hormones the body secretes to protect itself keep circulating, and the defensive movements and emotional responses keep getting played out."

(Van der Kolk, 2014, p. 66)

"The concept of a single, unitary 'self' is as misleading as the concept of a single unitary 'brain.' The left and right hemispheres process information in their own unique fashion and represent a conscious left brain self system and an unconscious right brain self system."

(Schore, A., 2011, p. 76)

In the 1950s, what was then called "multiple personality disorder" came to the attention of mental health professionals initially through books such as *The Three Faces of Eve* and *Sybil*. It was controversial and much disputed then, and today, dissociative disorders are still the subject of controversy. Even before therapists encounter a dissociative identity disorder (DID) client, they will have been affected by the anxiety and even hostility raised by any mention of the diagnosis among mental health professionals. The "countertransference" reaction to the idea that individuals can have multiple consciousness, parts with separate identities or separate lives often pits psychiatrists (least likely to believe such disorders exist) against psychologists and psychotherapists who have evidence that it does because they have encountered its distinctive symptoms and presentation. Since the 1950s, dissociative disorders have often been assumed to be "factitious disorders," an assumption that is rarely questioned—and rarely documented. In the context of the institutional bias against it, the field has overlooked or ignored research that validates the reliability of the diagnosis of DID and demonstrates that it is much more common in the population than hitherto believed (Brand et al., 2012; 2016). Though there has been more published research on dissociative symptoms in borderline personality disorder and more establishing the *under*-diagnosing of dissociative disorders than on demonstrating that DID is a factitious disorder, the field of trauma and dissociation has never been able to shed that stereotype. Korzekwa et al. (2009) and Zanarini (1998), for example, have consistently found statistically significant rates of dissociative symptoms in borderline personality and strong correlations between severity of dissociative symptoms and severity of borderline symptoms, including rates of self-injury and suicidality, depression, global psychopathology, behavior problems, and use of psychiatric services. That strong evidence base is rarely mentioned in the literature on borderline personality disorder. Despite the need for better, more effective models for treating clients diagnosed as borderline, their dissociative symptoms are rarely noted or treated. When I was asked in 2008 to consult to a state hospital and provide training in "trauma-informed care," I was told upfront, "We don't have DID patients here. Our trauma patients are all borderlines." I understood the message. It was clear: "Don't come in here and start diagnosing our patients with DID. If you want to work with us, leave that particular diagnosis at the door." I was untroubled, though. I was bringing to the hospital a training on trauma and a model for understanding unsafe behavior and suicidality, the Structural Dissociation model. To reassure the staff, I just kept saying, "This is a trauma model, not a dissociative disorders model. And it is the best approach to borderline personality that I have encountered in 25 years." If that is not enough to allay anxiety, I say, "The parts language gives clients a way to externalize the problem so they can change their relationship to it—the same way eating disordered clients do better when they externalize their eating disorders as 'Ed.'" All of these statements are true. Whether one believes that each part represents the implicit memories of a child or believes in using the language simply to externalize the behavior, the approach described in this book is helpful to the client. And that is what brings together the skeptics and the believers.

Recognizing the DID Client

Since the statistical probability of therapists encountering a DID or DDNOS client is fairly high (especially for those who treat trauma, borderline, or suicidal clients), it behooves therapists to be familiar with the diagnostic and treatment challenges of treating dissociative disorders (Brand et al., 2016). In this chapter, we will describe the special challenges of working with clients whose parts are not only structurally dissociated but also function autonomously, often with little to no awareness of the others. Although the theoretical model and the treatment are almost the same as described in previous chapters, a dissociative disorder brings with it special complications for the therapist, not just for the client.

DSM-5 and ICD-9 diagnostic systems both have a "bottom line" criterion for a diagnosis of DID: making the diagnosis requires "evidence of losses of consciousness: two or more parts of the personality take control of the body and operate outside of conscious awareness" (DSM-IV-R, p. 2000).

Assigned to the inpatient unit during my predoctoral internship, my very first patient was a 40-year-old writer diagnosed as acutely psychotic. Caitlyn was besieged by scathing, humiliating voices telling her to kill herself. "You're a cunt—a whore—you don't deserve to live—make this world a better place." Not knowing that clients with psychotic disorders are generally made worse when their delusions are questioned, I made the rookie mistake of suggesting that she take a stand: "Explain to the voices that they are not helping you get you discharged—you need them to back off a bit if they want you to get out of here."

To the amazement of both of us, the voices responded: by the next day, they had quieted enough to win her a discharge. Two admissions later, the reason for my spectacular success became clear: Caitlyn had a dissociative disorder, not a psychotic disorder. Arriving at the hospital to meet with her, I found my stout 40-year-old patient wandering around the unit wearing a lace tutu and combat boots! "It's been a strange day," she said in a lost confused tone, "This morning, I couldn't remember how to put my clothes on ..." and her voice trailed off. As I opened the door to the meeting room, she froze on the doorstep and started screaming, "What are you doing to me?! Who are you? Where's my mommy?!!!!"

When you've been a mother before becoming a therapist, you have certain instincts. One skill you never lose is the ability to know what to say when children are freaking out. "It's OK," I instinctively began speaking to her as if to a young child: "Your mom knows where you are. I talked to her today. [Which I had.] She knows you're with me, and she said it was OK—do you want me to call her?" Calming down a little but keeping her distance from me, she began to wander around the bare hospital office like a child exploring the room while I made conversation with a child in an adult's body: "Your mom didn't tell me how old you are or if you go to school."

CAITLYN: "I'm 6, and I'm in the red reading group!" [Smiles proudly] Everyone knows that's the best one." The big smile wasn't the smile of a proud woman—I could see the grin of that 6-year-old. My heart ached for her: 6 was the year in which this innocent little girl in the red reading group had been raped by her older brother, bullied by neighborhood boys, and emotionally abandoned and unprotected by her alcoholic mother. Before she was used and abused, my client had once been this confident little girl who was proud of how smart she was and eager to learn.

Thanks to Caitlyn, I learned some important lessons very quickly: first, DID (or multiple personality disorder [MPD] as we called it in the early 1990s) really does exist; second, my previous "job experience" raising small children and working with families was going to make working with dissociative disorders remarkably easier—not easy but easier. What I did not know (but would soon learn) was that my success with the little 6-year-old part of Caitlyn would very shortly stand in stark contrast to my ability to enrage other parts of her! Yet another lesson useful for the novice therapist I was then: "You can't please all the parts all of the time."

Diagnosing Dissociative Disorders

Steinberg (2013) describes five symptom clusters characteristically found in dissociative disorders that facilitate making the diagnosis:

- Dissociative amnesia or "missing time" (i.e., amnesia for periods of time after the age of nine or gaps in daily memory not explicable by ordinary forgetfulness).
- Dissociative fugue: finding one's self in an unfamiliar location with no memory of having planned to go there and no recognition of others around one. Sometimes, fugue episodes are accompanied by dissociative amnesia, the loss of memory for personal information, such as one's name, address, age, and job or significant others.
- Depersonalization (feeling disconnected from one's self or one's experience)
- Derealization (experiencing other people or familiar surroundings as "unreal")
- Identity confusion ("Who am I?"): Am I the person who functions? Or is that a false self? Am I needy and clingy? Or militantly independent? Do I want to live or do I want to die?
- Identity alteration: regression experiences, feelings or behavior that do not feel like "mine," being known by different names, evidence of child parts (stuffed animals, sucking ones thumb, being afraid to be alone), or evidence of activities for which one has no memory.

Psychotic-like symptoms, such as hearing voices, internal dialogues, intrusive voices, thoughts, images, and visual "hallucinations" of the trauma, are also potential signs of a dissociative disorder. These symptoms all represent implicit memory and/or manifestations of parts but unfortunately tend to be diagnosed as symptoms of schizophrenia despite demonstrable differences between trauma-related voices and auditory hallucinations. Dorahy et al. (2009) compared the voices described by two groups of schizophrenic patients (one with histories of trauma and one with no reported trauma) with the voices reported by a group of patients diagnosed with DID. The researchers found that, in this sample, the DID subjects reported hearing voices at a more frequent rate than did the schizophrenic subjects. They also described the voices as having different genders and ages, and they summarized the content of the voices' communications as generally negative and personally directed, focused on pointing out the individual's inadequacies, lack of worth, and using these accusations to justify "why you deserve to die." The voices reported by schizophrenic clients were fewer in number, did not have different ages or genders, and spoke from a more abstract spiritual or paranoid perspective, not a personal one, even if also encouraging self-destruction.

To Make or Not to Make the Diagnosis?

Making a DID diagnosis is not clinically essential if clients are already using trauma-informed treatment models in which the emphasis is on mindful awareness of the emotions, cognitions, body sensations, and action impulses of parts. The advantages or disadvantages of making a formal diagnosis should always be determined by the client's clinical presentation and source of distress: if the symptoms are leading the client to feel crazy and afraid of being "locked up," it may be reassuring to hear the diagnosis and learn that it is a treatable condition stemming from early traumatic experience. Annie illustrates a situation in which a diagnosis can be a supportive intervention:

> Annie was increasingly troubled by the dissociative amnesia caused by parts switching frantically to gain control of the body and drive their survival strategies. After she sustained a bad fall with no recall of how it happened, and after her husband told their couples therapist "she" had repeatedly asked for a divorce that Annie did not want or recall, she was alarmed. And then, after weeks of being unable to leave the house, brush her teeth, take a shower, or eat regular meals, it became clear that she needed some explanatory system for understanding what was happening to her.
>
> I greeted her at the next session with a big smile: "You know, Annie, I've been thinking about our last session and how you've been struggling to just do the simple things, and I'm excited to tell you I think I know why!" I always precede making the diagnosis with excitement or glee, as if I were about to tell my client he or she just won the lottery! Clients with child parts are often sensitive to adult mood changes: if I appear unusually serious or unsure of my words, their alarms will be triggered.
>
> Annie was eager to hear "why" she couldn't brush her teeth or eat breakfast or get through the day. After educating her about the structural dissociation model and sharing with her the diagnosis of DID, I explained: "Your parts developed a relay race system for surviving your childhood: one would grab the baton and run the next leg of the 'race,' while others were shielded from what was happening, and then another would grab the baton and run the next leg. It was automatic: the best 'runner' for a particular situation would be instinctively activated to run that leg, then the best runner for the next leg of the race would be triggered, and so on. No one was distracted by how the

others were running because each was separate and had little to no awareness of the others. You should thank your parts! It's thanks to them and the dissociative disorder that you and I are sitting here right now having this conversation!"

In contrast, there were many clinical disadvantages in making a formal diagnosis with Dustin: he had a lifelong phobia of being diagnosed psychotic after being raised by a schizophrenic mother and told by his father that he was "crazy—just like her." He also wrestled with deeply painful beliefs that he was inadequate and "less than," beliefs that could only be challenged by recalling his professional successes as an adult. Dustin had a very strong going on with normal life self, dating back to an early age, that was driven by the fear of being like his mother and fulfilling the negative expectations of his father. But he also had an intensely ashamed submit part that often took control of his body and led to acting out that part's wish to be invisible and avoid other people, much to his girlfriend's disappointment. She wanted him to be the dynamic professional man she had first dated, not the depressed, self-effacing, withdrawn little boy self he could become—especially in social situations. The little boy part just hoped that someone would be nice to him and not question his right to be there while his presence influenced Dustin to keep a distance from others under the belief that he was still "on the outside, looking in." Though Dustin's girlfriend frequently questioned this pattern, he never did; the physical action of anxious withdrawal to the periphery where he would not be noticed was all the evidence he needed to believe he was inadequate and unwelcome. The procedurally learned beliefs of childhood ("be seen and not heard," "you don't belong," "there's something wrong with you," "no one wants you") continued to condition his emotional and behavioral reactions to the social environment. To give him a diagnosis at this point in his therapy would only have given him ammunition with which to attack himself, rather than giving him hope and illuminating the path to recovery.

Assessment Tools for Diagnosing Dissociative Disorders

Because DID is such a controversial diagnosis in both the professional and lay worlds, using standardized, validated assessment tools to support making a diagnosis can be very important to clients' ability to accept it as true and useful information, rather than feeling shamed. Without the objectivity of a formal diagnostic instrument, they are likely to become suspicious of the therapist, anxious and defensive about the concept of parts, or apt to assume that it's simply another black mark being imposed upon them. When the therapist uses formal assessment measures, there is a reassurance of objectivity: we are not assessing them but assessing for a condition common to trauma survivors. It can even lend a sense of reassurance that they are not alone with this complex, baffling array of symptoms and are being taken seriously by the therapist. But knowing that formal assessment can be threatening to some parts, it is important that the therapist exude curiosity and enthusiasm as if this endeavor will be interesting and maybe even fun!

The most well-known assessment tool, the Dissociative Experiences Scale (Carlson et al., 1993), a self-report instrument, is the easiest to administer but unfortunately is also the least reliable tool. Clinicians using it report a high rate of false negatives (very low scores in clients who later demonstrate very obvious DID symptoms, e.g., switching of parts during a therapy session). These false negatives can be dangerous if they give the therapist a green light to go ahead with therapeutic work (e.g., memory processing) that exceeds the client's window of tolerance and activates the parts to act out self-destructively.

A more reliable measure is the Trauma Symptom Inventory (Briere et al., 1995), also a self-report instrument that elicits information about a range of symptoms from dissociation to intrusive images/sensations, anxiety and depression, and "tension-releasing" behaviors (e.g., self-harm, impulsive behavior, addictions). Although it does not explicitly diagnose DID, one of its measures is a severity of dissociation score and, when clients score high on that symptom cluster, the therapist has an objective statistic, usually along with other related scores, that provides a very natural entry point for a discussion of dissociation and dissociative disorders.

For making accurate and formal diagnoses of DID, there is no better assessment instrument than the Structured Clinical Interview for DSM-IV Dissociative Disorders (SCID-D) (Steinberg, 1994). Most challenging to administer because of its long, very complex interview format (it usually takes 3 to 4 hours to complete in one sitting), it is nonetheless a valuable experience for client and therapist because of the detailed, non-pathologizing discussion of dissociative symptoms it encourages. Many of the SCID-D diagnostic questions can also be introduced separately to elicit information about dissociation bit by bit as the therapy proceeds, rather than the entire interview completed in a formal way.

Diagnostic Criteria and Questions

Even when there is no immediate need for formal assessment and diagnosis, the therapist who is curious and concerned about a client's dissociative symptoms can still benefit from utilizing portions of the SCID-D (Steinberg, 1994) as the work of information-gathering in therapy naturally proceeds. Many of the SCID-D questions can simply be incorporated into the therapeutic dialogue. For example, Will could not remember the names of a single one of his colleagues or coherently describe what he did every day at work, causing his therapist to become curious about the possible role of dissociation in his self-acknowledged "absent-mindedness." When I suspect that the client may be experiencing transient time loss, I can ask some of the following SCID-D questions:

- Have you ever felt you had memory problems? Ever had gaps, small or large, in your remembering of things? For example, "I remember starting the project, but I don't remember finishing it."

- Is it ever hard to remember what you did yesterday or last week?
- Are there ever whole hours or days that seem to be missing or that you have difficulty accounting for?
- Have you ever found yourself having traveled somewhere without remembering how or why you went? (Steinberg, 1994)

Or for clients who frequently talk about being disconnected from themselves, questions eliciting information about depersonalization can be included into the discussion:

- Have you ever felt as if you were watching yourself from a point outside of your body, as if from a distance?
- Have you ever felt that you were going through the motions of living but the "real you" was far away?
- Have you ever felt like two different people? One going through the motions of living and the other just quietly observing?
- Have you ever heard yourself speaking and thought, "Is that me?"
- Have you ever felt that your words were out of your control? Your thoughts? Your actions? Your feelings? (Steinberg, 1994)

Questions about derealization often help detect parts that are disoriented in time and place. When they see the client's current environment, it looks unreal to them and unfamiliar, causing the client to complain of experiencing things as "unreal."

- Have you ever felt as if familiar surroundings or people seemed unfamiliar or unreal?
- Have you ever felt as if your surroundings were fading away?
- Have you ever had the experience of not recognizing close friends or relatives or even your own home? (Steinberg, 1994)

Eliciting information about internal struggles and conflicts always moves the therapy forward, regardless of diagnosis:

- Have you felt as if a struggle was going on inside you?
- Have you felt confused about who you really are?
- Have you ever felt as if there was a struggle going on about who really are, what you really want?

And if the answer to these questions is "yes," the therapist might want to ask more direct identity alteration questions:

- Have you ever felt or been told that you were acting like a different person?
- Have you ever referred to yourself or been referred to by different names?
- Have you ever found possessions inexplicitly missing? Or inexplicably appearing?

- Have you ever experienced rapid changes in your ability to function? Or does your mood ever change rapidly without clear reason?
- Do you ever have internal dialogues? Are these dialogues more like thoughts or voices? Do they increase under stress? (Steinberg, 1994)

Because the SCID-D questions are meant to elicit discussion of the client's day-to-day experience, rather than being primarily focused on obtaining a score, they facilitate gathering a detailed understanding of the client's symptoms and struggles that can be invaluable in any trauma therapy, regardless of diagnosis. The SCID-D is a qualitative measure with all the advantages and disadvantages inherent therein: it is thorough, detailed, allows the therapist leeway to inquire further or even compose spontaneous follow-up questions, and it is not limited by standardized questions. Even if the therapist prefers not to make a formal diagnosis, the dialogue facilitated by the SCID-D will be valuable and elicit valuable information needed for the treatment.

There Is No "She"—There Is No "He"

Many therapists are intimidated by the challenge of taking on their first DID clients because they have received so little exposure to or training on the treatment of dissociation or dissociative disorders. In addition, they are often presented immediately with serious and complicated symptoms: regressive behavior, losses of functioning, suicidal or self-harming behavior, dissociative fugue states. Quite quickly, however, they discover the biggest challenge: there is no one "she" or "he" in the client's chair. Though this client is a whole integrated *physical* being, he or she is not one integrated *psychological* being, and that proves to be not only confusing but also disturbing to even the most experienced of therapists.

The therapist is also hindered by the "information gap" inherent in the diagnosis. Clinicians are trained to rely on clients as the experts on their own internal states, to assume that they are the most credible source of information about both past history and moment-to-moment awareness. With DID clients, however, even very basic information can be inaccessible to the client or known to the client but censored by protector parts. Even more challenging is the unexpected, unrequested information the therapist is likely to receive from trauma-related parts seeking to promote their own agendas, usually either to push the therapist away or pull the therapist closer. Whereas adult clients infrequently use text and email as regular channels of communication, child parts driven to make contact with the therapist without the knowledge or consent of the normal life self regularly use these means of communication. When parts are free to act autonomously and secretly outside the awareness of the "observing ego" of the prefrontal cortex, when they are driven by primitive animal defense instincts in response to triggers associated with danger, there is often a loss of reality-testing, continuous consciousness, and behavioral control.

Keeping Secrets Even from One's Self

It is common for therapists working with DID clients to have secrets disclosed to them by individual parts communicating "behind the back of" (i.e., outside the consciousness of) the client's normal life self. Young child parts who feel endangered by triggering of implicit memories often hijack the body and can end up dominating the therapy in an attempt to elicit protection from the therapist, usually through disclosures of abuse or by having flashbacks in therapy. Fight- and flight-driven aspects of the personality might attempt to control the therapy in a different way, either by pushing the therapist away (devaluing, "firing," impulsively terminating) or punishing the young parts to prevent them from disclosing more secrets or becoming more dependent on the therapist. The therapist, confused by it all, can also inadvertently exacerbate the situation by unconsciously taking sides with young child parts that want a relationship or want to "tell what happened." When therapists continue encouraging disclosure of memory despite evidence that protector parts are alarmed by it, the result is most often increased instability.

> Sheila's therapist approached the treatment of DID using a model first developed in the 1990s and then discontinued because of the risks of decompensation and regression inherent in that way of working. Founded on an assumption that the "talking cure" would also work for trauma, child parts of DID clients were encouraged to "come out" in therapy and "tell their stories" to the therapist, who in turn would inform the going on with normal life self as if reporting child abuse to a parent. When clients had a sufficient window of tolerance, this method was reasonably effective, but few DID clients had sufficient affect tolerance to manage the intensified trauma responses or increased tendencies to fragment.
>
> Often, Sheila's normal life self did not want to hear the disclosures, fearing being swept away by a "tsunami" of emotions. That rejection in turn triggered the child parts' painful memories of not being heard or not being believed. The fight and flight parts became alarmed by the therapist's knowledge of the secrets, believing that meant she or he would use them against the client. As they became agitated and desperate to take action, the result was increased addictive and self-injuring behavior. Child parts were being "punished" through self-harm by a fight part determined not to allow further regression or vulnerability.

The case of Sheila provides a good example of the risks of a memory disclosure approach to the treatment of DID. The history of the trauma treatment field reflects a series of paradigm shifts as leaders in the field were forced to give up the memory retrieval and disclosure approach of the 1980s and 1990s because clients so often got worse instead of better. In the last 15 years, guided by the neuroscience and attachment research, treatments have moved away from an emphasis on event memory retrieval to focus on the legacy of implicit memory, and on mindful witnessing in lieu of narrative expression. Nowhere is the new paradigm more necessary than in the treatment of DID. Mindful self-witnessing is an antidote to difficulties in maintaining continuity of consciousness. Understanding the parts as disconnected "containers" of implicit memory driven by instinctive subcortical animal defense responses reduces the degree to which they feel weird and crazy. I tell the client, "A part is the child you once were at a certain age or the child you had to be in certain situations. It's the little you." That rarely feels strange to anyone. In this model, the stories told by parts about the trauma reflect the meaning they have made of what happened and how the legacy of those events lives on in the client's mind and body. The parts are not writing history. They are disclosing what they still dread, still feel, and the dangers they still watch out for.

> Sheila was frightened by the child parts' memories when they were disclosed to her by her therapist. She was very disturbed that she could go to therapy and not remember what happened after the first few minutes. When the therapist told her about parts that "came out" in therapy without her knowledge, she felt "possessed." And the injuries she kept finding on her body were frightening to see: how could that have happened? She didn't recall burning herself. Then, when the therapist disclosed that child parts were calling and emailing her between sessions, Sheila began to feel dangerously out of control. "I went to therapy to get better, but I feel like I'm getting worse!"

By developing an intense 1:1 relationship with the child parts and encouraging disclosure of memory, the therapist, Jennifer, had inadvertently dysregulated an already unstable system and triggered the attach part's desperate need to make contact between sessions. Alarmed by the deterioration in Sheila's condition, Jennifer assumed that what was needed was to meet more often so she could elicit more disclosure by the child parts and work on gaining acceptance of the memories by Sheila's normal life self. They were caught in a vicious circle: Sheila thought about leaving the therapy to stabilize, but when she had those thoughts, the attach parts panicked, shutting down her prefrontal cortex so that she "forgot" or filling her with fearful beliefs that she couldn't survive without Jennifer.

Although the treatment for DID clients should ideally be very much the same as that described earlier in this book, the therapist may have to be even more sensitive to the effects of disorganized attachment on the clients and parts. Because of the autonomous functioning of the parts, it is easier for the therapist to develop countertransferential relationships to each part as a separate "inner person": to become intimidated by the anger and devaluing of the fight part, as if it could harm him or her, or to feeling intense protective impulses, "wanting to help" the child who feels so alone and in so much pain.

The challenges of utilizing any treatment approach effectively become greater when amnesic barriers and/or intense conflicts between parts create an inability for the whole person or system to work with the therapist, much less work with itself.

Restoring Order to a Chaotic Inner World

The inner worlds or systems of most DID clients reflect the environments in which they were raised: harsh, secretive, critical, punitive, neglectful, intimidating, and/or terrorizing. To the extent that the client's parts survived by creating "smoke and mirrors" to hide secrets from each other as well as from family, neighbors, and teachers, the client will struggle to find stability. Each step forward addresses one layer of secrecy, followed by exposure of another layer—often maintained by saboteur parts that operate outside of consciousness to keep other parts intimidated, shamed, or invisible. As one such part told me, "It's easier to protect them if they're too afraid or ashamed to leave the house." To the extent that the individual and his or her parts survived by suppressing vulnerability or fighting for control, the inner world will be characterized by parts that fight to prevent vulnerability, for example, hurt, dependency, rejection. To the extent that the early environment was harsh, punitive, and neglectful, that world will be reflected in clients' habitual ways of treating themselves and their parts.

> Annie's inability to manage basic activities of daily living (grooming, showering, eating three meals a day, following a routine that included self-care) reflected the powerful influence of neglected child parts who longed to be taken care of and had no idea how (or were too ashamed) to take care of themselves. They had learned early in life to take care of others but associated self-care with the pain of being uncared for and unwanted. Annie learned from observing other children in school to wash her hair and to match tops and bottoms when she picked her clothing out of a pile of unwashed, ill-fitting dirty clothes all over the floor. No one made sure they were clean or ironed or free from stains and rips. Four children shared one toothbrush, two pairs of boots, and one umbrella. The only item of which there was always plenty in the house was alcohol.

Decades later, Annie's system of parts continued to recreate the hostile environment of her childhood: her attempts to get up in the morning, brush her teeth, eat breakfast, and plan her days were interrupted by the parts' "safety concerns." Depressed parts would feel too tired to get up and beg her to stay in bed. A part that used caretaking to elicit safety and connection, the Little Saint, would get anxious about who needed to be cared for. Although caretaking inflamed other parts to anger and feelings of oppression, it was associated with safety for the Little Saint. Annie's flight parts had yet another agenda: what was she going to do today that was meaningful and important enough to prove her worth in the world? Every day, they drove her to frantic activity, not stopping until her body ached and her limbs couldn't move anymore. The fight part's hypervigilant eye was on each part's performance, followed by a relentless negative critique of each and every activity, just as her mother had, triggering fear and shame in the little parts. At that point, her 16-year-old part would suggest a beer to anaesthetize them. Several cans of beer later, the little parts would quiet, as they had years ago when Annie's mother would feed the children beer because there was no food in the house. Because the parts were still defending against the old dangers, it still didn't feel safe inside.

When the Client Is Many Clients in One

"Restoring order" to the inner world and thus to the client's life circumstances begins with increasing the ability of the normal life self to observe the way the system of parts operates, including its struggles and conflicts. Brain scan research with DID subjects (Reinders et al., 2006) has demonstrated an association between the normal life self and the prefrontal cortex, while none of the trauma-related parts' brain scans showed cortical activity. This finding suggests that the therapist can make use of the prefrontal cortex as a way to connect to the normal life self. To facilitate unblending and manage the intense reactivity and emotional volatility of the trauma-related parts, the normal life self has to cultivate dual awareness.

In addition, to learn new models and new skills requires cortical activity. Because the prefrontal cortex is connected to the abilities to be mindful and curious, retrieve and manipulate already learned information, and to integrate new information, only the normal life part has the potential to learn new concepts or skills and bring that new learning to the parts. By engaging the prefrontal cortex, the normal life self can have access to information about both past and present, imagine parts he or she has never met, connect them to other information (such as childhood photographs), and even visualize them.

Teaching the Client's Normal Life Self How to Work with the Parts

As described in Chapters 4 and 5, the client is asked to make the assumption that all instincts, emotions, bodily reactions, and thoughts reflect communications from parts, even if they can only be "heard" retrospectively because of dissociation-related amnesia. Next, the client's normal life self is taught to observe these signs, to name each feeling state or belief as that of a part, and to validate the part's experience.

Particularly when safety is an issue, events in present time for which the normal life self has no memory must be "decoded": what triggered the intense emotions? Or the depressed part's hopelessness? When that hopeless feeling came up, what happened next? If the client has amnesia for what happened next, are there clues that fill in the gaps? For example, movie tickets, receipts, emails, Internet activity histories. Or if there is no memory and no clues, how does the therapist help the client gather more information?

With the use of structural dissociation model and some creative thinking about parts and animal defenses, therapist and client can also make educated guesses. Which part would have gone to the cemetery in the middle of the night? (It had to have been a part that could drive—i.e., an adolescent part.) Which part would have allowed itself to be picked up at the bar near the cemetery and taken to a seedy motel? (Probably not the part that went to the cemetery, but an attach part might have.) Which part would have been too afraid to ask the therapist for help? (Submit? Freeze? Not the attach part certainly!) And which part would have refused any offer of help? (Flight and fight would never yield their self-reliant, counterdependent stances to ask for help.) The simple act of naming overwhelming emotions as the feelings of a part usually decreases some of the client's emotional intensity. Developing the ability to observe, "A part of me is feeling this way" or "a part of me was desperate not to be alone" seems to have the same effect as a parent has in noticing a child's mood and naming it: there is relief in being seen by a compassionate "other." Being able to identify "who" is feeling that emotion, having that reaction, or about to act on a desperate impulse helps clients unblend, making easier the task of managing internal unrest.

To understand themselves and to make conscious decisions and choices, rather than be hijacked by their parts, DID clients will also need to learn to notice the comings and goings of different parts and to observe what triggers control each part's mysterious appearance and disappearance—even in therapy. Often, early in treatment, therapist and client can use the structural dissociation model as a guide: "Was that fight or flight that didn't want to come today? Was it submit or attach that came because they wanted to please?"

Because of the "information gap" inherent in the diagnosis, it is crucial to develop internal communication skills early in DID treatment, as well as the ability to observe intrusive feelings and physical phenomena and interpret these as communications from parts, rather than be frightened or ashamed of them. A sudden feeling of fear in response to thinking about the client's job must be reframed by the therapist as, "There seems to be a part of you that's anxious about your job," and then the client must be encouraged to obtain more information about this anxiety: "What could that part be feeling worried about? What triggers are you aware of in the workplace that would alarm a child?" In non-DID clients with structural dissociation, information-gathering will be much easier because the dissociative barriers between parts are not as impermeable. With DID clients, it is more difficult to know if a part is worried or lonely or ashamed because other parts may not be aware, and the normal life self has little access to inside information.

Although "switching" so that individual parts can "come out" and interact with others is more typical of DID, blending also takes place in DID clients. The normal life self might feel the intrusion of parts' feelings and thoughts but tend to interpret these as "my feelings." Feelings of depression, critical thoughts, or ruminations may not be experienced as parts but should always be attributed to them. With DID clients, just as with any traumatized client, the practice of noticing moments of being blended and then unblending is a crucial skill. For example, in response to the client's perseverating on "his" hopelessness, the therapist reflects, "It seems there's a part that believes he's worth nothing—a part that feels there's no hope for him, no way to belong or be accepted by others. Is that right? Do you notice him?" Feelings of anger, especially if they frighten the client or frighten others in the client's life, need to be named as indicators of a fight response: "Perhaps this reaction is coming from a very angry fight part determined to defend you verbally and physically … it would make sense that you would have needed a strong body-guard. We all need a protector."

Making Meaning of Moment-To-Moment Experience

In DID clients, not only do parts communicate their presence by intruding thoughts, feelings, images, body tension and sensations—they also "speak" through actions outside the awareness of the normal life adult. Finding evidence of actions one does recall is unsettling and often humiliating for clients, yet it is important that the disturbing feelings not interfere with curiosity, creativity, and therapeutic detective work. Curiosity is cultivated when the therapist repeatedly asks, "If this pattern of finding yourself in the kitchen late at night, _____ were a communication from a part of you, what would that part be telling you?" "If what you find yourself eating told you something more about this part, what would that be?" The "decoding" of parts activity outside the normal life self's consciousness is an extremely important focus of DID treatment that should never be conducted judgmentally, without empathy for the parts in question. And it helps the client become familiar with his or her own system—as important as meeting one's family for the first time.

Helping DID clients "unblend" from their parts also increases in importance when those parts have the ability to take over the body and take action independently outside of consciousness. The depressed, hopeless part is at risk to sacrifice her- or himself for others she perceives as more deserving despite the normal life self's determination to have healthy boundaries. The anxious part might inadvertently sabotage the client's first day at his or her new job by asking too many self-doubting questions. When those parts blend with the client's normal life self, it is crucial that the client not identify *with* them but instead differentiate them as child selves worried about "their" ability to cope with the demands of adult life or driven by triggered memories of being young, inadequate to grownup tasks, and in mortal danger.

> In therapy, Annie learned to language these phenomena in ways that helped her be more aware of how the parts affected her feelings, perspective, and abilities moment by moment. Initially, she and I worked

simply on reframing distressing feelings as communications from parts and trying to respond to them with reassurance that they were safe now. But her parts interpreted blanket reassurances as if they were the manipulative words of childhood perpetrators: they didn't trust words of comfort. Only when she validated why they were so distressed by acknowledging their traumatic experiences did they seem to relax a little bit as if to say, "If you really know what I'm afraid of and why I'm afraid of it, *then* I can believe you when you tell me I'm safe now." I reminded her, "You wouldn't have trusted what *I* said if you hadn't felt I understood, would you? Would the kids you've helped all these years have trusted you if you didn't 'get' what they were struggling with?"

At first, Annie's normal life self was resistant to even indirectly referencing the experiences of her childhood: "I don't want to remember all the terrible things that happened—I don't want to see those images and feel those feelings."

ME: "It's not required that you remember the details of what happened. It is only necessary to demonstrate that you 'get it'—they just need to know you *know* what happened. Because if you know what happened, it becomes credible when you say, 'I won't let that happen again—not in my world.' They really need help to see what's different about your world versus the world they still are stuck in. What shall we call their world? Where did you live growing up?"

ANNIE: "I grew up in New Jersey—they're afraid of *those* New Jersey people, of my mother and my father and Father O'Malley." [All of these individuals were deceased, but since their fears were implicit memories of the past, the parts were indifferent or resistant to thinking of them as dead.]

ME: "OK, that's wonderful that they can be so clear: they don't want to be in New Jersey, and they definitely don't want to be afraid of getting killed every day! Or scared of being abandoned or assaulted or used in some way. Of course, they don't—who would? And what shall we call where you live now? What shall we call the world you deliberately created as an adult?"

ANNIE: "Let's call my world 'Maine' because it's where I live, where my house and family are. It's a whole different culture in Maine—I made sure of that."

Creating a Present for Parts that Dwell in the Past

This example illustrates another related challenge facing DID clients and their therapists: the loss of time orientation, the confusion of past and present. With traumatized parts that are driven by animal defense survival responses, dissociatively disconnected from one another, and hypervigilantly alert for signs of the dangers each faced "then," it is not surprising that time orientation becomes distorted. The client might be engaging in the simplest of normal life tasks (getting out of bed in the morning, helping children get ready for school, washing the dishes, making a meal, driving a car) when that activity suddenly becomes triggering: driving activates implicit memories of being taken somewhere dangerous; washing dishes or cooking a meal triggers the shame and loneliness connected to being a Cinderella child, treated like a slave or expected to be the family drudge. In one moment, the body tenses in response to those triggering activities: the heart rate increases, legs begin to shake; stomach knots up; and shame washes over the client. Without a visual image to orient us to where we are in time and space, most individuals and most parts assume that something or someone just "made" them feel that way: right now, they must be in danger—about to be humiliated at best, killed at worst.

> For years, Annie woke up each morning to a feeling of dread, sick to her stomach as she faced another day. As she began her biological children's morning routine, the dread was replaced by intense anxiety. As she made their school lunches, the shaking and fear would intensify, so much so that she could barely make their sandwiches. She made meaning of the feelings in the same way she had as a child: "I'm going to fail again today—I still won't amount to anything— no one will want to be my friend—they'll think something is wrong with me." It was an automatic assumption that still operated as a "default setting." Without acknowledging where it came from, the belief felt just as true now as it had when she was a child: because she was a failure, something bad was going to happen.
>
> I asked her: "What was scary about going to school as a kid?" Immediately, Annie knew: "Because my father could get at us—the principal was his buddy who ignored the restraining order—he could just take us out of school and do what he wanted as long as we were back by the end of the school day."
>
> ME: "Can you see why the parts are afraid in the morning? Why it's scary to make 'school' lunches?"
> ANNIE: "Yes! And I had to make our school lunches every morning— I wanted to throw up!"

Most clients "get it" when therapists remind them to think, "Why might that have been frightening about that _____ when you were young?" or "What was special about that kind of situation or that time of day/day of the week/month/ year when you were young?" Note that these questions do not require a detailed narrative of past events for an answer: they promote awareness of the links between past and present by acknowledging what happened. Validating the feeling and body memories as normal responses to trauma ("Of course, that's scary,"

"Of course, that's extremely triggering!") is reassuring for clients, and few need "proof" to believe that they are triggered and their bodies are remembering.

Because of the denser dissociative barriers within, it is more challenging for DID clients to learn to recognize the shifts in mood, belief, and behavior that occur under the influence of their parts. It is challenging for them to accept that, unless they exhibit curiosity and interest in their inner worlds, a willingness to care about and care for their parts, they may be susceptible to "hijacking." "Hijacking" is a term developed by Pat Ogden (Ogden et al., 2006) to describe what happens when traumatized clients are exposed to triggers: the body mobilizes an emergency stress response, which "turns on" the sympathetic nervous system, stimulating a release of adrenaline and inhibition of the prefrontal cortex. As the parts are activated by the trigger, they can also stimulate the emergency stress response and animal defense responses. With the prefrontal cortex inhibited, the normal life self loses conscious awareness of the parts' actions and reactions, much less the ability to control or manage their behavior. When the normal life self loses all ability to keep normal life functioning intact, it is a clear sign that the client has been hijacked by parts. By reframing "I'm having a nervous breakdown" or "I'm falling apart" as "No, what you are feeling reflects the fact that your parts have staged a 'coup d'etat' and taken over," the therapist externalizes the crisis and empowers the normal life self. Most clients respond: "Well, I want my life back!" Especially with clients who are intimidated by their parts or ashamed of "how far I've fallen," it is important to evoke the drive to reclaim one's life, to take it back. I ask them: "Do you want a life determined by your parts and the trauma? Or do you want a life after trauma? A life you get to choose?"

Overcoming Conditioned Learning

Implicit reactions to triggers reflect conditioned or procedural learning to experiences that subjectively feel life-threatening. As a colleague once reminded me, "Trauma is the only single-incident conditioner of human behavior we know. Even one experience leaves indelible traces." These conditioned responses are very challenging to shift or alter. It is as if the body and nervous system are loathe to "give up" the automatic responses that ensured safety for another day. In addition, as a result of chronic dysregulation, made worse by repeated shutting down of the prefrontal cortex, the majority of trauma clients have difficulty retaining new information. They find it difficult to remember and utilize the same steps or skills that brought relief yesterday without being reminded or cued by others. It is as if the repeated inhibition of left brain activity makes encoding and retrieval of new information more difficult and also more unstable.

To add to their challenges, DID clients often have "eraser" parts, "thought-stopping" parts, or "information extractor" parts that actively interfere with encoding of new present-day-oriented information. It feels dangerous to trust it. In the dangerous world of their implicit memories, the parts fear that changing assumptions associated with survival will be foolhardy at best. In order to reduce fear and increase retention, DID clients need help practicing their observational and unblending skills in therapy. They benefit from and rarely complain about repetitive instructions to notice feelings and thoughts, make the assumption that the feeling belongs to a part, evoke curiosity about the part, name the feeling or thought as "his" or "her" thought/feeling, and increase dual awareness. And, if the parts take over control of the body, causing time loss and dissociative fugues, the therapist and client must also repetitively practice curiosity, asking over and over again: which part might have been triggered by what stimulus? And which part impulsively took the troubling action?

Continuous Consciousness: Knowing "Who I Am" Moment by Moment

Although more clearly fragmented and less in control of their responses, DID clients still present in one body with a narrative that is usually preceded by the word, "I." It is easier and more comfortable for any therapist to conceptualize this new kind of client in the same way that other clients are understood: as a "she" or a "he," rather than as "they." But for DID clients to stabilize and recover requires that both client and therapist stay focused on the ultimate goal of dissociative disorders treatment: the ability to have "continuous consciousness" with fewer breaks in time orientation, fewer instances of parts operating behind the backs of both therapist and client. Continuous consciousness can only be developed through repetition of new practices: focused concentration, awareness of being present in the body or "right here, right now," and habits of inner communication with parts so that information can be shared even if in fragmented pieces contributed by different parts.

Once DID clients have greater access to "continuous consciousness," when their parts are less activated and more willing to collaborate, they can stabilize. They can learn to know "who" they are moment to moment and make increasingly sound life decisions that are sensitive to their parts' feelings, likes, and dislikes but not constricted by post-traumatic paranoia. With increased ability for internal dialogue, it also becomes possible to bring switching under voluntary control. With the ability for inner communication, the normal life self can negotiate with parts who switch at problematic times to "let me do that job—that's not a job for kids." When dissociation is involuntary and unconscious, traumatic triggers determine "who" is out or, as I say to my clients, "who is driving the bus." Then I add: "Unless you want your life run by a 7-year-old or a 16-year-old, you might rather drive the bus yourself."

Dissociation as a Resource

As dual awareness and inner communication allow for internal trust and understanding to grow, involuntary switching tends to decrease or come under better control. Once DID clients realize that they have the ability to inhibit parts from switching, they understand that they can also choose to switch to summon "the right part for the right job." When DID clients begin to experience dissociative compartmentalization as a potential asset, not just a liability, the client's confidence grows. When the prospect of giving the toast at a best friend's wedding triggers terror among the parts, for example, the normal life self might ask inside: "Who would be willing to give the toast?" And a part unafraid of public speaking can be asked to take over that function. Often there is a feeling of triumph when the client and parts together feel the confidence of the "public speaking part" as he stands up in front of the group, poised and articulate, able to evoke a laugh. The normal life self might learn to enlist the fight part to support her in setting boundaries with others in the client's life who intentionally or unconsciously take advantage of her inability to say no. Sometimes, these "victories" trigger other parts: an ashamed part who feels undeserving: "I have no right to set boundaries." Or parts who are afraid to be seen and feel exposed by the public displays of mastery and confidence. With repeated experiences of mastery the conscious use of dissociation enables, the parts can feel something is different. At these points, it is very important for the therapist to remember that opaque dissociative boundaries between parts interfere with taking in new information: the normal life self must always be asked to "show the parts what happened just now. You promised them that you could say No, and nothing bad would happen. Ask them to notice: did they see you setting the boundary?? And is there anything bad happening now?"

Building Trust Inside

Trust begins to build with increased internal communication and experiences of mastery and competence. All their lives, the young parts have longed for someone who would hear, believe, and protect them—someone strong enough to keep the "bad people" away. The teenage parts have been waiting for someone strong enough to protect not only the younger parts but the adolescents, too. As the younger parts develop confidence in the normal life self, fight and flight's hypervigilance can relax a bit; their muscular tension loosens; they can "sit back" more easily. As the parts build increasing trust in an older and wiser grownup self, they can more easily believe the normal life part's reassurances and perspective. "It's not an emergency—nothing bad is happening" feels like reliable information, not a manipulative ploy. Healing their attachment wounds requires "basic trust" in a normal life self that is more palpable, who doesn't disappear each time the going gets tough, facilitating the ability of older parts to threaten the little ones. Trust is a prerequisite to being able to offer reparative experiences to young parts that transform or resolve their implicit and explicit memories and that offer them a felt sense of safety and welcome.

To feel safely welcomed, however, child parts have to experience the palpable sense of "who" is welcoming them. The parts have to be able to feel emotionally and physically that there really is an "other" who smiles at their entrance, who is glad to see them, who is tender where the child is wounded, and unafraid when he or she is angry and hostile.

> When Annie thought about the parts' world as "New Jersey," it reminded her why they were so hypervigilant and easily alarmed but without triggering the flashbacks she tried so hard always to avoid. She could more easily see, at first with my help, how they projected their New Jersey experience onto her environment in Maine. When the parts were in distress, she worked on remembering to ask herself, "Why would they have been worried about this in New Jersey? Why would it have been dangerous there?" As she did so, she discovered all kinds of connections her parts were making between her old world and the safe environment she had created for herself after fleeing New Jersey at the age of 19. Ironically, although she had created a life that soon became a refuge of safety for friends and family, she and her parts did not feel safe in it—because she was so often blended and identified with them. Sometimes she blended with their hopelessness and shame, sometimes with their fears and longing, and sometimes with their distrust.

Even more troubling were the parts that operated in secrecy, "behind her back." Following her curiosity about why she seemed unable to remember her therapy sessions almost as soon as she left my office, she heard other parts talking about the "eraser part." Then images and more internal conversation with the parts revealed the presence of a part who erased the blackboard of memory immediately when ever Annie had positive or empowering experiences so that she never remembered them again. It also erased information: her diagnosis of DID, the fact of her trauma history, her repertoire of skills, and her resources. She would learn a skill, only to find it had disappeared, and then relearn it again. Asking inside, she inquired, "What is the eraser part worried about if she lets what we talked about today stay up on the blackboard?" "It's different," said the eraser part. "And what are you worried about if the information is different or new?" "We know we can survive this way—but we don't know if we can survive this new way … It might not be safe." "Thank you for telling me," Annie responded. "All this time, I thought I was getting dementia, and it was just you trying to protect everyone!" From that day on, Annie and I tried to remember to contact the eraser part at the end of each session to ask: "Would you be willing to leave what we talked about today up on the blackboard? Do you have any concerns about it that we should know about?" And then Annie would ask the part, "What do you need from me—right here, right now—to feel safe leaving this information up?" We also developed some techniques for ensuring she could revisit ideas, skills, or insights that felt important: I might write on an index card a list of all the things she reported wanting to remember so she could take it with her. (I knew her attach parts wouldn't let it get thrown out!) Or I might ask her to send me an email after the session sharing what she wanted to take away from it. Or at times, I asked her to journal about the day's session or about particular parts and what they needed or what triggered them. I sometimes sent her emails summarizing what I had learned and thought might be useful to her. Earlier in the therapy, she and I used to wonder why those kinds of emails always disappeared from her email box! Then, at a session, I suggested to Annie, "Ask the eraser part if she would be willing to do two jobs?" "She says 'maybe, depending on the job.'" Annie reported.

> ME: "Tell the eraser part that we appreciate her working with us so nothing valuable gets erased. But her first job is still to erase anything 'bad.' (Maybe she could help erase some of the hurtful beliefs the little parts have about themselves.) But we also need someone who can help you [normal life self] save important information and store it in a safe place. That's hard for you to do when you're being overwhelmed by so many voices and so many feelings. So often, important moments and empowering experiences have gotten erased that might have been saved if we'd had her help."

In DID clients, the autonomous functioning of the parts causes problems with reality-testing, relationships, safety, and judgment, and the crises that result generally become the focus of therapy. The lack of conscious awareness of the parts' feelings, thoughts, bodily responses, and actions interferes with opportunities to get to know them in the way discussed in Chapters 4 and 5. With less severe compartmentalization, we can "know" a part by its feelings ("so sad"), its wishes ("it just wants someone to care"), its beliefs ("it's not safe to be alone"), and its body language and facial expression (a sad face, a child's shy body language). In a DID client, the manifestations of that part might be felt when the "client" has trouble leaving the office at the end of sessions or texts and calls repeatedly between sessions.

> When she was not blended with them and instead was consciously centered in her normal life self, she could perceive the differences between her perspective and that of the parts; she could feel the safe reality of her current life in her body—her heart rate slowed; her breathing was easier; she felt solid but not tense. It was a good feeling, even though the parts had always urged her not to trust it and for many years, she had accepted their reality: she believed their projection that she lived in a dirty, depressing, impoverished home with people who used and abused her and never tried to meet her needs. For many months, she and I worked on "orienting" (Ogden & Fisher, 2015) the parts: first asking them to show her images of "where" they were scared or paralyzed with dread or ashamed and humiliated. (Always, images of New Jersey would come to mind.) Then Annie would ask, "Would you like to see where I live?" and then she would bring up images of her home and

neighborhood now: an image of the fenced-in yard, the back door she had painted red, her flower garden, the river where she loved to swim and canoe in the summer. As the images associated with the traumatic past arose, she could feel the activation in her body, the shaking and trembling, tightening in her stomach, and feelings of wanting to run. As she oriented the parts to the details of her present environment (Ogden & Fisher, 2016), she could feel her autonomic arousal settle, the trembling lessen, and curiosity increase. As she repeatedly reoriented "them," she was less blended and better able to see her present objectively. By helping the parts to see where *they* were, she could finally appreciate where she was. Annie could now see the old rambling farmhouse in which she and her husband have lived for years as "quaint," instead of a "slum." Always in need of one repair or another because of its age, the parts had viewed the house as a blatant symbol of their neglect and lesser worth, like the torn and dirty clothes she wore to school as a child. Annie could now recognize its contents, the antiques and "found" objects she and her husband had refinished, as reflecting something about the person she became in the life she had created beyond trauma. She could even see the personal touches that reflected who she is as a person: a bright red back door to welcome her extended family of choice, a kitchen that is the center and heart of their home, colors and decorative touches that reflect her aesthetic sense. "I never knew this before," she said as she showed her parts images of "then" and "now": "Right here, I have what I always wanted—what I always dreamed of as a child ..., but I didn't know I had it." As long as the parts dominated her perceptions, she could not correctly identify what was before her very eyes—nor could they. Until Annie deliberately and consciously drew their attention to the details of the environment, the parts could not perceive, much less integrate, that they were no longer in New Jersey.

Annie is an example of how dissociative compartmentalization interferes with information flow even within one life and one body: while Annie's normal life part was creating a home with her husband, raising their children, and offering a safe haven for family members in distress, her parts believed that she was trapped in a hell-hole with a coercively controlling man forcing her every move. Their perceptions, biased by expectations of danger and chronically activated survival defenses, saw only what they expected to see: the same environment in which Annie had been raised.

Gathering Evidence: Establishing Retrospective Consciousness

Because a diagnosis of DID implies a loss of memory for personal information (especially for information about the autonomous activity of self-destructive parts), clients must learn to "fill in the blanks," to consciously gather evidence of what their bodies may have done outside of their awareness even if it is retrospective. Gazzaniga (1985) writes about the propensity as observed in "split brain" patients whose right and left hemispheres have been surgically separated by removal of the corpus callosum: the right brain might take action on impulse for which the left hemisphere would have no memory, but nonetheless, the left brain would construct a narrative to provide a rationale for the missing time or consequences of the action. The researchers were struck by the left brain's persistence in establishing a motive and meaning-making even when disconnected from the right hemisphere's actions and reactions.

A related challenge for clients with DID is the problem of what to do when parts are engaging in self-destructive or self-sabotaging behavior outside the awareness of the left brain normal life self. Gazzaniga (1985; 2015) emphasizes that the left brain's ability to use language to rationalize the actions of the right brain increases the chances of the behavior happening again, a potential risk to life in DID clients. Therapists working with such clients must be unafraid to ask directly, "Do you remember the details of what happened? Or just the outcome?" It is important for the treatment to distinguish: was the normal life self blended with the part that acted out last night? Or did the acting out part hijack the body and act outside of consciousness? If the answer is, "I guess I was blended with the suicidal part," therapist and client can begin to work on recognizing when the client is blended and practicing unblending strategies. If the part acts outside of left brain consciousness, then the work will have to focus on internal communication and increased ability to negotiate with the acting out part.

Therapists can also help their DID clients reconstruct what occurred either through diagramming (see Chapter 5) or by asking them to go "back in time" imaginatively to just before the crisis, identify the trigger, then move forward, frame by frame, with the therapist asking, "And what happened next?" Often, clients find gaps in the "video" for which they have no memory of what was happening. Then, the therapist's task is to remind them to ask inside, "Does anyone know what happened after that?" Being able to use internal communication to establish what triggered the parts, which ones responded and how, and why fight or flight parts "came to the rescue" is essential for establishing safety.

Building Skills to Overcome Gaps in Consciousness

Underlying the instability in the client's life is the capacity of each part for independent action and the lack of shared consciousness and memory. Without meta-awareness, without an observer keeping track of moment to moment experience, it is no wonder that trauma-related parts can inadvertently and unconsciously sabotage the client's normal life, believing that they are just trying to save their lives. Early in treatment, it is important to begin building the skills that clients will need to develop a continuous, unbroken consciousness for their daily experience. To restate Chapter 2, there is no focus at the stabilization phase of treatment on the client's consciousness of traumatic memory. The focus is on "now": the losses of conscious awareness in the past served the client's survival; the losses of consciousness now are destabilizing and sometimes unsafe.

> Gaby provides a good example: as she began to stabilize her life after years of drug addiction and high-risk behavior, she initially felt proud and energized. It felt like a vindication of what she had been through, not only in the childhood past but as an adult trying to survive after trauma. She was going to graduate school, in a stable relationship, shared a home with her partner, and even had just gotten a part-time job. It was then that she started to feel increasingly depressed. Many days, she could not get out of bed, missing classes and falling behind on her schoolwork. When she began to skip work, her partner became frustrated and critical: "Don't you know how much we need that income?" As she retreated under the covers in her bed (as she had as a child), memories began coming up: memories of the losses, the abuse, the loneliness, and the pain of having no one to care or comfort her. After several months of hopelessness and despair, Gaby's partner came home from work one day to find her unconscious. She had taken an overdose. Without having had a moment of conscious thought about suicide, Gaby had overdosed. Unbeknownst to her, the suicidal part had acted to end the suffering of the depressed part. She, of course, was too blended to even consider that her depression might belong to a part of her threatened by Gaby's successful going on with her life. Afraid of being left behind, the depressed part had come forward to let her know how badly she needed help.

Gaby's experience underscores the importance of building skills that increase conscious awareness across time. Had she been aware in advance of the suicidal part's intentions, her normal life self would have sought help. The first skill I teach clients with DID is to keep track of their daily activities by recording what they are doing or whatever is happening every hour on the hour on an hourly time schedule. If they encounter a gap in time (e.g., "I looked at the clock at 2 when I came back to work after lunch, and then the next thing I knew, it was 5 and the end of the day"), they are asked to look for clues to fill in the blanks. (For example, "I looked around to see what I had done from 2 to 5pm, and I could see I returned several emails, wrote a letter for my boss, and finished a report due tomorrow.") Simply the instruction to concentrate on what they are doing throughout the day and record it often by itself decreases the likelihood of switching. Clients learn a great deal from this assignment. They are often surprised how much focused concentration on tracking their activities helps to challenge automatic habits of switching or spacing out. Sometimes they are surprised by the activities they see written on the schedule: "I didn't think I spent that much time in bed …"

Another skill I often assign to DID clients who report missing time or frequent switching is learning to notice "who you are" moment by moment. In sessions, they are asked to observe the signs of blending with different parts, to notice the words, themes, emotions, and beliefs they verbalize, and to be curious about "which part is talking," "What part believes that?" or "What part is nervous that I won't like her?" As discussed in earlier chapters, a sentence preceded by the word "I" does not signify that the normal life is speaking or that all the parts feel exactly the same way. To know "who" is talking or feeling an emotion or believing a thought requires curiosity and at least brief exposure to the structural dissociation model to help foster the ability to recognize different parts. With clients who have issues with missing time or hijacking by parts, practicing this skill for one or two hours a week in psychotherapy is not nearly enough, especially when unsafe behavior is an issue. To reduce the memory and time gaps and to increase awareness of blending and switching, I often ask clients to purchase an inexpensive watch with an alarm function that can be set to automatically go off each hour. Each time the alarm rings, the client is instructed to pause and notice "who I am" or "who's here?" To make the task more structured, I often provide clients with a Dissociative Experiences Log to record what they observe. (See Appendix E.) When dissociative fugues occur during the night (i.e., the client discovers evidence that some part engaged in unsafe or unwanted behavior while he or she "slept"), the normal life self can be taught to set the car's trip odometers at the end of each day and then check in the morning to see if there has been any travel without his or her knowledge.

Some DID clients with parts that hold specialized abilities valuable for functioning can recruit a scheduling part to keep track of whatever they and other parts do in the course of the day or night. Or, when there is evidence that some activity must have occurred outside conscious awareness, clients can learn to ask inside, "Does anyone know why _____ happened? Who is responsible?" They are also taught to add, "And how was that part trying to help?"

No More "Bad Guys" and "Good Guys"

By framing the dialogue around the expectation that each part is motivated by the instinct to protect and help, the client and therapist communicate that no one will be blamed or penalized for having tried to "help" in his or her own way. Such language communicates, too, that this is a different environment and a different kind of grownup, one that is not punitive or shaming but instead wants to help all parts to feel safer and better appreciated. If the goal is to increase communication and develop trusting relationships, there can be no "bad guys." Parts can be asked to be sensitive or thoughtful of one another, but even parts that harm the body cannot be vilified. When parts are labeled as dangerous or abusive, no one can feel safe. If self-injuring parts are understood as trying to help bring relief to parts with overwhelming emotions or trying to numb the body or trying to teach everyone to "toughen up," they are framed as having inherently good intentions. If there is no judgment of their behavior or attempt to suppress or marginalize them, they and other parts are likely to share more and allow more to be shared. Most importantly, when treated as inherently collaborative in nature, the chances of their learning to become collaborators increases. For that reason, I am very adamant that there is no such entity as an "internalized perpetrator." Clients cannot "internalize" their abusers, though it might feel as if they have. The parts who can sound and act just like the perpetrator are reframed as protector or fight parts that "learned their ways" by modeling the perpetrator but whose intentions are always to protect the client and/or the little parts.

Coaching a Team

The need for collaboration and community is exponentially more important for DID clients than other structurally dissociated clients because there is no other way to create lasting safety and stability. With autonomous, disconnected parts that may not know each other, even the normal life part cannot enforce new rules—because he or she may not be present when they are broken. The therapist often needs to take on the role of a coach with a nearly impossible task: helping a chaotic conflicted "team" of individual parts, all unknowingly reacting to triggers of past experiences rather than to present moment threats. Each is perceptually biased by the legacy of traumatic experiences. Each is instinctively prepared to act according to automatic impulses and underlying animal defense. None of them is accustomed to collaboration, and none has had a coach before. Some parts will see the therapist not as a coach but as a godlike rescuer or protector; some will assume the therapist has nefarious ulterior motives; and only the normal life self or selves will be able to accurately understand the therapist's role, motivations, and even interventions. Because the normal life self can be more autonomous in DID clients and has greater access to prefrontal processing and learning, therapeutic "work" can most effectively be done when the normal life part is present in session. The therapist must create a therapeutic alliance based on here-and-now goals: teaching the going on with normal life part self-regulation skills, skill-building, offering psychoeducation that increases the client's ability to work with the system, to unblend, and to soothe or regulate vulnerable parts before their intense emotions drive fight and flight parts to act impulsively. Often, in the treatment of DID clients, the therapist is faced with what I call the "revolving door" of parts: he or she does not have one client who can be counted upon to predictably appear for the appointment. Many "clients" come, each of which has their own agenda: to elicit help and protection (attach), to please (submit), to fight for control (fight), to keep a safe distance or not come at all (flight), and to remain invisible (freeze). To prevent chaos in the therapy mirroring the chaos in the client's life, the therapist needs to balance welcoming whichever parts appear in the therapy hour with the therapeutic goal of empowering the normal life self and increasing his or her ability to form trusting relationships with the parts and eventually to help them become a team. Since one of the core issues in DID is hijacking by parts who act outside the normal life part's consciousness, the therapist must attempt to discourage the "revolving door" approach to therapy. There are several ways of accomplishing this goal without empathically failing the parts:

- Despite the absence of the normal life part during some or all of a session, the therapist can reference the client's adult self in conversations with each part: "Do you know Felicia? Oh, you'd like her! She's smart and funny, and she likes kids." "How can you say you don't trust Felicia if you don't talk to her? That doesn't make sense—you two have to get to know each other." "Does Felicia know how scared you are at night?"
- The therapist can insist on the normal life self or "wise resourceful adult self" being present in the therapy hour: "I really think Felicia should know how lonely and scared you feel," "It's really important for Felicia to know you're offering to kill the body to make the pain go away—maybe she could help the little parts with their pain so you wouldn't have to use your 'bail-out plan.' She would at least want to thank you for offering such a big thing." When parts resist, I emphasize that I myself need to talk to the normal life self because I want *their* concerns to be addressed: "How is she going to change this situation if she doesn't know it's a problem for you?"
- Creating a structure for each session that balances the needs of the parts with those of the normal life self: for example, the parts can be assigned the first 10 minutes of the session, the middle 20 minutes, or the last 15 minutes. (I prefer to have the younger parts present earlier in the session so the normal life self and I can work during the latter half.) The key is that the structure or norms for therapy are not couched in authoritarian terms: they are framed as concerns about the parts. "I know you want to tell me everything that's bothering you, but I also need time to talk to Felicia about how to help you with those things." Or, "I need time to teach Felicia how to help you." Notice that only the normal life self is acknowledged by using the given name of the client or the word "you."

Because the dissociative barriers are more impermeable in DID clients, it is even easier for clients to disown some parts and over-identify with others. It is also easier for parts to be unaware of each other, hypervigilantly aware, or even to disown other parts that threaten them.

Increasing the Presence of a Normal Life Adult

It can be particularly challenging for DID clients to believe they have a normal life self, much less to feel connected to its strengths and competencies. The parts may remember a normal life child equally powerless to protect herself whose role was foreign to them. While they prepared to fight, flee, freeze, submit, or cry for help, the normal life child kept moving forward along a normal developmental path, more focused on the multiplication tables or playing baseball or taking care of younger siblings. If the client has been more identified with younger parts (e.g., the attach part's loneliness and distress, the submit part's shame and depression), it may feel ego-dystonic to think of the normal life self as "me." Many clients have become so accustomed to feeling overwhelmed, shaky, crazy, or defective (the outcome of being blended with or hijacked by their parts) that any positive qualities or skills they possess have been thrown into doubt. It would be challenging for any human being to hold on to feelings of being normal or successful or competent when one is flooded with panic, shame, despair, rageful feelings, and impulses to harm—all at the same time. It would be difficult for anyone to maintain accurate self-esteem with judgmental parts communicating day after day that one is stupid, worthless, disgusting, or undeserving. Often, the therapist, too, is hard-pressed to remember that the client cannot lack a normal life part as long as he or she has an intact prefrontal cortex, areas of daily functioning, or even the wish or vision for a normal life. The example of Cecilia illustrates how therapists can work to strengthen the capacity of the normal life even when competency and executive functioning are limited:

> Cecilia had never experienced "normal life." From the day of her birth, to two drug-addicted parents, there was nothing safe or normal in her life experience. She was in foster care by age 5, identified as "disturbed" by her teachers by the 3rd grade; and, by the age of 12, she had her first hospitalization. She had rarely been out of residential environments since. But as her therapist explained the structural dissociation model, she had a flash of excited recognition. "I do have a going on with normal life part! That's the part of me that's always wanted to have a normal family, to live in a home instead of a hospital—that's the part that wants to go to college! I remember that part from my first foster home—that's the part that kept telling me that someday I wouldn't have to live under the thumb of crazy people— I could make my own life if I could just live long enough." Inspired by feeling emotionally connected to her desire to be whole and healthy and have a normal life, Cecilia immediately knew she wanted to help her trauma-related parts learn to feel safer and stable. She felt a physical determination and drive she had never consciously felt before. For the first time that she could recall, she asked her therapist, "What do I have to do to have a normal life?"

The therapist's job is to hold the belief that human beings have an instinct to "keep on going," to keep the home fires burning, even to self-actualize—even if it is hard to believe or hard to convince the client to believe. Cecilia's treaters were understandably skeptical when she presented them with her question: they were aware that, before she could live a normal life, she would have to resolve her eating disorder, refrain from self-injury and suicidal threat, and get "clean and sober." As the supervising therapist, I was confident. "Tell her that her first task is to begin noticing each part separately and naming them according to what they do or feel, like 'the shame part,' the 'sad part,' 'the little girl part,' 'the suicidal part.' She can use the structural dissociation model diagram to remind her of what kinds of parts to look for."

Even in the face of the client's adamancy that there is no adult self or normal life part, the therapist must remain a believer. As long as the client's prefrontal cortex is intact, he or she is capable of curiosity, mindful awareness, compassion, creativity, confidence, courage, and commitment (Schwartz, 2001). If there is normal functioning in any arena of the client's life, some aspect of self must be responsible for it. Which part of the client takes the car to be serviced? Who takes care of the children? Who goes to parent-teacher conferences at school? Who walks the dog? Who pays the bills? Can he remember even one time when he had patience? Or one time she was curious or creative? Or one time she extended compassion to another human being? Or were sought out by others for support or advice?

> Maggie suffered painful bouts of self-doubt, shame, and aloneness re-
> lated to the belief, "I don't belong." The feeling memory of a frighten-
> ing childhood in a family that made her feel as if she wasn't wanted
> pervaded her consciousness, interfering with incoming data that might
> have told her parts that, in her adult world, she was welcomed warmly.
> I asked her if she would be willing to do some research as a homework
> project for the following week: would she be willing to look for any and all
> evidence that might maybe, possibly mean that she did belong? And as
> an addendum: would she be willing not to critique her list or to question
> the evidence she found? She came back for her next appointment with a
> list and lots of questions: "Does having friends and family calling you up
> to ask for advice count as 'belonging'?" she asked. "Absolutely!" I said.
> "How about being asked to represent your school at a teachers' confer-
> ence?" "Wow! That would be evidence of belonging *and* being seen as
> valuable," I clarified. "And how about being asked to become a deacon in
> my church? I guess that counts, too. How could they ask me to take such
> an important role if they didn't think I belonged?" "So, Maggie, we've
> learned something important," I said. "You now have hard evidence that
> you do belong here—in the world you made for yourself and the life in
> which you *choose* to participate—now it's a question of conveying that
> to the parts: pointing out to them each and every time one of these mo-
> ments occurs that you do belong. Could you bring their attention to the
> moment you see the evidence and share it with them? Otherwise, they
> will continue to feel that painful sense of being on the outside, looking in."

Bringing Parts Up-to-Date: The "Trickle-Down Effect"

When amnestic barriers around dissociated self-states prevent communication from part to part, information about current life experience cannot

be integrated. The attach part feels a longing to be important to friends, spouse, or children, causing the normal life part to prioritize relationships in her life that evoke feelings of being cared about. But the news that there are now caring people in the client's life never reaches the attach part, much less the fight and flight parts or the depressed submit part. The attach part still feels little and vulnerable to abandonment, never having gotten the news that she is part of a body that is now 43, not 5 years old. The normal life part may not be aware that the suicidal fight part, triggered by the submit part's shame, is planning to take an overdose. Other parts feel nervous, sensing that something bad is about to happen but unaware of what exactly will unfold. The normal life plans a summer vacation and makes reservations, unbeknownst to the suicidal part. Had the suicidal part known the depression was a memory, not evidence of all hope lost, the suicidal impulses might have subsided. As one client put it, "So much in my life has changed, but obviously there has been no trickle-down effect—the news hasn't yet reached the parts."

Annie provides us with an example of how to help clients work on "the trickle-down effect," on techniques that can help provide information about present time to parts lost in the traumatic past.

Annie found herself wandering around her backyard with blood oozing from a cut on her leg after "coming to" after dark one night. The last thing she recalled was an afternoon conversation with her therapist about the latter's upcoming vacation/absence. As they talked, she had felt a rush of anxiety; her back tightened up; and she felt a sense of dread. "How are the parts feeling about this?" I asked. "They're scared," Annie said. "If you're around, they feel there's some protection against danger—if you're not here, anyone could hurt them." "Annie, where do they think they are? Ask them to show you a picture of where they are right now."

ANNIE: "A picture of my childhood home comes up."
ME: "That makes sense. They're afraid the bad people will hurt them again. Who would I have been back in New Jersey in those days? What would my absence have meant to them?"
ANNIE: "They think you're Wonder Woman—or some combination of the school guidance counselor who kept asking me if I was OK and Wonder Woman."
ME: "So, in their eyes, I'm the person with the power to rescue them if the bad guys come for them? Didn't anyone ever tell them that **you** rescued them a long, long time ago? Don't tell me no one has ever brought them up to date! Annie, you never told them?! All this time, they've been safe, but no one told them!" [I deliberately speak with a slightly horrified tone, as if appalled by this oversight.]

ANNIE: "That's right—but I never told the parts because I didn't know they were there."

ME: "Annie, it's so important to tell them now. Could I talk to them? Maybe they'll believe me. Could you ask if everyone can hear me? [Pauses while Annie attunes inside to make sure all parts are listening.] There is something very, very, very important that I think you all should know—some good news! Great news! A long, long time ago, almost 20 years ago, Annie left that scary house in New Jersey where so many bad things happened and went far, far away to Maine, so far away that your mother was really mad and told her she could never come back to that house! Does anyone remember when your mother did that?" [Waits for parts to respond to the question and gets a nod. She goes on.]

"Once she was far away from New Jersey, Annie realized that the bad people who hurt all of you couldn't do that anymore if they didn't know where you were, so she decided not to tell anyone where she was. It was a secret to protect you and her, and it's never been broken. The bad people have never known where you all are, and now they are all too old to hurt you as long as Annie is here—she has a tall strong body now, much taller and stronger than they have. Annie, what's it like for the parts to hear me give them this news?"

ANNIE: "There's a kind of stunned silence inside—they're taking it in … It's hard to believe, but they want to."

ME: "Show them a picture of your home today. Explain that it's where you live. Ask them to look around each room very slowly and notice if your house is like New Jersey or different."

ANNIE: "Oh no, they think it's very different—it's clean and pretty and homey. Just what they always wanted … But the little ones want to know if they have to be alone in this house because they don't like being alone—it's scary."

ME: "Tell them who lives in this house and why you allow your husband, son, and Ethan to live there …"

Annie brings up images of her husband, son, and nephew and invites the parts to share their reactions: "They like the idea that there are strong men who want to protect me in this house …"

ME: "Of course they do! It's good to have strong men who want to protect you, who would fight for you—your sons would; your nephew Ethan would; your husband would."

ANNIE: "That's true—I have bodyguards!" Laughs delightedly. "Can you imagine? I have all these males around me who are over 6 feet tall who all depend on me. Imagine that?!"

ME: "Now, the challenge is going to be this: helping the parts take this news in. Each time they automatically react to your home and neighborhood as if they're still in New Jersey, ask them to pause, open their eyes, look around, and focus very carefully so they can see where they are. Ask them: is this New Jersey or Maine? How can you tell? Yes, the red door tells you you're in Maine—the white paint on the house, the smells of cooking coming from the kitchen, the quiet, the sound of laughter—that's not New Jersey. That has to be Maine." And each time Annie asked her parts to look around the room or around the house, she could feel a calming of her body as the parts recognized the signs of where they were now and breathed a sigh of relief.

Changing Patterns and Roles

Survival behavior, learned in the context of life threat, is often difficult to change: the body resists relaxing patterns of clenching, bracing, increases in heart rate and respiration, impulses to punch or kick or claw (Ogden et al., 2006). Lowering one's guard, softening tension, opening the heart can all feel threatening, thanks to the implicit memories connected to the threats of the past. As soon as the client's body relaxes, anxiety escalates. Without the ability to modify those automatic, instinctive threat responses, trauma survivors cannot feel safe, can't feel a sense that "it's over" (Ogden & Fisher, 2015; Ogden et al., 2006). These challenges are compounded when the client is dissociatively compartmentalized, especially when there are parts amnestic for each other's behavior and/or engaged in a life-or-death internal struggle. Even the most basic skills of trauma recovery are difficult to remember, much less utilize, under these circumstances. If we want to help clients with dissociative disorders, the best approach is to rely on:

- Increasing conscious mindful awareness of parts, as discussed in Chapter 4, and of the signs of triggering, switching, and blending.
- Psychoeducation.
- Helping clients learn to speak the "language of parts."
- Piecing together a continuous sense of consciousness, challenging the client to observe the emotional, cognitive, and action patterns connected to different parts.
- Emphasizing practice and repetition of new patterns or actions until they become familiar.
- Renegotiating internal relationships: using internal communication to develop greater trust and collaboration among the parts.

Typically, with a client presenting with multiple serious symptoms and issues, therapists often try to address the problems causing the highest risk first. In DID clients, that means addressing the amnesia, the internal conflicts, problems with self-regulation, and the attachment issues of the fight and attach parts that can fuel self-injurious behavior—all complex and multifaceted challenges that cannot be effectively met at first—not until the client has developed dual awareness, the ability to unblend, at least rudimentary inner communication skills, and a capacity to convey empathy to the parts. (See Chapters 4 and 5.)

To renegotiate the role of a fight part from that of suicide threat to one of stabilizing protector requires that the client learn to differentiate the suicidal part from the normal life self who "keeps on keeping on" in spite of everything, and then to unblend from the suicidal part, learn how to manage the conscious impulses of that part (as well as any pulls to switch), to communicate a respect for and a wish to build relationships with both the angry or suicidal part and the wounded child selves it protects, find ways of comforting and bonding with the attach parts to reduce their vulnerability to painful emotion, and then to build up the somatic sense of protection connected to the fight response (aligned energized spine, readiness for action, muscular strength, movement impulses to punch, push away or block in the arms and shoulders) (Ogden & Fisher, 2015).

The most sophisticated interventions depend for their success on the building blocks of DID treatment: awareness of shifts in emotion and sensation connected to parts, mindful naming of each part's function or attributes, unblending from parts' impulses and emotions, "befriending each part," developing interest in and compassion for them, learning through inner dialogue to decipher their intentions and motivations, allying with the "best self" of each part, and then negotiating new resolutions to old issues. Annie gives us an example of how much patience and repetition is necessary for DID clients to become proficient in these skills—and the way in which layers of parts defending other parts result in patterns of stuckness.

> Annie found that, even after what felt like years of practicing the basic skills of working with her parts, she kept encountering new road blocks: first, she discovered teenage parts who distrusted my every word or piece of advice, believing I would ultimately use or abuse them. Once they were reassured that, even if she listened to me, Annie was strong enough to hold her own opinion, no matter how much the young parts wanted to please me, the protectors relented and allowed her to keep growing. A year later, she encountered a part that fought to deny the trauma and abuse she had suffered, a part responsible for her "forgetting" that she had parts and therefore forgetting to unblend. Most recently, she identified the "eraser part," the part that deliberately caused amnesia for new ideas, skills, information, and especially for any positive change in her life, in order to protect her from changing the status quo that had allowed her to survive not only familial abuse but also ritual abuse. By erasing the memories of all positive change and even positive experiences, this

part reinforced the feelings of hopelessness, shame and guilt, avoidance of being seen, and a sense of isolation and not belonging—all
of which had kept the traumatic secrets "locked down" for so many
years that Annie only learned what had happened to her in her 30s.

In DID, amnestic barriers between parts interfere with the client's ability
to know his or her own inner world and the parts that make it up, creating
ripe opportunities for guerilla warfare or sabotage by parts of whom even the
normal life is often unaware. In addition, the amnesia helps ensure that the
trauma-related parts are equally unaware of the safety, stability, and comfort
of the normal life part's consciously constructed adult life.

Working with Regression and Aggression

Two of the strongest drives in any human being are the attachment drive
and the fight response. Both are crucial to survival. Proximity-seeking as an
attachment drive and its corollary, the cling for survival response, are necessary for the protection of the young. Fight is the animal defense that gives
us the strength to protect ourselves as well as others. Both of these drives
tend to be dramatically intensified in DID clients, a diagnosis that is statistically associated with disorganized or traumatic attachment in childhood
(Lyons-Ruth et al., 2006). With an attach for survival part dissociatively en-
capsulated and forever a tiny child, unaware that he or she is protected by a
grownup body or has interpersonal power in relationships, fear of rejection
and abandonment are easily activated and feel "present now," not a memory
of the past. The emotional pain or anxiety associated with loss of proximity
in turn triggers the fight part to anger, hypervigilance, mistrust, even paranoia. Disoriented in time, the fight part comes to the defense of the attach
part, both parts assuming that the therapist, friend, or significant other is
the cause of these feelings of hurt and anger. This "other" is rejected as "cold
and uncaring," "insensitive," or "condescending," with the implied demand
to remediate these failings because they are "wrong." Or the opposite may
occur: the client may come to therapy blended with the attach part, shy and
mute or highly distressed and agitated. In either case, the therapist will feel
a pull or yearning to help when faced with the neediness and "littleness" of
the attach part or, conversely, may feel pushed back or defensive in the face
of the fight part's accusations. Some therapists draw their boundaries more
clearly in the face of the regressive or aggressive behavior, while other therapists try to prove their trustworthiness and caring by giving and doing more
for the client. Both extremes tend to intensify the traumatic transference: the
setting of boundaries inflames the fight part as a challenge for control and
triggers feelings of rejection in the attach part. Giving and doing more is also
threatening because it inflames the attach parts' longing and fear of loss, a
red flag to the fight part. In many trauma therapies, these issues complicate
the treatment but, in therapy with DID clients, they can more dramatically

intensify because of the greater autonomy of the parts. When the neediness and fear of abandonment are held by a young part unintegrated with competent, protective, or nurturing parts, the communication of need and vulnerability is palpable and hard for the therapist to resist without feeling guilty and abandoning. When anger and outrage are held by an unintegrated fight part, the anger is more intimidating and unleavened by perspective, empathy, or gratitude. Some therapists have trouble holding the boundaries in the face of the onslaught; some rigidify the boundaries and tighten the treatment frame. Either extreme tends to be triggering to the parts. The challenge in both cases is that of holding in mind a paradox: each part is separate in its perspective, its sensitivities, and its defenses; each can take over the body and drive action as if it were a separate person, yet each is part of a whole, a whole that is fully able to function and care for itself. The therapist must try to hold onto this double perspective in order to avoid treating the child parts as if the whole client were young and unable to function on his or her own—or, even worse, treat the whole client as if she or he were only angry, accusatory, and devaluing.

To treat the paradox, rather than treating each part separately, requires that the therapist be able to resonate with the young part and communicate at his or her developmental level and also be able to resonate with the angry part as if it were an individuating adolescent, in need of respect for its insight and sense of fairness as well as its courage. The angry part's positive intentions, the wish to protect the child, must be acknowledged. Most of all, working with disorganized attachment in DID clients requires restraint on the part of the therapist: a holding back of the impulse to soothe the child, to offer the reassurance requested, to become a go-between for the normal life self and the angry part. If we as therapists can restrain ourselves from over-reacting to either regression or aggression, then we can facilitate a growing relationship and dialogue between the normal life aspect of the client and his or her traumatized younger selves. If the normal life self learns to soothe the child and provide the feeling of specialness so necessary in secure attachment, then the fight part will not have to be the only protector. If the normal life part is able to negotiate with the fight part and take over the protector function, then fight's aggressive behavior will not be activated so automatically by the sense of threat to the child. If therapists substitute themselves for the normal life part, then the system becomes dependent upon the therapist—which fuels the disorganized attachment. The fight part's sense that the therapist is a threat intensifies when the client as a whole becomes more dependent on us; the attach part's fear of abandonment also intensifies. The parts are then caught in a vicious circle, and so is the therapist. Without restraint and repeated self-reassurance that the client knows how to survive (is an expert at it, in fact) and we need only to teach him or her how to manage the internal forces triggered by relationships, we cannot help clients weather the storms caused by trauma-related disorganized attachment.

Patience, Persistence, and a Good Seat Belt

If we as therapists exercise the appropriate restraint of both nurturing and self-protective impulses, it means that we don't become responsible for the parts that want to live, the parts that want someone to whom they can attach or tell their stories or feel special. We don't "take on" the angry protectors on behalf of the normal life self or on behalf of the child parts. If we are exercising the kind of "economy" that communicates our commitment, care, and compassion while avoiding induction into the system or taking on the roles of rescuer, victimizer, or victim, all the parts will feel safer. The normal life self can more easily shoulder the responsibility of caring for the young parts if the therapist is not competing for that job. If the therapist can hold warmth in the heart for the little attach part, respect for the fight part and admiration for its courage, and can see the signs of a normal life self with the potential to become a healer and comforter, then it becomes easier not to feel pressure to "fix" the problems and crises. This requires patience on the part of the therapist, persistence, and holding on tight as the system tests our consistency in being caring and compassionate but not caretaking—even when the suicidal part is threatening, the child feels lost and alone, the normal life part is so blended that it can't be mindful, engaged with the parts, or able to prevent switching and acting out.

Treating the Child by Enlisting the "Parent"

Clients and their fight or attach parts sometimes take issue with my emphasis on the client's normal life part working directly with the parts, while my role, as I describe it to the parts, is to "teach the grownup how to take care of you." I am the coach for this team, the parent educator. All involved would much rather that I help each and every part myself. An understandable wish, of course, but one that is challenged by the necessity for mindfulness as an antidote to trauma. Without an observing witness that resides in the client's body, a "part that can see all the parts," the child and adolescent selves will still be "home alone." The parts' locus of control will still be external. The loss of control associated with trauma will persist as a need for an external resource to regulate the nervous system and transform negative feelings into positive.

I realized one day while working with Annie why this issue felt so important to me beyond an intellectual commitment to self-regulation and mindfulness-based treatment. Her little parts were begging me to "say something nice," interrupting the work Annie and I were doing to address the parts responsible for her inability to have daily structure. I asked Annie if *she* would be willing to say something nice to the child parts so we could go back to the structure issue. "But they want *you* to say something nice—they need a good feeling today." These little parts communicated an important message: "Our feelings are not our own. Other people make us feel bad, and only other people can make us feel good." This is one of the lessons taught by trauma. Thanks to those child parts, I have been committed to ensuring that my clients would leave therapy with the ability to manage bad feelings and evoke good feelings—without having to depend upon others to "make" them feel good or bad. If I work using primarily "direct access" (the IFS term for 1:1 work with the parts), then client and parts will learn that they can depend on me to feel good feelings. But if I am away on a speaking trip or between sessions, the parts have no resource for good feelings unless I provide outside-of-therapy contact—thereby risking exacerbated disorganized attachment. The unrelenting fears of abandonment of the attach part are heightened: without "her," they believe, there is no source of good feelings. But if, on the other hand, the work of building relationships with the parts, earning their trust, and developing warm attachment bonds is an internal experience, then control rests with the client. The attach parts do not have to worry about abandonment because the wise, caring normal life self of the client is always there. He or she becomes the source of the warm, pleasurable safe feelings. Dependency is safe when child parts depend upon a caring adult self available in the same body.

Self-Healing, Rather than Interpersonal Healing

It can be hard for therapists accustomed to working with the relationship between client and clinician to take the more "backseat" role of family therapist. But although it can be very effective to use the relationship as the vehicle for healing with one individual client, there is no "one" therapeutic relationship with fragmented or DID clients. We are dealing with many "clients," all of whom are part of a family system that must heal itself to be free of the past, just as a biological family must do. This value is also central to the work of Sensorimotor Psychotherapy as the principle of "organicity" (Ogden & Fisher, 2015), referring to the body's innate drive toward healing and growth, toward "righting itself" when off-balance, growing new skin cells after a cut, or automatically compensating when there is an injury to some part of the body. In Internal Family Systems, the same principle is called "self-leadership": the belief that we heal ourselves through access to the innate capacities for compassion, curiosity, clarity, creativity, courage, calm, confidence, and commitment to all of our selves. Young, traumatized parts impacted by trauma and neglect have long been deprived of the compassion and calm they deserved; they have needed someone to courageously protect them, and they have suffered from the failure of adults to make a deeply felt commitment to them. On top of that rejection, their banishment as "not me" parts by the normal life self has reenacted the failure of commitment day after day ever since.

What both Sensorimotor Psychotherapy and IFS teach is that the therapist must provide a "container" or "growth-facilitating" environment that evokes these natural tendencies necessary for healing. In IFS, the therapist's own use of the qualities of self (Schwartz, 2001) is meant to stimulate the client's natural access to states of curiosity or commitment or compassion. In Sensorimotor Psychotherapy, these same qualities are not specifically named, but they are cultivated. The therapist's commitment to staying embodied and mindful and his or her palpable curiosity has a contagion effect, spontaneously engaging the client's curiosity and attentional focus, facilitating organic change (Ogden & Fisher, 2015).

Even without taking over the role of healer, the therapist nonetheless contributes to the sense of safety in the therapy via the social engagement system (Porges, 2011). The social engagement system is a neural system connected to the ventral vagus or ventral portion of the vagus nerve, controlling the movements of the eyes and eyelids, the muscles governing facial expression, the larynx, middle ear, and the tilting and turning movements of the head and neck. These are the channels of communication between babies and parents: a mother holds the baby's gaze, smiles and laughs, her eyes sparkling. Then the baby coos, and the mother imitates his vocalizations, and the baby echoes hers. She tilts her head and smiles again; the baby smiles back. The child feels safe and warm.

By using the social engagement system to communicate welcome, warmth, and understanding to every part, particularly to those parts with whom the client is uncomfortable, the therapist creates a felt sense of safety. Not only can the child part can hear the caring tone of voice but also sees a softness in the therapist's eyes or face, automatically returns the smile, and is soothed by the soft tone of voice. If the therapist says with warmth and sadness, "Of course the little part is scared in an empty house—how could she not be? With no one taking care of her and so many people who were mean to her, it must be terrifying to be by herself," the child is reassured not just by the words but by the tone of voice, the normal life self is educated, and there is modeling of how to attune to a child. If therapists use a tone of respect or even delight when referring to the fight part, rather than a tone of concern or authority, they will communicate that they are not scared away by the threats of the fight part but admire that part's adversarial protectiveness or willingness to fall on its own sword if the battle is lost. "Wow! The angry part really shut me down and put me right in my place—and that's not easy to do. That part definitely has your back!" "Could you thank the suicidal part for its generous offer? Maybe that part believes that you're not strong enough to handle all the feelings and memories, so it has to intervene, but you could explain that you'd like to be strong enough to tolerate them, and you can't learn to do that if the fight part is always bailing you out."

In the role of family therapist or coach, the therapist can contribute to strengthening the connection between the normal life self and both attach and fight. Therapists can urge clients to make a special place in their lives or hearts for the littlest self, the part that is innocent, trusting, and the most vulnerable. Use of facial expression, tone of voice, and softening of gaze can all support the communication of empathy or evoke it in the client.

Facilitating Reunion

Because the prefrontal cortex is associated with neutrality, observing presence, and access to compassion, I can be confident that, if I am talking to the normal life part, I will hear more integrated responses: "I'm a little ambivalent about dealing with these little parts. I'm afraid of them, I guess." When I hear, "I wish they'd go away and never come back," I can be sure that exposure to the vulnerability of attach has triggered a distancing or gatekeeper part that "hates the other parts." Hostile, punitive remarks can only mean one thing: an intrusion by a part that is phobic of the traumatized parts. In those moments, I know the wise, compassionate "best self" of the client is not speaking. And I feel confident challenging the "I" as unrepresentative of the client, as I did in the following example with Tom. Because my belief in his "best self" is a compliment, it is hard for him to argue with my remarks and even harder to take offense.

> Tom was adamant: "I never asked for these parts to help me survive, and I don't want them now. I wish they were dead!"
>
> ME: "Why do you wish they were dead, Tom?" I asked.
> CLIENT: "Because they embarrass me—they look sad; they're scared of their own shadows; they want me to depend on people. I did that once before, and look how that turned out!"
> ME: "Tom, I know you. And I know that you would never, ever turn your back on a child who was hurting! I refuse to believe that you of all people would make fun of a child who was crying or looked sad. You always try to help everyone! Imagine for a moment that there is a little boy standing right here in front of you [I point to a spot on the floor]. He's looking lost and he's crying and looking around [I imitate the same movements as if I were scared]—what's your impulse? To say 'Shut up, kid' and just walk on by? Or is there another impulse?"
> TOM: "No, my impulse is to stop and ask him, 'What's wrong?'"
> ME: "Of course it is! I knew it—you'd never turn your back on a child in need! What is he saying?"
> TOM: "He's saying that he ran away from home because bad things were happening, but now he's lost, and he's scared."
> ME: "That was very brave of him to run away—for such a little guy, too. What's your impulse? What are your body and your feelings telling you?"
> TOM: "I want to say, 'Come with me—I'll take care of you—no one gets hurt at my house ...'"
> ME: "And what goes with those words? Do you want to take his hand? Pick him up? Or ask him to follow you?"
> TOM: "I feel like I want to pick him up ..."
> ME: "Then follow that instinct—just reach out to him and see if he'd like that."
> TOM: "He's already jumped into my arms—as soon as I said I wanted to pick him up!"

ME: "Then just feel him in your arms—feel the warmth of his little body—see if he likes that feeling of being held ..."

TOM: "I can feel him relaxing—like he knows I'm safe—I won't hurt him."

ME: "Feel his knowing that ... Yes, he can relax—he's in good hands now—is that a pleasurable feeling?"

TOM: "It's the best—it feels so good to hold him."

ME: "Well, I'm glad it feels so good because he really needs to be held—it's been a long time coming. He needs someone to hold him, to notice when he feels bad, to greet him every morning with a big smile and hugs and kisses."

TOM: [tearing up] "Yeah, no one ever looked happy to see me every morning ..."

ME: "That was his experience and yours, wasn't it? And what's it like to see him and feel him with you right now?

TOM: [through his tears] "He's asking if it's OK to cry—he doesn't know why he's crying, so he's saying 'sorry.' That's so sad. I told him it's OK—I'm crying, too, because I'm happy."

ME: "It's the grief of relief. He's finally getting what every baby and every little kid wants: for someone's eyes to light up when they see him coming—to feel so very special to someone. And just feel it in your body ... you are giving him something he's always wanted, and it feels just as good to you as it does to him!"

References

American Psychiatric Association (2000). *Diagnostic and statistical handbook of mental disorders-TR.* Washington, D.C.: American Psychiatric Association.

Brand, B.L., Lanius, R. Loewenstein, R.J., Vermetten, E., & Spiegel, D. (2012). Where are we going? An update on assessment, treatment, and neurobiological research in dissociative disorders as we move towards the DSM-5. *Journal of Trauma & Dissociation*, 13, 9–31.

Brand, B.L., Sar, V., Stavropoulos, P., Kruger, C., Korzekwa, M., Martinez-Taboas, A., & Middleton, W. (2016). Separating fact from fiction: an empirical examination of six myths about dissociative identity disorder. *Harvard Review of Psychiatry*, 24(4), 257–270.

Briere, J., Elliott, D.M., Harris, K., & Cotman, A. (1995). Trauma Symptom Inventory: psychometrics and association with childhood and adult trauma in clinical samples. *Journal of Interpersonal Violence*, 10, 387–401.

Carlson, E.B., Putnam, F.W., Ross, C.A., & Torem, M. (1993). Validity of the Dissociative Experiences Scale in screening for multiple personality disorder: a multicenter study. *American Journal of Psychiatry*, 150, 1030–1036.

Dorahy, M.J., Shannon, C., Seager, L., Corr, M., Stewart, K., Hanna, D., Mulholland, C., & Middleton, W. (2009). Auditory hallucinations in dissociative identity disorder and schizophrenia with and without a childhood trauma history. *Journal of Nervous and Mental Disease*, 197, 892–898.

Gazzaniga, M. S. (1985). *The social brain: discovering the networks of the mind*. New York: Basic Books.

Gazzaniga, M. S. (2015). *Tales from both sides of the brain: a life of neuroscience*. New York: Harper-Collins.

Korzekwa, M., Dell, P.F., Links, P.S., Thabane, L., & Fougere, P. (2009). Dissociation in borderline personality disorder: a detailed look. *Journal of Trauma and Dissociation*, 10(3), 346–367.

LeDoux, J. (2002). *The synaptic self: how our brains become who we are*. New York: Guilford Press.

Lyons-Ruth, K. et al. (2006). From infant attachment disorganization to adult dissociation: relational adaptations or traumatic experiences? *Psychiatric Clinics of North America*, 29(1).

Ogden, P. & Fisher, J. (2015). *Sensorimotor Psychotherapy: interventions for trauma and attachment*. New York: W.W. Norton.

Ogden, P., Minton, K. & Pain, C. (2006). *Trauma and the body: a sensorimotor approach to psychotherapy*. New York: W.W. Norton.

Reinders, A.T.T.S., Nijenhuis, E.R.S., Quak, J., Korp, J., Haaksma, J. Paans, M.J., Willemsen, A.T.M., & den Boer, J.A. (2006). Psychobiological characteristics of dissociative identity disorder: a symptom provocation study. *Biological Psychiatry*, 60, 730–740.

Schwartz, R. (2001). *Introduction to the internal family systems model*. Oak Park, IL: Trailheads Publications.

Steinberg M. (1994). *The structured clinical interview for DSM-IV dissociative disorders-revised (SCID-D)*. Washington, D.C.: American Psychiatric Press.

Steinberg, M. (2013). In-depth: understanding dissociative disorders. *Psych Central*. Retrieved on September 13, 2015 from http://psychcentral.com/lib/in-depth-understanding-dissociative-disorders/.

Zanarini, M.C., Frankenberg, F.R., Dubo, E.D., Sickel, A.E., Trikha, A., Levin, A., & Reynolds, V. (1998). Axis I co-morbidity of borderline personality disorder. *American Journal of Psychiatry*, 155, 1733–1739.

CHAPTER **9**

Repairing the Past: Embracing Our Selves

"At the moment of the trauma, the [child] is utterly helpless. Unable to defend herself, she cries for help, but no one comes to her aid. … The memory of this experience pervades all subsequent relationships. The greater the [child's] emotional conviction of helplessness and abandonment, the more desperately she feels the need for an omnipotent rescuer … [But] because [she] feels as if her life depends on her rescuer, she cannot afford to be tolerant; there is no room for human error. …"

(Herman, 1992, p. 137)

Regardless of whatever cruelties or losses they encounter, human beings are born with the capacities necessary to "keep on keeping on," even to live a full, rich, meaningful life—in spite of adversity. We come into the world with innate drives to attach, explore, laugh and play, bond with our social group, and nurture the young. Even as young children, we have a developing brain that offers us such resources as curiosity, compassion, creativity, and wonder (Schwartz, 2001). We also have the mental ability of imagination: if all is lost, we can still dream, still imagine a life we've never known.

But, under chronic conditions of neglect, trauma, or frightened and frightening parenting, our bodies organize to prioritize the mobilization of animal defense survival responses and anticipation of danger (Ogden et al., 2006; Van der Kolk, 2014). The "luxuries" of normal attachment, exploration and learning, play, even sleeping and eating, take a back seat to hypervigilant attention to potential triggers and a readiness for defensive reactions. As important as it is to have parts whose hypervigilance and preparedness for action support survival under threat, it is equally important to have a part able to "make do" in even the worst of circumstances. The normal life child self smiles for family photographs and events, cares for siblings (or even for parents), goes to school, finds pleasure or mastery in the normal developmental "tasks" of childhood (playing with other kids, exploring nature, engaging in athletic or academic competition, getting lost in books, learning a musical instrument, and "adopting" supportive surrogate parents, such as teachers, neighbors, grandparents).

Often, in taking a client's history, the therapist is drawn to the details of neglect, abuse, and family dysfunction that "need to be addressed" in therapy. Never trained to listen for the indicators of the child's drive for normality, their peer relationships, school life, or what kept that child "going on," therapist and client unwittingly paint a shared portrait of the client as a wounded victim, not a ingenious survivor. Annie provides us with a good example of what happens when the therapist neglects to be curious about the side of the child who "kept on keeping on" and focuses the therapy on the wounds and wounded parts. Despite the severity and chronicity of her neglect and trauma, despite coming from the "wrong side of the tracks," or perhaps because of these things, Annie's normal life self was always strongly driven to make the most out of whatever "normal" she could create or emulate.

> An eager, bright sociable little girl, Annie's normal life self naturally evoked the support and attention of her teachers. Physically active and good at athletics, she discovered early on that owning a baseball mitt or bat was the best ticket to social connection with her peers. Although handicapped in peer relationships by the stigmata of neglect and poverty (dirty hair, unwashed second-hand clothes that didn't fit or match), she managed to compensate with the help of an exuberant personality and sports equipment purchased with her paper route and babysitting money. By the age of 8, as her mother's alcoholism worsened, she was put in charge of running her family's entire household and caring for two younger siblings, a burden to which she submitted for fear of physical abuse but which also earned her a repertoire of precocious competencies in cooking, cleaning, and childcare. Caring for two younger siblings who adored her and to whom she was safely attached provided an important normal developmental experience, one that most likely contributed to her later ability to raise two securely attached children and then "adopt" a series of surrogate children who found safe haven in her home. As an adult, friends, relatives, and neighbors consistently sought refuge and support in Annie's home. She often felt confused about why they would seek her out. The fight parts tried to tell her it was only because they wanted to use her since she was such an easy mark. The person she identified as "I" would never have drawn others to her, would never have been a "wise woman" to whom they would come for safety and support.

Despite the strengths and resources of her normal life self, Annie found her day-to-day experience dominated by traumatized child parts, with dramatic ramifications. Although she wished for more contact with others (and so did her attach part), the fight and flight parts held her back from acting on that wish. Instead, she was internally compelled to isolate, avoid going outside, cancel dates with potential friends, and never, ever answer the door or the telephone. Only those individuals seeking caretaking in her home were allowed to have contact with her. Ironically, caretaking had been the safest role she knew in childhood, and many parts did not want to give it up despite the scathing criticism of judgmental protector parts. Although Annie's normal life self wanted to have a routine that balanced regular eating and sleeping habits, household responsibilities and pleasurable activities, following a schedule was impossible. She and I constructed schedule after schedule to no avail. Any type of structure was assiduously avoided by her parts—a phenomenon often seen in clients with histories of neglect, even those with graduate degrees and professional careers. The case of Josh illustrates another example of what happens when the parts' implicit memories and perspectives dominate the individual and pre-empt functioning of the prefrontal cortex, disempowering the normal life self. Without the cortical ability to differentiate his grown-up self from trauma-related parts, he could not see his life or himself in perspective.

Josh was a very competent, successful, well-liked man in his forties. Respected by his colleagues, loved by his wife and daughters, accepted as "one of the guys" by his Wednesday night basketball buddies, a combination of intelligence, kindness, humility and humor endeared him to most people in his life. At times, he could see glimpses of this man others knew so well, but more often, the positive responses he evoked in others triggered a child part holding anxiety and self-doubt. "It's hard to take in anything positive, not when you know you're inadequate—when you know you come from nothing—or worse. I know the positive things are true of me, but I can't believe them." Attending a positive psychology weekend for couples, he found himself skeptical and at times even cynical: "It's so woo-woo. Say something nice to yourself and you'll feel better. But what if it's not true? I couldn't tolerate saying it and then finding out it's not true." Each time he had a glimpse of something beyond the inadequacy endorsed by his child parts, his cynical part would convince him there was no data to support any positive qualities in himself.

Dawn also found her perspective distorted by whichever parts' intense emotions and reactivity "hijacked" her body and drove her impulsive behavior.

Dawn was 12 when she was taken out of the foster care system and sent to a Department of Child Mental Health residential placement. That was OK with her. Life had hardly been normal up to that point, nor had it been safe, and even though it didn't always feel that way, residential programs meant safety. Now 22, she had spent the intervening ten years in and out of residential care and hospitals. There, her chronic self-injury and eating disorder were treated as symptoms of borderline personality disorder and evidence of manipulative, attention-seeking behavior. Each time, her normal life part took a step forward, wanting more out of life, it triggered parts frightened of being seen, harmed, or abandoned. Without a window of tolerance, Dawn had no way of managing either her post-traumatic hyperarousal symptoms or her loneliness and emotional pain, which then tended to trigger vigorous efforts by the drug-seeking and eating disordered parts to alter her state. And if that didn't work, her self-injurious part would use cutting to mobilize adrenaline and thereby counteract the fear and vulnerability. Each time these parts hijacked her body and drove her to relapse or self-harm, it confirmed for the young terrified child part that there was no safety anywhere, increasing the panic that the fight and flight parts tried to shut down. Shown a diagram of the structural dissociation model by her new therapist, Dawn was surprised to feel an instant sense of recognition as the normal life self was described to her. "Oh yeah, I know that part! That's the part of me that used to promise myself that someday I'd get out of 'the system' and have a real home and family of my own. That's the part that kept me trying to get better all this time." Dawn, unlike Josh, immediately identified with her normal life part and felt relieved to give it a name and a purpose. It even began to feel real to her that maybe, after all, she could have a normal life!

Each of these clients had normal life selves with inherent inborn strengths and resources. Despite having never known "normality," even Dawn had the same drive to be her best self, the same curiosity and compassion for others, the same determination despite all the obstacles she had faced. All three normal life selves were strong-willed, creative, and instinctively knew what "normal life" signified for each of them. When their left-brained normal life selves were in charge, their personalities, identities, and values were well-defined. Sadly, because the normal life self blended so easily with the traumatized parts, yet also related to them as "not me" aspects, there was little communication or collaboration with the right brain-related parts. Feeling a sense of defectiveness because of their symptoms and difficulties, they were distracted from seeing how blending with their parts' trauma-related implicit memories and survival defenses was impacting their lives and sense of identity.

Instead, the inner worlds of each tended to be more like battlegrounds: Annie's normal life self wrestled with parts terrified of the world they imagined lay outside her home, a world she had deliberately chosen for a normal life because it was so benign and gave her access to nature. Believing it would be as malevolent as the traumatic environment of childhood, her parts wanted none of it. Josh's intelligent, thoughtful normal life part lost conflict after conflict to critical and ashamed parts holding the conviction that no accomplishment or acceptance could erase the stain of having been "less than." Dawn's normal life self was quite literally on "lockdown," in and out of specialized programs, no match for the violence of her addicted, self-injuring, and eating disordered parts. The traumatic or disorganized attachment they had each experienced early in life created especially intense internal conflicts between the attach part's fear of abandonment and yearning for care versus the fight part's determination to defend against any and all vulnerability. Subsequently, traumatic events of all kinds (from bullying to human trafficking, homelessness to sexual abuse to domestic violence) had exacerbated these fears and further polarized the parts: parts holding implicit memories of fear, dread, and shame triggered parts driven by impulses to flee or fight for life—and vice versa. It was an endless cycle. Each part's belief system, reactivity, defensive responses, and emotions implicitly described its place in their histories and embodied the defensive responses needed at the time. Their conscious childhood memories were the tales of how they were victimized, never seen or never loved. Each failed to mention how they survived. Josh's story was that he would never outlive the humiliation, poverty, abuse, and neglect that characterized his childhood: he would never belong. Dawn's story was similar: she had never been wanted, never been safe, and she never would be. She might as well be dead. Not only were their normal life parts missing in their daily consciousness but also missing from their childhood memories. Flooded with the traumatized parts' emotions, impulses, and beliefs, each normal life self had automatically identified with the parts' implicit memories. Each was disconnected from a felt sense of ownership of the aspects of life he or she had deliberately created to support "keeping on" despite it all. Blended with the parts, all three identified with the traumatic lives of their childhoods rather than with their consciously created "life after trauma."

The parts' disordered attachment and need for the approval and acceptance by others created a vulnerability to depending on others, leading fight and flight parts to perceive that they were still being used and abused—or could be. Their fight parts attacked their bodies, their credibility, even those closest to them—demoralizing the normal life selves and affecting their ability to be effective or to feel effective or both. None of the three could gain perspective without a trusting relationship between the parts and the self who could create safety, stability, and a life after trauma. When Dawn identified the little girl inside who had been left alone and unprotected to become prey for pedophiles, she was finally able to make the connection between her nightfall terrors and unsafe behavior. She felt an immediate protectiveness that impelled her to buy a little girl doll and doll bed so she could "see her and tell her I'm going to take care of her." But when Dawn's normal life part tried to reassure the little girl who got terrified every night as soon as it got dark, there was no emotional impact. The only interventions that eased the panic caused by blending with the child were restricting food intake and drinking alcohol. Not knowing that she would have to befriend the little girl first and win her trust before she would be able to believe the words of reassurance, Dawn was discouraged and, blended with her depressed submit part, she gave up trying.

When Josh's judgmental, humiliating fight part was triggered by social situations, Josh's prefrontal cortex could not compete with its emotional intensity. Nor could he reassure the ashamed part or the part that felt he didn't belong. He was too blended with them. The normal life self on whom others relied for words of support and wisdom could not "be there" for his child selves. The parts did not seek him out either. The ashamed little boy and depressed 12-year-old parts had a long though troubled relationship with the fight part; they had no relationship at all with Josh's normal life self. How could they know he was there when he was blended with them?

Although Annie went through the motions of relating to her parts, she had no emotional connection to the words she spoke to them. In fact, she was afraid to feel too much for her young selves, having found it overwhelming in the past. Historically, once she began to feel their fear or sadness, it would escalate into a tsunami wave of emotion. Her normal life self was exceptionally gifted with her surrogate children and students, had a sensitivity to their trauma, and knew just how to help them find their own normal life selves. She took on more surrogate children of an alcoholic mother in the neighborhood and began to teach them how to survive as she had taught herself. She fed them healthy snacks, made them do their homework, and, over time, went to their parent-teacher conferences. As teenagers, she drove them to work or school activities to make sure they got all the skills and capacities they would need for eventual independence. Annie taught me an important lesson about the effects of neglect: seeing that they had no support or structure but also no help in developing the capacities to feel safe on their own, independent of their mother, she could see that without help, they would never be able to leave. To be on their own without any skills for self-regulation or functioning was terrifying and made a big world feel even bigger.

But Annie couldn't access these insights and abilities on behalf of her own parts, especially when overwhelmed by the emotions of younger parts or the defensive responses of fight and flight parts. The result: when she was triggered, she couldn't forge a relationship with her parts because she blended with them and could not stay present. For the parts, it was as if they had just cried for help, and the person to whom they called out heard their screams and then walked away. The parts felt abandoned, just as they had when their favorite aunt "walked away" back to her own life even after she had seen what was being done to them at home. When she could feel differentiated and separate, Annie's normal life self kept a safe distance from the parts' emotions—aided and abetted by a professional self, the teacher, who preferred a left-brain understanding of the parts to any emotional connection. But to the parts holding memories of yearning for some sign of care or kindness, the teacher's unemotional reassurance that they were safe now was as often alarming as it was reassuring.

> Midway through a discussion of her fear of leaving the house or yard, I asked Annie to be curious about why some protector parts were still holding her on "house arrest," the term I used for her agoraphobia. I wanted to communicate that it was more than the fears of the young part that wouldn't even let her open the door. She was also being prevented from leaving by some unidentified protector part. As she reassured the frightened part and headed toward the door, her body would suddenly tense up until she was frozen and couldn't move.

Asking "inside" to find out more about why she was on "house arrest," she got the following communication: "They're worried about the bad people outside the house like the ones who grabbed you as a kid."

I ASKED HER: "That makes sense—they were very dangerous people, very dangerous. And you were very little. But didn't anyone ever *tell* the parts that they're safe from those people now? Did anyone bother to tell them that *you* took them far away from New Jersey a long time ago and brought them to a place where no one could find them? *You* did that for them and you. Did anyone ever tell them that you changed your name so you couldn't be followed? Do they know *anything* about the life you've built here for the past 40 years?"

ANNIE: "It didn't occur to me that I had to tell them—I thought they'd just know."

I challenged her but with a tone that spoke to the parts' needs to be told, not her failure to tell them: "How *could* they have known? As far as they know, they're still in New Jersey, and they are still little. No one takes care of them, and *anyone* could take them. They were fair game for any creepy person, and they believe they still are. That's why they're so scared." Reassuring her that she hadn't failed (she hadn't known about the parts then), I appeal to her compassion for children: "You didn't know it, Annie, but they experienced it as you leaving them there. If you didn't tell them you were going, didn't say you were taking them away from all that—if you didn't tell them where they were when you arrived in Maine, then they don't know!"

On another day in a session with Josh, discussing his shame and fear of failure after he'd been triggered by a business meeting with male peers, I asked Josh a similar question: "Josh, does that little boy *know* that he doesn't live in that place anymore? Does he *know* that he doesn't have to wear clothes that are too big for him anymore? That no one will make fun of him now? I bet he doesn't even know that people here look up to you! He just remembers being fat, not having the right clothes, not being able to play sports with the other boys—and he remembers the shame of being bullied. This, your life, isn't real to him ... only the bullying feels real."

Annie and Josh both identified with their ashamed parts early in adulthood, facilitating their ability to be "seen but not heard" and minimizing the abuse in their families. They had a need for a "damage limitation strategy" (Gilbert & Andrews, 1998) to survive that conditioned judgmental parts and ashamed parts to dominate their inner lives and sense of identity for many years. Looking through the telescopic lens of their ashamed parts, neither could recognize, much less integrate, the healthy normality they had created in their lives as adults, the way they drew people to them. Both were inspiring examples of how the inborn drive to be healthy, conscious, compassionate, kind, and do meaningful work could surmount poverty, abuse, socioeconomic status, and post-traumatic stress. Neither, of course, could relate to such descriptions of themselves, so I kept these insights to myself and instead tried to evoke their interest and curiosity in the parts holding the shame. I encouraged each to thank those parts for helping them survive without losing their hearts or their souls.

Dawn, having never known "normality" outside of the mental health system, was especially out of touch with her normal life self's ability to function and to persevere. But, unlike Annie or Josh, she could unblend from her parts and have warm feelings toward the frightened part and respect for her fight and flight parts. Her treatment team took every opportunity to point out signs of the normal life part so Dawn could begin to recognize it as a force in her life despite the up's and down's caused by the parts' strong triggered reactions to her attempts to go forward.

Accessing the Resources of a Wise Adult

For many trauma survivors, the past as conveyed by the incessantly triggered implicit memories of the parts continues to be experienced as more "real" than the present. When that happens, the parts continue to relive and relive, over and over, the neglect, abuse, rage, fear, and dread—and to re-experience being abandoned by the normal life self just as they were abandoned by their caretakers years and decades ago. Annie, Josh, and Dawn illustrate this phenomenon.

To break the cycle requires several steps on the part of the therapist: first, the therapist must challenge the client's automatic beliefs and habitual patterns so that the tendency to identify with the autonomically activated emotions and drives of the parts is inhibited.

> Carla came to therapy in a highly activated state, having just had to take a leave of absence at work after she became too overwhelmed with fear, sadness, and a sense of numb unreality. As she described the past year of her life, it became clear that she had functioned highly for so long because her normal life self was supported by two trauma-related parts, one afraid of failure and one equally determined to succeed. This team drove her to develop a successful professional career and long-term relationship with her partner, but, I explained, "It was held together with rubber bands and chewing gum." Then her partner had an affair; she was mugged at knifepoint in her own neighborhood; and her father died, activating the trauma-related parts and completely incapacitating the normal life part. "No wonder you have been feeling 'not yourself.' Your parts staged a coup d'etat—probably

right after you found out about the affair," I commented. "These emotions that have been overwhelming you belong to very young distressed parts."

At the next session, as Carla made connections between her reaction to the affair and a childhood spent parenting her mother and soothing her father to ensure her safety, I translated her narrative into the language of parts: "So that little girl was all on her own—with no one to help her take care of her mother or protect her from her father—she had to grow up very fast, didn't she?" Carla responded immediately to the language of parts: "She did—she couldn't afford to feel lonely and scared—she had to take care of herself because no one else was going to."

"That's how it felt when I found out Amelia was cheating on me. I felt all alone again."

Concerned about how overwhelmed she was by her feelings and their parts, I drew on her strong prefrontal cortex and scientific background to begin deconstructing the situation: we subdivided the stressors, differentiated her reactions to each, and then connected the different sets of feelings to the different parts communicating them. By dividing an overwhelming situation into smaller components, each could be experienced as more manageable. "So not only were the losses hard for the strong normal life part of you to come to terms with," I validated, "they were devastating for this young girl." I added, "Remember: a betrayal would be deeply distressing for any adult, but on top of that, it triggered the worst fears of your younger parts. Children are so much more vulnerable to feeling unimportant and unseen. They fear being abandoned more than they fear attack."

CARLA: "True, but even though the little girl was heartbroken, I put up a wall with Amelia—'you can't hurt me anymore because I am not really connected to you.'"

ME: "That sounds like a bodyguard part that didn't want that little girl's heart broken again! But if I recall, your normal life self also got on the phone and found a couples therapist right away. It doesn't sound as if *you* were putting up a wall—just trying to save your relationship. But someone clearly was! If you feel the wall there in your body, some part is responsible for it."

CARLA: "The wall is still there—I can't take it down—I've tried. But maybe that makes sense if I didn't put it up?"

A week later, Carla was back with good news: "I've been thinking a lot about the little girl and meditating—and crying a lot for her. I've been remembering what it was like. Before, I was so focused on my career that I never thought of what she had been through and how lonely she was, which is just what Amelia complained about! [She chuckled with recognition of the irony.] I've been taking good care of the little girl this week, holding her close to me, and the wall is softening a little—just a little. The wall wants me to know that it doesn't trust me yet to protect her."

It took very little for Carla to resonate immediately to her little girl part rather than identify with her. It was as if she had been waiting for someone to give her the language for something she already knew or sensed. Her compassion for the little girl was easily accessible, and perhaps because of her meditation practice, she could experience a felt connection to her mindful observer self while also feeling connected to the little girl and to the protective wall. Over the weeks to come, Carla guided the therapy herself from a wise mindful place, and I had only the job of supporting and commenting on the work she was doing. Sometimes, she chose to work on her relationship to the little girl and sometimes on strengthening her capacity to be calm, curious, accepting, and centered (what Richard Schwartz [2001] calls "self-energy") through her meditation practice. She felt her heart increasingly open and, with that, she was able to observe without judgment how closed it had been before. "I thought of myself as gentle and caring, but I'm sure that's not how other people saw me. They just saw the professional distance that I rationalized as the price I paid for success in my work."

Not all clients have the immediate response to or compassionate understanding of their parts as Carla did—or the intuitive access to her "wise mind" (what would be termed "self" or "self-energy" in the language of Internal Family Systems). Carla, for example, intuitively sensed the need to meditate as a way of developing a mindful relationship to the multitude of painful thoughts, feelings, and body sensations she and her parts were experiencing.

For other clients, simply shifting from a narrative approach to a mindful dual awareness stance might have taken many months. Clients are used to equating therapy with talking, "getting things off my chest," or "venting." Even certain parts can be very attached to narrative therapy because it gives them an opportunity "to be heard" or "heard and believed." Normal life parts may be attached to talking because their priority is problem solving the issues that are most troubling or most triggering on a daily basis and avoiding the "not-me" feelings. Child parts yearning for connection may feel soothed by the quality of the therapist's listening and empathy; parts focused on avoiding the trauma (or the emotions connected to it) might be attached to complaining and/or analyzing. But since the key ingredient in a parts approach is mindful, compassionate noticing of thoughts, feelings, and bodily reactions as communications from parts, the shift from narrating to noticing is crucial for the success of the work. Narrating will yield an understanding of a part's role in the client's trauma history or even in day-to-day life, but it will not heal that part's wounds or "earn" secure attachment. Just think of a small child crying: if the adult responds by saying, "The child is crying," or "I am crying," the child is unlikely to feel any comfort or relief. If the adult hears the teenager's anger and comments, "I am angry about that," or "It made me angry, too," or

"Why did that make me so angry?" it is unlikely to have an effect other than to make the adolescent angrier. But these are what the parts hear when *their* feelings and reactions are narrated by the client as "my feelings."

Listening to Children Builds Attachment Bonds

To develop a trusting relationship, like all children, they need someone to respond to *them*. Often, simply asking the client to try out the language of parts, replacing "I'm freaked out" with "There's a part of me that's freaked out," results in an easing of distressing feelings. The settling and relaxation effect is also increased when the normal life self is encouraged to respond to the parts' complaints at a level of intensity just above or just below theirs and with a tone of genuine concern about their feelings: "You're really upset about something—I can tell. What's bothering you? What's hurting you?" The answer, of course, is that dissociated child parts need what any distressed child would need from an adult: a caring someone who will ask concerned questions, respond in a way that communicates "I get it," or try out different supportive responses until there is a "repair" in the child's state. Clients who have children of their own find they have immediate access to skills and abilities that help their young parts, and I encourage them to use what they know for "this child," too.

Whose Feelings Are These?

The greatest obstacle for clients in successfully "repairing" the distress of their trauma-related parts is the automatic, unconscious tendency to blend with the parts and identify with their feelings. Because their emotions and those of the parts are experienced in the same body and the same mind, they continue to feel like "my feelings," not "a part's feelings," long after the client understands the concept of parts and can identify them. Disidentifying from cognitive schemas held by different parts can be equally or more challenging. For some clients, it is difficult to question beliefs that have felt familiar and "true" for many years, even if they can be connected on an intellectual level to parts. Questioning "what *feels* true" can be experienced as threatening—or threatening to certain parts. When therapists challenge beliefs in worth, belonging, deserving, or adequacy, for example, and reframe those as trauma-related beliefs held by parts, the parts to whom they belong may feel anxiety. For them, safety is equated with beliefs in being worthless or undeserving, which provided the rationale for survival habits of holding back, being seen and not heard, or not rocking the boat. It is easier for children to believe they are bad than to believe they are alone in a dangerous world. It is also easier to be submissive, ashamed, and take the punishment being meted out when flooded with shame and self-loathing. There are two steps to the process of helping clients embrace the parts whose defensive responses or ingenious use of them helped them survive. First, they must learn to observe the signs of being blended and learn the skills of unblending. Next, they must access their innate compassion and "feeling for" these young parts, including overcoming conditioned habits of disowning, disparaging, or failing to notice the "not me" parts. Here, the therapist's skill lies in making sure that a client unblends before trying to help his or her parts. Only dual awareness allows the client to hold a "meeting of the minds" between the normal life self on the left brain side and trauma-related parts on the right brain side. As the therapist explains each side to the other, building curiosity and empathy, encouraging respect for their differences, and engaging in team-building for the parts, shifts often begin to occur.

> Wanting to trust me even though she was new to my practice, Jenny would try to ignore feelings of mistrust or questions about the therapy that kept cropping up in each session. I might say something apparently benign, and she would feel herself tensing against it. Or she might find herself getting uncomfortable and changing the subject. She often had thoughts about what my intentions really were: "What is she trying to sell me? Can I trust this?" As she was entertaining those thoughts one day, she heard me say, "You might find that parts of you want to trust me and parts of you don't—I just want to say how natural and normal it is that they feel that way. Many clients don't want to talk about these thoughts for fear of hurting my feelings. But I'm relieved if there's a part that's holding out trust until I've earned your trust!" Jenny felt a tremendous relief. Maybe it wasn't "bad" after all to have trouble trusting. "Think of it this way, Jenny. After all you've been through, you and your parts have earned the right not to trust me. My job is simple by comparison: to keep demonstrating that I'm trustworthy even if some parts never believe it."

Notice that I utilize an "equal opportunity" approach, supporting the parts who find it hard to trust as much or more as the parts who trust without question. My purpose is to ensure that the therapeutic environment offers a clear-cut welcome to *all* the parts, whatever their conflicts or perspectives, not just to the parts that are best suited to engage in therapy. I was also conscious of wanting to model the quality of empathy and curiosity that Jenny's normal life self would need to earn their trust, too. Rather than reacting negatively to the parts that don't trust, don't collaborate, don't allow vulnerability, or re-enact old solutions over and over again, the normal life self (like a good parent) must learn to ask: why might these parts withhold trust? Why would collaboration have been unsafe in their world? Why would it have been important to stay disconnected? To stay afraid? To stay angry?

In secure attachment, the parent mirrors his or her intuitive understanding back to the child: "You just wanted to feel special," "You had to wait such a long, long time for me—it was too long, huh?" "That made you mad, didn't it?" The child's reaction determines the parent's next response: "Oh, I hurt your feelings—of course—it didn't make you mad—it made you *sad*. I'm so sorry!" Secure attachment is built not on what caregivers say but through the experience of co-regulation (Fogel & Garvey, 2007; Hughes, 2007). The child feels something distressing (or pleasurable) to which the parent's nervous system, body, and emotions respond. The parent then "digests" these communications, puts words to them, and communicates their meaning back to the child, who is either soothed, dysregulated, or unmoved. The child's response in turn calms, dysregulates, confuses, or frustrates the parent, leading to another attempt at resonance and repair to which the child may respond positively or negatively. In attuned co-regulation, the parent is able to manage his or her dysregulation or frustration well enough to stay open to the child's feelings and refine each attempt at repair until attunement is achieved. The moment of "attunement"—when both child and parent drop into a deeply relaxed calm, when the child's small body melts into the parent's grownup body, when both are caught up in mutual gazing, smiling, and laughing— feels blissful to both parties. Most of all, it feels safe. In the human brain and body, the sense of safety is neurobiologically connected to the social engagement or ventral vagal system (Ogden et al., 2006; Porges, 2005), the neural system controlling the muscles of the face, movements of the eyes and eyelids, larynx, middle ear, and the tilting and turning movements of the head and neck. Attuned co-regulation depends upon this system, and its availability depends on the body's neuroception of danger versus safety. When clients say, "I don't feel safe here," they are describing neuroception, the "sixth sense" that all is not right—based on their experiences of the past. When other clients say, "I'm perfectly safe here," they really mean, "I am not neurocepting any danger here." Because it is a physiological response, not an intellectual evaluation, neuroception overrides the evaluations made by the prefrontal cortex: for example, "I know I'm safe here, but it sure doesn't feel that way." For a traumatized individual to know, "I'm safe here—I can feel it," requires both accurate cognitive appraisal of the environment and unbiased neuroception.

But reorganizing neuroception biased by trauma so that clients can experience safe environments as "safe" is not possible without the creation of attachment bonds with their traumatized parts. For children too young to protect themselves and dependent upon those who care for them, attachment equals safety. As long as the parts hold the non-verbal implicit memories of failed or traumatic attachment without reparative moments of attunement, the normal life self will continue either to experience intrusive anxiety, mistrust, loneliness, anger, and hypervigilance or to shut down emotionally and constrict life activities. Feeling truly safe requires "soul retrieval."

Sarah had none of the obvious signs of structural dissociation: she was functioning well in the organizational world, had a stable, satisfying family life with her partner and two dogs, and described her PTSD symptoms as much reduced since an EMDR treatment two years prior. Why was she in my office now? She described the one remaining issue in her life this way: "It's anxiety—no, more like a terror—that comes over me sometimes, like when I'm alone in the house or there's a lot of stress at work. I want to just curl up in a ball and wait for it to be over—but I'm not sure what I'm waiting for." (My ears perked up, and I made a mental note: "Perhaps a child part? Still alone and afraid?") As we concluded this first session and Sarah stood up to leave, she paused for a moment: "Do you believe in soul retrieval?" she asked. I smiled, sensing she and I were talking about the same thing: "Yes, I do—that's part of what therapy is all about: retrieving the lost children inside ourselves and bringing them to safety." Sarah smiled, too. I felt an implicit understanding had been reached. The parts had interviewed me, not just Sarah, and I had heard them and made them welcome.

Despite all the work she had done processing memories of events, Sarah had never addressed the lingering implicit memories held by certain parts. She was unaware consciously that she was fragmented and has no idea of the unmet attachment needs that contributed to the frightened part's terror. Only the fact that she felt so powerfully drawn to the concept of soul retrieval (and the communications from the frightened part) gave away an inkling of the parts hidden inside her. Later, when they were at last known to her, thanked for their contributions, welcomed as honored guests, and made safe inside, her relationship to them was what she most valued.

Describing drawings of the parts she had made to understand them better, Sarah observed, "Now I draw them three-dimensionally, not as stick figures—now they are real to me, and I am real to them. We can see each other in the drawings." Unseen and unsafe as a child, invisible except when her parents were angry, Sarah's final drawing in the latter stages of therapy depicts the child parts on a theater stage, while she as the normal life self watches with a smile from the audience. The children on stage seem relaxed, unafraid, and unselfconscious as the adult gazes fondly at them, communicating enjoyment and appreciation of their efforts.

Reaching Out to Parts from Places of Strength

Sarah as an adult was known for her ability to take younger colleagues "under her wing" and nurture them personally and professionally. Josh's strengths also lay in his ability to resonate to younger, more vulnerable beings, particularly his own young children. Dawn was known as the person to come to with a problem about which her friends could tell no one else. When she was out of the hospital, she volunteered at an animal shelter. Annie's kitchen was the safe haven for struggling friends and family, injured animals, and surrogate children who found their way to her home when theirs were violent or neglectful. Instinctively, she provided exactly what she had needed as a child: someone who "got it" and quietly supplied needs they didn't know how to verbalize or felt too ashamed to ask, ranging from new sneakers or school supplies to help with their homework or offering a shoulder on which to cry. Sarah had been an educator before she began working in organizations; Annie had been a junior high school teacher; Josh was a hospital administrator who mentored 11- and 12-year-old boys in a basketball league for inner city children at the YMCA. Now it was time for them to offer the resources they had been bestowing on others to their own child and adolescent parts. Having learned to unblend, notice and empathize with their parts, and to engage in an internal conversation, they could take their work one step further and offer those parts a reparative experience of acceptance, comfort, validation, and support.

Although the client may protest that he or she doesn't know how to take care of a child, or what to say or how to reach them, the therapist must hold the confidence that each client has access to all the qualities he or she could need: each is inherently curious, caring, capable of compassion and creativity, all the capacities "their" children needed from adults in the past. Often there are arenas in the client's life where those abilities flourish when he or she is in the normal life part. Josh engaged in a number of roles in which he used his capacity for empathy, attunement, interpersonal connection, and the courage of his convictions: he was a parent; his professional life centered on advocating for others; he volunteered as an athletic coach for his children's sports teams; he was an AA sponsor. I felt confident that, in those roles, Josh had developed all the resources he needed to "be there" for his parts. Annie was not only a mother and surrogate mother but also a teacher, so I challenged her: "Annie, what did you do when your 13- and 14-year-old students acted up in class? When no one was listening, and no one could hear you? Did you just try to ignore them and carry on? Or did you do something?"

Annie was quick to respond: "I couldn't ignore them, or it would have been pandemonium! I had to get them back into some kind of order. So sometimes I would do a distracting activity that got them focused on something else. Or I stopped talking and just stared at them until they got the message that it was time to settle down."

"Annie," I said. "This is so interesting! I've never known you to offer your parts that kind of creativity or consistent structure. The structure must be important in a classroom, huh? Think for a moment about your parts: imagine there's a classroom inside you, but it's more complicated than an 8th grade classroom because it has kids of all ages in one room!" In an instant, Annie was in her normal life self, pondering what she would do if her inner family of parts were a classroom of children.

Accessing the Resources of Normal Life

If the normal life part is a parent or caretaker, the therapist can make connections to his or her fund of knowledge about those roles. I ask clients who have children, "What happens with your children if you try to ignore them when they're upset or scared?" The response is always, "They get more upset—that's why you can't ignore them!" Then, I can suggest: "Yes, you are absolutely right! And just like your kids, these child parts inside get more scared when you try to ignore them ... What would you do if they were your biological children?" If the client is a manager or administrator, I might ask, "Think about what the folks you manage need from you to give their best at work ..." Or, "Imagine what you would say if one of the people who report to you were struggling with this kind of anxiety?"

> Determined to have a normal life despite her childhood trauma and the series of crises that marked her early adult years, Rachel finished her university education in between hospitalizations, got married, and was midway through graduate school when her parts suddenly hijacked her ability to function again. Her therapist noticed a pattern in these crises: bright and ambitious, Rachel would do well in her classes or at a job (despite the inevitable triggers) until she seemed to finally be at a stable place—which seemed to be the signal for an uprising among her parts. It wasn't clear if they became afraid of being left behind or afraid of her success and consequent visibility (two common triggers for traumatized parts), but as she learned to unblend, she began to see another theme emerge: a young part of her was afraid of what would happen if Rachel became confident and unworried. Using the Four Befriending Questions [see Appendix F], she discovered that this young, anxious, helpless part had once been instrumental in providing protection against her father's rage. Although he was triggered each time his young daughter was confident, proud, and held her ground against him, he melted when she was helpless and needy, unthreatened when he could rescue her—from his own abuse. The result was a split inside Rachel between a strong normal life self and proud angry parts versus the helpless, needy, frightened parts that had helped her survive and adapt. The strong, proud contingent supported her ambition and drive, while the needy, scared parts were threatened by her success because, to them, it would evoke violence and rejection.
>
> What both sides needed was a sense of a steady inner presence, someone with compassion for the young parts who could hold her own when they became hysterical and clingy or judgmental parts got angry and scathing. Certain adult activities provided that feeling of a steady inner presence: doing yoga, running, caring for her dog, and socializing with friends. As a first step to "being there" for her parts in ways her mother had not been, Rachel committed to spending evenings after work at yoga class or running with her dog. Something as simple as a commitment that she honored consistently (no matter how much the little parts longed to go home or to bed after work) seemed to bring a feeling of centeredness and lessened vulnerability that helped all the parts.

Where Rachel and many other clients struggle is the point at which the parts' strong emotions require compassion to feel safe or soothed. Curiosity provides some mindful distance by activating the medial prefrontal cortex, regulating the autonomic arousal or emotion of a part. Building the resources of a normal life self also supports the ability to differentiate between child parts' implicit memories and adult capacities. But when the observing normal life self is moved by the emotions of the child, when a felt sense of compassion and deeper connection is evoked, that mental space diminishes, potentiating opportunities for other parts to intrude or for flooding by distressing feelings, leading to loss of dual awareness. These are moments when the therapist can suggest some simple somatic interventions (Ogden & Fisher, 2015) that help regulate the nervous system while also communicating commitment and compassion to the parts.

- When young parts are anxious or distressed, asking clients to place a hand over the heart or chest, or "over the place where you notice the little part's grief" has a calming, regulating effect on most clients and enables them to send a somatic message to the parts: "It's going to be OK—I'm here for you." This simple intervention reaches below the habits of self-alienation and rejection of the not-me parts. Non-threatening to most parts, it communicates a caring that clients often have not yet learned to feel toward their young selves.
- When intense inner conflicts between parts or overwhelming emotional memories cause difficulty regulating or even staying present, the therapist can ask clients to experiment with opening their arms and making a big circle as if about to catch a big beach ball or hug a child. I like to wait to introduce this skill until the client complains about overwhelm or too many internal struggles so that I can say, "I get it—all those feelings are too much to hold all at once sometimes." And then I suggest we experiment: "See what happens when you make a container big enough to hold all the parts—just the right size to hold all of their feelings, all their points of view, all their beliefs, all the needs." This gesture opens the chest, sending a somatic message: "All are welcome—no one will be forgotten." The parts usually breathe a sigh of relief. They can feel the bodily sense of being "all together," the feeling of the arms encircling them yet making room for each one. And then they feel the sense of welcome.

Taking Young Parts "Under the Wing" of Someone Who Cares

Annie was invariably flooded by her child parts' emotions as soon as she tried to move from intellectual conceptualizing of their distress to feeling for them. At times, the surge of emotion was so intense and sudden she could hardly breathe. It often felt that the parts were afraid that, if she differentiated enough from the highly protective fight parts and reached out to the vulnerable young ones, harm would come to them all. Rachel also found it hard to make the leap from identifying her parts by their feelings of distress, negative thoughts, and physical ailments (headaches, dizziness, fatigue) to engaging with them emotionally. She could use unblending skills to differentiate her normal life self from the intense reactions of her parts, but she couldn't take the next step. She could not emotionally connect to them—almost as if there were a wall separating the normal life self and the trauma-related parts.

Sarah, too, could talk compassionately and even affectionately about her parts, and she could express her understanding of them intellectually, but she had trouble making a felt connection that would allow her calm, strength, confidence, and clarity to communicate safety and empathic understanding to them. Each needed an intermediate step between being able to recognize a part and appreciate its dilemma, on the one hand, and emotionally meeting that part with enough sense of felt connection to create the building blocks of earned secure attachment, on the other. Equally important was that this intermediate step be in some way attachment-oriented or related to attachment-building.

> Without commenting negatively on Sarah's pattern of relating to her parts from a safe distance, I began to talk about the need to "take them under your wing." "You're doing such a beautiful job of noticing which parts get triggered and thanking the parts who contribute their resources to supporting your normal life, but the one thing we haven't addressed yet is how to take the little distressed ones under your wing when they get frightened. You know, they have never had anyone, not parents or grandparents or aunts and uncles, ever take them under their wings." Each time I said the words, "your wing," I reached out with my right arm as if to shelter someone under my arm. Without asking Sarah to do the same, I kept my arm outstretched as we talked more about what it would mean to "offer a wing" to her little parts. "They get scared of so many things," Sarah said, "and then there's one who reacts to that by being fearless, and she triggers them more because she shows them pictures of daredevil things she used to do when I was a kid."
>
> ME: "Hmmm … Do you think it would help her if you took the scared part under your wing so she didn't have to be so brave? Or do you think she could use a wing?"
> SARAH: [face lit up] "I think she could use a wing! She's only 7—you shouldn't have to be that brave at her age." Like many clients, Sarah felt connected to some parts and had more trouble with proximity to others, presumably the ones she had had to disown as a young girl.

ME: "OK, great. You have a clear sense of her, don't you? You really 'get' her! If she thought for a moment you felt sorry for her, she'd be so humiliated. So, offer her a wing from that place in you that 'gets' her."

SARAH: [speaking to the child] "You know, you were one daring little kid! I would have been too scared to climb a tree that high." [Laughs] "She's telling me I must not have been as scared of her mother as she was! That's what gave her the courage to climb it."

ME: "Maybe you could explain that you are now just as old as her mother was then. She probably doesn't know that. Now that you are a grownup, it's a different story. See if she'd like you to protect her from people who might yell at her and threaten her. Tell her you could take her under your wing when scary people are around—if she wants, of course."

SARAH: "She likes that idea—she is asking if my wing is big enough for her to hide behind!"

ME: "She's such a bright spirit, isn't she? What did you tell her?"

SARAH: "I told her, 'Of course it's big enough! Go ahead and hide behind it.'" [Gazing down fondly, as if the little girl were sitting beside her on the sofa, Sarah was smiling, too.] "You know, I'm so proud of her—she was so brave, and I know she helped me keep my head high."

ME: "Tell her that—with your feelings and your body. She's very special, and she needs to know that."

Sarah's humor, warmth, and down-to-earth qualities as an adult were just what her young tomboy part needed, and the surge of fierce pride and tenderness she felt for the little girl surprised Sarah and warmed her heart. For the scared parts, the visceral feeling of her pride and warmth felt like an antidote to their chronic anxiety and hopelessness. Especially because her daring child part's emotions were less overwhelming, she could feel emotionally close to her while still staying centered in her normal life self. Offering the child "a wing" was non-threatening to both, yet it conveyed the sense of safety craved even by a fearless child self.

When clients are blended with their parts and lose touch with the perspective, information, and abilities acquired in adulthood by the normal life self, it feels undeniably true that they would never be able to care for their parts, never have the confidence to make decisions, never feel enough conviction in their ability to create safety, never be able to feel anything for the parts but fear and loathing. The list of things "I could never do" is a lengthy one when it reflects the views of traumatized parts. But, somehow, when the client's normal life self is asked from a place of mindful dual awareness if he or she would be willing to "offer a wing" to a young child self, the words evoke non-threatening images. It is a harmless phrase, describing an action that doesn't require effort or faith, and it conveys both differentiation and protectiveness.

Better yet, judgmental "parts that hate the other parts" (who, at any mention of vulnerability, usually intrude with scathing rejections of any kindness or compassion) do not object to the language of "offering a wing" as they often do to the language of "caring for" or "taking care of." The therapist's demonstration of holding open an arm like a wing rarely threatens fight or flight parts either, and the ease of making the gesture communicates without words the sense of how easy it is to offer a wing to someone in need. Because it is a somatic communication, it avoids discussion or intellectual analysis of what it might mean to take someone under one's wing, and it speaks directly to young child parts yearning for contact and comfort.

Attachment Bonds Are Built through Body Experience

The formation of secure attachment in childhood always begins from the "bottom up," starting with the way infants are held, reached for, rocked, fed, soothed, or gazed upon (Ogden et al., 2006). Attachment bonds develop organically through the repetition of small somatic transactions over weeks, months, and years; verbal communication about attachment experiences do not occur much later in development. When parents reach out their arms and say "Up?" babies and toddlers reach up in response—not in reaction to the word but to the gesture. The arms are a potent conveyer of safety, insecurity, or threat in childhood: whether and how parents reach out, whether their arms are limp or half-hearted or are used to intimidate, the way muscle tension conveys the quality of the parent's experience of holding and closeness (Ogden et al., 2006). These same somatic communications can also be applied to developing earned secure attachment in child parts.

Inviting Parts "Here" Instead of "Going There"

In contrast to early models of trauma treatment, the focus of internal attachment work is on being "here," not "there." Rather than revisiting the early traumatic experiences, attention stays focused on how the normal life self can "stay present in the present" so that the part of the client that kept developing at a distance from the traumatic events can now contribute to repairing the past through the provision of crucial "missing experiences" (Kurtz, 1990; Ogden & Fisher, 2015). Neglect, trauma, and frightened and frightening caregiving involve not only harmful, inappropriate experiences but also the loss of positive experiences that are just as crucial for children to feel safe. For Sarah's parts, the sense of being under her wing, feeling her pride and protectiveness, relaxing rather than having to brace against harsh words or blows, provided an emotional, relational, and somatic experience unquestionably missing in her childhood. Under the wing of her normal life part, the attach part could feel a sense of someone "there," the ashamed part could feel Sarah's pride challenging her automatic feeling of "less than," the fearless child part could feel admired and visible, and protector parts might even be able to relax.

The provision of a missing experience, of course, does not involve the actual event. There is no way to turn back in time and provide for an adult the holding an infant should have had. There is no way for a 5-year-part to go back to the first day of school and have someone there to hold her hand. But what can be done is to make an emotional, physically felt connection to that 5-year-old self, then imaginatively recreate a felt sense of the experience she should have had by evoking the emotional and somatic components of it: the sensation of someone bigger next to her, feeling warmth and solidity, then imagining the big hand taking the little hand, and noticing the feelings and sensations. With the therapist's help in supporting dual awareness and differentiation of child and adult, each connects viscerally and emotionally to the experience of the other and mirrors it back. Each mentalizes the other: What is it like for the big self to feel the little boy next to him? What happens for the little boy when the big self reaches for his hand? How does that little hand feel in the big hand? What's it like to feel the child leaning into his body? What happens when the child hears him talk about how good it feels to hold the little boy's hand?

> Elizabeth was quiet and thoughtful as she said to her therapist, "You know, I used to think I was the wrong child born into a good family, the right family—I thought the problem was that I was 'wrong'. Now,"[she lifted her head and met her therapist's gaze] "I know that I was a right child born into the wrong family."

That feeling of being "the right child" was a missing experience for Elizabeth all through her childhood, but, as she took it in, she felt how "wrong" her family of origin was for a child like her.

> Her belief that she didn't belong was no longer real: "Of course, I didn't belong! Thank God. Those were not people I would want to belong to." Holding that present moment perspective, Elizabeth then included her parts, "The parts belong with me now—I'm the right family for them, just like I'm the right family for my own kids."

> ME: "Can you connect to the part that has always had that inner feeling of wrongness and not belonging? Can you feel her here with you right now?"
> ELIZABETH: "She's there—still feeling sick about herself ..."
> ME: "Ask her if she'd be willing to show you a picture of the home and family where she doesn't belong ..."
> ELIZABETH: "There's an image coming up: it's the apartment where I grew up—not much furniture, very bare—I just hear the sound

of my grandmother's oxygen tank. She's little, like kindergarten age, and there's no one to welcome her home from school. She's lonely, but she's also relieved. If I'm just alone with my grandmother, I won't get hurt."

ME: "Let her know that you 'get' it—in that home, it was better to be lonely than scared."

ELIZABETH: "It was ..." [sadly]

ME: "How do you feel toward her as you see that 'home' she has to live in?"

ELIZABETH: "It breaks my heart ..."

ME: "And what's that like for her to hear you? Hear that it makes you sad to see her sad."

ELIZABETH: "It feels strange but good-strange—no one ever knew she was sad before. No one seemed to care. She imagined that her grandmother cared, and that helped."

ME: "Now ask her if she'd like to see a different picture. Would she like to see where you live?"

ELIZABETH: "She's curious—I'm showing her a family photograph with my partner and kids and me out on the deck—you can see the geraniums in bloom and the trees in back and the sun is shining ..."

ME: "What's that like for her to see your home? Does she like it?"

ELIZABETH: "She's interested but a little confused about who 'these people' (my partner and kids) are ... I'm explaining to her that this is my family and it could be her family, too, if she likes it here." [Smiling at the little part's delight] "She says she likes the red flowers and the sun on her face. I'm telling her that she can stay here if she wants ... She's saying, "Really????" like I just invited her to Disneyland!" [She laughs, enjoying this moment with her little part.]

ME: "Such a tender moment: notice that feeling of her innocence and delight. This little girl takes nothing for granted, does she?" [I am deliberately directing her attention to the positive feelings being shared between little girl and adult so they can amplify each other's pleasurable experience.]

ELIZABETH: "I can feel her holding my hand very tightly—she'd like to stay here, but she's afraid 'those people,' meaning my family, won't like it. And if they don't like it, they'll be mean to her."

ME: "Of course she'd be a little afraid to trust this—the people she knew didn't need much of an excuse to be mean to her."

ELIZABETH: "It's so sad—how do I tell her that no one will hurt her here? She'll never believe me ..."

ME: "Tell her with your arms, your feelings, your body—she won't believe the words, but she might believe how it feels. Can you see her?"

ELIZABETH: "She's pulling at my hand—she wants me to go to the far side of the deck, away from my partner and kids. She looks scared to go near them—it's just so sad—she thinks they would hurt her, and she's not taking any chances."

ME: "What's your impulse, Elizabeth? Just see her frightened eyes and little face, and do whatever your motherly instincts tell you to do ..."

ELIZABETH: "I just picked her up, and I'm holding her in my arms ... [Takes a cushion and holds it tenderly.] 'I'm here with you—no one can hurt you now' ..." [Tears come up.] "'You can come here and see the red flowers whenever you want—I'll be here.'"

The key to the emotional connection developing between Elizabeth and the child part is the evoking of a multisensory experience: seeing the child's face, hearing the hiss of her grandmother's oxygen tank, re-experiencing the sense of loneliness, feeling the child's hand in hers, sensing an impulse to reach out and hold her, hearing the tenderness in Elizabeth's voice, the exchanging of images, the color of the red flowers, the emotions of grief, and the physical sense of relief. Each of these sensory components is in and of itself non-threatening, and the emotions of sadness and grief are muted by the warm, comforting feelings growing between adult and child. Alienation from her parts no longer feels imperative in these moments: there are no overwhelming emotions or horrifying images from which distance is needed. If there had been, it would have been a more difficult session, but many of the same multisensory elements would have modulated the distress: images of "here" to balance traumatic images, more focus on Elizabeth's comforting presence and connection to the child.

Fears and Phobias of Internal Attachment

As Carl visualized his boyhood self and recalled how lost and lonely he had been, he often felt sadness for that boy—but immediately afterward, before he had a chance to communicate empathy, he would have an intrusive thought, such as, "This is ridiculous—what's this about trauma and lost boys? You have more important things to think about!" It was like being jolted out of a reverie. Suddenly, Carl could feel all his muscles tightening and a feeling of disgust—then he would become very analytical. This analytical part would begin to question the theoretical rationale for the work he and I were doing, request references to the literature, and suggest other treatment options (including some Carl had tried before without success). Week after week, the cycle continued: Carl would become curious about what part was communicating through the distress he was experiencing; he would ask some Befriending Questions of the part, begin to feel increased warmth and protectiveness toward the little boy—and then the irritability would intrude once again, "What are you doing? Why are you wasting your time on this?"

Carl had discovered a "gatekeeper" part whose job it was to block him from forming attachment bonds with young, vulnerable parts. The gatekeeper had clearly learned the rules from Carl's parents: nothing but rational, goal-oriented behavior was welcome in their home. Their son, however, was a sensitive, anxious child (aware that he didn't fit in the way other boys did, though not yet aware he was gay), struggling with separation anxiety from his mother and intimidated by his father. Their message was: no son of theirs would be a "sissy"; that is, if he wanted their love, he would have to measure up to their standards. The gatekeeper part had evolved to protect the little boy from rejection: "Keep your eyes on the 'important things,' and you will be accepted and respected."

The high point of the gatekeeper's efforts was Carl's successful graduation from law school amidst the congratulations of his parents. Then a series of rejections in relationships with men triggered the little boy so powerfully that Carl was flooded with fears of abandonment and an intense yearning to feel special to someone. The gatekeeper's judgments and distractions were no longer enough to block the child's hurt and neediness. Next followed a series of sessions in which yet another kind of gatekeeper erected stumbling blocks to thwart Carl's attachment to the child part.

> Carl could feel the child's fear in his body: "He wants to call Nick [his former boyfriend] so badly—he wants to beg him to come back."
>
> ME: "Ask him what he's worried about if Nick isn't here ..."
> CARL: "He says if Nick isn't here, then no one loves him ..."
> ME: "And, what's he worried about if no one loves him?"
> CARL: "He'll be alone—he's too little—it's too scary for him to be alone."
> ME: [using the Four Befriending Questions] "Ask him: what is he worried about if he can't do things by himself because it's too scary?"
> CARL: "That he'll be humiliated—people will laugh at him, and they won't want to be around him—he'll be all alone." [The core fear]
> ME: "That is scary for a small boy ... Ask him what he needs from you, right here, right now, to not be so afraid of being rejected and left all alone."
> CARL: [doubles over and cries out in a younger voice] "This is too hard—I can't do this!"
> ME: "Carl, are you still here? Can you hear the little boy calling out to you, Carl? He's telling you how hard this is for him—of course, it is! He's too young to take care of himself. He needs someone to be here for him." [I deliberately repeat his given name several times to cue his normal life self to stay present with the child part rather than dissociate or shut down.]
> CARL: [still in the child state] "I want to go—this is too hard."

ME: [speaking directly to the child part as if I were talking to a young boy] "Of course it's too hard for a little boy. Children need a grownup—they shouldn't be left all alone." Then shifting to a tone of voice geared to an adult: "Carl, are you still there? I want you to notice the little boy ... We can't leave him all alone—he's very scared and so hurt. Carl, are you there? [Carl nods.] Great—this little boy needs you, and you're blended with him so it's hard to help him. See what happens if you say the words, "He is feeling scared—this is too much for him."

CARL: [now in his adult voice] "That's a little better, but he's pretty upset."

ME: "That's all the more reason why he needs you to stay present and not abandon him by blending with him. He really needs you to hang in there. Let him know you're here—with your feelings and your body—make sure he can feel you with him. Can he?"

CARL: "Yes, he says he can feel me trying ..."

ME: "That's really important, huh? He can feel that you are there and you are trying, and that's new for him. No one even tried to do that for him before ..."

CARL: "I'm telling him that I will keep trying—I may not be good at it right away, but I won't stop trying."

ME: "What's it like for him to hear you say that? I bet no one ever said that before: 'I will keep trying to be there—'"

CARL: "It feels good to him—which makes me feel good—but then he's saying that he's afraid to believe me, and that makes me want to give up."

ME: "That's what your mother did: she gave up because she didn't have the bandwidth to accept her son as he was. You can do better than that. Think for a moment: why would this little boy be afraid to believe you? How would that make sense?"

CARL: "Well, sometimes my mother was loving—when I was the son she wanted. But I couldn't count on her. That's probably why he doesn't trust anyone. And I guess I haven't been exactly reliable myself ..."

ME: "Yes, that's true—you haven't been reliable—you didn't know, and I can tell that you feel badly about that. Let him hear that. ..."

CARL: [tears come to his eyes] "He wants to cry when I tell him it was my fault that his feelings got ignored. He always felt there was something wrong with him—he made his mom upset just by being scared and wanting her near him."

ME: [speaking to the child] "He didn't know it wasn't him—he was just a little boy doing the best he could to make his mom understand he needed her." [Then speaking to the adult] "You know it wasn't his fault, too, Carl—would you ever expect your little boy to adapt to you instead of the other way around?"

CARL: [tearful] "I just want to reach out and hold him—"

ME: [interrupting him to add] "Just follow that impulse to reach out to him ..."

CARL: "I feel so sad for him—I just want to protect him ... [starts to sob]"

ME: "Let him know with your feelings and your body how much you want to protect him and keep him safe with you ..." [keeps talking to Carl and the young part while he cries] "He's waited such a long time for this ... and now there's finally someone here ... so many feelings he's been waiting to tell someone ... and now, finally, at last, someone is here. Notice the tears of relief: finally someone's here, and he can cry now."

CARL: "He's so sad, but relieved, too—I keep telling him I'm not going anywhere, and I won't forget about him again. He won't be alone." [Another burst of tears as the little boy hears Carl's words.] "I'm telling him that I like having him here with me—no one likes being alone, even grownups."

ME: "That's right—no one likes being alone—and now he has you, and you have him. That's important: he never ever has to be alone again because he has you, and you have him." [I deliberately repeat this phrase because it describes the essence of feeling attached, and I want both child and adult selves to feel what it's like to have the other. "Notice what it feels like to have his little body in your strong arms, feel his tears against your chest ..."

CARL: "It feels so good. I can feel him. He's starting to relax finally—like he can trust me a little. Before, he kept asking, 'You're not going away, are you?' [Tears come up again] That's heartbreaking—I don't want him to have to worry about that—it shouldn't be the first thing on a kid's mind."

ME: "You are so right, Carl—he shouldn't have to worry about being left. I want you to notice how good you are at naturally knowing what he feels and wants. You have such an intuitive sense of what kids need. Your mother certainly didn't have that, but you do."

CARL: "I do—it's a protectiveness—feeling how little he is and wanting to make sure he's not hurt. My mother definitely didn't have that. But how do I keep this going?" [Notice the shift in tone to the very practical normal life way of thinking.]

ME: "The key is making him a priority, just as you would if you adopted a child of your own. You would keep him in mind from the time you woke up in the morning to the time you went to bed at night. You would wonder, 'How's my little boy doing?' Try that. And if you forget to do that, make sure you apologize to him!"

We end the session with a discussion of "parenting tips," ways that Carl could remind himself that this boy, like any child, needs to feel held in the mind of the caregiver, to feel seen or "recognized" (Benjamin, 1994), to have his feelings noticed and comforted, validated, and regulated. I offer him a menu of ideas: starting each day by saying "good morning" to the little boy; relating to him "face to face" by putting out a picture of himself at the age he senses the little boy to be; going to a toy store to find a stuffed animal for him based on what toy lights up his eyes or keeps drawing his attention; carrying with him a small object (a stone or tiny toy animal, for example) that symbolizes the child as a way of holding him close, imaginatively tucking the child in at night as a way of making sure he feels safe. Just as we do with parents and families, it is important for the therapist to remember that what happens outside each session is just as important as what happens during the therapy. Especially for fragmented individuals with histories of trauma, it is important to be attentive to how they carry the work of therapy past the hour.

Touching moments of heart-to-heart connection between a small child part and a compassionate adult self are important, but to facilitate the shift from internal alienation to earned secure attachment is "10% inspiration and 90% perspiration," as the saying goes. Repetition over and over again of the same steps (connecting to a part, creating moments of repair and attunement, and deepening the bond between child and adult selves) and then integrating the experience by evoking it again and again are the most important ingredients in lasting change. In the 1980s and 1990s, we believed that the intensity of the emotional experience would result in a transformative shift. Now, informed by research from the neuroscience world, we know that neuralplasticity or actual change in the brain is best facilitated by intensive repetition of new patterns of action and reaction (Schwartz & Begley, 2002).

Rupture and Repair of Internal Attachment Relationships

Knowing that "healing" cannot result from re-experiencing old emotional pain provides a different sense of direction to the therapy beyond stabilization and memory processing, the traditional ingredients associated with trauma treatment. Without efforts to repair emotional ruptures, bring solace to parts in distress, and combat self-alienation and self-loathing with internal attachment bonding, traumatized clients cannot feel whole, safe and welcome. Deeply felt self-acceptance and self-compassion can only develop when our young, wounded parts experience the safety of a here-and-now adult's unconditional attachment to them, when they sense that they now have a protector and advocate. Because there will inevitably be competing, equally intense drives to seek connection and to defend against potential harm or rejection, the therapist must shoulder responsibility for keeping in mind the ultimate purpose of the work: "repairing" the implicit memories of early attachment rupture being communicated by the part's shame, fear, sadness, anger, or emotional pain. Although each client and each part is unique, each manifestation of internal self-alienation subtly different, the building blocks of internal attachment repair remain the same:

- As the client reports emotional distress, negative thoughts, or physical reactions to a trigger, *the therapist asks the client to recognize these symptoms as a part.* "There's a part of you that's really overwhelmed by shame, huh? Can you feel her with you now? What's telling you she's there?" The therapist first helps the client mindfully differentiate traumatized part versus adult observer, then poses questions that build a felt sense or portrait of this part, bringing it alive in such a way that the client can spontaneously feel interest in or concern for the part and respond empathically to the question, "And how do you feel toward this part now?" If the answer isn't mindful or compassionate, the therapist assumes that there is another part intruding that also needs to be named and welcomed, needs someone more interested in whatever parts are present than in the goals of today's session.

- *Try to elicit a felt sense of each part,* not an intellectual interpretation. "Notice how she speaks to you through feelings or words or physical sensations—that's her way of communicating—let her know you're listening—you want to know what she's trying to tell you. And if you're not sure, just ask her ..."

- *Place greater emphasis on the togetherness of adult client and child* than on the content of their conversation. "What's it like for that child to feel you here with him? To feel your interest and concern?" Questions such as these help clients notice the effect of their attention, words, and concern on the part, to realize the impact they have when parts experience being seen or mentalized. "It's very special for him, huh? And how does it feel inside you to sense how much your caring means to him?" The therapist takes advantage of opportunities to bring to the attention of the normal life part to how pleasurable mutuality in attachment feels: the warm and loving feelings that reward us for taking the time to meet a child's needs is the "payoff" that fuels us to greater efforts to be attuned.

- *Encourage inner reciprocal communication.* "Ask her: Can she feel you there with her now? Good, she can—that's great. Let her know that we're both listening, and we want to understand how upset she is." Make sure "inner communication" is not a guess or intellectualized interpretation: "Don't try to think about what she would answer—ask her and then just listen inside. You might hear words, feel an emotion, get an image or memory. He's giving you a picture of his room ... maybe he's trying to say that he's upset about something that happened here." The therapist guides the client's normal life self to interpret the child's non-verbal communications and then asks for correction: "Did I get that right? I really want to understand."

- *Cultivate trust.* "Let her know you understand completely: she *wants* to trust you but it's hard—she's been hurt so much. Communicate to her that you know—really, really know—why she'd be afraid to trust you. Because you do. You absolutely know what it was like in that home." The therapist needs to capitalize on these moments of emotional recognition and use them to deepen the sense of connection. "What's it like for her to sense that you 'get' it? Does she like it when you understand? When you believe her?"

- *Use what doesn't work as an attachment-building moment.* Repairs are even more powerful when they follow from what goes wrong relationally. "He's retreating, huh? He's so afraid of being hurt that he's backing away from what he most wants. Let him know that's OK—you understand, right? See what it's like if you reassure him you won't go away. You'll stay right here, and he can take all the time he needs to be sure he can trust you." Feeling the importance of the moment, I speak for the child and guide the adult to an attuned response. I want to help my client gain confidence as a "parent" in interpreting the child's signals and responding empathically.

- *Use the Four Befriending Questions* (see Appendix F) to explore the parts' fears, conflicts, mistrust, hypervigilance, shame, or anger. "Could you ask that part what he's worried about [if he comes closer to you] [if he tells you how angry he is]?" Even when therapists feel confident they know the answers already, they need to remember that the purpose of the four questions is to increase dual awareness, deepen the internal dialogue, discover the child's core fear and highlight it, and then teach a model for needs-meeting by asking the child to verbalize one concrete in-the-moment need that could address the core fear. No therapist can turn back the clock and prevent heartbreaking, horrifying events from taking place, but we can help clients and their parts to experience how little moments of safety, care, or heartfelt connection in present time can build warm, nourishing implicit memories side by side with the memories of abandonment and abuse.

- *Each response by a part becomes another chance for repair* facilitated by the therapist's guidance. "So she's telling you that she wants to believe you 'get it,' but she's afraid you'll just take advantage of her trust—they all do ... Do you get that, too? Let her know that with your feelings and your body that you completely understand why she expects people to use her instead of help her ..."

- *Insist on responsibility and accountability.* The internal community of parts has often unconsciously recreated the hostile environment of the client's family of origin: the normal life self is likely to have neglected the parts, allowed hostile or sadistic parts to persecute them, or expressed wishes to be "normal" (i.e., to not have parts). When parts say, "I don't trust you because you only care about going on without us" or "How can I trust you when you've never listened? Never even seemed to care what I felt?" the therapist must encourage the client to connect to that complaint: "Do you think there's some truth to what this part is saying? Is he right that you didn't want to listen, didn't want to care? If so, let him know that—you're the kind of person who can say, 'I made a mistake, and I'm sorry.' Tell him."

- *Use these mistakes and empathic failures in the service of repair.* "What's it like for him to have you take responsibility? To hear you say that you realize you have been pushing him away?" "Yes, you can feel him relaxing just a little bit when you acknowledge the truth ... Not many grownups ever did that, huh?"

- *Maximize the moments of attunement* so they are experienced physically and emotionally. "If this little girl were standing in front of you right this minute, what would you want to do? Reach out to her? Take her hand? Or pick her up and hold her?" "Feel what that's like to have this little boy in your arms. To feel his hand in yours. Is it a good feeling?" "Take in the warmth of his body and the feeling of holding him safely ... Ask him if he would feel less scared if you did this every time he got afraid."
- *Avoid the tendency to shift away from mindful connection to a part* to habitual insight-oriented discussion. It is the therapist's job to remind clients that there is a child right there, listening to every word spoken, who needs to know he or she will not be forgotten again: "As we are talking, check in with that little boy and see how he's doing now. He needs to feel that he won't be forgotten this time, and the only way he'll know is for you not to forget him. Remember that children learn what they live. You can say you won't forget him—now you'll have to live your life without forgetting him. It may be hard, but you can't break a promise to a child—every safe, caring parent knows that ..."

When these steps are repeated over and over again, the normal life self feels increasingly differentiated from the trauma-driven emotions of the parts and can therefore feel more spontaneously caring and compassionate toward them. The parts in turn increasingly feel "held" by someone older and wiser. Each feels needed and wanted by each other, just as parents and children in a secure attachment relationship feel. "Earned secure attachment" bestows on the human mind and body the same qualities and resources as secure attachment in childhood: an ability to tolerate closeness and distance, giving and receiving, empathic attunement and empathic failure, the ability to see shades of grey, and the ability to tolerate disappointment.

References

Epstein, M. (1995). *Thoughts without a thinker: psychotherapy from a Buddhist perspective*. New York: Basic Books.

Fogel, A. & Garvey, A. (2007). Alive communication. *Infant Behavior and Development*, 30, 251–257.

Gilbert, P. & Andrews, B. (1998). *Shame: interpersonal behaviour, pychopathology & culture*. New York: Oxford University Press.

Herman, J. L. (1992). *Trauma and recovery*. New York: Basic Books.

Hughes, D. (2007). *Attachment-focused family therapy*. New York: W.W. Norton.

Kurtz, R. (1990). *Body-centered psychotherapy: the Hakomi method*. Updated edition. Mendocino, CA: Life Rhythm.

Ogden, P. & Fisher, J. (2015). *Sensorimotor Psychotherapy: interventions for trauma and attachment*. New York: W.W. Norton.

Ogden, P., Minton, K., & Pain, C. (2006). *Trauma and the body: a sensorimotor approach to psychotherapy*. New York: W.W. Norton.

Porges, S. W. (2011). *The polyvagal theory: neurophysiological foundations of emotions, attachment, communication, and self-regulation.* New York: W.W. Norton.

Schwartz, J. & Begley, S. (2002). *The mind and the brain: neuralplasticity and the power of mental force.* New York: Harper-Collins.

Schwartz, R. (2001). *Introduction to the internal family systems model.* Oak Park, IL: Trailhead Publications.

Van der Kolk, B.A. (2014). *The body keeps the score: brain, mind and body in the healing of trauma.* New York: Viking Press.

CHAPTER 10

Restoring What Was Lost: Deepening the Connection to Our Young Selves

"When those aspects [of ourselves] that have been unconsciously refused are returned, when they are made conscious, accepted, tolerated or integrated, the self can then be at one, the need to maintain the self-conscious edifice disappears, and the force of compassion [is] automatically unleashed."

(Epstein, 1995, p. 19)

As clients learn to speak the language of parts, increase their ability to unblend, and cultivate a dual awareness relationship characterized by curiosity rather than aversion, there is often a spontaneous settling of the nervous system, calming trauma-related parts. The habit of mindful noticing creates a little space between the young child and a wise adult who finds it much easier to be curious now that he or she is less overwhelmed. Cause-and-effect relationships become clearer. The client feels less "crazy" when "over-reactions" are reframed as normal reactions of traumatized children. Now, the client can observe the influence of the parts on their actions and reactions and practice being aware of impulses to blend and make a conscious choice: "If I blend with the despair of the depressed part, it will upset the little parts and trigger the suicidal part—maybe I don't want to 'give in' to the feeling of hopelessness after all." With a conscious, voluntary separation from trauma-related parts and a more regulated nervous system, clients begin to develop less aversion and more compassion for them—or at least perspective toward them. Particularly with clients with chronic high-risk symptoms, self-destructive behavior, substance-abuse, and/or eating disorders, stabilization is almost entirely dependent upon acquiring the ability to differentiate the aims and goals of a normal life versus those of a desperate flight or fight part more afraid of trauma-related vulnerability than of death. Traditional treatments for these issues typically focus on cessation of unsafe behavior, thereby alienating and polarizing the fight and flight parts and often jeopardizing stabilization. Similarly, shame, exhaustion, and self-doubt are most often treated as indications of chronic depression or low self-esteem, rather than understood as communications from parts who bear the burden of submission and humiliation. Worse yet, when client symptoms are chronic or treatment-resistant, they are often labeled as "personality disordered," confirming already held beliefs in their defectiveness and not belonging. But stabilization of even the most dysregulated, dissociated clients can gradually be achieved with repeated practice of the following simple steps described in more detail in Chapters 4 and 5:

- Learning to recognize triggered emotional and somatic reactions as "triggering" and avoid interpreting them as here-and-now responses to the environment.
- Evoking curiosity by reframing these responses as "communications from parts."
- Increasing client ability to mindfully notice moment-to-moment interactions between triggering stimuli and triggered parts.
- Differentiating the qualities of an observing normal life self with either the ability or desire for a life beyond trauma from the characteristic signs and symptoms of traumatically activated parts.
- Cultivating not only the ability to name the parts but growing compassion for their youth and ability to survive in the face of "what happened."
- Learning to communicate internally, building trust, and making felt connections to the parts.

These simple initial tasks are the foundation upon which any deeper work must be built, and it is well worth the therapist taking the extra time to stabilize these abilities until the client can use them independently outside of therapy, not just with the therapist present. It is not helpful to clients to move ahead to "the deeper work," only to discover in hindsight that the client was more dysregulated and more blended with his or her parts than the therapist realized and now is overwhelmed by emotions or traumatic memories.

Therapists (and sometimes their clients, too) put enormous pressure on themselves to accomplish therapeutic goals quickly. Often, the sense of urgency is driven by the client's suffering and the empathic wish to relieve it, sometimes by the pressures of limited sessions and/or insurance coverage. Sometimes, we push ourselves because we believe or are led to believe that a particular method "should" work in just a short time, and we question ourselves rather than the method when it does not generate quick results. We also do not take into account the role of structural dissociation: structurally dissociated clients cannot integrate new information or tolerate emotional intensity, and they are also hindered by the internal conflicts between parts. Always in trauma work, the therapist's motto should be, "Slower is faster." Taking the time to build a foundation for each piece of work allows a steady progression toward resolution, rather than a great leap forward followed by two steps back—a pattern to which traumatized clients are all too prone.

In traditional phase-oriented treatment, stabilization is followed by a phase of "memory-processing" based on the assumption that unmetabolized memories of traumatic events are the active ingredient in post-traumatic stress. However, as discussed throughout this book, research suggests that the "active ingredients" underlying post-traumatic disorders are chronic autonomic dysregulation, situationally activated implicit memories without words, and fragmented parts that experience themselves as still in danger of annihilation or abandonment or both (Van der Kolk, 2014; Ogden et al., 2006). "Trauma processing" must therefore include the body and the parts, and it must focus on reorganizing the individual's implicit memories and *relationship* to the traumatic past. For clients to transform their relationship to frightening, overwhelming, humiliating events necessitates acquiring the ability to be "on speaking terms" with the traumatic past without fear of being overwhelmed or humiliated. In Sensorimotor Psychotherapy (Ogden et al., 2006), the litmus test for assessing client readiness to process memory is the question, "What happens when you just 'think about thinking about it?'" I once asked that question of Annie, and the next week, she reported that she'd been having flashbacks all day and all night ever since. Clearly, the question was very premature.

To "process memory" requires preparation: learning to overcome the fear of emotional vulnerability, of the body, and of the parts, reduce sensitivity to traumatic triggering, and inhibit the automatic tendency to "self-defeating stories" or self-blame. While stabilization requires the ability to notice, identify, and differentiate one's parts, the healing of traumatic wounds necessitates an additional step: making an emotional connection to the parts and providing reparative experiences that serve as antidotes to the past.

Reorganizing the Relationship to the Past

Developing compassionate relationships with parts who are hurt, lonely, consumed by rage, frightened, and ashamed is a challenging job, however. Because their emotions are so raw and overwhelming, welcoming them requires tolerating their traumatic activation, learning how to remain unblended despite the distraction of strong physical impulses, and regulating their over- or underwhelming affects. In practical terms, this means that the therapist must help clients maintain their ability to stay curious, despite the intense internal struggles, and cultivate enough compassion to communicate welcome to each part. Therapists will be challenged here by training that prioritizes the felt connection to strong emotions over other types of experience, but it is important to be patient. If the client feels "too much" for the parts, he or she will become flooded with their emotions. To the extent that the normal life self has been able to develop confidence in being able to stay present, has learned to recover from when flooded and "come back," has slowly come to appreciate each part's role in surviving the traumatic past, and has the ability to offer a healing or "loving presence" (Kurtz, 1990) to wounded selves, he or she will be prepared to offer reparative experiences to the parts. "Loving presence" is a state of being: warm, compassionate, curious, looking for what is right instead of what's wrong, unconditionally accepting. Ron Kurtz emphasizes the importance of the therapist cultivating a "loving presence," that is, finding something to "love" in all clients, even those who are stuck, resistant, devaluing, narcissistic, or demanding. In that state of consciousness, time slows down; our bodies relax; there is a feeling of warmth—all is "OK." As important as this concept is in the therapeutic relationship, it is equally important in individuals' relationships to their parts. They must find something to love about each one.

The Role of Memory

Although processing traumatic memory is not the objective of this work, often memories of specific events come up spontaneously as information is obtained about a part's fears, doubts, and longings. Rather than being the "target" of the therapy, memories and images should be capitalized upon to provide a context for evoking compassion for the young child who felt the loneliness, fear, pain, or shattered faith in those he or she loved.

The most important therapeutic purpose of such memories is to deepen a heartfelt bond between a normal life self and the young child he or she once was. Transformation of the client's relationship to the unfinished past often happens spontaneously when the normal life self suddenly connects to the felt experience of the child and immediately feels sadness or protectiveness. Tears spring up spontaneously; the chest or heart opens; the client's arms feel the impulse to reach out to the child; words of compassion arise spontaneously. There is a feeling of welcome and attunement in the client's body—the child in that memory can "come home" now. It's safe. In my mind, these moments are what it means to "process" memory: the client can tolerate the memory when he or she observes it as "what happened" to the little part, and creating the new ending to that event transforms the experience. Now, it ends with the child safely in the arms of someone safe and caring. Both adult and child feel a warm and loving connection to each other.

If clients are helped to notice those moments, to identify how it feels emotionally and somatically to connect empathically to young parts, and then to focus on these new feelings for 30 seconds or more, the brain will begin to encode them as memory (Hanson, 2014; Ogden & Fisher, 2015). These new experiences are further deepened when new meaning is made of them: "Notice that when the parts feel your caring and protectiveness, they can relax a little bit. Ask them: do they feel safer when they feel heard and understood?" Asking child parts about their feelings in response to the adult self's protectiveness is an intimate question, one that can only enhance the felt sense of closeness and attunement. When the child part says "Yes!" or even "I wish I could believe you," clients experience a stronger felt sense of bonding and a felt sense of responsibility to stay present and protective.

Unable to unblend from parts afraid of leaving the house, Annie tried to go back to work by opening a tutoring business in her home. That way, she didn't have to leave the house because children came to her for their lessons. Nonetheless, her ability to create lesson plans was constantly interrupted by inexplicable deletions of material from her computer, anxious predictions of failure ("You'll be found out"), and a fear so intense she literally shook like a leaf before her student arrived.

Asking Annie to notice what the parts were trying to tell her, I asked, "What are they afraid of? Ask inside ..."

After listening for a minute, Annie said: "A lot of things—making a mistake, not knowing enough, even just having someone in the house."

ME: "Ask them: what did it mean in their home to make a mistake or not know enough?"

ANNIE: "They say it meant that you got punished—or you didn't see things coming before it was too late."

ME: "And what did it mean to have people in the house?"

Annie, after a pause: "It meant that they had come to take you somewhere bad or do something bad to you." [Notice that events are validated but not explored to keep the emphasis on how such experiences would make a child feel.]

I try to translate the parts' communication to help Annie "get" these fears at a more visceral level: "Annie, do you see what they're saying? Your parts aren't just worried about being embarrassed or 'failing.' They are worried about being killed. They just want to make it out alive! Is that right? Ask them if that's true."

ANNIE: "They say you're right: they don't think it's safe out there. They don't want to risk it. I didn't realize what it meant from their point of view. I just thought they felt ashamed of me, so I tried to push through their objections and just get the job done."

ME: "Ask them: what did it mean to them to be so scared and have their fears ignored?" [Annie pauses as if listening inside to the parts.]

ANNIE: "It means that they still aren't safe if no one cares enough about them to listen."

ME: "And how are you feeling toward them now as you 'get' that?"

ANNIE: "I feel badly. I didn't mean to scare them."

ME: "Let them know that—with your feelings and your body, not just your words. Let them know you feel badly that they were so scared."

ANNIE: "It's hard—I just feel their anxiety. When I try to feel for them, I just blend with them."

The therapist now models an intervention for Annie to try out with her parts: "Ask them if you could have their full attention because you have an important announcement for them, a very serious announcement. See how they respond if you say it both with your words and with your body very emphatically, 'I would never let anyone in this house who would hurt you—*never*. No one bad is ever allowed in this house.' [I model the emphatic tone I want her to use.] Don't say it if you don't believe it, but I think that's the rule you created years ago, even before you had children."

Annie could feel her body relax a little, so I asked her to repeat the same words again: "I would never, *ever* let anyone in this house who would hurt you." A calm began to settle in her body.

ANNIE: "I've spent so many years trying to ignore the parts or just being blended with them—I never thought about *why* they were so scared. It never occurred to me that they thought they were still in New Jersey."

"See what happens," her therapist suggested, "if each time you sit down at the computer or are expecting kids for lessons, you start by making the same announcement: 'I wouldn't be doing this if it wasn't safe. I will never allow anyone to enter this house who would hurt you. Never, *ever.*'"

When Annie remembered the meaning of her parts' alarm reactions to her students and reassured them using the same words over and over again, the parts relaxed and more easily allowed her to do her job without interruption. When she forgot, lost connection to the felt sense of wanting to protect and reassure them, and automatically tried to push through their fears, she would immediately experience renewed difficulty once again. Pushing through their fears was necessary when she was young, but it was a cruel re-enactment of the traumatic past now.

"Me Now" versus "That Part of Me Then"

Because traumatized and normal life parts share the same mind and body, because triggered responses activate the body and nervous system as a whole, most clients are accustomed to being blended with their parts, losing connection to their experiences of competency, mastery, or enjoyment of life. When Annie was asked, "Why might the parts have been afraid to do this then? Why would it have been frightening in New Jersey? In that house? With that family?" she was reminded that she, as an adult, now lived in another house with another family (her family of procreation), in a different state, even in a different decade. And when the parts reminded her that they lived under constant threat of physical, sexual, and emotional abuse, she felt a sense of surprise. For the normal life part of Annie, the trauma was far away, a distant memory that she did not care to revisit or even think about. In her adulthood, she hadn't stopped to ask herself, "Why don't I want to revisit those memories?" She had been too busy raising children, tending to her home and garden, participating in the community, and being a surrogate parent to students and neighborhood children. Almost all of those activities involved some kind of repair of the traumatic past: giving her children and surrogate children the experiences of care and understanding she had never had, creating an environment in her home that communicated safety, keeping her home and yard well-tended (as unlike her neglected childhood family home as possible). At this stage of the work, it is particularly important for the therapist to challenge any "false self" assumptions that come up. Because the left brain normal life part is not connected to strong trauma-driven emotions, unless blended with them, and is fearful of overwhelm, it is easy for clients to feel a sense of being an empty shell just going through the motions of life and to conclude that their ability to function is a pseudo-self. Annie illustrates how unwise that conclusion can be: believing that she had created a false self, she failed to see how closely her values and priorities as an adult reflected her, how she had unconsciously made meaning of the past by creating a very healthy, creative, compassionate environment for her family of choice, very different from that of her family of origin.

> For Sam, the sense of his "real self" was most connected to a young depressed boy part who just wanted to read and daydream and to a teenager whose mood depended on regular access to "sex, drugs, and rock 'n roll." His normal life self was less palpable to him despite the evidence of his professional achievements, marriage, friends, and young son. He had a tendency to ignore adult commitments and minimize his normal life self as just a persona he needed to get through the day—mostly to humor others. As often happens, the minimizing of the normal life self increased the power of the younger parts to influence his decisions: rather than paying bills or taking the car to be serviced, the child part would pull him to read another chapter in his book or watch a movie on TV. Days passed in sexual fantasy or lost in the exploits of fictional characters.

Challenging "false self" assumptions requires the therapist to believe that the ability to function is just as important as the ability to feel emotion, an attitude not always taught in therapist training programs. Functioning and feeling each represent a different hemisphere of the brain: the left brain prioritizes order, sequence, organization, and good judgment, while the right brain is driven by emotional and survival imperatives. The left brain is more positive in outlook because it has access to facts, while the right brain, though deeply emotional, is also more focused on the negative and on threat (Hanson, 2014). Both sides of the brain and both priorities are necessary to living a full, rich life. Additionally, as I remind my clients, a false self is a physiological impossibility: even when different individuals emulate the same person or borrow the same verbal expressions or mannerisms, each will be unique. Each imitation will be molded by the individual's own brain, body, and personality—which in turn reflects his or her unique developmental history. The therapist must help clients to appreciate how, lacking normal role models in the family, the normal life part nonetheless persevered. Borrowing role models from other families or imitating valued qualities missing in traumatic and neglectful environments was a manifestation of the normal life self's determination to build a new life no matter how insurmountable the odds. Helping clients to appreciate the qualities and resources of their normal life selves and be more aware of their capacity for curiosity, compassion, clarity, creativity, confidence, and commitment is an important responsibility for the therapist. Without explicit attention to befriending the normal life "me now," clients will continue to assume that the "me then" conveyed by their parts' feelings and dysregulation is "who I am."

> To challenge entrenched cognitive schemas centered on her worthlessness and failure, I asked Gilda if we could work on the practice of "just owning" or acknowledging the facts of her adult life and normal life self. I made the first "thing to own" very factual and easy for her. "Just take a moment to 'own' that you are the mother of three children." "They are the best thing that ever happened to me," replied Gilda.
>
> ME: "Yes, they feel like the best thing that's ever happened to you—and just 'own' that feeling. Is that a good feeling?"
> GILDA: "Yes, it is—I'm so proud of them. By the way, I've been helping out in my daughter's class once a week. Those kids are so cute."
> ME: "They are, aren't they? Such a cute age. So 'own' that, too. You love kids, and you like helping out in Julie's class. I bet you never had a parent who'd have come to your first grade class!"
> GILDA: (laughs) "That's for sure, and I'm not sure I'd have wanted them to come. It would have been mortifying."
> ME: "But your daughter doesn't have to feel that way, does she? I bet she likes it when you come. 'Own' that, too. You've been a parent whose daughter is proud to have helping out in her classroom."

Owning the facts of one's life is a left brain activity: gathering information and categorizing it. Gilda had been confused by her experience of the parts' strong, right brain-related emotions coupled with an emotionally disconnected left brain functioning self. It made her feel fraudulent to feel so vulnerable and dysregulated at some times and to feel nothing at other times—a perception she held as a belief for many years without ever taking the time to orient to the facts of her history, her life now, and her environment. Though she worked as an accountant, a job for which her left brain was an asset, the overwhelming nature of the parts' feelings made her normal life self feel "dead" inside. By being asked to "own" the pleasure she took in her daughter as well as her daughter's friends and classmates, she could experience that her normal life left brain self did have emotions. She just hadn't recognized them before because they were less intense and quite enjoyable—and because she had endorsed self-defeating story about herself without ever adding up the facts. Week after week, she noticed and practiced "owning" facts about herself, many of which surprised her. "You have been asked to host three weddings and a graduation party at your home—could you take a moment to 'own' that fact?" "Wow," she said, "people must really love me or love my home or both ... and now I can hear a part saying, 'They are just using her, Gilda—face it,' and the pleasure I just felt went away."

I commented: "Well, I think you and I just got a glimpse into why it's hard to own the facts of your life now—it brings up 'too much' pleasure to feel the richness of your chosen life, and your fight part gets alarmed."

Establishing Internal Communication with Dysregulated Parts

While continuing to identify their roles, resources, capacities, and daily activities as evidence of a strong normal life part, the therapist also repeatedly continues to remind clients to assume that day-to-day difficulties with feelings or functioning are an expression of parts being triggered by normal life trauma-related stimuli. Next, as the normal life self "listens" with curiosity or compassion or both to the dysregulated emotions being conveyed by parts, he or she is taught to respond to these communications by asking the parts to say more about their feelings: What are they worried about? Notice that the term "worried about" is consistently used in response to expressions of fear, shame, anger, sadness, even numbing and shutdown. The assumption is that all feeling responses represent a worry about something. "Worry" is a term familiar to children and adults alike. Perhaps more importantly, it is a word that does not threaten any of the parts: "anger" would be a threatening word for attach and submit; "scared" would be difficult for fight and flight parts to endorse. The expression, "What are you worried about if _____," can be used to gather more information about almost any situation therapist or client is likely to encounter. I can ask, "What is the little part worried about if I go on vacation?" "What is the ashamed part worried about if he gives up the shame and holds his head high?" "What is the hopeless part worried about if she were to be hopeful?" "What is the suicidal part worried about if Felicia makes a commitment to live?"

Usually, the worries initially expressed by parts are concrete or superficial: afraid of making a mistake, afraid of being hurt, afraid of being judged or rejected, afraid things will fall apart. Just like children, child parts tend to be more concrete and stimulus-bound. The next step is to inquire more deeply, just as we would with any child: What is he worried about if someone judges him? What is she worried about if she makes a mistake? Then the normal life self is asked to make a connection between the parts' fears and the childhood environment in which the trauma occurred: why would a child be scared of being judged in that world? Why would he be terrified of making a mistake in that family? The purpose of this step is not to retrieve memory. Making a connection between past and present always reflects the goal of increasing empathic connections to the parts' emotions and cultivating attunement. The memory is not explored in detail but serves as a vehicle for empathy: "No wonder the ashamed part won't give up her shame—it kept her safe. Maybe you could let her know that it's OK if she feels safer keeping it as long as she knows that it's just a way to survive—it doesn't mean it's true."

However, initiating and sustaining an internal dialogue with parts autonomically activated by perceived threat is not always simple. It requires helping clients maintain dual awareness in the face of intrusive anxiety-provoking thoughts, shaking and jitters, elevated heart rate, tightness in the chest, sick feelings in the stomach, constriction in the throat, and impulses to run away, crawl under the covers, punch a wall, or claw at one's own skin. These somatic reactions are challenging for most clients to tolerate and often exceed their ability to describe, much less regulate. As unaccustomed as they are to the vocabulary of emotion, traumatized individuals are even more at a loss for words when it comes to their bodies (Ogden & Fisher, 2015). Even the word "body" can be so triggering that it evokes more activation rather than less.

The therapist's job is to assume that these challenges are just part of the work, not a risk to life or a "deal breaker." Anytime we help clients learn a new skill outside of their current repertoire or try out a new approach, it is often triggering for the parts. As many clients describe it, "I know I can survive this way, but if I try something different, what if it doesn't work? What if I can't survive?" Clearly, these are the voices of parts anticipating attack or annihilation, but their strong reactions to change often paralyze both the therapist and the normal life self. The therapist asks: Is this new step or skill too much? Should the fears be ignored, acknowledged, or are they a sign that the client is not ready?

Rupture and Repair

Therapists can be reassured by the research demonstrating that even as infants, the window of tolerance expands and resilience increases when infants are exposed to experiences or stimuli just slightly outside their comfort zone and then are soothed and re-regulated. (Tronick, 2007) In the attachment literature, this phenomenon is labeled "rupture and repair": the child's experience of discomfort is followed by some kind of repair (encouragement, soothing, reassurance, distraction) that reinstates attunement and facilitates positive feeling states. When these are repeated experiences, the body and mind begin to develop an expectation that repair will come: that someone will soothe the rupture, that good experiences will follow bad, and that fear will be reassured by safety.

When we as therapists assume that, as much as something new might be welcomed by the normal life self, it is likely to be threatening to trauma-related parts, we will be better prepared to help clients. When the parts "resist" our interventions, it is because they are afraid of change: after all, trauma is a sudden "change." One minute, nothing was happening, and the next minute, it all changed. When the therapist helps the client notice the resistance as the parts' understandable hesitation or hypervigilance, there is an opportunity for increasing internal compassion. When therapeutic work is complicated by the client's hyper- or hypoarousal, by a narrow window of tolerance, or by parts triggered by the process occurring in the session, it is crucially important that the therapist attend more to helping the client regulate distress or dysregulation than to the content or focus of the session. Just as a parent often has to interrupt a conversation to attend to a child's distress, the same goal also serves to build the bonds of attachment to the parts.

A very important principle of internal attachment work is that all difficulties that arise in the session become opportunities to increase compassion and acceptance and foster a repair of the past. If clients are having trouble maintaining dual awareness as parts intrude thoughts, images, and intense emotions, the therapist can help them regulate autonomic activation without losing focus on attachment issues. For example, a Sensorimotor Psychotherapy somatic intervention could be reframed as a way to support the parts: "See what happens if you feel your feet on the ground … like you are communicating to the freaked out parts that you are solid on your feet. Does it help if you also lengthen your spine? Try it—put a little space between the vertebrae in your lower back, and see what happens. Maybe then they can feel how tall you are and how strong your body is" (Ogden & Fisher, 2015). Notice that the interventions are explicitly worded to communicate that they are not being used to silence or stop the parts' dysregulated input: the message is that all interventions are in the service of helping them as well as the normal life part.

Another way of helping clients regulate activation stemming from triggered parts is to use a technique drawn from Internal Family Systems (Schwartz, 2001): asking the parts to "step back" or "sit back." In the IFS model, this technique can be used to get past parts defending the status quo in order to access deeply hidden exiled parts. In this instance, it is used to help the client maintain a window of tolerance and maintain an ongoing dialogue with all parts. As the client reports "too much activation," "too much noise in my head," "too many thoughts going too fast," or "critical voices humiliating me," the therapist asks her to see what happens if she asks the parts to "just sit back a little" or "sit back and make more room for you. Explain that you can help them better if they will sit back just a little." Framed in this way, the parts are not threatened, and there is something in it for them—the availability of help. When clients report no response, they are instructed to be curious: "Ask the part: What is it afraid of if it does sit back?" Most often, parts reply, "If I sit back, I'll be ignored—no one will hear me." Often these responses reflect implicit memory of the past (of not having a voice, not being able to cry for help, not being heard), but often they are accurate reflections of past experience. The normal life part has been trying to ignore them, suppress their feelings, or deny hearing their voices. The therapist has to validate that fact: "You know, it's true—not knowing that they were parts, not knowing they were young and frightened, most people do exactly what you did: try to ignore them. How sad, huh? Would you like to be the first person these parts have ever known to admit having hurt them? I know it would mean a lot to them …" By universalizing the description of what has happened ("most people," "not knowing"), clients can hear these truths without the therapist triggering ashamed parts. Notice that the normal life self is always treated as a sane, competent, caring adult capable of learning and responsible for his or her actions; the parts are always described with empathy as children or adolescents whose magical thinking, fears, idealism, and traumatic wounding make them act impulsively and emotionally. Less is expected of them, but more is expected from the adult normal life self because, just as in biological adults, he or she has access to the prefrontal cortex, to states of curiosity and compassion, and has the functional abilities to take responsibility for the parts' safety in the body and in the world.

Communicating Compassion toward Wounded Child Parts

Children and adults alike believe the reassuring words of others only if they feel "gotten"; that is, when they sense that they are believed, understood, cared about, or important to someone. Empty reassurances not only fail to comfort but are often a trigger, evoking emotional memories of abusers whose reassurances were a way of "grooming" the child. Clients can learn the right words to tell their parts, "You are safe now—no one can hurt you—this is now, not then," but without empathic attunement, these clarifications literally fall on deaf ears. Even in therapeutic relationships, our ability to successfully reassure is directly proportional to our emotional resonance to the client's feelings and fears. If the therapist can teach the client the ability to stay connected to states of curiosity and compassion without losing the sense of boundary differentiating parts from wise 'self," they can begin to offer their parts the "missing experiences" (Kurtz, 1990; Ogden & Fisher, 2015) that repair the past, elicit "the grief of relief," and cultivate secure internal attachment.

For that reason, internal communication aimed at "repairing" the trauma-related implicit memories of parts is always focused on eliciting just the right amount of emotional connection between the normal life self and the parts: not so much connection that the normal life self gets blended or flooded but enough that there is a growing emotional resonance. First, based on the assumption that the parts' emotions, impulses, and behaviors are their "language," the normal life part is asked to "hear" each channel of communication as a message from a young, wounded part and to remain interested and curious in their reaching out. The therapist's responses to the part's communications should reflect the child's apparent age, feelings, and predicament. In normal life, adults rarely use the same "language" to talk to or about a 2-year-old as they would with a 16-year-old. When we communicate with little children, we use simple words, express concern not just verbally but with our body language, and we use words familiar to young children, such as "scary," "bad people," "mad," "not fair." With teenagers, the therapist has to be sufficiently connected to his or her own rebellious or adolescent self so his or her communications do not feel condescending or therapizing. "Oh shit, really?!" is far more effective with an adolescent, for example, than, "That must have been hard for you." Then the normal life part is coached to respond compassionately and to convey understanding or, if he or she doesn't understand, to ask the questions we would ask any child. As a next step, the normal life part is encouraged to explore the part's feelings or reactions by inquiring, "What are you worried about? What's scary? What makes you so sad?" Sometimes, parts reply with a traumatic or hurtful image, sometimes in words such as, "I'm bad—that's why people are mean to me," and sometimes with feelings like, "I need a friend—I'm lonely." It can be helpful at this point for the therapist to encourage the normal life part to think: Why would it make sense for a child part to feel that way? What was happening at that point in my life that made him feel so ashamed?

As the normal life self takes in the fear, shame, confusion, anger, or vulnerability that lives on in the child part and seems to be making an emotional connection to the part, the therapist asks an IFS question, "How do you feel toward that part now?" (Schwartz, 2001). If clients have truly connected with the part, compassion and empathy are evoked spontaneously by that question, and the responses reflect the growing attachment to the young part: "I feel sad for her," "I want to help him," "I want to protect that little one."

For internal attachment work to be successful, it is important to use the exact wording above. "How do you feel about?" is a different question than, "How do you feel toward?" "Feeling about" involves left brain information retrieval reflected in clients who reply, "I don't know—let me think about it." "How do you feel toward" accesses right brain intuitive responses that can be felt by the part as true and authentic. As "feeling toward" the part transforms the normal life self's habitual alienation, the therapist guides the client's normal life self to connect to feeling sad or protective or proud toward the child and to communicate that empathic connection back. Often, the part simply needs to hear, "I believe you" or, better yet, "I know how bad it was."

Because communication involves reciprocity, an experience missing from the lives of most traumatized children, the therapist concentrates on the mutuality of the exchange: "What's it like for the little boy to feel your sadness? He isn't used to people feeling for him ..." "What's it like for her to hear that you want to protect her? Does that feel good or a little scary?" Most often, the child part expresses positive feelings, either in words or in emotions and body sensations. As the client is guided to ask, "What's it like for the child part to hear us expressing concern about her feelings?" they often feel a spontaneous change in body experience: relaxation, warmth, a smile, a deep breath. The therapist, like a good family therapist, underscores all positive changes in family relationships: "Yes, she can breathe—knowing you want to protect her must be a relief, I think. Ask her if that's correct." "It feels good to him to feel that someone cares about his feelings, huh?"

Equally important is the question that should always follow, "And what's it like for you to feel how much it means to him?" As mutuality is built interaction by interaction, just as it is in parent-child relationships, this dialogue can continue: "It feels very special and heartwarming to know he's so touched … And what's it like for him to hear you say it warms your heart to have this connection with him?" "When he says he wishes he could go home with you, what's that like for you?" "OK, you're ready to take him home?! That was immediate—you're 'on that' right away, huh? How does he like that?"

Especially when the part has shown the normal life self an image or there is some connection to memory, the normal life self is asked to validate the part's event-specific emotions: "I 'get' how afraid you are of leaving the house and being seen, and I understand it completely. It wasn't a good idea then to have people watching you—it was creepy." Or, "I completely understand—it wasn't a good idea to try something new unless you were absolutely sure you knew what would happen." When the parts feel the empathic "getting it" as an emotional communication, not just verbal one, there is relief and a building of trust in the normal life self.

Interference with Reparative Experiences

The next step is to help clients stay connected to the reparative experience they are providing for a young traumatized child self, whether it is the felt sense of being understood, of being genuinely moved by the child's hurt and fear, or the somatic experience of warmth, muscles relaxing, heart-rate slowing. Inner dialogues can deepen as trust builds between child and adult parts, but often, just at these moments of deepening, other parts intrude to cause distraction from the moments of attunement occurring between the normal life self and the wounded child. Threatened by the feelings of attunement, warmth, loving presence, softness, and vulnerability, the critical voices of fight parts often intervene, as do annoyed parts, confused parts, superior parts ("I don't need to be here—I know all this"), or anxious parts. Generally, the normal life self is coached through these interruptions by the therapist: "Seems as if the critical part is not so comfortable with the closeness between you and the little part … Would you like to find out more about what the critical part worried about? Or would you rather ask the critical part to sit back while you finish talking to this young boy?" Notice that a choice is given as a way of supporting the new learning: when clients have to make a choice or initiate an action, they exercise weakened muscles. Having had to be passive, or to overcompensate by being impulsive, developing habits of intentionality and choice is an important part of recovery.

The Four Befriending Questions

Many clients have the capacity for engaging in internal dialogues with their parts: those who are less dysregulated or dissociative, clients with a wider window of tolerance, those with more ability to be meditative or mindful. These individuals often benefit from the Meditation Circle technique (see Appendix

B) in which they imagine a meditation circle with a place in it for each part and then wait in silence to observe each part as it arrives and takes its seat. Having a place in the circle, being asked to express their feelings and worries, hearing concern in the normal life part's voice, even the experience of being able to count on a predictable way to be heard are all reparative experiences for young trauma-related parts and contribute to an increased feeling of safety inside. When parts feel safer and more trusting, their autonomic dysregulation settles, the window of tolerance expands, and with it, there is more activity in the prefrontal cortex, increasing the ability of the normal life self to be curious, creative, calm, compassionate, and hold onto perspective.

For clients who are more dysregulated, more phobic of their parts, or who have fight parts preoccupied with limiting the therapist's power or attach parts focused on the therapist's caring, being able to engage in a compassionate dialogue with parts is more challenging. With clients who cannot establish free-flowing inner communication or who are in the early stages of learning to do so, it is helpful to have a more structured internal dialogue that does not require as much capacity on the client's part. The "Four Befriending Questions" address the need for a structured, easy-to-learn technique for carrying on internal conversation even in the context of dissociation or dysregulation. The name for this technique is a headline for its intent: to befriend the parts so they feel heard and welcome. The first three questions are all focused on understanding a part's core fears, usually either the fear of harm and annihilation or the fear of abandonment. What prompts the use of the Four Befriending Questions is any feeling or issue that represents a communication from a part. I often use this dialoguing technique with clients who are getting hijacked in their daily lives as a way to intervene and re-establish stability. It is also helpful when their lives are being constricted by parts afraid of the day-to-day triggers. Here is an example:

> As she is discussing whether or not to accept a birthday invitation from an old friend whom she hasn't seen for many years, Annie is overcome with shame at the very thought of going. Invited to assume that this shame belongs to a part and to focus on the feelings as a message from that part, I coach her through the following steps:
>
> - Ask this part that feels so ashamed what she's worried about if you go to the party?
>   Annie: "She says she's worried people will see me."
> - Ask her what she's worried about if people see her?
>   "They won't like what they see. They'll be grossed out."
> - "And what is she worried about if they don't like what they see?"
>   "She says 'They'll reject me, and then I'll be all alone.'" [The core fear.]
> - And then the fourth and final question: "Ask her what she needs from you right here, right now to not be so afraid of being rejected

and abandoned." [It is important that this final question include the exact words of the part and clearly communicate that it is asking what the normal life self can do this in very minute to relieve those feelings and fears.]

Annie heard a voice inside saying sadly: "I need you not to be ashamed of me." As Annie took in the words of this young girl, tears came up: "I feel so badly for her! She's right—I have been ashamed of her, and I don't want to do that to her anymore."

- "Tell her that—let her know how badly you feel about having been ashamed of her all these years—and tell her with your body and your feelings so she knows you mean it ..."

In the following weeks, Annie tried to remember to express support and reassurance to the 13-year-old part: to apologize for having made her feel more ashamed and to promise her that Annie would not abandon her or let anyone reject her. To her surprise, she felt strangely calm the day of the party. Rather than anxiously obsessing about how awful it was going to be or shaming herself in advance, she reminded herself (and the 13-year-old) that she didn't *have* to stay but she *could* if she was enjoying herself.

The next week, she described her experience: "It was fun! Lynn was glad to see me, and, for the first time ever, I didn't feel like I had to work hard to impress people. In fact, I listened a lot more than I normally would—I just spoke when I had something to say. I didn't have to keep talking to make sure they couldn't reject me."

ME: "And what was that like for the 13-year-old to feel your ability to just be yourself, knowing you didn't need to impress anyone? Ask her now ..."

ANNIE: "She says it made her feel proud. If I belong, she belongs. If people accept me, she's more confident they will accept her."

ME: "Well, it probably helped that you were focused on her feeling comfortable instead of being ashamed! All the anxious parts who'd be coaching you and the critical part who'd be telling you that you were failing couldn't get a word in edgewise because you were focused on her. She helped you out!"

Notice that the therapist leads her through the four Befriending Questions, step by step, and then helps her focus on the moment of repair with the 13-year-old: "Tell her how badly you feel ... What is it like for her to feel someone's distress over having hurt her?" In these moments, only the therapist will be able to fully grasp the meaning of each step: with the meta-awareness of the witness, the therapist can understand that Annie would feel badly for hurting any child but also understand that, for the 13-year-old, it is a yearned for but also very new and strange experience to matter to anyone or for anyone to feel badly about hurting her. Often, the child parts feel nourished, warmed, or "held" by the caring of the normal life self but then suddenly pause and hold back, anxious or hesitant, afraid to believe that it is true or unwilling to let themselves believe it to be true. How can they trust someone who cares when all they have known is a lack of caring?

The therapist will need to help clients capitalize on these moments by validating the part's fears and lack of trust: "This is so new—ask her, does it feel good to know that you hurt for her? That you don't like hurting her? Or is it a little uncomfortable?" The client's normal life self might respond: "It feels like she wants to trust me—wants to believe I'll be here for her—but she keeps relaxing and then stiffening again and pulling back." The therapist may need to translate the child part's responses in such a way that more compassion is evoked: "Maybe she's pulling back because she *wants* to trust you … Ask her: would she like to trust you? Would she like to believe that you won't leave and you won't hurt her?"

When therapists begin guiding clients through repair work with their parts, they may feel uncomfortable "putting words in the client's mouth" or assuming they know what the child part might be feeling. It is important to remember that, in trauma work, we provide psychoeducationally informed explanations for clients because they don't have the words for their trauma responses: past and present are intertwined, the language spoken by the normal life self is a different language from that spoken by the child part, and we are faced with the choice of supplying words to make sense of their experience or leaving traumatized clients in confusion. Therapist bias or client over-compliance is counteracted by asking clients to observe the effects of each intervention (Ogden & Fisher, 2015) and by asking them to check in and ask the part if "that feels right." With clients capable of tracking their emotions or body experience in more detail, the therapist can ask more detailed questions: "What happens to the tension (or fear, hypervigilance, or shakiness) when you tell her that you're here now to protect her?" With clients whose ability to observe or feel is limited, the therapist may have to provide more language or more structure or both. A simple technique for ensuring that the therapist is not "leading the witness" to a harmful extent is to give clients a menu of possibilities (Ogden & Fisher, 2015): "Does she feel more tense or more relaxed? More guarded or more anxious? Does the fight part agree or disagree with your offering comfort to the little part?" The therapist can also offer a menu of emotions: "Is he more ashamed or more sad?" Or body responses: "Does the fight part's anger feel more like energy? More like strength? Or does it want to do something?" We can even offer a menu of parts: "Does that sadness feel more connected to the attach part or to the depressed part?"

The importance of encouraging embodied communication cannot be stressed too much:

- "Let the little boy know with your feelings and your body that you completely understand why he feels that way."

- "Use your feelings to tell her that you're here now, and you mean to stay."
- "Just hold him gently so he gets the message that he's not alone."

Building Impulses to Care

Often, in trying to educate clients about young parts and their need to be cared for, therapists offer generalizations, such as "the child parts will need you to take care of them" or "when you learn how to make them feel safe," but psychoeducation such as this is frequently too abstract to grasp even by the normal life self: what does it actually mean to "take care of" or "make a child part feel safe?" Not only can those words intimidate the normal life self but can also be triggering for child parts, evoking fears of failure or beliefs that the therapist wants nothing to do with taking care of them. On the other hand, providing concrete suggestions for what exactly to say or do with young parts can be useful, especially when given in multiple choice or "menu" form (Ogden & Fisher, 2015): "You could tell him that you're a grownup now—or that the bad people have gone away—or that you're here to protect him so he doesn't get hurt again." By offering a set of choices, we can evoke the client's intuitive sense of what this young part might need: for example, "I think I should start by telling him that I'm a grownup now—that I'm not little like he is anymore. That's the only way he could believe I'm actually capable of protecting him."

Overcoming Internal Distrust and Fear

A frequent deterrent to restoring a sense of hope and safety to child parts comes from either skeptical, hypervigilant parts or from young parts afraid to trust that they are now finally getting what they have most desired. It would make sense that fight and flight parts might manifest as suspicious, mistrustful, cynical, or sabotaging parts. It would be understandable that the protector parts of some clients (e.g., those whose abusers were exceptionally sadistic, manipulative, or malevolent) would be more vigilant in armoring themselves against taking in anything positive or allowing vulnerable parts to let down their guard. This phenomenon is particularly common in clients with dissociative disorders (see Chapter 8) but also occurs in clients whose parts are more integrated and less dissociatively compartmentalized. The internal distrust of protector parts manifests very differently from that of vulnerable parts. For example, when the normal life part asks a question inside and gets no response, he or she is generally encouraged to ask the question again or to change the words slightly. But when the result is still the same, the best assumption is that the silence *is* a communication. It could mean, "I'm not talking to you," or "I'm afraid to talk to you," or "I don't know who you are." Or there might be a response that appears silent at first because it comes without words. The client might notice an emotion, such as anxiety or sadness or anger, or a body response, for example, tensing, going numb, a change in heartbeat or breathing. Sometimes, when the emotion is sadness and there is a physical sense of vulnerability, these communications without words are coming from a preverbal child part. In that case, the therapist coaches the normal life part to communicate just the way an adult would with any infant or toddler and to use the part's nonverbal responses to gauge the success or failure of repair.

But if the normal life self asks inside, "What is this part worried about?" and the answer is silence coupled with anger, muscle tension, or numbing, it is safest to assume that this is a message from a hypervigilant or angry part: "Perhaps there is a part communicating that it doesn't trust you." Often, it is helpful at this point to externalize the part by asking the normal life self to imagine a similar scenario and notice his intuitive sense about the silent part: "If you had just adopted a traumatized child, and he wasn't talking to you when you tried to get closer to him, what would you make of that?" Most clients in their normal life parts immediately respond: "He doesn't trust me yet, of course." "And what would you do next?" "I'd tell him that I understand— how could he trust me this quickly? I'd tell him he can take his time and get to know me before he makes up his mind." Even clients who insist that they don't know how to understand or what to do about a child part very quickly access "expertise" when asked to imagine being the foster parent of traumatized children and teenagers or the director of a group home for traumatized youth.

The therapist can support the client's intuition and insight by helping the normal life self share them with the part: "That makes total sense—now, can you communicate this same message to the part that's not speaking to you right now? Let him know that it's up to him—there's no pressure coming from you—you understand why it's hard for him to trust anyone." Using the client's report of body and emotional responses to interpret the part's reaction, clients can be encouraged to just keep talking to the "silent part" and to experiment with different approaches. Perhaps the silent part could be asked, "What would you need from me [the normal life self] to be willing to tell me more?" Or the client could affirm the part's caution: "I want the silent part to know that I appreciate his cautiousness. Better to say less than say more until you know who you're talking to." Often, when protector parts are given respect and greater control, they are more willing to engage in a dialogue.

> It became clear in Jennifer's therapy that her protector part shut down everything it perceived as threatening. She could be in mid-sentence when a voice would interrupt with: "And what is the point of this? Why are we talking about it? Where are we going?" When asked, "What are you worried about if we talk about this?" the part fell silent. I suggested that her "evaluator part" was obviously concerned about wasting time in therapy and had correctly perceived that she and Jennifer jumped around from topic to topic quite frequently. Jennifer was asked to thank the evaluator part for its efforts—still silence. Then I suggested that Jennifer propose a topic to discuss and ask the evaluator part if it was OK to talk about it. To her surprise, Jennifer

heard an "OK" from inside. Each time she wanted to explore some-thing more deeply or change the subject, she was encouraged to ask the evaluator part if it was OK. Both she and I began to see that the evaluator was almost always willing to OK the request, and when it didn't, there was often a useful reason. A reparative dialogue had begun: the evaluator had been unable to protect her from parents who manipulated her little girl part's attachment strivings, but this part could protect her now—as long as Jennifer remembered to give it a place in her life.

Creating a New Purpose and Mission for Each Part

When protector parts are given power and control consciously and volun-tarily by the client's normal life self, there are many positive benefits. A better balance of vulnerability versus feelings of mastery is achieved; protector parts are more willing to allow access to young wounded or innocent parts; internal communication improves; and the client receives help in becoming more re-sourced, self-protective, and better boundaried—all from an unlikely source, his or her own fight and flight parts. The most frequent mistake likely to be made by the therapist is to give up in the face of the protector's silence, resis-tance, or devaluing of the client or the therapy, rather than reframing these responses as natural, normal, and protective in intent. The other common error results when client, therapist, or both "demonize" the protector parts: that is, see them as an interference in therapy rather than as part of the work. When the therapist urges the client to push through the objections of the fight parts or try to ignore them, it further polarizes them and reinforces their dis-trust. When the therapist expresses respect, gratitude, and understanding of the fight and flight parts' actions and reactions, and encourages the client to do the same, protector parts begin to be more open to collaboration. And as client and therapist persist in their efforts to make contact with the fight part, no matter how often rebuffed, it sends an important nonverbal message, one that might make even the most hypervigilant protector more curious, that they are committed and willing to have that commitment tested.

Researchers have noted that one of the characteristics of mothers who pro-mote secure attachment in their children is the ability to resonate to the baby's state, modulate their own states to avert infant distress or enhance positive affect, and simultaneously mirror both states back to the child (Kim et al., 2014). The mirroring of the infant's state along with the mother's correspond-ing feelings of concern, enjoyment, empathy, or warmth seems to have the ef-fect of communicating "I understand" but also "and I can help." If the mother simply mirrors the infant's state, both appear stuck in the same distress. They "blend" as does the normal life self with parts in distress. If the mother reflects back only her different, more positive state, there is no comforting sense of being "gotten." It is more like an empty reassurance: "I don't get it, but don't worry—you'll feel better soon."

The literature on secure attachment suggests that both resonance and repair are equally important aspects of what has been called "attunement." This concept can be applied to the relationship between parts and normal life self. Just as with mothers and infants, "blending" with the feelings of a part simply leaves that child alone with the distressing emotions, as do disembodied words of reassurance or hope. Not only is it crucial for parts to feel a visceral sense that the normal life "gets" how scared, ashamed, angry, or hurt they are but also to feel the effect of the latter's curiosity, compassion, calm, strength, and protectiveness. But because these are traumatized parts, the need for an adult self to consistently provide "attunement" in this sense will take time and persistence.

> Mason was eager to work on the issue of his phobia of getting sick, which led him to hyper-focus on avoiding "germs"—creating a chronic anxiety that distracted him from being able to enjoy an otherwise satisfying life beyond trauma. As he tuned in to the fear in his body and the sinking feeling that he was getting sick, he noticed the intrusive thoughts that kept coming up ("Why did you touch the door knob? Didn't you notice that man blowing his nose?"), and a childhood image spontaneously arose. He was in a second grade classroom watching a cartoon on germs and hand washing: in each frame, there were flashes of red as the film showed examples of where germs lurked in a child's life, and the voiceover kept saying, "Watch out for germs! Wash your hands after touching surfaces—stay away from sneezing and coughing." He could see his 7-year-old self in the memory becoming more and more panicky, and he could feel the heightened anxiety in his body. As Mason remained mindful and curious about the intensity of this fear, I translated the boy's experience into trauma-related terms: "He has so many bad things happening at home, and now he's being told that there are more bad things to watch out for. No wonder he's scared! But to him, a bad thing is really bad—really traumatic. He must be terrified, huh? How do you feel toward him as you sense how scared he is?"
>
> MASON: "I feel sad for him—he never had a safe place or a safe person in his world." [Mason is beginning to mirror both the boy's anxiety and his own empathy.]
> ME: "Yes, he never, ever had a safe place or a safe person … and when you feel the sadness for him, what impulse do you have? To come closer to him? To just let him know you're there?"
> MASON: "I just want to pick him up and hold him—but I can sense that he doesn't trust me." [His mirroring gets more attuned, communicating both his wish to hold and comfort and his sensitivity to the boy's fears of being too close.]

ME: "How could he trust any grownup? He never met an adult like you … Maybe just let him know you're there and you want to help …"

MASON: "I can feel he wants to trust me, but he's afraid to let down his guard."

ME: "Ask him if you're right—would he like it if he could trust you?"

MASON: "Yes, he's saying that he has to pay attention to bad things like germs—he has to be watchful—he can't relax."

ME: "Tell him you could help him with that—assuming you're willing, of course. Ask him if it would be OK if you took over the job of watching out for him—just for a few minutes to see if maybe it helps him out …" [She demonstrated the action of carefully scanning the environment a full 180 degrees to take in the whole room.]

Mason began to turn his head and neck very slowly and carefully, demonstrating for the 7-year-old how thorough and watchful he could be.

"How did I do?" he asked inside.

"Not as good as me but pretty good," the boy responded.

"Show me how you would do it," Mason said inside to the 7-year-old. He could immediately feel his concentration heighten and his gaze seek out spots like doorknobs so prominent in the film. Then he tried intentionally to duplicate the same deliberate focusing of the child: "How was that?" he asked the boy.

He could feel a sense of the boy moving closer to him, a slight relaxation of bodily tension, and then a wave of fatigue hit him. "I don't know what's wrong with me—I just want to go to sleep," he said.

Again I translated, "Maybe this little boy can relax now because you're watching out for him, and you're doing it just the way he needed … He must be exhausted from all that hypervigilance."

"I can feel him leaning up against me—he is tired. I just keep saying, 'You can rest—I'm watching out for you—you don't have to do it anymore." Tears came to Mason's eyes as he heard his own words, and his son came to mind: "My son has never had to watch out for himself—no 7-year-old should have to."

ME: "That's right—and that's why it's important not to forget this boy, just as you don't forget about your son even if he's quiet. Let's think about how you're going to keep an eye out for this little boy and how you can keep letting him know you're there …"

In this example, therapist and client had to become creative because the child part didn't want just proximity and comfort; he wanted protection. Simply reassuring the little boy that Mason would be there for him would have

communicated that the normal life self had failed to understand his fundamental concern: once he had seen the film in class, no place was safe anymore.
He had to watch out for abusive grownups at home and watch out for dangerous germs outside the home. Notice the importance of my translating the
child part's communication which facilitated the suggestion of "taking over"
the boy's hypervigilance (Ogden & Fisher, 2015), allowing him to rest. Each
child part will be different: each will have different needs for repair of traumatic wounding based on age, developmental stage, experiences of trauma
and/or neglect, and the animal defense to which they are connected. For example, a fight part might need a sense of purpose, control, and mastery; an attach part yearns to feel protected, loved, and safe from abandonment; a freeze
or fear part could simply crave safety from harm or threat of death; submit
parts need to feel worth, autonomy, and initiative; and a flight part might wish
freedom from entrapment.

In the next chapter, we will address how the work of emotional connection, communication, and repair of dysregulated memory states can become
something even more fundamental to children and adults of all ages, whether
they are parts of an individual or his or her children. Through repeated experiences of sessions like these and the practice of these same techniques at
home, we can help clients "grow" secure attachment—just as attuned parents
"grow" attachment bonds with their infants. Each time, the adult self of the
client attunes to the child part's unmet need, fear, or painful emotion and "repairs" the distressing experience, attachment bonds are built, piece by piece,
experience by experience. With infants, it is the baby's calming and relaxing
into the parent's arms that generates a shared felt sense of closeness, safety,
and warmth that we label "attunement." As the parent feels the blissful feeling
of the infant's little body "melting into" her arms, in turn relaxing her body
and engendering feelings of warmth and loving presence, the shared sense of
closeness communicates itself back to the infant, enhancing the child's experience, and deepening the parent's sense of well-being and intimacy. The
transmission back and forth of the feelings and body sensations that convey
"secure attachment" deepens their shared experience, lingers on it so that it
can be encoded and internalized as a somatic memory of what it means to feel
"safe and welcome."

When repeated experiences of "safe and welcome" are shared by a compassionate, caring normal life self and a wounded child part, the client experiences the deep sensory and emotional connection evoked by their mutual
attunement as a bodily state. Although it is now many years later, the young
child at last feels securely held and the client's sense of resilience more stable,
just as it is in individuals whose secure attachment experiences happened at
the developmentally appropriate times. The client has encoded a bodily and
emotional state that conveys love and safety, the certainty of feeling cherished,
and the comfort of a warm felt presence of another. At the worst of times, we
can "be there" for our selves—like a parent to whom one can turn at any age
or stage of life.

"Earned secure attachment" is a concept that has been discussed for many years in the literature and refers to the unique ability of human beings to heal their own wounds by evoking healing experiences that have been missing from their lives. Regardless of our early attachment experiences, we have an opportunity as adults to "earn" the secure attachment that was not available to us when we were young and dependent for a sense of safety on the attachment status of our parents.

When our adult selves provide attuned experience of secure attachment to our younger parts, though, there is an added benefit, just as there is for parents who nurture secure attachment in their children. Not only do the child selves feel the safety and loving presence of a securely attached adult but so does that adult. Both are nourished and comforted—both can relax into the moments of attunement—the hearts of both can open.

References

Hanson, R. (2014). *Hardwiring happiness: the new brain science of contentment, calm, and confidence.* New York: Harmony Publications.

Kim, S., Fonagy, P., Allen, J., Martinez, S., Iyengar, U., & Strathearn, L. (2014). Mothers who are securely attached in pregnancy show more attuned infant mirroring 7 months postpartum. *Infant Behavior and Development,* 37(4), 491–504.

Kurtz, R. (1990). *Body-centered psychotherapy: the Hakomi method.* Updated edition. Mendocino, CA: Life Rhythm.

Ogden, P. & Fisher, J. (2015). *Sensorimotor Psychotherapy: interventions for trauma and attachment.* New York: W.W. Norton.

Ogden, P., Minton, K., & Pain, C. (2006). *Trauma and the body: a sensorimotor approach to psychotherapy.* New York: W.W. Norton.

CHAPTER 11

Safety and Welcome: The Experience of Earned Secure Attachment

"In attuning to another being, we bring a feeling or empathy with another's feelings as well as a kinesthetic and emotional sensing of another. The listener defixates from his or her experience and lets go of the mind's thinking long enough to enter into another's experience and world. We engage in a reciprocal interaction of emotional expression or affect and an exchange of felt resonance—we feel 'felt.'"

(Friedman, 2012)

"The observed takes in the observer having taken her in, and the two become joined. This is resonance. The boundaries of oneself and another become permeable and the sense of being a separate self softens and loosens. ... This is how we feel 'felt,' and this is how two individuals become a 'we.'"

(Siegel, 2010b, pp. 54–55)

The terms "dissociation" and "integration" have long been synonymous with one another—meant to signify that the only reasonable goal in working with splitting and compartmentalization must be the fusing together of dissociated parts to create one single "homogenized" adult. Daniel Siegel, however, makes a strong case against defining integration as fusion. He asserts (2010a) a different view: "Integration requires differentiation *and* linkage." Before we can integrate two phenomena, we have to differentiate them and "own" them as separate entities. We can't simply "act as if" they are connected without noticing their separateness. But, having clearly differentiated them so they can be studied and befriended, we then have to link them together in a way that fosters a transformed sense of the client's experience, facilitating healing and reconnection. A part can be connected to the past, to a physical movement or body sensation, to particular emotions. Another emotion can be noticed, related to a younger or older part, and then linked to the reaction of other parts to those same feelings. In the wake of trauma, individuals need to be able to connect implicit memory to trigger and link the trigger to an explicit context. New information about the present must be linked with old perceptions shaped by the past. To feel safe today, a felt connection must be made between the "child I was then" and the "adult I became today." Trauma-related vulnerability feels less painful when it is linked to new body experiences of mastery or to a somatic sense that "it's over—finally, now it's over" (Ogden & Fisher, 2015). Using Siegel's definition of integration, fusion is not necessary nor is it as empowering as coherence, collaboration, and overcoming self-alienation. In this chapter, we will focus on how to foster integration by differentiating parts previously denied, ignored, or disowned, connecting to them emotionally, and providing experiences that replace self-alienation and self-rejection with self-compassion and secure internal attachment relationships.

When the emphasis in the therapy is not on the recall of traumatic events but on identifying trauma-related parts connected to the implicit memories that still affect the client's current experience, the need to disown the parts is diminished. When clients are helped to see their ashamed parts as "real" children of particular ages and to empathize with their littleness, their bravery, or their pain, disgust and fear give way to empathy.

"She looks so little," clients say. "He is trying so hard to be brave, but he's really afraid." "He's too ashamed to let me own anything nice—because if it's too nice, he's afraid that someone will take it away because he doesn't deserve it." Moments before they made these observations, all three clients had been blended with their parts.

Diane described being appalled that she had burst into tears when her boss criticized her performance: "I can't believe I humiliated myself by being so weak." Josh had been trying to replace his old car with a brand new one, only to find that his ashamed part could not let him buy something "nice." Mark came to therapy to talk about his "speechless terror" of speaking in public and the impact of this deficit on his professional life. In each case, the problem could be traced to a young part connected to particular times and events in the client's lives. Interestingly enough, I have a very clear sense of those young parts, but many of the events that wounded them were never described to me. I let the symptoms and the parts tell the client's story.

"The Symptoms Tell the Story Better than 'the Story'"

Because the trauma treatment field has historically been focused on traumatic events and the roles of memory and narrative, therapists and clients alike often forget to listen to the story told by the symptoms and the parts. Taught to be stimulus-bound by the narrative, most therapists use the story to frame the treatment.

"It's her mother," my colleague said of her 55-year-old patient. "Really? She still is being abused by her mother??" I asked, shocked at the thought. "Oh no, her mother died 20 years ago, but she's afraid to do anything because of her mother. She's even afraid to go home after work for fear she'll be criticized and ridiculed." I thought for a moment and then had a realization: "Actually, it no longer has anything to do with her mother. It did once when she was small.

But now what's troubling her is how the effect of what her mother did lives on right now in present time in her child selves and in their body memories. It's no longer about the past."

My colleague had gotten inducted into the interpretation of event memories as described by the client. She hadn't listened for what story the symptoms told—a somewhat different story. The client's most troubling symptom consisted of intrusive shame connected to a yearning to feel "as one" with those she loved, usually her male partners. The client often sobbed for hours after a date that did not include moments of blissful closeness to the man taking her out. Her yearning for contact resulted in numerous close friendships and intimate relationships, but the accompanying rejection sensitivity created conflicts in those relationships and sometimes a self-fulfilling prophecy when they ended because of the boyfriend's frustration over not being able to please her. As I heard the story "narrated" by the symptoms, I was struck that the story I heard had nothing in it regarding harsh criticism and frightening anger. The symptoms told a very different story of disrupted attachment, leaving a small child deeply hungry for contact, yet also frightened of her scary mother. The child who was in need of missing experiences of closeness and attunement was not being "seen" as she lived on in the client's body and emotional life. The therapist encouraged the client to share her recollections of childhood experience but never realized that remembering the events that caused the little girl's pain would not heal and comfort her.

Having listened carefully to the story told by Mark's symptoms, it was clear events had taught him it wasn't safe to speak or safe to express his opinions as if they merited a hearing. Josh often made references to the poverty and neglect he experienced, the humiliating verbal abuse, and being bullied by kids at school, but his symptoms added some details he hadn't mentioned: he had had to survive by lying low, by pleasing his parents and placating the bullies. His intelligence, combined with a drive to learn and fear of failure, made him a superior student. Though it didn't help him feel a sense of belonging anywhere, his intellectual resources "got him out of Dodge" and gave him the chance to start a new life. That was the story his symptoms told, just as Diane's described a world in which it was imperative never to show weakness—even as a small child. In each case, the events were only important to create a context for understanding and empathizing with the parts. Trauma resolution occurred organically in the context of attachment repair with each part.

Capitalizing on Dissociative Symptoms to Heal Dissociative Fragmentation

The essence of dissociative fragmentation is the ability to split off unbearable emotions from the memory of what happened, to encapsulate and disown "not me" parts and experiences, and to be guided by cognitive schemas that exacerbate self-alienation but help children survive and adapt. Most therapists and clients therefore do not realize that dissociative splitting is a mental ability, not just a symptom.

The ability to quickly retrieve information and act on it automatically and efficiently, without interference from emotion or intrusive thoughts, is central to the medical professional's ability to save lives. Dissociative splitting is also a prerequisite for the athlete on whom the team depends at a critical moment; it contributes to the ability for peak performance enjoyed by actors, musicians, public speakers, and politicians. Dissociation becomes pathological only when it is unconscious and involuntary, under the control of triggers. As a mental ability, it can be used consciously, thoughtfully, and voluntarily. The goal is not to "cure it" or prevent it but to help clients use it wisely in the service of healing and recovery.

Creating Safe Places for Child Parts in an Adult's Normal Life

Often, the difficulty functioning reported by so many survivors of trauma, especially in work settings, can be traced back in retrospect to trauma-related triggers inherent in "normal life": authority figures, work demands (whether reasonable or unreasonable), challenge and change, success or failure, visibility or invisibility, pressure, working in groups, lack of social support, feeling "too little" for the responsibilities being given to us. In each instance, the trigger stimulates a part or parts that hijack or blend with the normal life self, impairing its ability to function.

Frances was a distinguished-looking, well-dressed professional woman in her early 60s, known in her industry for the large and successful business she established providing services to corporations. Ironically, a divorce led her to therapy; her abuse history was revealed; and her first therapist embarked on a trauma treatment, unaware that she was highly dissociative and fragmented. Within months, she was struggling to function at work and curled up in a fetal position at home, sobbing for hours. "I knew I couldn't do it anymore the day I went into work, and I didn't know how to turn on the computer—I didn't know how the copy machine worked—I couldn't concentrate, and I didn't know whom to trust." Frances had been hijacked by child parts connected to the abuse memories she had been processing in therapy. The severity of her fragmentation, symptoms such as the dramatic "loss of well-learned functions," gaps in memory, and preoccupation with suicide all suggested that she might have dissociative identity disorder (DID). As I began to treat her, evidence of parts' activity was dramatic. She described coming home from work or a therapy session, collapsing in her front hall in sobs, and then having no recall of what happened until she "woke up" on the cold stone floor hours later. The suicidality was cleared related to a suicidal part that, she reported, had had a suicide plan for the last 40 years—along with the means to carry it out.

"I go to the firing range every 6 months to renew my license to carry," she reported proudly as she walked in late to her therapy session. I smiled to myself, noting that this part did not have the same boundaries as Frances did. The latter was punctual to the minute. "She" referred to the gun as her "suicide kit" and assured me she took it everywhere. It was unnerving to hear Frances identify with the suicidal part, but I could not risk alienating that part by questioning this pattern. If she is identified with the suicidal part, I wondered, who has been disowned? Because Frances was so destabilized, I simplified the treatment to the bare minimum: she described her difficulties getting through the day, and I encouraged her to be mindful and aware of the parts whose feelings and symptoms overwhelmed her. One day, she was so blended with a young, grieving part that longed for her father (the father who had sexually abused her but had also loved her and been her "safe" attachment figure) that I spontaneously suggested that we stand up and "rock the baby." We both stood up, facing each other, and rocked from foot to foot, each holding an imaginary baby in our arms.

I could see her body calming, her feelings settling a little bit, as we rocked: "How does she like being held, Frances?" I asked. "She loves it," Frances reported. "Wonderful—she's needed this, hasn't she? She's been so desperate these last few months, poor little thing." "This is good for her—and good for me. It reminds me of rocking my babies 30 years ago—as much as it soothed them, it soothed me. I guess she must have loved it, too."

The next week, she reported that she was rocking the baby part rather than let her cry herself to sleep on the hallway floor. "I guess I can't ignore her anymore—she'll play havoc with my life. ... Oh, by the way, it's my birthday this weekend, and the suicidal part is already thinking about how to celebrate it ..."

Frances in her dignified professional normal life self had asked me a question at our first session: "Would you ever commit one of your patients to a hospital if he or she were suicidal?" And I answered, "I'm proud to say that I've never committed anyone to a hospital against their will in 30 years of practice, and I'm determined to keep that record until I retire. Patients of mine have gone to the hospital when needed," I clarified, "but always on their own volition." Now I had to discuss the suicidal part's views on birthday celebrations still bound by my policy of avoiding involuntary commitment of any patient. I had told Frances that I "always work it out with each individual."

ME: "I'm not sure the suicidal part's idea of a birthday celebration is quite what the little parts of you are dreaming about, and their needs should be uppermost on a birthday. Older kids don't care about birthdays, but little ones do. What were birthdays like in your family?"

FRANCES: "They were extravaganzas of my mother's making—kids were always envious of me because of them. They didn't know the price I paid: I used to dread my birthday. I'd get a party that just embarrassed me, and then I'd 'get' something 'special' from my father." [She shuddered at the thought.]

ME: "It doesn't sound like they ever got what a child wants! A child just wants to feel loved and special, to be the center of attention in a good way, or to get to choose what kind of party she wants, who she wants there, and to be in charge." Then I had an idea. "Why don't you give the child parts a special birthday? They have been waiting a long time to celebrate their birthday 'their way.' First, they need a present—from you. Just go to a nice toy store and walk through it, allowing your eyes to gaze wherever they wish and noticing where they stop and stare or the toy they keep going back to look at. That can be something special you do with them, too—they never had anyone do something special for *them*."

The next week, Frances arrived, glowing and excited. "You'll never guess what I bought for the parts—I can't get over it! This is 'not me'—it's definitely for them." Reaching into her purse, she proudly pulled out a beautiful pink pig, a stuffed animal representation of Olivia, the pink pig heroine of a children's story. "Can you believe it? Me? A pink pig named Olivia?!! You know that I did this just for them ..." And then she paused: "But I have to tell you: I love her, too. Isn't she beautiful?" To this day, whenever I see an Olivia, I think of Frances and how Olivia changed her life. For the first time, the parts were given what they wanted instead of what their parents wanted to gratify narcissistic and pedophile impulses. Something fundamental changed in their sense of safety on that birthday: they could feel someone was there for them. Someone cared enough to buy them Olivia and brought comfort to the crying infant part and a smile to the little girl.

Just before her next business trip, Frances casually commented, "You know, I think I'll take Olivia on this trip instead of my suicide kit ..."

"That would be lovely for 'the kids.' Do you think that will be a problem for your suicidal part?" I asked.

"No, I don't think so—he's pretty calm as long as they are OK."

Frances used her dissociative abilities to allow the eager eyes of the little parts a separation from her more critical eye so they could look around the toy store without her influencing their choices. Then, still maintaining a voluntary and deliberate split, the normal life part's judgments about a pink pig could be kept separate from the little girl who fell in love "at first sight" with Olivia, allowing the purchase to be made. Frances had been a good mother figure: she put her child parts' feelings first, thanks to the voluntary use of the dissociative splits.

Supporting a Functioning Adult Normal Life Self

Josh's ashamed little boy part was asked to orient to the adult Josh's environment: his business office, his home, wife, and three children. Josh asked the little boy to notice how people treated him now that he was an adult: "They act like you're important!" the little boy noticed with awe. He observed how Josh was welcomed by his amateur baseball team, his church community, and his family of choice. It was clear to the boy that Josh "belonged." "You're with me now," Josh kept saying. "No one here is going to take away something nice of mine."

Mark and I realized that the frightened little boy "trying so hard to be brave" about his upcoming speaking engagement had not been asked to speak—the normal life Mark had! (Many traumatized clients report the same phenomenon: child parts that once had to be precociously adult often confuse adult roles and activities as "things they have to do.") As I coached him, Mark explained to the boy that he was a grownup, and grownups *like* to speak in public because they want to tell people about their work and share their ideas. *"Really?"* said the little boy.

> MARK: "It's because no one will hurt a grownup like they hurt kids or say mean things, like the other kids do. Grownups like to do a lot of things that are scary for children, but *you* don't have to do those things. You're just a little boy, and kids shouldn't have to do scary grownup stuff." I asked Mark to propose a plan that might work for both him and the child:
>
> MARK: "Would it be OK if I spoke at the meeting next week, and you could stay home. You don't have to go to scary things grownups choose to do."
>
> "I guess so," said the little boy.
>
> "Maybe he'd like to watch you speak," I hinted.
>
> After a moment of silence, Mark's face lit up. "He says he would like to stay home with the cat and watch me on TV!"
>
> We both laughed: "Why not?" I said. "Dissociation is a wonderful ability. It's just as possible for him to stay home and watch you on 'TV' as it is for him to still be trapped in that house in Virginia while you go on with life in New York." Subsequently, Mark's career blossomed: each time he encountered a "scary" challenge, at least scary to the boy, he would have the same discussion. "I know it's very scary for you to get on a plane with so many people and feel trapped inside, but you don't have to do that. Business trips are for grownups because they have jobs. Kids don't have to have jobs, but grownups do. Where would you like to be when I'm on the plane and at my meeting?"
>
> "I want to be home with the cat," the little boy said. "But I'll miss you."

This simple technique (making conscious, voluntary use of the existing dissociative compartmentalization in the service of growth and healing) has allowed numerous clients of mine to undertake what otherwise would have been very triggering, even overwhelming normal life experiences. One client was able to take her husband and children to visit her parents, a thought that initially caused panic and nausea, communicating how alarmed the parts were at the very thought. By leaving them "at home," she and her family had a short but uneventful visit, and the parts felt heard and protected.

Another client was able to finish law school when parts that were intimidated and terrified were allowed to stay home while "she" went. "Law school is something grownups choose—not a place for kids," she told them each morning. She used the same technique when it came time to find a job, buy a home with her husband, adopt a rescue dog, and have a baby. Whenever aspects of her normal life were threatening, the parts were given a choice: "You can come on the job interview if you want—you can help me with the baby if you want ... but if you don't want to, you can all stay home." The parts felt a sense of protection and understanding: they were little, too little for law school and home-buying and babies. For the client, it was an empowering experience: she continued growing as a mature adult without always having to battle her parts just to be able to function.

"Earned Secure Attachment"

In research on earned secure attachment or "earned security," attachment status is evaluated according to the degree of "coherence" in the subjects' narratives as they reflect back on early attachment experience. Siegel, D. J. (2010b). The mindful therapist: a clinician's guide to mindsight and neural integration. New York: W.W. Norton. "Coherence" is the opposite of having fragmented, conflicting, and polarized points of view within one individual. Coherence means arriving at a place where the sum of many views come together—as they did when Mark and the little boy agreed that the child should be spared having to participate in frightening, overwhelming grownup activities. Each time they made that agreement, Mark felt liberated from the past: he could pursue his career, unafraid that its demands would trigger incapacitating feeling memories. Rather than having to be a precocious miniature adult as he had throughout childhood, the child part was offered a very new, previously missing experience. Someone was taking care of *him*. He could be a little boy and still be safe.

Changing the Paradigm: The Effects of the Past Are Not Indelible

"Narrative coherence," the standard for adult secure attachment, whether continuous or earned, is defined as the ability to describe childhood experiences of insecure or traumatic attachment in an integrated, regulated way, just as those with "continuous secure attachment" do in describing their attachment histories (Roisman et al., 2002.) It is not that the earned secure have had "good" attachment experiences. The subjects in these studies reported failed or suboptimal early attachment, painful experiences with attachment figures, even traumatic experiences. Coherence reflects having come to terms with the past, repaired its worst damage, and found a way to accept the missing experiences or childhood wounding as "the best they could do," "it wasn't about me," "they were lucky to have me—they just couldn't see that." Notice that coherence involves the ability to construct a "healing story" to explain what happened. A healing story is likely to be comforting, regulating, and to promote acceptance of "what is," thereby increasing coherence. To the extent that coherence reflects a reconstruction or transformation of painful memories, it supports the encoding of new, more positive feelings.

What makes earned secure attachment unique, however, is its correlation with parenting that promotes secure attachment in the next generation (Roisman et al., 2002). This research challenges the prevailing view that suboptimal attachment in the parent generation predicts the likelihood of providing less-than-optimal attachment experiences for the next generation. Instead, it suggests that human beings can transform the implicit memories and explicit narrative of the past by internalizing healthy adult attachment experiences until they achieve the benefits conferred by secure attachment. The fact that earned secure attachment transmits the ability to offer the same to the next generation is a hopeful sign. It implies that we can help our clients bring a stop to the intergenerational legacy of trauma in their families and create a new legacy through the intergenerational transmission of secure attachment.

An Intergenerational Legacy of Secure Attachment

What either type of secure attachment endows is increased relational flexibility, the ability to modulate emotional up's and down's, to tolerate disappointment and hurt, distance and closeness, to have the capacity for interdependence, and to see the world in shades of gray. Most of all, earned or continuous secure attachment allows us to internalize reassuring and comforting voices or presences that help us tolerate the times when no one is there. And it helps us to keep our hearts open when the people in our lives reappear.

When the child part feels the loving gaze and shining eyes of the normal life self, experiences the visceral sense of being held in the arms of a strong, safe, protective adult, the building blocks of secure attachment are in place: a physical sense of being held safely, an emotional sense of closeness and specialness, "heartbeat-to-heartbeat communication," the felt sense of "being with" this small being of our implicit memory. There is mutual attunement between a caring and committed normal life adult and the child who longed for moments like this, even if afraid to believe or grasp them now. In order to be mutual and reciprocal, this process requires both self-resonance and other-resonance. With our feelings and our bodies, we must convey that finally we do understand, and we want to make it right now. In this way, the human brain uses its inherent split to heal traumatic injuries to attachment. First, the left brain reconceptualizes the emotional distress as a child's, then the right brain has a compassionate, caring emotional response to the child; the feelings of closeness and attunement become reciprocal, creating a more intensely pleasurable state; then the left brain encodes the "feeling of what happened": the feeling of being held and safe and welcomed by smiling faces with open arms. We have just provided ourselves with a "missing experience" (Ogden & Fisher, 2015) of love and safety and retrieved the "souls" of the lost "not-me" children. Each of us is transformed.

Laura provides a good example of how a therapy focused on changing an alienated relationship to her parts provided them with an experience of secure attachment, and how that in turn transformed her relationship to the past, not just to the wounded places inside her.

> Initially unaware of having a dissociative disorder, Laura experienced her stressful job as threatening, rather than triggering, and interpreted lack of concern for the threats she forecast as "denial." When her superiors did not see the threats, she felt unprotected and at the mercy of incompetent authority figures—just as she had been as a child. I "knew" intuitively she was describing the distorted perspective of structurally dissociated parts, especially a frightened part that I sensed when she talked about how quickly fear could bring her high-functioning professional self to her knees. As I began to talk about the young parts of her that got so triggered by incompetent, unethical adults in her corporate world, I connected them to her descriptions of the daily stressors that triggered her. "No wonder they don't feel safe in your job—no one will listen to their fears of attack." At first, she could relate to the parts intellectually and/ or connect them to narratives from her childhood, but she couldn't relate emotionally to them because each emotional connection resulted in blending with their feelings so quickly that she and they both felt overwhelmed. But as Laura doggedly and persistently sought to connect to her young parts and to offer them a home with her, their fear and rigidity began to soften. The first time she felt their interest in her was through a series of images of her younger parts peeking out at her from behind trees and bushes, the same kinds of hiding places she remembered finding as a young girl. Like a secure attachment-promoting parent, Laura was attuned and creative. She trusted her intuitive sense that they weren't yet ready to be seen but first needed to be acknowledged. So she engaged them in an imaginary game of hide-and-seek in which they had permission to seek her but she wouldn't find them until they were ready! She would call into the woods to thank them for all they had done for her—the professional respect they had gained her, the honors she had won, the courage to leave home and build a life on her own. And as she visualized herself sitting in a clearing, talking to the children hidden

in the woods, she could increasingly feel the sincerity in her voice and the emotions of gratitude, not just the words. Another day, as she was talking about how deeply grateful she was to them, she spontaneously reached out with her right hand as if to grasp the hand of one of the parts, and as I said, "Notice to whom you're intuitively reaching out right now," she could feel a small hand against hers. "It's a little one," she said.

Me: "Just feel her hand in yours, and sense what this child inside you needs."

Implicit memory (the tiny hand) and implicit emotions (the longing she could feel in the little girl to be held) suddenly "met" adult presence: she could feel her need to convey that she knew exactly what this child had been through. Her other hand reached over and grasped the one reaching out, holding onto it as if to a lifeline. She could feel the little girl's grief and pain but had no impulse to pull away from it. The moment felt like confirmation of the spiritual sense of certainty she had been increasingly having: that she could not heal until she finally brought all the children home again—home to *her*. I just echoed her mindful observations: "Yes, you've known for some time that you needed to bring them home ... Let her know that—make her welcome. She's never known what it would be like to be welcomed home. ..." Laura sat holding the little girl's hand in hers, while tears that seemed to belong to both ran down her cheeks.

I kept narrating the moment-by-moment experience as it unfolded, trying deliberately to articulate the feelings of both the wise compassionate adult Laura and the small Laura inside, wanting to make sure that this moment was remembered and could be called upon over and over again:

"Yes, someone is finally here, someone finally gets it—that's why she's crying. And you are crying for all she's been through ... She's finally home, and someone is crying for her, not making her cry. What's that like for her? ... She snuggles in closer when you ask her that, huh? I guess that's an answer for you ... I think she likes this feeling—and how about you? What's it like for you?" The softness of Laura's face, the loving gaze, and the relaxation in her body told me the answer. It felt deeply pleasurable and special.

By putting words to the experience between the little girl and Laura, by asking both to notice "what it's like" to have the other respond (i.e., to mentalize each other), I try to keep the focus on deepening the emotional attunement between child and adult, making meaning of the moment-to-moment transactions as attachment-building experience unfolding "right here, right now"

(Ogden & Fisher, 2015) in present time, trying to create a word picture that can be encoded as a new memory connected to the felt sense of security, warmth, and closeness she and the child were enjoying in this moment. I kept trying to simultaneously convey attunement to the child's "grief of relief" and to the adult's grief on behalf of the child, while emphasizing their shared tears and sense of closeness. The therapist's role is to be a "broker of secure attachment" between adult self and child self, helping each partner in the relationship attune more precisely to the other, deepening their mutual sense of closeness, conveying a sense of the future unfolding in a new way now that they are finally connected with each other.

This is how the healing of early attachment wounds can lead to earned secure attachment. By deepening and embodying the feelings and images associated with moments of felt attunement, we facilitate development and encoding of new implicit memories. The "earned" newly encoded experience includes body sensations of softness and warmth (contact comfort), emotions of pleasure yet also grief (what I call the "grief of relief"), the sense of being "gotten" and unconditionally accepted, a feeling of nourishment, safety and security, and "feeling for" and with the other. Attunement to one's child parts creates a sense of closeness and peacefulness, an "OK-ness" that refuels clients to create more resonant attachment experiences even with their challenging parts. Attunement doesn't just feel good to children—it feels good to parents as well.

Secure Attachment Is a Somatic and Emotional Experience, Not an Event

Secure attachment is not an objective goal—it is a physical and emotional state that one can call by many names: "safe," "close," "connected," "recognized," "understood." Secure attachment is cocreated and unintentional in its unfolding. It emerges from repeated moments of felt resonance, from the delighted feeling of "speaking the same language." It thrives on pattern and consistency. This is why children love to play the same games of peek-a-boo and hide-and-seek that Laura played imaginatively with her parts in the woods. They thrive on hearing the same words repeated in the same tone over and over, hearing the same song or nursery rhyme or joke, having the same goodnight routine every night. Providing secure attachment experiences to a child requires flexibility of response, a spacious window of tolerance, and the ability to "coregulate," to make little adjustments to the other as the other adjusts to us—until the "fit" feels "just right." In parent-child relationships, this process is aided by the fact that there are two separate bodies, two separate smiles, two sets of arms and legs. It is perceptually clear to both that they are separate beings.

When it comes to attuning to their younger selves, traumatized clients are hampered by automatic tendencies to instinctively recoil from the parts' painful emotions and fears. The fact that these emotions and implicit memories are not separate is also challenging: both sets of feelings arise within the boundaries of one body. That biological fact creates difficulties in knowing whose feeling is whose and supports the tendency to "blend" with each other's emotions. As clients often say to me when I notice an emotion and name it as a part's feeling memory: "No, *I* am having the feeling, and I am having it *now.*" When they identify with the feeling, it usually intensifies—as it also does when they disown the feeling, believing that it's not theirs, and disown the part whose wounding it tells us about. The same thing happens when they are flooded with a tsunami of intense feelings without words that seems to be theirs, no matter how much they would prefer otherwise. Blending and disowning are different strategies that both serve a survival function. Blending enables quick actions and reactions in response to emotions. Disowning preserves the sense of self and allows a parallel "not trauma" track in the midst of the worst moments in our lives.

Avoiding Enmeshment and Alienation

Attunement to another requires that we neither reject nor merge: we retain our own sense of selfhood while resonating at the other's frequency and allowing them to resonate at ours. This generalization is equally true in romantic relationships, parenthood, or in relationship to our younger selves. The tendency to merge or to become enmeshed with traumatized or abandoned young parts is natural: we sense a feeling or bodily reaction and we naturally give it a name preceded by the word "I." "I'm tired—I'm anxious—I feel very alone—I am furious." The more intense the feeling state and the more frequently experienced, the more likely we are to preface it with an "I," the more likely it is to be contagious, and the more likely we are to merge with it—a challenge encountered on a daily basis by parents of young children. Equally problematic is the disowning or rejection of some parts (e.g., the vulnerable ones) and/or the identification with the parts who are hostile (e.g., controlling, judgmental, aggressive parts) or hopeless, regressed, and childlike. When either occurs, there is a loss of balance in the system—as well as a loss of reality-testing, perspective, and compassion. If our client identifies with ashamed, submissive, compliant parts, he or she runs the risk of failing to perceive signs of healthy anger or defensive responses; if the client identifies with angry or suicidal parts, he or she runs the risk of anger management issues, self-destructive behavior, or internally recreating the early hostile environment.

Helping clients to attune to parts they loathe or feel intimidated by is just as important as bringing secure attachment experiences to young child parts for whom empathy is easy. It is more challenging to foster empathy for judgmental or scathingly critical parts and harder for clients to want to reach out to an angry part whose sharp tongue and intimidating manner costs them jobs, friendships, and neighborly relationships. Because earned secure attachment is dependent upon acceptance and compassion for all of our "selves," the therapist must insist that clients at the very least thank those "harder to love" parts for their protection. The therapist, like a parent or coach, must often be creative in brokering attachment relationships between the normal life self and more dysregulated or disowned parts.

Linda had come a long way—from suicidal despair to stabilization, from accepting her traumatic childhood to realizing what happened thanks to the parts who finally told her about the events she had not remembered. What was missing in her life was the ability to have needs: she could be generous, but she could not accept generosity; she could be kind, but she couldn't accept kindness. Her 11-year-old parentified child part wanted nothing for herself: kindness was for those who deserved it. The other "missing person" was an angry part. She knew about her suicidal part and had thanked it for its offers of help during the darkest of days, but she insisted repeatedly that there was no angry part, no feelings of anger, and she was glad! Her stance was: anger is destructive; I am not a destructive person; therefore, I have no anger. Ironically, this was the only stand she had ever taken in opposition to me over many years of therapy! "No," she said, "I am never angry." Then, one day, as we were talking about the issue of anger, she heard a rough, scathing voice inside, saying, "Oh, isn't she [referring to me] so 'nice'?—this bitch is just too nice! I want to puke!" Linda startled.

"What are you noticing?" I asked.

"Some part just called you a bitch!"

"Hooray! That's cause for celebration—the angry part is in the house! [Laughing] You were wondering if you really had an angry part—I think it just showed up. But before you dismiss it, hear me out: some part of you has to be cynical; some part has to keep an eye on the people who act "so nice" and then knife you when you're not looking. Who else is going to have your back? And furthermore, that part is right—I can sound too sickly sweet sometimes."

The next week, Linda came back, excited to tell me something. She had recently been promoted to CFO of a large corporation, a mixed blessing because the job came with the challenge of dealing with the competitive behavior of male colleagues who repeatedly sabotaged her efforts to work with them as a collaborator. "Do you remember I told you that they schedule meetings and deliberately don't include me in the email announcements?" "I do." "Well, luckily, the secretaries are on my side, so they're letting me know when it happens. This week, something amazing happened. As the time for the mystery meeting came up, I suddenly felt powerful—like I didn't have to let them get away with this shit! So I marched myself down to the conference room, walked in, sat down at the table with all the confidence in the world, and said ever so sweetly, 'I knew you'd want me in on this.' What could they say?! I won!"

ME: "And are you having the same thought I am?"

LINDA: "You mean, was that the angry part? You better believe it was! I felt so calm, powerful, determined, and clear-headed. I could be fake-sweet, but I felt like I had steel inside me. That was definitely not me!"

ME: "Then a high five to the angry part ..."

LINDA: "No, not enough. The angry part gets an Olympic gold medal!"

In the weeks and months following, Linda matter-of-factly challenged her male colleagues by simply taking her place among them, no matter how hard they tried to prevent it. Simultaneously, she began to feel more deserving of the life she had worked so hard to achieve, better able to take pleasure in its perks rather than blending with the 11-year-old submit part who felt worthless and undeserving. The angry part of her had brought to the system a much-needed sense of having rights and boundaries. Linda had always gotten ahead by working harder than everyone else. The fight part helped her learn to get ahead by standing her ground, holding her head high, and refusing to take responsibility for others who were not doing their jobs. While the angry part contributed "backbone," the sweetness of her attach part and the collaborative willingness of submit made it hard for her peers to react angrily. By accepting the angry part and trusting it, despite her wish to disown it, Linda created safety for herself and her parts even in the corporate "jungle."

Earned Secure Attachment and the Resolution of Trauma

"The fact that these adults [with earned secure attachment status] are capable of sensitive, attuned caregiving of their children, even under stress, suggests that this 'earned' status is more than just being able to 'talk the talk'; they can also 'walk the walk' of being emotionally connected with their own children, despite not having such experiences in their own childhoods. We may serve a vital role for this and future generations in enabling each other to achieve the more reflective, integrated functioning that facilitates secure attachments."

(Siegel, 1999, p. 11)

If helping traumatized clients "earn" secure attachment by forging bonds of affection and connection to their young selves can help prevent attachment failure in the next generation, then the work described here will also serve a preventive function. Therapist and client can take pride in knowing that they are not only healing old wounds but also protecting their children from another generation of parenting by dysregulated, attachment-disordered adults.

Whereas disorganized attachment is associated with autonomic dysregulation, controlling attachment strategies, internal conflicts between distance and closeness, and difficulties with identity formation, both earned and continuous secure attachment are associated with resilience. Studies report an association between secure attachment and greater affect tolerance, as well as increased ability to bounce back from hurt, stress, rejection, or disappointment, tolerate both closeness and distance, and internalize positive attachment figures. In studies of earned secure attachment, two findings are particularly relevant to a parts approach: first, although earned secure attachment was associated with depressive symptoms and emotional distress in some parents studied, they nonetheless evidenced an ability to provide good attachment to their children, suggesting that their earned secure attachment status allowed them to tolerate higher levels of internal discomfort without their parenting ability being compromised. The second finding was that the benefits of earned secure attachment were virtually indistinguishable from the benefits of what researchers called "continuous secure attachment" (Roisman et al., 2002), that is, childhood secure attachment. These findings fit well with the model presented in this book. Long after internal attachment bonds have been established, clients and their trauma-related parts may still periodically suffer distress, still be vulnerable to depression and anxiety, and even have destructive impulses. But earned secure attachment provides a stable base that enables individuals to tolerate grief, loss, betrayal, and other stressful normal life experiences—without loss of their capacity to parent the next generation or to soothe and reassure themselves—or their "selves."

This is very good news for trauma survivors who have struggled with the painful effects of disrupted, disorganized attachment. As they overcome trauma-related self-alienation, their internal sense of safety and well-being will be equal to that of adults born to securely attached parents. So often, clients fear that they have been irreparably damaged by the abuse and attachment failure. The research says otherwise. If trauma survivors are willing to overcome trauma-related tendencies to fear and loathe some parts and over-identify with others, if they can welcome all the "children" without having favorites or scapegoats, the ending can be different. If traumatized individuals are willing to embrace intimidating judgmental parts, frightening suicidal parts, and parts who wound the body or "pour whiskey in the baby bottle" to silence the little parts, the seeds of earned secure attachment are sown. There need be no pressure to love or nurture hostile or aggressive parts because that would be to fail them empathically. An adopted teenager would need different kinds of experiences to feel safely attached than a 3-year-old. Attunement arises from a sensitivity to each part and to the "missing experiences" necessary for each to transform and heal wounded or broken places. The "missing experience" (Ogden & Fisher, 2015) for a fight part, as Linda demonstrates, is not being held and soothed; it is the experience of control over threat, the feeling of being respected for its strength and its need for clear boundaries that ensure safety. When the normal life self of the client overcomes the tendency to ignore the fight part's injunctions against vulnerability or caretaking of others and instead works to develop increasing ability to set boundaries and insist on fairness in relationships, the relationship between the two begins to shift.

When the safety concerns of the fight parts are heard, when they are treated as heroes rather than perpetrators, they become committed, loyal, and bonded. Being ignored or engaged in a power struggle inflames them; being heard and taken seriously tames them. The same is true for the flight parts: attempting to force closeness or commitment on them pushes them away; acceptance of their needs for control over interpersonal distance relaxes their guard.

No matter how their implicit memories and animal defenses manifest, all parts, like all human beings, desire acceptance and attunement. Even though a mother might find one child temperamentally easier to parent than another, her job is to forge an attachment bond to both the "easy" and the "hard" babies equally. For individuals to experience the internal stability and well-being endowed by earned secure attachment, all parts must be embraced—from the grouchy, distancing adolescent flight part to the endearing and innocent attach part to the always depressed and hopeless submit part to the silent, terrified freeze part and the "take no prisoners" fight part. When the client can find something to love about each and every part, the internal world begins to transform. Just as therapists are not trained to ask clients, "How did you survive? How did you do it?" they are also rarely trained to ask, "What could you love about that part that won't let you sleep? That won't let you eat? That won't let anyone get close to you?"

Earned secure attachment, according to researchers, is most often built through healthy, meaningful relationships in adulthood (such as that with a spouse or therapist) or through the vicarious experience of secure attachment available through parenting one's own children. To add to that list, earned secure attachment can also be cultivated through healthy, attuned relationships to our "selves." The ingredients are the same: the willingness to prioritize the needs of the other, the ability to communicate welcome and acceptance, attunement and coregulation, emotional closeness, compassion, loving presence, and the ability to maintain a felt connection to the other even when one is dysregulated, frustrated, or overwhelmed. Whether we bring these capacities to a newborn baby of our own, or to an infant or child self, they have neurobiological effects. The cornerstone of infant attachment is what Allan Schore (2001) calls "adaptive projective identification." That term refers to the way in which the infant's distress, projected via dysregulation, is experienced by parents as their own distress. The baby cries; the parent is dysregulated by the cries. She feels uncomfortable, so much so that she is driven to pick the baby up, soothe, comfort, and distract, until the repair effort hits on the infant's unmet need and the baby calms and settles into the parent's arms. Only then does the parental nervous system calm and settle. All is well now—both are regulated and soothed. Sometimes, the infant's unmet need might be for up-regulation made possible by the parent's making funny faces and sounds, eliciting infant smiles and laughter, until the point at which the parent also feels an uplift in mood. Parent and child feel a shared, reciprocal pleasure hard to capture in words other than to call it "attunement bliss."

Hearing the Child's Cry

Child parts, too, feel distress, and they too "project" their discomfort to signal for help. In a two-person system in one biological body, it is more difficult for child parts to be heard, other than via blending and/or reciprocal dysregulation. For that reason, practice of the skills described in Chapters 4 and 5 is the crux of the treatment. Having mastered these skills in the therapist's office, the normal life self can hear the child's cry as a signal to unblend from the distress, recognizing that "she" or "he" is upset. Curious because of the discomfort of her own state, the client is motivated to be interested in this child self who is so unhappy, rather than avoidant. Curiosity helps regulate the mutual dysregulation and distress and keeps adult and child in contact, challenging habitual self-alienation tendencies to ignore, disown or reblend with the part's feelings.

Then the normal life self learns to do what any good secure attachment-promoting parent would do when a small child is crying: he or she experiments to find a repair for the child's distressed state. The measure of a successful repair lies in the body: if a repair is successfully made, the little boy or girl will take a breath, heart rate will slow, the nervous system will settle, and there will be a sense of relief in the body. If the therapist allows the client to identify that state of relief as "I feel better now," the opportunity to build secure attachment will be lost, at least for the moment. Only by staying "present" in relationship to the child can the client foster a secure attachment experience. Soothing distress or evoking positive feelings does not build resilience in young children or parts when it is followed by a quick, "OK, that's done. Now I have other things more important to do." Even securely attached children need to feel "held in mind" by their parents, even when they are not physically present.

To heal the fragmented selves of traumatized clients entails a therapist willing to "see" the parts in an individual's whole physical body, able to be "relentless" in helping clients learn to interpret distress as "theirs," and skilled in gently and non-coercively insisting on a focus on the needs of wounded children. Just as therapists do in treating traumatic attachment in children, clients have to be helped to consistently provide reparative interventions to parts whose presence is felt "now" because some stimulus has activated their implicit memories, causing pain. Each repair reclaims a part that was once left behind, "retrieves" a lost "soul," no longer disowned and phobically avoided. There is no need for parts whose job was to loathe and fear the vulnerable parts to ensure the self-alienation. There is no need to fear the vulnerability and no need for self-loathing as a protection. Better yet, by helping clients identify the somatic signs that "the little one feels better," sharing in the felt sense of "better," communicating the shared enjoyment of "better" back to the child, and continuing to deepen the mutually felt sense of safety, closeness, and welcome, there is an unexpected reward. There is an experience of relaxation, safety, and "attunement bliss" that pulls not for avoidance but for embracing the child, making her welcome, finding a place for him at the table of the client's life.

Healing the fragmented selves of traumatized clients requires only that the positivity-oriented left brain-related normal life self befriend right brain-related parts, both "owned" and disowned, and become curious about their ages, stages, fears, and strengths, and learn to be in relation to them. This is an apparently small, non-threatening step but it challenges trauma-related conditioned learning by increasing communication and collaboration between the two hemispheres, the opposite of splitting. Healing our broken places and fragmented parts happens naturally as an organic process—much like plants grow toward the light. All that is needed is the willingness to "see" the parts, hear their fears and feelings, and be curious even if not yet compassionate. Guided by a therapist who can speak for all the parts and for the system as a whole, the normal life self's conditioned avoidance of the parts is challenged. Mindful dual awareness decreases the automatic tendency to disown the parts by regulating autonomic arousal and facilitating being able to "see" each other.

Like nations at war, like families in conflict, sitting down together elicits the commonalities and prevents "demonizing" each other. With a therapist who facilitates dual awareness, who is determined to repair the fault lines between the emotionally driven parts and logic-driven normal lfe part, who is willing to see each side as worthy and deserving of a place at the table, and whose own compassion and attunement is palpable, there is a softening toward not-me parts. When both client and therapist can appreciate the ways in which every part has supported the survival of the whole, how the internal struggles that still occur are simply a reflection of parts trying to defend against the threats "then," there is more softening. Much like planting and tending a garden, internal attachment-building involves patience, repetition, and a deep conviction that healing is normal, natural, and cannot be rushed. It requires only the right "soil" and patient, compassionate "gardeners" to evoke innate healing tendencies in even the most wounded of living beings.

> "I am still every age that I have been. Because I was once a child, I am always a child. Because I was once an adolescent, given to moods and ecstasies, these are still part of me, and always will be. ... This does not mean that I ought to be trapped or enclosed in any of these ages, ... but that they are in me to be drawn on ... my past is part of what makes the present ... and must not be denied or rejected."
>
> (L'Engle, 1972, pp. 199–200)

References

Friedman, W.J. (2012). Resonance: welcoming you in me—a core therapeutic competency. *Undivided, the Online Journal of Unduality and Psychology*, 1(3).

L'Engle, M. (1972). *A circle of quiet.* New York: Harper Collins.

Ogden, P. & Fisher, J. (2015). *Sensorimotor Psychotherapy: interventions for trauma and attachment.* New York: W.W. Norton.

Roisman, G. I., Padron, E., Sroufe, L.A., & Egeland, B. (2002). Earned-secure attachment status in retrospect and prospect. *Child Development*, 73(4), 1204–1219.

Schore, A. N. (2001). Neurobiology, developmental psychology, and psychoanalysis: convergent findings on the subject of projective identification. In Edwards, J. (Ed.). *Being alive: building on the work of Anne Alvarez*. New York: Brunner-Routledge.

Siegel, D. J. (2010a). *The neurobiology of 'we.'* Keynote address, Psychotherapy Networker Symposium, Washington, D.C., March 2010.

Siegel, D. J. (2010b). *The mindful therapist: a clinician's guide to mindsight and neural integration*. New York: W.W. Norton.

Five Steps to "Unblending"

When we are triggered by something and our traumatized parts get activated, their feelings flood the body with intense and overwhelming feelings and impulses to act or react in ways that are not "us" or who we intend to be. That experience is called "blending." To find our adult selves again, we need to "unblend," to mindfully separate from the intense reactions of the parts until we have a felt sense of "I'm here" and also "he or she is still here, too." Here are the five steps to unblending:

1 First, assume that any and all upsetting or overwhelming feelings and thoughts are a communication from parts—and try to make that assumption even if you are not sure it is true.

2 Describe the feelings and thoughts as "their" reaction: "They are upset—they are having a hard time—they are overwhelmed." See what happens when you speak for the parts by talking about "their" feelings.

3 Create a little more separation from them, just enough so you can feel their feelings less intensely *and* you can feel yourself, too. Change your position, lengthen your spine, engage your core, or sit back. Keep repeating, "They are feeling _____."

4 Use your wise grownup mind, the part of you that is a compassionate friend or organized professional, to have a reassuring conversation with whomever is upset. Acknowledge that the part or parts are afraid, overwhelmed, ashamed, or sad. Imagine: if these were the fears of your colleagues, clients, or friends, how would you respond? What would you tell them? Ask them what they need from you to be a little less afraid.

5 Get their feedback and opinions: Is what you are doing helping even a little? What do they need right in this moment to feel a little less alone, a little less afraid, a little less angry? Do they like it when you listen and show concern? Promise them that you will check in with them, make more of an effort to remember they are in distress, or be more protective.

The key to the success of this technique is consistency, repetition, and a willingness to keep using it even if you have days when it does not work.

Meditation Circle for Parts

This intervention can help in a number of ways: it encourages daily or almost daily mindfulness meditation (a good treatment for a traumatized nervous system). It promotes internal awareness of parts that might otherwise disrupt or destabilize your normal life part, and it increases self-compassion and compassion for the traumatized parts.

All it takes is willingness to trust that any pain, loneliness, shame, overwhelm, or threat you feel is a communication from dissociated child parts. Rather than wait until they get triggered or until you are overwhelmed by their feelings, the meditation circle practice helps to build internal dialogue, create trust, and reassure the parts that someone cares and prevent problems from escalating.

Once a day, preferably at the same time each day, find a comfortable quiet place to sit. Relax or close your eyes, take a breath, and then make an internal announcement, for example: "I want to ask every part of me to come into the meditation circle … this is not to criticize or judge or control you. I want to get to know you—I want to know when you're having a hard time—I want to know what's bothering you so I can learn to help you more." Then pause and visualize the meditation circle, communicate welcome to the parts, and be curious about the children and teenagers who slowly join it. Do you recognize the parts that slowly gather together? Are you surprised at who shows up or how they communicate who they are through their body language and facial expression?

Many people are surprised by what they see: more parts than they expected, more obvious pain and vulnerability, younger or older ages. Assume that everything you notice (ages, facial expressions, dress, even body language) will tell you more about them. Your job is to welcome them, to be curious about what they need, hope, or fear.

Sometimes there is no clear image, just a sensation of the parts joining you, or no one shows up at all. This is not a problem. You can still validate them and what they have endured: "I bet some or all of you don't trust this—maybe you are worried that it's a trap—or that you will have to let your guard down."

Once you have an image or sense of parts gathered in the circle, invite them to tell you what they are worried about—is there anything they want you to know about their worries?

Try to be a good listener: try to really "get" what they're telling you about themselves. Take their fears and feelings seriously. If they express feelings of abandonment or hurt that you haven't been there, try to "own" it if you recognize some truth to their perception. Try to take responsibility: "I should have been there—I can see why that was hard for you." Be an "equal opportunity" welcomer: even if you are "turned off" by a particular part's shame, vulnerability, or anger, try to accept all feelings and beliefs expressed by the parts as a natural and normal emotion any traumatized child might be likely to have.

To the extent that you can, try to come up with the support and validation the parts need to assuage their fears and frustrations: "I will remember how scared it makes you when people get angry—maybe you can stand behind me so you don't have to worry about someone blaming you." "Maybe I can help you look out for bad things—maybe I can promise to protect you from ..." "You've been alone a long time—I won't forget that." Try to keep the focus on today or right now: "Notice that right here, right now, I am here and I'm not leaving." Traumatized children have many fears, and it doesn't help *them* to open them all up at once or try to solve them all at once. Equally, it is natural that some parts won't trust you at first, will hesitate to hear you, or even be angry. You can tell them, "Every day we will meet, and you can tell me more about your worries and what I can do each day to help or understand or be there. Maybe over time, you will trust me. ... There is no rush—take all the time you need."

Internal Dialogue Technique

Step 1: Focus on the thoughts and feelings that are causing you distress right this minute, and assume that they belong to a part. Tune into that part for a few moments and see what you notice about it: it is speaking to you right now through the thoughts, feelings, beliefs, and gut responses that you are experiencing. What kind of part would feel or think this way? A very young one? A middle-sized child? A teenager? Connect to that part by letting it know you are there.

Step 2: If you are feeling too blended with that part to have a conversation, then create a little bit more space by asking the part to "sit back" or "relax a little bit," and make room for you, the adult, to listen to what this part has to say. This step can be repeated whenever you get too "blended" or start to get confusion or overwhelm. Confusion, overwhelm, and anxiety always mean that parts are confused or overwhelmed. They are talking to you by communicating their feelings. The same is true when you feel depression, shame, anger, or self-criticism. If ashamed, depressed, angry, or judgmental parts jump up at any time, just repeat Step 1.

Step 3: Be curious. Ask the part what she or he is worried about. The assumption is that parts are activated because they are triggered and experiencing past-related fears. Children need to know that people hear their worries and take them seriously, or they don't feel safe. Listen to the words that come up, even if they don't make sense to you, and then reflect the words back to the part: "It sounds as if you feel really worthless and unlovable." Make sure to ask: "Is that right? Am I getting it?" That lets the part know that you are really listening and really trying to connect and help. Sometimes, parts worry that they will have no place in the adult's current life, and those fears must be reassured for Step II to be effective. Sometimes when you have parts that are very young, they don't speak in words: they speak through feelings and body sensations. For example, you might ask, "What are you worried about if I go to my friend's birthday celebration?" and then get no verbal response but instead a physical response, like fear or shame. Assume the feeling or tension is a communication, and reflect it back, "It sounds like you're afraid that people will see you ... Is that right?"

Step 4: Explore the underlying fears. Usually, the underlying fear is a variant on the theme of "something bad will happen" which has gotten projected onto current triggers. Often we have to explore several levels of fear to get to the core fear. Ask the part again:

"What are you worried about?" No matter what feeling or words come up (anger, sadness, shame, guilt, fear), assume that this part is not comfortable with the feeling and is worried about something.

Then, once you have that next layer of worry, ask: "And if that were to come true, what would you be worried about?" (The questions should be as concrete as possible and tied to the expressed fear of the part, even if the fear doesn't make sense.) Usually, the answer is "safety," which then requires another question: "How would he or she be unsafe if this happened?"

It usually takes 2 to 4 questions along these lines to get to the core fear, usually a fear connected to the trauma in some way: "I'll be alone," "I would be trapped," "It would be too much—I would just shatter."

Step 5: Identify some type of corrective experience that can be provided by the adult self directly to the part, something that the part didn't get back then, like validation, support, comfort, care, reassurance, or protection. These fears come from long ago, even though they *feel* connected to *right now* because they are happening in the present moment. They are the fears of child parts who don't know that you are an adult with strengths and resources *and* who has safety under your control most of the time, certainly compared to when you were a child. Ask the worried part, "What do you need from me right here, right now, to not be so afraid of _____?" In most cases, the answer the part gives is: "I need to feel that you, the adult, are there with me and not as scared as I am."

Step 6: Focus on how the adult you are today can provide a corrective experience for the child you once were. Child parts can be afraid that if the adult is scared, too, or overwhelmed, there really will be danger, and no one will be there to help the child part. I stress to my clients that an adult would only be afraid of a real danger, not afraid of past dangers happening again exactly the same way. The adult can reassure the child parts that right now they are not alone—they're with you. Or reassure them that nothing bad is happening—they're just remembering how scary it was then. If words don't calm the body or the emotions, you can do something physical to communicate safety: for example, put a hand over the part of the body where the anxiety is felt (the chest, stomach) or lengthen your spine by gently stretching it from the middle of the back upward or stand up and walk around to demonstrate how tall and strong you are. You can also reassure the part through imagining being there with her … What would you want to do if you saw him feeling this way? Take his hand? Pick her up? Take her away from that place?

Step 7:   Practice! The more you practice these skills, the easier it will be to recover from crises and avoid them. Remember every crisis results from some part getting triggered and reacting out of fear or shame or anger.

The key is communicating a real commitment to the parts that, from now on, you will listen to them, take their fears seriously, connect to them with compassion, and try to provide the protection and support they have been waiting for.

Treatment Paradigm for Internal Attachment Repair

The premise of this paradigm or protocol is that dissociative disorder clients, borderline clients with dissociative features, and structurally dissociated complex PTSD clients all come to therapy because their parts are intruding upon the consciousness of their going on with normal life selves. The presenting problem described to the therapist by the client will in some way reflect the activation of a part holding trauma-related implicit memories: depression might be a sign that a depressed child has been triggered by a loss; anxiety might be the communication from an anxious part whose implicit memories have been activated by the birth of a child; relationship difficulties may be an indication of conflict between parts about trust/mistrust, closeness/distance. Whatever implicit memories underlie the presenting problem, therapy is apt to further activate the parts because it is a promise of help from an authority figure, something for which they have been waiting many years. By its very nature, therapy will evoke impulses to disclose but also exacerbate procedurally learned secrecy. It will stimulate the yearning to trust and connect but also trigger hesitancy and hypervigilance. Closeness to the therapist and the invitation to "open up" will trigger implicit memories, and separation or distance will also be triggering.

The therapist's job is to give both sides "a voice":

1 At each session, as the client arrives with a presenting problem or distress of the day, *the therapist's job is first to tie that distress to a part*, that is, if the client is feeling more anxious, the therapist reframes the anxiety as the child part's nervousness or fear and expresses empathy *for the part* rather than empathy for the "client." Although it may be important to spend some time listening to what the clients are feeling, it is also important to avoid reinforcing their procedurally learned "stories" about themselves and to help them become more mindful and curious about the part in distress.

2 Next, *switch pronouns* so that "you" now describes the adult self of the client and "he" or "she" describes the part: "Yes, she's really scared, isn't she? Do you know what triggered her? Or did you just wake up to find her in this state?"

3 Evoke curiosity about the part that is in distress: Is he or she very young? Are his or her feelings familiar? What is going on in the client's life that might trigger these emotions? [Notice that there is no attempt to place the part in childhood history or in the traumatic context. The emphasis is on the part's experience *now* in the context of the client's daily life and the relationship between the normal life self and the part.]

4 Use language and tones of voice that speak to not only the adult but also to the age of that part, whether a young child, teenager, or latency-aged child.

5 Be prepared for other parts to get triggered by the attention to vulnerability: A skeptical part that questions the use of parts language, an angry part that feels condescended to, a "shutdown" part that stops talking and goes mute.

6 Notice and name parts that distract or shut down the conversation with or about a vulnerable part: "Interesting—there's a part that thinks I'm condescending, huh? I wonder what in my tone of voice or words gave her that message ..." "I appreciate the skeptical part's questioning of what we're doing here ... that's important." "Notice how protective these parts are of the anxious part—they don't want us to get too close to her."

7 Be the voice or spokesperson for all the parts: "Remember that all parts are welcome here ..." "Keep in mind this is a child—no wonder she is so upset ..."

8 As the client expresses feelings and thoughts or describes physical reactions, images, or impulses (whether in parts language or not), keep reminding him or her that all of these sources of information can be communications from parts: "If this belief/feeling/impulse/image were a communication from a part, what would that part be trying to tell you?"

9 Then have the client check with the parts by asking to him or herself: "Is that right? Is that true?" If the answer is "no," then have client invite the part to correct the statement until it is "right."

10 Invite the client to ask inside, "Are you tired of feeling this way?" or "Are you tired of being in the past?"

11 If the answer is "yes," then whatever interventions are offered should be framed as an attempt to help the parts. Often, especially when clients shut down or refuse to speak, our interventions are framed as attempts to get the adult back in control of the body. But that approach sends a negative message to parts that they are not welcome. The same intervention (e.g., grounding) done on behalf of the parts will be much more successful.

12 After each intervention tried, ask the client to check inside with the parts: "Does that help?" "Does this feel better or worse?" If the answer is positive, repeat the intervention or affirm the part's feelings: "Yes, it feels good to me, too—I like holding your hand." Or "I want to protect you."

Dissociative Experiences Log

Time/Day	Thoughts I'm having	Feelings I'm having	How I'm acting	What's happening in my body?	Am I older? Younger?	What does this tell me about which part I am right now?

The Four Befriending Questions

Step 1: The client is asked to identify a part that is in some kind of distress. Then the therapist initiates the dialogue by inviting the client to: "Ask this distressed part what she's worried about if you _____ _____? [e.g., go to the party, say "No," get angry, stand up to your boss, etc.]

Step 2: "Ask her what she's worried will happen next if her worry *[repeat the part's exact description of it]* really does come true."

Step 3: "Ask her: if those worries that *[repeat the part's exact description]* really do happen, what is she worried will happen next?"

Keep repeating Step 3 until a core fear is reached: usually either the fear of annihilation or the fear of abandonment.

Step 4: "Acknowledge her fear by mirroring it back to her, then ask the part: what does she need from you right here, *right now* to not be so afraid of _____?" "Right here, right now" is the operative word: the need must be small enough and sufficiently concrete that it can be met by the normal life part with coaching as appropriate from the therapist.

Index

abandonment, fear of 7, 12, 27, 109–11, 142, 179–80, 182, 190–1, 232–3
acting in 67
acting out 67
action systems 24–25
adaptation of body and mind 2, 67–69
adaptive projective identification 258
addictive behavior 111; associated with trauma 127; neurobiological basis for 13; producing relief 131–2, 136–7; as symptom for internal splitting 29–31
adrenaline 35, 130
Adult Attachment Inventory 17
affect tolerance 55–56, 104
aggression and therapist working with 179–80
alienation from self 5, 7, 15, 66–67, 75, 77, 100, 142, 213; avoiding 254–6
amygdala: activated 36–37, 45, 51; and mindfulness 78; in survival response 34–35
animal defense responses 25, 68, 136
anorexia 131
ashamed part 80, 84–88, 91, 142, 189–93
attachment 16–17; building bonds 206; to caregiver becoming frightening 105–9; continuous secure 249, 250,

257; controlling strategies 107, 132–3; cultivating internal 228–31; disorganized 103, 105–8, 115–16, 179–80, 191; manifestations of 113–15; recontextualizing 110–12; drive 65; earned secure 13, 16, 17, 63, 77, 104–5, 241, 242–60; fears of internal 209–13; formation as a child 55–56; internal 209–10, 228–31, 259–60, 269–70; remembering early 104–5; repairing internal attachment relationships 213–16, 259–60, 269–70; secure 15, 198–9, 206, 228–31; developing 239–41; intergenerational legacy of 250–3; mother resonating to baby 237–8; as a somatic and emotional experience 253–5; seeking part 70; and self-destructive behavior 132–3; traumatic 5–6, 12–13, 103–24; Type D, 105
attachment figures: conflicting proximate-seeking drive and fight and flight responses 24, 132–3; creating secure attachment 198–9; as source of danger 105–9
attach part 78, 87–88, 109–11, 132–3, 175, 179–80; relationship with the fight part 115–16; and transferences 112

273